A MAN AMONG OTHER MEN

A MAN AMONG OTHER MEN

The Crisis of Black Masculinity in
Racial Capitalism

Jordanna Matlon

CORNELL UNIVERSITY PRESS   ITHACA AND LONDON

Some of these chapters have appeared in previous forms in: *Antipode; American Sociological Review; Boston Review; CODESRIA Bulletin; Contexts; Ethnography; Global Dialogue; Laboratorium; Poetics; and Wiley Blackwell Encyclopedia.*

First published 2022 by Cornell University Press

Library of Congress Cataloging-in-Publication Data

Names: Matlon, Jordanna, author.
Title: A man among other men : the crisis of Black masculinity in racial capitalism / Jordanna Matlon.
Description: Ithaca [New York] : Cornell University Press, 2022. | Includes bibliographical references and index.
Identifiers: LCCN 2021039981 (print) | LCCN 2021039982 (ebook) | ISBN 9781501762864 (hardcover) | ISBN 9781501762932 (paperback) | ISBN 9781501762888 (ebook) | ISBN 9781501762871 (pdf)
Subjects: LCSH: Masculinity—Economic aspects—Côte d'Ivoire—Abidjan. | Blacks—Race identity—Economic aspects—Côte d'Ivoire—Abidjan. | Capitalism—Social aspects—Côte d'Ivoire—Abidjan.
Classification: LCC HQ1090.7.C8 M37 2022 (print) | LCC HQ1090.7.C8 (ebook) | DDC 155.3/32—dc23
LC record available at https://lccn.loc.gov/2021039981
LC ebook record available at https://lccn.loc.gov/2021039982

On that day, completely dislocated, unable to be abroad with the other, the white man, who unmercifully imprisoned me, I took myself far off from my own presence, far indeed, and made myself an object. What else could it be for me but an amputation, an excision, a hemorrhage that spattered my whole body with black blood? But I did not want this revision, this thematization. All I wanted was to be a man among other men. I wanted to come lithe and young into a world that was ours and to help to build it together.

— Frantz Fanon, *Black Skin, White Masks*

Contents

Acknowledgments

This book culminates a project that began well before I stepped into the field and continued for years after I had anticipated its natural ending, adopting along the way new intellectual traditions and expanding my theoretical horizon. It is the product of many conversations. At times I mostly spoke, and at other times I mostly listened.

My book owes its greatest debts to the orators and vendors who shared their reflections and experiences and invited me to learn about their lives. Brilliant and patient, Raka Ray, Ananya Roy, and Peter Evans were pivotal in bringing form to this project, and in thanking them I extend additional gratitude to Raka for being the gravitational force around which an enduring intellectual community was formed. I thank also my other mentors and interlocutors at UC Berkeley: Michael Burawoy, Nazanin Shahrokni, Jennifer Carlson, Kimberly Kay Hoang, Abigail Andrews, and Oluwakemi Balogun. The generous support of the Jacob K. Javits Fellowship and the National Science Foundation Graduate Research Fellowship funded my fieldwork. My family in Abidjan made that fieldwork both possible and wonderful; thanks to Mowa Botembe, Achi Atsain, Isabelle Atsain, Felicia Atsain, Elodie Kadisha, Marc Kadisha, Tatiana Kadisha, Itzhak Ashkenazi, Clement Zêkê, Tino, and MC.

My journey continued at the Institute for Advanced Study in Toulouse, and for the gift of three incredible years of insights and friendship I thank Alissa MacMillan, Mohamed Saleh, Jonathan Klingler, Sean Bottomley, and Paul Seabright. I also thank Edgar Pieterse for welcoming me to the University of Cape Town's African Centre for Cities during this period.

At American University's School of International Service (SIS), I am inspired by the intelligence and grateful for the camaraderie of the Ethnographers of Empire: Malini Ranganathan, Garrett Graddy-Lovelace, Erin Collins, Randolph Persaud, Marcelo Bohrt, James Mittleman, Carolyn Gallaher, Susan Shepler, Lauren Carrruth, and Kendra Salois. I thank Rachel Robinson and Christine Chin for their mentorship, and Allison Beaufort for being such an exceptional mentee. I thank Olayinka Martins who went from student to interlocutor as the manuscript took shape, and I am eager to read his book. Thanks also to my hardworking research assistants who over the years have helped along this project in its various stages: Kimberly Tower, Megan Prybyl, Bertha Nibigira, Julie Geiger, Jason Farr, Clement Mutambo, and Zeinabou Saidou Baraze. Institutionally, the free rein that SIS gave me to develop my courses "Seeing Africa," "Racial Capitalism," and "Race in the World Political Economy" enabled me to engage literatures to which I had not been previously exposed. The book incubator that SIS Research hosted on my behalf was one of my best days, and I thank Caleb Schmotter for the labor he put in to make it happen. Words cannot sufficiently express my gratitude to my incubator participants, Randolph Persaud and guests Ch. Didier Gondola, Robin Kelley, Jodi Melamed, and Jesse Weaver Shipley for privileging my manuscript with their insights and energies. I was humbled to be in this meeting of giants, and they steered me toward my goal with care and confidence.

I thank the Woodrow Wilson Foundation (now Citizens and Scholars) Career Enhancement Fellowship for allowing me the time to put my ideas into words and for my mentor, Chandan Reddy, a stellar mind and a fantastic human being. Many years ago I asked one of my heroes, AbdouMaliq Simone, to be my mentor for a fellowship that never happened, and I thank him for his constant encouragement since then of me and my scholarship.

The careful editorial and reviewer suggestions of my previously published articles advanced several of the ideas in this book. For that I thank *American Sociological Review* under the editorship of Omar Lizardo, Rory McVeigh, and Sarah Mustillo, *Antipode* under Sharad Chari, the *Boston Review* under Deborah Chasman, Chloe Fox, and Adam McGee, *CODESRIA Bulletin* under Divine Fuh, *Contexts* under Douglas Harper, *Ethnography* under Paul Willis, *Global Dialogue* under Michael Burawoy, *Laboratorium* under Anna Isakova and guest editors Natalia Samutina and Oksana Zaporozhets, *Poetics* under Timothy Dowd, and the *Wiley Blackwell Encyclopedia* under George Ritzer.

The book began once I had published that "big picture" piece in that flagship journal, an accomplishment that gave me closure in saying what needed to be said from what I had learned thus far, and the freedom to explore how to more deeply connect my empirics to history and theory. What came next was a lengthy process of rethinking, relearning, recomposing, and rearticulating. The more formal conversations that occurred over this period provided structure, exposure, feedback, and deadlines, and I am grateful to the dedicated organizers, thoughtful discussants, and enthusiastic participants at each of these gatherings. My special thanks to Hannah Schilling and re:work at Humboldt University and the Center for Metropolitan Studies at the Technical University of Berlin; Janet Roitman at the SIS Ethnographies of Empire Spring Symposium; Yang Zhang and Elizabeth Thompson and the SIS Historical International Studies Research Cluster; Mary Clark and Theresa Runstedtler at the American University Critical Race, Gender, and Class Theory Workshop; Jovan Lewis, Camille Hawthorne, Sharad Chari, and Brandi Thompson Summers at the UC Berkeley Black Geographies Workshop; Fiona Greenland and Isaac Ariail Reed at the University of Virginia

Sociological Working Group on Aesthetics, Meaning, and Power; Chambi Cha-chage, Jessica Levy, and Melissa Tandiwe Myambo at the Princeton University Symposium on Africa and Racial Capitalism; the Gender/Power/Theory Work-shops at UC Berkeley, the University of Chicago, and the University of Southern California; Ann Orloff and the Northwestern University Sociology Colloquium; Kendra Salois and Kwaku Nuamah at the DC Area Africanists Workshop; Ricardo Cardoso and the Mariners, Renegades, and Capitalism: Researching the Urban Atlantic for the Coming Century conference at New York University; Sara Berry and the Johns Hopkins University Africa Seminar; Kopano Ratele and the Sum-mer School at the University of South Africa African Masculinities Stream; with the American Sociological Association: Emily Barman and the 2019 Session on Race in Organizations; Ruben Gaztambide-Fernandez and the 2017 Session on Culture and Inequality; with the African Studies Association: Reginold Royston and the 2017 Session on Creativity and Disruption: The Polyvalence of Afri-ca's New Political Economies; with the American Association of Geographers: Camille Hawthorne and the 2018 Session on Representations of the Black Spatial Imaginary; Daniel Esser and the 2017 Session on Labor Narratives and Urban Informality in the Global South; and with the International Sociological Asso-ciation World Congress, Lynn Spillman and the 2018 Session on Theorizing and Historicizing Economic Culture.

For making the book's cover possible, the statues that made their pandemic journey from Abidjan to Paris to Washington, DC, I thank the intercontinental and intergenerational generosity of Assiatou Bah Diallo and Fatoumata Barry Diallo.

In its final stage my thanks to Jim Lance, Clare Jones, Karen Laun, and all those at Cornell University Press who believed in my vision and supported me in seeing it through.

And to my family, with love and always my deepest thanks—Carlos Carmona Medina, for listening, for helping, for teaching, for everything and still more; Tolosa Amelia Carmona, for your life and for filling mine with so much joy, beauty, and gratitude; Colleen Thomas-Matlon, for your creativity and grit; Mina Para Matlon, for modeling the courage to forge your own path; Penelope Thomas, for always a good story; Joyce Cacho, for making our family your own; and Peter Matlon, for showing me conviction in principles and rigor in inquiry and for always being willing to read my drafts.

INTRODUCTION
Greatness in Each Man

Pont Général de Gaulle is a bridge that connects Plateau, Abidjan's center and proud bastion of wide, leafy boulevards and steel-and-concrete modernity, with Treichville, the city's original African district, or *quartier populaire*, following the segregated spatial logic of the colonial city.[1] Treichville is named after Marcel Treich-Laplène, early French explorer and first colonial administrator of Côte d'Ivoire (Daddieh 2016). Like Treichville, scattered throughout Abidjan are roads, bridges, and neighborhoods that preserve the appellations of the colonial era.[2] Unlike those postcolonial states that indigenized the naming of their quotidian urban spaces, in Abidjan durable affirmations of European influence and the decades of *Françafrique* that dominate political, economic, and cultural relations between ex-colony and metropole endure.[3] Pont Général de Gaulle honors the president of France when Côte d'Ivoire gained its independence. Throughout his political life Charles de Gaulle esteemed the first Ivoirian president, Félix Houphouët-Boigny, as his close confidante. Côte d'Ivoire, the "Coast of Ivory," alludes to a resource of brilliant whiteness whose violent extraction of bone from flesh is now firmly coupled with the dark side of the global economy. Yet Côte d'Ivoire's most forceful assertion with respect to its name has involved not this association, but rather the maintenance of an unyielding Frenchness: it declared, in 1986, a refusal to recognize any translations of its name—the English Ivory Coast, the Spanish Costa de Marfil—in formal diplomatic exchanges (Lea and Rowe 2001).[4]

After reaching land in Treichville, Pont Général de Gaulle arrives at the Jardin Bourse du Travail, translated roughly as the "Labor Exchange" or "Labor Placement" Garden.[5] The bridge terminates in a roundabout adjacent to the Solibra beer-and-soft-drink factory, a prominent manufacturing and distribution company with a near monopoly over the Ivoirian beverage market.[6] Crossing this bridge in 2008, one would have looked up to find a billboard advertising Guinness, an Irish beer locally bottled and distributed by Solibra (see figure 0.01). Eight Black men stand on either side of a man-sized Guinness bottle. The label reads, in English, "Foreign Extra." Each proud and distinguished looking, the men from left to right appear to be, first, a retiree, invoking a lifetime of steady work and a pension in old age, followed by men whose sartorial expressions suggest various accumulation strategies: a businessman, an athlete, a mechanic, a man whose casual T-shirt and jeans indicate no discernible trade, a pilot, a doctor, and a DJ. The man in jeans holds a banner declaring, *Il y a de la GREATNESS en chaque homme* (There is GREATNESS in each man). Unlike the obdurate Francophonie of the name Côte d'Ivoire, here the roots of greatness bow to an Anglophone foreignness.

That the average man whose work is unmarked bears the banner for all men illustrates how Guinness has tapped into an African predicament of jobless men. A validation, this advertisement lays claim to parity among men irrespective of work, when otherwise empty time, waiting time, is made full with consumer time, momentary fixes of meaning-making. A man's worth, then, is contingent on something else: in this case, a Guinness beer. The Guinness brand bestows this resignified worth; this branding feeds a familiar narrative of branded Black bodies in the capitalist economy.

In 2008 Côte d'Ivoire was in the sixth year of a civil war that had split it into a rebel-held north and a government-controlled south. Already in its third decade of precipitous economic decline, the war exacerbated *la crise* (the crisis), justified the grounded economy, scared away much of the French and other expatriate populations who had long monopolized the inchoate business sector, and swelled an already strained urban labor market with displaced persons from the hinterland.[7] Once the "Paris of West Africa," Abidjan had become a decadent city, decadent in the double sense of the excessive indulgence the state lavished on the city center during its heyday and in the dilapidated condition of the majority of its urban space, constituted not by the planned colonial city but by the *quartiers populaires*.[8]

This was a time when, by official counts, three-quarters of Abidjan's four million residents were self-employed informally, earning their keep through luck and a hustler's sensibility (Union Économique et Monétaire Ouest-Africaine 2001–2002, United Nations Population Division 2009). To find work in a factory

FIGURE 0.01. Guinness billboard. Author's photo, Abidjan (2008).

like Solibra was inconceivable for the average man with poor social networks. Job seekers greatly outnumbered jobs, and the broker who connected them invariably demanded a hefty finder's fee. Once hired, a worker's earnings were subject to a regular cut for the manager. With so many desperate for these coveted positions, after two or three months Solibra was at liberty to fire one and hire another itinerant worker, thwarting the emergence of permanent employees who might then be entitled to full wages and benefits.

So recounted the *vendeurs ambulants*, or mobile street vendors, who sold along this stretch of road. Concentrated, with no shortage of irony, around the Jardin Bourse du Travail, at an intersection duly nicknamed "Solibra," these vendors sold inflatable balls, car mats, camcorders, toilet paper, phone recharge cards, and other assorted bric-a-brac to motorists stalled in rush-hour traffic. Just above them, as if to garner some dignity out of their uncertain status, stood that Guinness billboard. It offered an alternative possibility, an imaginary that reflected the shifting occupational realities and aspirations of Abidjanais men during a time in which finding a steady job was as unlikely as striking media stardom. In this imaginary established professionals rub shoulders with the new figures of the crisis economy: equivalent, then, are the pilot and the DJ, the athlete and the mechanic, the businessman and the street vendor. What they have in common—what makes them all great—is a Guinness in their hands. Here, Guinness has explicitly invoked greatness outside of wage labor, a realm demarcated by the colonial project.

This greatness was also rooted in the history of conquest. The imperial mission sought out foreign possessions not only as a source of land and labor but also as a market for European products. Undergirding this mission was a civilizational narrative that portrayed the consumption of foreign goods as Africans' path up the gilded evolutionary staircase. In late capitalism, a time when the reality of permanent contraction surpasses the anticipatory moment of an expanding wage economy, incorporation of the world's "bottom billion" renders proof of its triumph (Collier 2007, Prahalad 2006). An entrepreneurial-by-necessity, petty consumer class emerges as capitalism's final frontier. Supplanting the promise of wage labor under a regulated, planned economy, every man is now free to achieve greatness, making and spending on his own accord. His capacity to do so is a test of his self-worth. For those Treichville men who worked underneath this billboard, earning a few dollars on a good day, to be branded by Guinness was to gain status. In the absence of more durable lifestyle indicators, local hierarchies ranked who drinks a Guinness, who drinks a local beer, and who drinks at all.

The Guinness advertisement extolled a vision of corporate empire and citizen-consumer. Yet residuals of other imperial etchings coexisted in this space. Pont Général de Gaulle, the quartier Treichville, the name Côte d'Ivoire: all marked Abidjan as a bulwark of Françafrique, solidified through the extractive and exploitative relations of metropole and colony. These etchings overlaid different eras in the continuous story of racial capitalism, eras that differentially incorporated Black men into processes of production, consumption, and commodification. The story of Abidjan is a story of racial capitalism told in the exaggerated hierarchies of work and in the racialized imaginaries that these hierarchies produced as men sought survival and status. During the interregnum, the miracle-turned-mirage (cf. Hecht 1983) that became known as la crise, imaginaries circulated in lieu of probable expectations. These imaginaries bore the legacies of Black men's incorporation into racial capitalism, as would-be workers and would-be consumers in a modern economy—and in an enduring relationship to commodification as value.

The Dissolution of Work, So Conceived

Stuart Hall has said that race is the modality through which class is lived. Gender, then, is surely the modality through which race is lived.[9] The theory of racial capitalism establishes that capitalism and race are co-constituted, and racialization is the means by which capitalism continues to extract and distribute surplus, to allocate costs and benefits, gains and losses (Robinson 2000). This book advances the theory of racial capitalism by examining the hegemonic imaginaries that channel how Black men insert themselves as active subjects in the global economy. I use a Gramscian framework to unravel how exploited and excluded individuals consent to an oppressive system by virtue of dominant forms of racial and gender expression. Tracing the imaginaries that reinforce and contest the lived experience of Black manhood and that manifest in transatlantic exchanges, I establish the principal narratives among Black men in economies of severe un- and underemployment. In particular, I investigate the relationship between Blackness, masculinity, and economic agency in Abidjan, Côte d'Ivoire. Like the Guinness billboard and its surrounds, sites across Abidjan gain meaning from their historical significance and contemporary uses. The street corner, the speakers' corner, locales of leisure and diversion, the visual terrain of the sign, the body itself: all emerge as spaces for particular performances of manhood, performances that reinforce a survival-status nexus for precarious, underemployed men.

My empirical case begins from the premise that the global economy has moved away from a wage labor model, one that conceived of jobs to enable a decent quality of life for a man and his family.[10] I say "man" because historically wage labor was gendered: born in the industrialized global north and reproduced by colonial regimes in cities in the global south, capitalist norms established bread-winning as a rite of passage into responsible, modern manhood. But labor was also racialized: despite appearing as normative, the family wage has in fact been an aspiration realized in significant proportions only for men of a dominant race and class status. Incorporated into the capitalist world system as slaves or colonial subjects, the penalty of Blackness situated men from Africa and the African dias-pora at a severe structural disadvantage, and the majority of those inducted into modern economies never attained breadwinner status. Situated in this marginal position, their experiences portend the contemporary regime of informality and surplus labor: the loss, for would-have-been workers across the globe, of what some once took as a birthright. I contend that Blackness and projects of racial capitalism generally offer theoretically rich insights for this moment of prolifer-ating wage labor exclusion, a moment in which the crisis of work is doubly the crisis of masculinity.

By centering (post)colonial Abídjanais men, I illuminate the fundamental role of wage labor in producing dominant and oppositional imaginaries of Black masculinity in racial capitalism. Similarly, I emphasize that breadwinning ide-ology and access have been essential tools through which racial capitalism has established racial difference across masculinities and has excluded Black men. The African city in the European colonial project draws out how racialized con-ceptualizations of being civilized and citizen are woven into gendered norms. As the Paris of West Africa, Abidjan in particular was conceived as an ideal type in the post–World War II capitalist experiment. There, those incorporated into a state-regulated economy, entitled to family wages and social welfare, comprised the colonial and independent-era évolué (evolved) elite. For those left out, évolué livelihoods and lifestyles structured social hierarchies and were deeply aspira-tional. Abidjan's évolués were an experiment in social planning, the proliferation of French empire by way of a stratum of acculturated African civil servants who would uphold the colonial and neocolonial state and reproduce its norms and culture. Firmly established as the hegemonic ideal, this state-sponsored bread-winner circumscribed a universe of possible masculinities in which opposition would itself be rooted in economic aspiration. Transmitted across the Black Atlantic (Gilroy 1993) as media simulacra, diaspora men became icons of late capitalist success and potentiality for men excluded from this colonial experi-ment.[11] Defying the premises of the social contract, the seductive individualism of these icons offered a way to ascend hierarchies predicated on economic worth while bypassing Abidjan's entrenched évolué norms. However oppositional, economic agency remained a precondition to masculinity. I examine these two constructions, the évolué and the mass-media icon, the lived experience and the media imaginary, to trace one story of the long crisis of Black masculinity in racial capitalism. This story, as told from Abidjan, critiques the explicitly racialized and gendered system of wage labor as well as the alternatives that emerge out of value making in the capitalist world system.

The Crisis of Black Masculinity

> Breadwinning makes a real man.
> Black men are not breadwinners.
> Black men are not real men.

Unpacking the meaning of Black masculinity requires first anchoring the noun, "masculinity," and its modifier, "black," in capitalism, the system through which their common understanding gains salience. Thus posited, Black masculinity is an identity in contradiction, "Black" implying deficit or deviance from "masculinity." The noun and its modifier figure on opposing sides of the privileges accorded to capitalist subjectivities. As such, Black masculinity appears in perpetual crisis.

Conceptually, "masculinity" alludes to the power infused in the roles that men play and to the multiple dimensions through which this power embeds itself in society (Brown, W. 1995). It infers a dominant position in a set of social relations and establishes the behaviors, practices, and desires that are assumed to follow, even when structural conditions make them untenable. In capitalism, masculinity is associated with men's presumed economic dominance. This dominance emerged as a consequence of the gendered division of labor established in the European transition to industrial capitalism, remunerating men and leaving women's activities outside the regulated, state-sanctioned economy. Wages buttressed an idealized, heteronormative construction of masculinity within a patriarchal socioeconomic structure that positioned men as producers and providers. Intended to facilitate these co-constituted roles, the apex of social policy in the golden years of an expanding post–World War II global capitalism was the male entitlement to a family wage.

The rationale for dispossessing non-Europeans of their lands and forcefully compelling their labor was that capitalist expansion was simultaneously civilizational expansion.[12] "Whiteness," a designation that, while never fixed, was used as cause and consequence for claims to power, became shorthand for civilization and enabled agency within the world capitalist economy. Race acted as the key ideological tool to justify, while ensconced within a universalistic, egalitarian narrative, those who gained and lost from the extractive and exploitative tendencies of global capitalism. Civilized societies were distinct from and entitled to subordinate those that lived in a state of nature—savage or childlike. Blackness was defined in opposition to whiteness as a total civilizational absence. The transatlantic slave trade was particularly formative in that it reduced the Black body to the permanent state of unfreedom and propertylessness. Its source of value was as a commodity object, to labor in the total service of another. Blackness, as negation, precluded the conditions to full personhood.

By the Darwinian intersectionalities of the Victorian era, gender and race demarcated the makers of history and its others. Men, purportedly positioned in a higher stage of evolution, were to be the bearers of civilization, while women existed in a base state of nature, "too far behind men to be agents of history" (McClintock 1995, 223). Black Africans, Europeans theorized, comprised a "female race" (Cohen, W. 2003, 236). European conquest of Africa was a masculinist endeavor, posed as the penetration of a dark and virgin continent. In short, the logic of capitalism from its inception established gender and race as the categories that would organize individuals along a hierarchy of social and economic value and privileged those designated as male and white. As a deficit, Blackness revoked the masculine entitlements to work and property. Reinforcing this logic, a civilizational framework affiliated Black masculinity with immaturity and savagery, physical force over mental capacity, and implied deviance: irrationality, excessive or perverse sexuality and violence. Black men's supposed bestiality generated an uncontrollable, corporally located, hypermasculinity that necessitated their subjection to bodily discipline and control, to labor under the command of the whip or to be incapacitated behind the bars of a prison cell.

These depictions of Black masculinity, as deficient and deviant, elucidate why Black masculinity the world over is frequently associated with crisis: of formal or licit employment, of fatherhood and the nuclear family, of prison populations, and of marginalized and violently targeted quasi citizens. These crises originate in the racial capitalist and patriarchal political economy and in the disparate realities that Black men faced—and continue to face—vis-à-vis the fundamental processes of labor and capital accumulation.

A vast body of scholarship has emerged to document the deficiencies of Black masculinity and to chronicle the deviant behaviors that result. The pages that follow instead trace this "crisis" of Black masculinity and examine the consequences with respect to its structural roots: Black masculinity understood as a dilemma of economic participation for those Black men who aspire but fail to achieve this patriarchal, heteronormative expression of masculine identity in capitalism. Interrogating the twin legacies of slavery and colonialism, the diaspora and Africa, the imaginary and lived experience, under a singular analysis of Black masculinity in racial capitalism, this book will examine how the politics of representing Black masculinity has interacted and continues to interact with political economy vis-à-vis processes of production, constructed around wage labor and its alternatives in the informal economy and as entrepreneurial strategies; consumption, access to and denial of property; and commodification, the Black body valued in its object-state. In doing so these pages will relate "then" and "now": property regimes and failed breadwinners and conspicuous consumers; civil servants and entrepreneurs; objectified Black male bodies and tropes of Blackness. I will examine how Black men's incorporation as acting subjects—and commodity subjects—vows to resolve the contradictory location of Blackness and masculinity vis-à-vis their capitalist formulations.

What emerges is the story of a minor term. Blackness is "the Remainder—the ultimate sign of the dissimilar, of difference and the pure power of the negative—constituted the manifestation of existence as an object" (Mbembe 2017, 11). Blackness is racial capitalism's *other*, the minor term in a set of racial binary oppositions; from this subordinated location springs forth an anomalous iteration of masculinity. If masculinity is construed as dominant, then Black masculinity is set up to fail. Hence I introduced this discussion with a categorical syllogism. I presented a set of logical propositions where the major term is "real men," the middle term is "breadwinners," and the minor term is "Black men." If breadwinning makes a real man, and Black men are not breadwinners, the conclusion is that Black men are not, in fact, real men. It is a conclusion that derives from the racial and gendered logic of capitalism.

FIGURE 0.02. "We are tired of our men being emasculated so that our wives and daughters have to go out and work in the white lady's kitchen," declared Martin Luther King, Jr., to the men at the 1968 sanitation workers strike in Memphis (quoted in Honey 1999, 287). *I Am a Man*, March 28, 1968. Copyright Richard L. Copley.

Black Masculinity and the Production of Consent

Foundational to the emergence of liberal political economy was the principal of the codependence of patriarchy and property (Shilliam 2018). Figuring centrally in the liberal position on abolition, leading thinkers such as Adam Smith and jurist William Blackstone were pivotal in formulating wage labor as a socially necessary form of patriarchal servitude, the morally paternalistic expression of the master-servant (and juxtaposed to the master-slave) relationship. Wage labor enabled the unpropertied man to become a "small patriarch" in the domestic sphere and to assume "his orderly place in the hierarchy of paternalistic dependencies" (12). The "natural" inequality of gender, "considered to positively restrain the actions of all men," would therefore have a civilizing influence (16). But as property himself, the Black male slave was barred from marrying and thus unable to become a patriarch. This made him the subject of deep anxiety, for only patriarchy could avoid the mutually reinforcing tendencies toward anarchy in public and private life (Shilliam 2018). The solution to his predicament was not self-sufficiency, in other words, to be without a master.[13] In contradistinction to "masterless men" (13), wage labor was to produce a proletariat class of "deserving poor" indoctrinated in the principles of "industriousness, prudence, [and] patriarchy," and through which the system of private property would be reproduced and commercial society—capitalism—expanded (15, 16).[14]

While imperialism eventually disseminated the patriarchal ideology of breadwinning across classes, races, and continents, the labor conditions and legislations to facilitate family wages have always, often intentionally, been out of reach for the majority of men from formerly colonized and enslaved populations. Thus foreclosed, Black men have long been compelled to seek out alternative means to demonstrate the requisite economic agency upon which their masculinities are at stake.

The incorporation of Black men into capitalism disproportionately subjected them to nonnormative masculinities as they survived and garnered status outside the boundaries circumscribing "good" or "dignified" work.[15] As opportunities to amass wealth were more likely to bypass the wage labor route, the strategies of Black men preempted the market fundamentalism of the neoliberal economy, associating financial potency not with free labor power but with the freedom to make and to spend.[16] Independent of the regulatory protections of wage employment, they were poised as potential entrepreneurs. Their relative access or depravity moreover blurred the lines between citizen and consumer.

In premising modern manhood on economic participation, capitalism has played an essential mediating role in social relations. Codifying work as masculine while also normalizing Black men's restricted access to such work and their participation in alternative accumulation strategies were hegemonic projects: the ideological axes of capitalist domination. They were the means by which the unequal capitalist world order appeared natural, appropriate, and just. To draw from Gramsci's (1971) theory of hegemony, these were ideologies of the dominant group that produced a common sense understanding of the world and generated consent to domination. One's own social position, be it dominant or subordinate, was located in a logic that emerged out of those economic conditions. That logic produced consent.

Building on Gramsci, Hall (1986) developed a fuller understanding of superstructure beyond the economic structure, encompassing private relations and identity formations as composites of what Gramsci established as the ethical, moral, and cultural terrains of struggle. The emergence of civil society led to "a diversification of social antagonisms," with race and gender becoming "for the art of politics . . . the 'trenches' and the permanent fortifications of the front in the war of position" (18). The global law of value, Hall explains, "operates through and *because* of the culturally specific character of labour power" (24; emphasis in original). Here he (24) identifies the theoretical basis for a "non-reductive approach to . . . the inter-relationship between class and race" attentive to the "culturally specific quality of class formations in any historically specific society." He further observes that racial and ethnic stratifications "have provided the means for differentiated forms of exploitation of the different sectors of a fractured labour force [with profound] economic, political and social effects" (24). In this way Hall establishes how hegemony operates along the mutually constitutive realms of race and class in what I refer to as "racial capitalism."

Slavery and colonialism were the historically specific modes through which Black bodies were incorporated into capitalism, and they shaped the culturally specific quality of class formations in economies built on those foundations. "In the colonies," Fanon (1963, 40) explained, "the economic substructure is also a superstructure. The cause is the consequence; you are rich because you are white, you are white because you are rich." Yet on the African continent, unlike on slave plantations in the Americas, bestowing the privileges of whiteness was instrumental to consolidating consensus to racialized colonial oppression and promoted a kind of racial passing among those Africans who adopted the ways of the colonizer. A small number of Europeans were on the ground to enforce foreign rule over a vast inhabited territory, so that soliciting consensus and thereby promoting an elite African stratum designated évolué was in the West African colonies a necessary strategy.[17] Opportunities for improved livelihoods if not basic recognition of one's humanity immersed in this schema, African subjects swept into the white man's world faced the imperative to "turn white or disappear" (Fanon 1967, 100). "Mimicry and membership" (Ferguson 2006) thus entangled, colonial rule was not only a matter of violent coercion but also consent, and it carved out of indigenous society an évolué elite with allegiances and identities oriented toward the metropole. The pressure to conform to cultural norms upheld an economic order constructed of white dominance and Black subordination and rendered the politics of representation a crucial component of this colonialist-capitalist exploitation. Hegemony clarifies "the 'subjection' of the victims of racism to the mystifications of the very racist ideologies which imprison and define them" (Hall 1986, 27).

Devaluing Blackness satisfied explicitly capitalist logics of imperial expansion and its accordant, racialized social stratification. The Black body was both reified for its labor power and commodified for its difference. Implying a deficit of full personhood, Blackness constituted a global law of value that embodied a permanent state of extractability, exploitability, and ultimately disposability. Again, however, the terrain of struggle involved not only coercion but also consent—the construction of common sense. Culture constitutes the repertoire of representations in social life and comprises "the contradictory forms of 'common sense' which have taken root in and helped to shape popular life" (Hall 1986, 26). This framework illuminates the contradictory location of Black masculinity: the dual yet opposing common sense positioning of masculine entitlement and devalued Blackness. Black masculinity epitomizes how "subordinated ideologies are necessarily and inevitably contradictory, . . . the so-called 'self' which underpins ideological formations is not a unified but a contradictory subject and a social construction" (27).

Focused on how race complicates class solidarity, Hall's reformulation of Gramsci recognizes but does not task itself with theorizing gender as a fundamental mechanism of difference in the constitution of labor. However, the differentiated forms of exploitation and labor stratifications in European capitalism were from their inception already gendered. Fanon observed a colonial corollary of being white and being rich; he might have added that in the colonies, as influenced by the metropole, to be a man was to have money and to have money was to be a man.

In gender theory Connell (2005, 77) defines hegemonic masculinity as "the configuration of gender practice which embodies the currently accepted answer to the problem of the legitimacy of patriarchy, which guarantees (or is taken to guarantee) the dominant position of men and the subordination of women."[18] The breadwinner is, by extension, the hegemonic masculine working ideal. Masculine identities and practices establish meaning through "the common sense about breadwinning and manhood" (Donaldson 1993, 645). On a structural level whiteness facilitates access to this role. Rather than a "parallel problem about gender relations" (Connell and Messerschmidt 2005, 831), hegemony, within the context of gender expression—and racial difference, assumes its particular form and can thus only be understood within capitalist relations.[19]

In Connell's (2005, 79) framework, complicit masculinity, though not achieving hegemony itself, supports the "hegemonic project," thus "realiz[ing] the patriarchal dividend." Theorizing complicity as a gendered analogue to consent situates complicit masculinity as an ideological orientation through which structurally dislocated men reinforce hegemonic norms. Complicit masculinity underscores how Black men make claims to male dominance in a system of racial capitalism, even if that entails adopting differential aspirational models in the context of severe un- and underemployment and the failure of the classic breadwinner model for Black men globally. Crucially, complicit masculinity affirms that agency is located within capitalism so that, borrowing from Margaret Thatcher, *there is no alternative* to being a real man that is not rooted foremost in this relationship, despite one's own marginal position.

For Connell marginalized masculinity indicates a disadvantaged structural location, a point she (80) illustrates with regard to Black American men's persistent barriers of widespread unemployment, urban poverty, and institutional racism. As with men in other devalued racial groups or in the lower classes, these barriers prevent Black men from achieving hegemonic masculinity even though they may subscribe to dominant group norms. Connell (80–81; emphasis in original) argues that because marginalization exists "relative to the *authorization* of the dominant group," individuals like celebrity athletes may be hegemonic; still, their success fails to "trickle-down" and "yield social authority to black men generally." Instead, these select individuals become anomalous "exemplars of hegemonic masculinity" (81).

Thinking about how capitalism constructs gender identity and mediates social relations underscores how, on a structural level, Blackness signifies exclusion from the patriarchal dividend and thus masculine agency. Simultaneously, however, when individual Black men become icons through one-in-a-million livelihoods and millionaire lifestyles, as representative tropes they embody alternative expressions of masculine agency in the global economy—namely, as entrepreneurs and consumers. Centering Blackness in these celebrity tropes enables otherwise marginal Black men to also assert dominant identities despite their historical and contemporary structural exclusion from the breadwinning ideal. Instead of "critiqu[ing] the dominant culture's norms of masculine identity," they allow men to "rewor[k] those norms to suit their social situation" (hooks 1992, 96). Far from being situated outside or opposing capitalist hegemony, Black men who participate in underground economies or practice forms of conspicuous consumption use this agency to affirm their manhood.[20] Yet common sense portrays such assertions of economic agency as oppositional stances—in other words, dialectics of domination and opposition, negation and affirmation, are bound together within hegemonic common sense. Hegemony thus operates by appealing to strategies of domination and by generating its most obvious response. Resistance, in turn, is speciously articulated as financial achievement and consumer capacity, rather than as an assertion of masculine identity altogether outside economic registers of worth. Masculinity, absent these common sense associations, might for example include reconstructing the fatherhood role or elder status as provision of care rather than material resources (e.g., Burton 2021; Edin and Nelson 2013; Enderstein and Boonzaier 2012; hooks 2004; Johnson and Young 2016; Morrell and Jewkes 2011; Neal 2006; Wilson 2006). It is a challenge of uplifting a Black masculinity that is not constructed by and through the expectations of capital and its failures, racism, and patriarchy (Ratele 2015).

Responding to "white colonizers' notions of manhood and masculinity" and therefore "acting in complicity with the *status quo*, many black people have passively absorbed narrow representations of black masculinity, perpetuated stereotypes, myths, and offered one-dimensional accounts" (hooks 1992, 90, 89). Hegemony and consent provide a vocabulary to examine Black masculine subjectivity in racial capitalism from colonial conquest to economies of surplus labor.

The Argument

This book builds upon and expands these theoretical foundations on the racial and gender dimensions of hegemony. It explores labor narratives and imaginaries of Black masculinity in Abidjan, a city where modern manhood was strongly linked to French colonial norms of work, while also engaging the histories and expressive identities of men across the Black Atlantic to make a broad argument about Black masculinity in racial capitalism. I establish how racialized imaginaries of the ideal man shifted in response to changing capitalist regimes. I examine the period from colonialism to la crise as a narrative arc, illuminating the sustained power of imaginaries even while capitalism affords a deficit of real opportunities.

Parts I and II take as their departure the troubled expression of Black masculinity in racial capitalism examined thus far to probe Blackness as a signifier and a structural location within the political economy of patriarchy. I write within conversations on racial capitalism that interrogate individuals as active economic agents (or not) in the public sphere, conversations that often take male identity for granted. Indeed, the story I tell of Blackness as the minor term is one that has already subsumed masculinity into the construction of its normalized protagonist. I therefore encourage my readers to maintain at the fore of this discussion, when it is not itself manifest, the always intersecting, and contradictory, location of Black masculinity. It is this premise that will center Part III, when I examine Abidjanais men's performative masculinities. I add, moreover, that my account of Black masculinity is set within a heteronormative, cisgender framework. This was the universe as articulated by the men I encountered. Yet I remind the reader that these silences speak loudly about the assumptions that pertain to the rigid, imperial formulation of masculine identity and to the alternative, often liberatory, possibilities these assumptions foreclose.[21]

Part I traces the long crisis of Black masculinity in racial capitalism from slavery and colonial subjugation to the postwork economy. I argue that Blackness has been symbolically positioned against white supremacy as a manifestation of capitalist hegemony, locating the terrain of Black struggle in the arenas of representation and political economy. In doing so, I consider the Black male body's historical roles as undervalued labor power, as a commodity object, and as a fraught consumer whose access to commodities has been constrained or denied. Chapter 1 establishes the évolué and the media icon as the two tropes that constitute idealized masculinities for Abidjanais men, and around which I construct my argument. In chapter 2 I trace the evolution of the wage labor ideal in French West Africa from the slave economy to the breadwinning family wage at the moment of independence to show how colonization offered the privileges of whiteness to a stratum of African évolué men. Next, chapter 3 demonstrates how the location of the Black body as a primary site of struggle, the pervasive value of Blackness-as-commodity despite the exploitation and increasing exclusion of its productive potential, and the dual presence of hegemony and counterhegemony, most visibly expressed in the Black American celebrity, create the conditions for the media trope.

In Part II I provide a historical account of labor from colonialism to la crise in the African city with an emphasis on Abidjan. I complement this colonial past and present by tracing lineages of Black Atlantic imaginaries. This parallel analysis sketches the incorporation of Blackness in racial capitalism to examine its multiple and dialectical potentialities: as negation and affirmation, and in the form of Blackness commodified, synthesis. These are the origin stories of the colonial évolué and the global media icon.

Attentive to the double commodification of Blackness, as productive potential and cultural artifact, together defining the project of racial capitalism, I examine how these representations shape aspirational Abidjanais masculinities vis-à-vis capitalist processes of labor, consumption, and commodification. My analysis of imaginaries in chapters 4 and 6 reveals mechanisms of racialization and, with an emphasis on aesthetic practices, interrogates expressions of Black masculinity in former slave and colonial economies from inception to the present. Hegemonic racial constructions compelled particular responses, and I uncover how claims to agency via a repertoire of colonial and Black Atlantic imaginaries, negated or affirmed, operated within this dialectic. These imaginaries formed subjectivities and inspired subcultures alongside social movements. Yet the very gains won in the politics of representing Black masculinity, modes of value-rendering affirmation that contest racialized negation, threaten to fracture unified opposition to whiteness and capitalism.

I put this analysis of imaginaries in dialogue with the material conditions, spatial distinctions, and ideological framework that structured experiences of labor and manhood in Abidjan—in other words, the lived experience of racial capitalism for Abidjanais men. In French colonial Africa, racial signifiers took on cultural overtones, such that those men earliest incorporated into the imperial economy, as interlocutors of the colonial state, attained the select status of évolué and were conferred special rights and entitlements. Among this group were the first urban wage laborers. The évolué was the "main subordinate variant" of the European in the racially exclusive order that underscored "a phallocentric vision of colonial modernity" (Gondola 2016, 9, 122). Évolué identity carried over into "expectations of domesticity," with salaried work anticipating breadwinning and effectively collapsing the categories of man and worker (Ferguson 1999; see also Ferguson 2015). Across urban Africa wages came to validate a man's image of himself as provider and acted as a conduit to marriage, itself a prerequisite for "adult masculinity" (Lindsay and Miescher 2003). In short, economic participation predicated évolué masculinity, with the European notion of man-as-worker facilitating the African designation of man-as-husband. Africans not similarly favored were absorbed into capitalism under the brutal regime of forced labor or simply excluded as social juniors if not "savages."

What was the colonial economy of civilized wage labor became the "formal" economy upon independence, the consequences of which I take up in chapter 5. Despite always constituting the bulk of the urban labor market, informal activities were feminized and made incongruous for masculine identity. I draw on this framework to establish how the évolué shaped modern Abidjanais masculinity. I explore how the French civilizing mission, or *mission civilisatrice*, sought to acculturate African men into whiteness, a pursuit that rendered registers of race and culture equivalent and was expressed through men's livelihoods and lifestyles. By negating their Blackness, Abidjanais men asserted their agency.

Sustained Franco-Ivoirian neocolonial relations, embedded within an extreme instance of state-led development, buttressed economic prosperity and political stability in the first decades after Ivoirian independence in 1960, a period known as *le miracle ivoirien* (the Ivoirian miracle). Ideologically, this relationship generated an image of Abidjan as a "stepping stone" between Africa and the

West (Newell 2009a, 179). And it maintained the évolué ideal in Abidjan even while rallying cries of "Black Power" and "Black is beautiful" were igniting the decolonial and antiracist struggles of the mid-twentieth century elsewhere. Such affirmations of Blackness were frequently anchored in anticapitalist traditions to critique whiteness as an expression of capitalist hegemony. These affirmations occurred during a moment in which Black men's productive potential was in the process of asserting claims to greater value and agential participation in the global economy. Black men's labor had not yet been rendered redundant. I juxtapose these negations and affirmations as competing imaginaries for Black male potentiality in racial capitalism. In Abidjan acculturated évolués accepted the terms of the imperial political economy to redefine their own positions within but without contesting the representational repertoire of Blackness. Elsewhere, Black men derived value in opposition to whiteness and capitalism as a singular project, identifying racial capitalism as mutually constitutive of negating representations and an exploitative political economy. In other contexts Black men embraced those same racialized representations to exalt their agency as capitalist subjects.

My analysis of imaginaries establishes how ideological moments of Blackness are refracted through the Black male body—laboring or not—in the city, the locus of capitalist modernity in Africa. From there, I arrive at chapter 7, which discusses a period of economic stasis, protracted civil war, and political interregnum, precipitated by the debt crisis and the fall of commodity prices. Abidjan entered the twenty-first century with nearly 75 percent of its working-age population involved in the informal economy (Union Économique et Monétaire Ouest-Africaine 2001–2002). While this figure was the double consequence of a colonial legacy and structural adjustment seen across urban Africa, similar patterns of un- and underemployment have occurred for Black men in postindustrial cities in the global North and together reflect the "disposability" (cf. Wright, M. 2006) of Black men in late capitalism. Dissociated from the formal economy, men not only face formidable livelihood challenges but also stigma that directly target their sense of masculine worth. In turn, many dissociate as fathers and husbands and are resigned to remain social juniors in the public and private spheres. I theorize that men on both sides of the Black Atlantic, formerly positioned as exploited and undervalued labor, have now entered an economic regime of overwhelming exclusion.

La crise entrenched the negation of Black men's potential as wage laborers and breadwinners. The imaginaries that emerged reflect the transition from exploitation to exclusion as well as the legacy of the Black Atlantic struggle to affirm Blackness in the politics of representation. In what I call imaginaries commodified, Black men employ the hegemonic representational repertoire of Blackness to access the dominant political economic order, thereby signaling a return to commodification as a source of Black value. Mass-media icons, as tropes, are exemplary: rejecting the wage labor ideal, they embody extreme expressions of alternative livelihoods and lifestyles of celebrity entrepreneurship and hyper-consumerism and vindicate un- and underemployed Black men globally. These responses to denigrated representations of Blackness fracture the singular oppo-sition to racial capitalism as a politics of representation—against whiteness, and political economy—now, celebrating capitalism. Entrepreneurialism and citizen-consumers supplant wage labor and transform the évolué ideal. In doing so, the particular configuration of the colonial political economy is rejected, but the racial hierarchy of the world political economy remains.

Imaginaries that circulate throughout the Black Atlantic are not simply abstract representational repertoires; rather, they structure how men express their lived experiences, narrating their livelihood strategies and shaping their lifestyles. Part II outlines imaginaries of Blackness set within the dialectical strug-gle between negation and affirmation in racial capitalism. In Part III I examine how the évolué and media trope, as resolutions to that struggle, contributed to the construction of masculinities in Abidjan amid civil war and sustained eco-nomic decline. I use ethnographic fieldwork and interviews with political propa-gandists, or orators (orateurs), for former President Laurent Gbagbo and mobile street vendors (vendeurs ambulants) in Abidjan from 2008 to 2009, supple-mented by visual analysis, to demonstrate how underemployed Abidjanais men asserted economic agency, and accordant registers of public value and self-worth, outside of wage labor. Having thus far shown the capacity for racial capitalism to elicit consent via ideologies of masculine dignity, value, and success, in these empirical chapters I demonstrate how marginalized Abidjanais men, even as they fail to achieve breadwinning masculinity, remain committed to patriarchal tenets that uphold the structures of racial capitalism and the generalized subordination of Black men within it. By situating my study within the narrative arc of racial capitalism, I establish how, far from indicating a novel formulation of African masculinity in late capitalism, orators' and vendors' struggles to assert dignity, value, and success were contiguous in conflict and character with those faced by Black men since slavery and colonialism.

Orators gained renown in Abidjan as President Gbagbo entrenched his reign during Côte d'Ivoire's 2002–2011 civil war, a contested battle over Ivoirian iden-tity that excluded regional migrants, northern Ivoirians, and with an awakened hostility, the French. Positioning themselves as President Gbagbo's street propa-gandists, orators were well-known public symbols of the country's political crisis. Highly educated men who a generation prior would have constituted an ascen-dant middle class of civil servants, they now faced dwindled opportunities. They frequented the Sorbonne, a public space in the urban core, where they espoused nationalist and misogynist speech to audiences of predominantly un- and under-employed men. Rejecting racialized colonial narratives that limited évolué status to salaried men, particularly civil servants, orators used anti-French rhetoric and patronage relations with the Gbagbo regime to assert entrepreneurial identities and thus redefine the évolué in the economy of la crise. These men accounted for the failures of the Ivoirian developmental model that had been predicated on the public sector and articulated a vision of the future role of the state as generating employment opportunities by way of financing entrepreneurial projects. Yet by declaring themselves évolué, they upheld the terminology and deep significance of the colonial social imaginary in the Ivoirian postcolony.

Mobile street vendors (hereon vendors) sold their wares between cars at busy traffic intersections. Their activities were highly denigrated and of dubious legality, and their growing prevalence in Abidjan offered a striking, public symbol of Côte d'Ivoire's economic crisis. The stigma attached to such informal work in a city where the wage-earning évolué identity was so closely linked to citizenship translated into the social classification of vendors as noncitizens, although many were Ivoirian. Seeing little hope for upward mobility or dignity in their work, many found inspiration from men in global Black popular culture who had themselves escaped poverty to garner immense wealth. On an everyday basis socially aspirant vendors "bluffed" (Newell 2012) their way through Abidjan's hierarchy as conspicuous consumers, and in the longer term they hoped to transform their hobbies in the worlds of music and sport into viable professions.

Orators and vendors both adhered to a market ethos, according value to the capacity to buy or to sell. Dismissing as a prior generational ideal the worker entitled to social protections, they exalted the entrepreneur and consumer of the laissez-faire state. I examine how orators and vendors performed these subjectivities: orators by way of political imaginaries and vendors by way of VIP imaginaries. How these men navigated urban sociality in an Abidjan of la crise demonstrated the emergence of a market ethos from the racial and gender order of the colonial African city. This order underscores how hegemony operates around unattainable producer-provider norms of masculinity and through tropes of Blackness. Beyond Abidjan and the African city, my examination elucidates the challenges that Black men face as excluded men in a global system of racial capitalism. I assert that Blackness, initially subjected to "thingification" (Césaire 2000, 42), and Black masculinity in particular, incorporated into capitalism absent the value-rendering agency of the laboring subject, comes to personify the ideals of making and spending—the ultimate market freedoms. While the évolué, and breadwinning generally, predominate as masculine aspirations, un- and under-employed men in Abidjan and elsewhere also emulate the Black man-as-trope, an identity entrenched in legacies of commodification and consumption. I draw a line from the évolué and the media trope to the aspirational and performative masculinities of orators and vendors. I conclude that Black men, who as a majority have been structurally impeded from achieving the salaried breadwinner ideal, have developed alternative models of success that prefigure the ideal subject in the contemporary postwage economy.

Following a co-constitutive trajectory of social coherence, cultural worth, and accumulation rooted in racial capitalism, the elevation of évolués and media icons emerged out of many possible ways for Abidjanais men to assert dignity and value. The coexistence of other Abidjanais masculinities, from those expressed through the exchange and care networks of Sufi *zawiyyah* at home and abroad (Simone 2001, 2004a) to those derived from the sexual and physical aggrandizement of gang membership (De Latour 2001), belies how "in the same place and time, another set of conditions, another way of doing things, and another reality have always already been possible" (Simone 2010, 8). The means to achieve limitless becoming is the hope that Abidjan, like all cities of migrants, offers. Yet in the "time of the 'postcolonial'" (Simone 2010, 9), the limiting register of racial capitalism so often dominates the horizon, foreclosing alternative ways of being under the cover of market freedoms, the social enfolded tightly within the economic. Just as they exemplify these market freedoms, orators and vendors are then simultaneously manifestations of Abidjan's promises and failures.

Racial capitalism, as it materializes through power and differentiation, is spatialized across multiple geographic scales. Each scale reinforces the civilizing mission as a project incompletely realized in the African city and structures place and imaginaries in a "here, not there" hierarchy from denigration to aspiration,

TABLE 0.01 Situating Blackness vis-à-vis economies of exploitation and exclusion

Economy of exploitation	Colonial évolué: Blackness negated; accepts the terms of the imperial political economy to redefine its position within the representational repertoire by way of acculturation	Blackness-as-resistance: Blackness affirmed; opposes whiteness and capitalism as a singular expression of hegemony through representation and political economy
Economy of exclusion	Market fundamentalist évolué: shift from wage labor to entrepreneurialism accepts the terms of the world political economy while rejecting the colonial legacy	Media icon: Blackness commodified; employs the representational repertoire of Blackness to access the dominant political economic order—extols livelihoods (celebrity entrepreneur) and lifestyles (hyperconsumer) of iconic Black men

negation to affirmation. By elucidating this imperial composition in Part II, I anticipate my ethnographic approach, in which I identify sites in Abidjan that reflect, reinforce, and contest the metropole/colony distinction as urban center/ periphery modalities. Positing orators and vendors as protagonists in this story of racial capitalism in an Abidjan of la crise, I therefore construct my empirical discussion around particular sites in the city that constitute their spaces of sociality and economic livelihood: nodes along these men's survival-status nexus. I concentrated my fieldwork in three quartiers: Plateau, the urban core and former colonial settler's city, and peripheral Yopougon and Abobo. As center and periphery they represent the "two separate ideas" of France and Africa (Naipaul 1984, 80), contemporaneous axes of postcolonial urbanity.

Chapter 8 describes my methods and sample. Chapter 9 examines the Sorbonne, a predominantly male, nationalist, and pro-Gbagbo speakers' corner in Plateau, and the organization of orators who made it their place of work. There, a market iteration of the évolué ideal maintained a firm grip on men's aspirational identities and livelihood strategies. While socially and financially dependent on their political networks, orators aspired to enter the world of business as state-financed entrepreneurs in a postconflict Côte d'Ivoire. The privileged relationship they had forged with the Gbagbo regime provided little steady work in the present, still this was an advantage that helped them survive in the tenuous and unpredictable economy. With those who listened and socialized at the Sorbonne, orators performed being in the world and the city that centered Ivoirian citizenship and political partisanship. Orators and audience members alike adhered to scripts of modern manhood in the public and private spheres of politics, the economy, and the home, creating within the Sorbonne a fictive social world of their own masculine dominance. In doing so, they collapsed narratives of modernity, masculinity, and citizenship.

Chapter 10 explores peripheral Abidjan—the streets and intersections where vendors peddled their goods and the leisure spaces and social worlds where they escaped the stigma of their trade. Vending was a marginalizing activity designated outside the realm of work and deemed inappropriate for men and citizens. To contend with this stigma, vendors employed coping strategies from denial to resignification. In particular, many vendors identified with activities outside of work, aspiring to realize hobby-based alter egos that mirrored the livelihoods and lifestyles of mass-media tropes, namely those of iconic athletes and musicians. They consumed Black popular cultural production and in doing so, developed an Abidjanais vernacular that circumvented established narratives of évolué identity to articulate an urban belonging that connected their experiences to a Black Atlantic periphery. Like the Sorbonne's orators, vendors constructed aspirational identities in masculine spaces. But these were boys' worlds, in the double sense that vendors lacked the means to attract women and they were unable to convert their fantasized alter egos into adult masculinities.

For orators and vendors alike failure was an unforgiving truth that struck against their aspired imaginaries. Unlike vendors, orators came from better-off families, were more highly educated, and had grander expectations of what might come of their lives. Nevertheless, like the vendors, those expectations constituted a "what might have been" in the era of le miracle ivoirien. If orators were the would-be middle class, vendors were the would-be working class. The realities of their lives—unmarried and unmarriageable, surviving month to month if not day to day—stood in sharp relief to their fantasized lives as successful entrepreneurs and conspicuous consumers.

Chapter 11 interrogates sartorial expression, the brand, and the space of the sign as extensions of the media icon. First I examine how marginal men employ their bodies to approximate the icons they so admire. Next I highlight one brand, Dolce & Gabbana, that had been appropriated and made ubiquitous in the Abidjanais lexicon. Finally, I look at the art of the hand-painted barbershop sign and the *gbaka* (privately operated minibus), demonstrating how portraits of Black Atlantic icons redefined spaces that represented contemporary African urbanity and the un- and semiskilled jobs available to its men. These visual narratives of Black masculinity on Abidjan's periphery underscore how the registers of Black, male, and global act as signifiers of value and belonging.

These original empirical chapters reveal expressions of masculinity "as embodied performances entangled in a maze of social contexts and as exhibiting bodies that are both objects of and agents engaged in social practice" (Gondola 2016, 11). I demonstrate how performances of Abidjanais masculinity relied on entrepreneurial and consumer narratives to secure social and monetary rewards. Simultaneous to the negation of Black men's productive potential, Abidjanais men embraced alternative imaginaries that contested their exclusion from the wage economy. In my conclusion I situate my account of Abidjanais men within the narrative arc of Black masculinity in racial capitalism and consider what is at stake for identities both rooted in and negated by processes of capitalist accumulation and disposability, as well as for the world at large. My postscript explores the politics of my own positionality in the field.

This investigation of underemployed Abidjanais men and the colonial and Black Atlantic imaginaries that shaped their livelihood and lifestyle aspirations provides an account of how racial capitalism operates through the mutually reinforcing realms of labor and ideology. Attending to the ways that hegemony is secured for Black men who confront the failed breadwinner model, I show that the double imperative for survival and status manifests through common sense constructions of racial and gender identity. Intervening in the longstanding debate of the crisis of Black masculinity, in urban Africa and throughout the Black Atlantic, this book demonstrates how gendered labor narratives and racialized imaginaries produce consent among Black men and sustain a global system of racial capitalism.

A Note on the Narrative and Rethinking the Ethnographic "Object"

The theoretical work that this text performs began with my fieldwork in Abidjan, with encounters that will doubtlessly be familiar to students of postcoloniality and popular culture in African cities. I take a lengthy detour to arrive at that point, however, on a course that interrogates Abidjanais men's subjectivities not in themselves but rather as they are formed in dialectical tension, by and through existing relations of power. These subjectivities recall the direct, Franco-Ivoirian colonial lineage, as well as invoke distant, Black Atlantic imaginaries whose own respective struggles I am compelled to reconstruct to make sense of present contradictions. I historicize the subject formation of underemployed Abidjanais men as a means to theorize more broadly the co-constitution of Black masculinity's economic and social value in racial capitalism. To do so requires telling a story that is equal parts theory and history before finally arriving at—or rather, returning to—ethnography. In that sense my narrative proceeds in reverse order from my scholarly journey, an inductive methodology refashioned into a deductive analysis.

This book takes as its ethnographic object capitalist hegemony. By seeking primarily to understand how production, consumption, and commodification suture value to Blackness and masculinity, I direct attention to capitalist hegemony as a composite of ideological and material relations. Beyond this study I offer this analysis as a call, in the tradition of "ethnography of global connection" (Tsing 2005), to reconsider the ethnographic approach. When ethnography emerged as a colonial device for knowing the other in the pursuit of conquest, the presumption of "us" as both the authoritative voice and the intended audience of acquired knowledge was clear. Difference and inferiority were likewise assumed. Thus by pronouncing our common humanity, when EuroAmerican allies of the "native" cause initially insisted that the cultural practices and social norms of the other made sense, that they were more same than different, they were engaging in acts of political insurrection. Yet doing so maintained the a priori "us," this act of translation embedded in a transfer of knowledge from one group to another. The compulsion to give visibility, to document how those who are different from and have materially less than the presumptive "we" live meaningful lives, however well intentioned, betrays this residual colonial logic. The baseline assumption of ethnography, like any endeavor to study the human, must always be our common humanity. This was never a discovery to be made. Once the ethnographer dismantles accepted geographies of voice and audience, she can no longer be satisfied with chronicling and interpreting symbols, rituals, or subjectivities. The task is rather to unveil the historically constituted and geopolitically situated dynamics of power, be they macro-, meso-, or micro-, that structure these othered life-worlds. This call transcends studying "up" and "one's own" to fundamentally to rethink the ethnographic object itself. It is a call to substitute the object as persons or groups for that of the circuits and relations through which materialities and ideologies of sameness and difference travel.

A Note on "Blackness"

My use of the term "Black" in this book fundamentally refers to African and African-descended populations. It is a term that is nevertheless highly fluid and contingent on the national/local, temporal, and situational context, in actuality operating within a "logic of coupling . . . black *and*," even as hegemonic ideologies demand a "logic of a binary opposition" (Hall 1993, 111). For people of mixed race, being socially or legally classified as Black has and continues to depend on who makes up the majority group and the political and economic relations on the ground. Black in this sense is a relational identity associated with marginal status. Further, the malleability with which Blackness can be either claimed or disposed of has much to do with skin color; the darker one is, the harder it is to identity as other than Black, although even this is mediated by other factors such as class, nationality, or culture.

A variety of racial formulations have manifested in the Black Atlantic according to the imperatives of different forms of slavery and colonialism. In Côte d'Ivoire, the *métis* (mixed-race) category applies and may be more likely to be grouped alongside, though not the same as, whites. In the French Antilles the legal definition of Black, and slave, shifted by historical era. Black identity in metropolitan France is formally expressed as cultural difference from an otherwise French nativist-universal norm, an albeit-denied racialized understanding of citizenship that almost fully overlaps with the divisions constructed during imperial conquest. Black identities in the United States are distinctive for their broad reach due to the legacy of hypodescent, whereby the slave woman's offspring reproduced the category of racial unfreedom in perpetuity.[22] In other words, being partially Black meant one was wholly Black, and hence, in the antebellum South, a slave. In many Latin American countries a plethora of fine distinctions among white settlers, slaves, and indigenous populations were codified during the colonial period and persist in the contemporary social imaginary. In colonial Africa, where control by a small white population necessitated local alliances, mixed-race children acted as powerful intermediaries and were highly advantaged vis-à-vis the majority Black Africans; this produced a set of relations and racial understandings whose social legacy persists today. An exception to this is South Africa, where "coloureds" became a distinct middle stratum.

For the above reasons my use of the term "Blackness" is not to be reified but rather understood as a fluid and sociohistorical construction. And while I have restricted my designation "Black" to African or African-descended populations in the preceding pages, as a larger political project I recognize that the European imperial racial order was global, and I therefore emphasize the relational and hegemonic construction of Black-as-other. It is a claim of otherness that is sometimes asserted and at other times imposed. An umbrella of Blackness forges alliances among formerly colonized, albeit disparate populations, not all of whom are African-descended, and I find the designation fruitful for thinking through subjected and marginalized positionalities and solidarities.

Finally, I capitalize "Black." Harris, C. (1993, 1710), drawing on Kimberlé Crenshaw, observes that in the US context "Black" denotes a minority group and is thus a proper noun. Moreover, "the use of the upper case and lower case in reference to racial identity has a particular political history," such that "'Black' is a naming that is part of counterhegemonic practice" (1710). Yet I also note that centering the experiences of continental Africans rather than the African-descended diaspora compels a major shift in the use and meaning of Blackness. In most sub-Saharan African contexts, ethnicity, region, or nationality are far more prevalent; Blackness is not derived from the erasure of these other complex identities. Moreover, while the imposition of Black identity was foremost an act of imperial negation, beyond any strict counterhegemonic practice, within a framework of racial capitalism the Black-white opposition is not a totality but a particular expression of capitalist hegemony. Blackness as it is presently lived has multiple ideological purposes, including, I argue in these pages, as a hegemonic counternarrative. In that context, the reification of Black identity has also been an instrument of commodification.

Part I

THEORIZING BLACK MASCULINITY IN RACIAL CAPITALISM

Capital can only be capital when it is accumulating, and it can only accumulate by producing and moving through relations of severe inequality among human groups. . . . These antinomies of accumulation require loss, disposability, and the unequal differentiation of human value, and racism enshrines the inequalities that capitalism requires. Most obviously, it does this by displacing the uneven life chances that are inescapably part of capitalist social relations onto fictions of differing human capacities, historically race.

—Jodi Melamed, *Racial Capitalism*

The very obviousness of the visibility of race convinces me that it functions as a signifying system, as a text we can read.

—Stuart Hall, *Race, The Floating Signifier*

TROPES OF BLACK MASCULINITY

Racialization and racism are intrinsic to capitalist development and reproduction (Robinson 2000). Race colonizes social hierarchies and strategies of capital accumulation, enabling some bodies to command property while others are commodified. Race provides "the raw materials from which difference and *surplus*—a kind of life that can be wasted and spent without limit—are produced" (Mbembe 2017, 34). From capitalism's originary moment reaching beyond Europe to encapsulate the land and labor of peoples it rendered subject, Blackness operated as the minor term, the acute and diminished other, of a binary worldview: white/black, civilized/savage, beautiful/ugly, good/evil. Henceforth paired, these oppositions normalized social and economic inequality within the dominant purview. Toward peoples of African descent, racialization has justified, and racism is thereby a consequence of, the exploitation of Black bodies in the transatlantic slave economy. "The features of the man, his hair, color and dentrifice, his 'subhuman' characteristics so widely pleaded, were only the later rationalizations to justify a simple economic fact: that the colonies needed labor and resorted to Negro labor" (Williams 1994, 20). With the experiences of Black humanity in stark juxtaposition to the liberal ideology of freedom in the emergent discourse of free wage labor, the slave posed from the outset as its primitive and necessary exterior.[1] Appealing thus to ideology and imaginary, capitalism generates value out of—and devalues—Blackness in regimes where whiteness is both immediately and symbolically hegemonic.[2] The social is in every instance embedded in the economic.

To trace the means by which capitalism situates Black labor, and how accordant imaginaries of Blackness structure the social order and legitimize domination, is to document the hegemonic order of racial capitalism. To further demonstrate the production of consent among Black populations requires critically interrogating value creation in racial capitalism, attentive to how inclusion on one axis may preclude resistance on another. Integral to these considerations is the fact that capitalism codes labor, and economic participation generally, as masculine.

The incorporation of Black men in capitalism occurred under severe structural disadvantage, generating an enduring crisis of Black masculinity. Part I assembles the theoretical components of Blackness, and particularly Black masculinity, in racial capitalism to examine the production of hegemony and consent. To begin, I situate the two frames that compose my argument: the construction of the French West African évolué, and the Black Atlantic media icon, both of which disseminated as idealized imaginaries for Abidjanais men.

Representation of Consent: The *évolué*

In French colonial discourse, race was at the center of cultural contestation, the site of hegemonic struggle. Civilization peddled a whitening effect, ascendance up an evolutionary ladder from commodity to collaborator, the pinnacle a "not quite/not white" (Bhabha 1994) évolué: translated, literally, as "evolved."[3] The term "reflected the permeation of social Darwinist discourse throughout European societies by the late nineteenth century" and the belief in the teleological journey from savage to civilized/citizen, an idea that "animated France's overseas expansion . . . and provided an ideological framework through which to legitimize the fact of imperial rule. Consequently, those people the French colonizers decided had made the first steps out of their initial state toward becoming French were said to have 'evolved' in comparison to their countrymen" (Genova 2004, 21–22). Thereafter entitled to seek the rights of a citizen, evolution presumed an inherent "biological handicap" of Africanity that fused colonial "racial criteria and sociological criteria" (Urban 2009, 452).

Acting as material and ideological interlocutors of colonial regimes in Africa, the évolué was a means by which "racial capitalism deploy[ed] . . . terms of inclusion to value and devalue forms of humanity differentially to fit the needs of reigning state-capital orders" (Melamed 2015, 77). The évolué realized the mission civilisatrice by becoming a modern, capitalist subject: a man who would approximate the Frenchman in public and private life, providing for his wife and children with the wages he earned in the new, colonial economy. To exchange free labor in the white man's image, a capitalist realm whose parameters were defined by and largely interchangeable with the colonial state—was to become an acting subject of history. At its base membership ensured consent.

When colonial territories achieved independence, civilization, evidenced by economic and political parity and the social benefits such parity was to accrue, became the charge of the new regimes. The mission civilisatrice assumed the discourse of "development." In Côte d'Ivoire as elsewhere in the colonies of French West Africa, or AOF (Afrique Occidentale Française), a peaceful transition to independence was driven by and saw the évolué assume power, consolidating political and economic interests and maintaining a neocolonial relationship with France under the elite complicity of Françafrique.[4] The public sector encompassed a somewhat wider but nonetheless minor stratum of wage earners. Neither fully bourgeoisie nor proletariat by the prototype of European industrial capitalism, this constituency of bureaucrats and unionized workers constituted a relatively privileged "nucleus of the colonized population . . . most pampered by the colonial regime" (Fanon 1963, 108). The measure of a successful state—and the implicit state-society social contract—would be whether modern workers' livelihoods and lifestyles would proliferate widely, supplanting noncapitalist arrangements otherwise labeled nonmodern, traditional, or African. External to the wage economy, these latter arrangements, such as market trade, were relegated to what women did—and posited as something other than work. The state being the major employer of wage labor, these steady and dignifying jobs became crucial sources of patronage (Cooper 1996, Mbembe 2001). At the level of man and state, global belonging was largely a question of the character of one's economic incorporation into the domestic and international realms (Ferguson 2006).

Relations between individuals and the state as well as between states were in these ways embedded in political arrangements that originated in the colonial project. In Côte d'Ivoire close ties to France and full coffers from a booming cocoa sector in its early years of independence enabled first President Houphouët-Boigny to maintain an expansive civil service and buttressed its position as the regional hegemon, le miracle ivoirien. With a large, regional migrant population working in low-status, informal occupations, wage labor was a proxy not only for manhood but also citizenship. In Côte d'Ivoire the idea of civilization translated into the language of development and state-sponsored employment. Racial capitalism, with its political economy of Françafrique and impetus to civilize Africans in the image of the French colonizer, was inextricably linked to gender and nation. Being évolué was a matter of man's relationship to the intertwined state and economy.

Representation of Consent: The Media Icon

Another means of contesting Black subjugation has entailed not sociocultural whitening but rather resignifying bodily commodification as economic agency. From the outset, racial capitalism engaged a politics of representation to devalue

Blackness in the world political economy, thereby aligning white supremacy and capitalist hegemony. A coalition of antiracist and anticapitalist struggles has frequently met this coupling while also lending to a common sense understanding of Blackness as oppositional to both forms of oppression. Yet asserting an equivalence between Black value and economic agency decouples antiracist and anticapitalist agendas. Within the racial capitalist world order, these assertions appear to undermine racial domination even while its structural inequalities persist.

Black men's breadwinning aspirations meet their disproportionate marginalization in the global economy. In urban Africa the informal economy has inadequately absorbed surplus laborers, leaving the great majority of men underemployed, while men across the Black Atlantic are more likely to be under- and unemployed or illicitly employed than the white majority.[5] Nevertheless, icons of Black manhood appear prominently as skilled entrepreneurs and conspicuous consumers, their celebrity status articulating corporate culture (see, e.g., Carrington 2010, Shipley 2013). Figuring within a long tradition of glorified Black entertainers and athletes when Black people are otherwise excluded from mainstream social, political, and economic life, these icons operate as tropes of Blackness that provide authoritative, mass-mediated counternarratives to racialized dispossession. In doing so, they model a path to full citizenship that bypasses wage labor. And like the évolué, theirs are gendered tropes: economic participation simultaneously makes Blackness visible and facilitates patriarchal entitlement.

As celebrity icons, African Americans are key agents of global popular culture and direct the "standards, desires and passions" (Gilroy 2001, 100) of Black culture globally. Yet as a demographic, African Americans do not profit from the commodification of Black culture. The "paradoxical location" (Hanchard 1990, 32) of American Blackness is thus inextricable from histories of capitalist excess and negation. Disseminated across media circuits, it appears simultaneously hegemonic—as American, imperialist, and capitalist, and counterhegemonic—as African, colonized, and resistant if not revolutionary. The latter, in its "stylish opposition" (Ebron 2008, 319), obscures the former. This expression of Blackness neither identifies nor opposes white supremacy as a tool of capital accumulation. A double entendre, American Blackness provides a productive tension for the pursuit of capital accumulation on a global scale.

Colonial formulations and global media circulations represent idealized imaginaries of Blackness amid la crise. Abidjanais men drew on these imaginaries as they aspired to become évolués and celebrity icons. Together, they comprised the spectrum of Black masculinity vis-à-vis production, consumption, and commodification. And, by creating an illusion of opportunities that were in fact out of reach for the vast majority of Black men, together they obscured the overarching structures of racial capitalist exploitation.

THE EVOLUTION OF THE WAGE LABOR IDEAL

History shows us that every civilization originates from the white race, that none could exist without the help of this race, and that a society is only great and brilliant in proportion to its sustained contact with this noble race.

—Arthur de Gobineau, *Essai sur l'inégalité des races humaines*

What reassures France is that she holds light and freedom; for a savage people, to be enslaved by France is to begin to be free, for a city of barbarians, to be burned by France is to begin to be enlightened!

—Charles Hugo, *Un coté de la question d'Afrique*

In 1441 Portuguese sailors offered ten Africans from the Guinean coast to their expedition's benefactor, Prince Henry of Portugal.[1] Within three years the Portuguese were systematically trafficking and enslaving African men, women, and children. Other European nations soon joined in the lucrative sale of human flesh, and with the growing importance of sugar production in the West Indies and Brazil and the dependence on African slave labor for its cultivation, the slave trade quickly became central to the emerging global capitalist economy. After Britain and Portugal, France commanded the third-largest transatlantic slave trade.[2] By the 1620s the French had established colonial plantations in the West Indies to breed cattle and cultivate tobacco and sugar. Settlers introduced African slaves prior to the territory's falling under formal French jurisdiction, and within a half century "it was clear that slavery would become the dominant form of labor and the basis for French wealth in the Caribbean," with the "institutions, customs, and laws that developed around black slavery in the French West Indies confirm[ing] the inequality between the races" (Cohen, W. 2003, xxii).

Having already granted concessions to private companies in the Senegal and Gambia region during the previous decade, in 1638 France established a trade port on the Senegal River that became its first sub-Saharan African colony in 1659. French traders commenced slave trading there in the 1670s, and France brought it under government control in 1685, at which point the trade

FIGURE 2.01. Map of Afrique Occidentale (West Africa) featuring natural resources (1897). Credit: Bibliothèque Nationale de France.

constituted France's primary economic interest in Africa (Schneider 1982). The first French expedition to present-day Côte d'Ivoire, in search of slaves and gold, occurred in 1687 (Cohen, W. 2003, 158). There, the French coordinated its slave trade predominantly from the port of Assinie, abducting bodies for transatlantic transport as well as for continental labor in mines (Loucou 2012).[3] The slave trade in the region peaked from 1720–1760; when it declined, so too did the French presence (Atger 1960, Loucou 2012). From the start of the slave trade to its end, the French enslaved approximately 400,000 Africans from what is now Côte d'Ivoire (Loucou 2012).

The transatlantic enslavement of African-descended people ended in three general phases: first, European nations sequentially abolished slavery in the metropole beginning in the early 1700s; next, they abolished the slave trade in the early 1800s; and finally, over a period of several decades in the mid-nineteenth century, they abolished slavery in their colonies. France abolished colonial slavery in 1848. Rather than Europe's departure from Africa, however, manumission signaled a renewed orientation toward colonial rule, trade monopolies, and varying forms of forced labor. From the slave trade through colonization, the known territory of Africa was for Europeans a continent to be understood and carved up according to commercial interests.

French conquest of the territory, originally called Côte d'Or and renamed Côte d'Ivoire in 1893, was initiated through treaties with chiefs along the coastal region.[4] In 1832 France returned to its post at Assinie and began fortification in 1842 under the guise of securing the region from slave traders (Daddieh 2016). Assinie was inaugurated as Fort Joinville in a treaty the next year with Attacla, its king. The initial terms were stock colonial arrangements: ceded African territory, French legal authority over disputes between French and natives, and a commitment to "free" trade—in other words, French control over the terms of trade and monopoly access to native products (Atger 1960, 446).[5] In the earliest years commerce was mostly an individual affair. Arriving in Grand Bassam in 1862, the merchant Arthur Verdier became the first permanent French settler in 1871. At this point France had, by decree, extended its sovereignty over much of contemporary Ivoirian territory (Atger 1960, Loucou 2012). It drew formal colonial borders and appointed Louis-Gustave Binger, a vocal advocate of European control as a remedy for the "despoil[ing]" effects of the indigenous slave trade (Cooper 2000, 115), as the first governor of Côte d'Ivoire on March 10, 1893.

No longer primarily a reservoir for the trade of Black bodies, Africa's new value was to be in the exploitation of labor and the extraction of land and resources in equal measure. France pursued this value in response to the erosion of "order and prosperity" in its Antillean slave colonies, transforming its civilizational narrative into "coherent [administrative] doctrine" on the continent (Conklin 1997, 15).[6] It was a shift justified on moral grounds: as enlightened protectors, the French were compelled to end the barbaric practice of slavery and introduce its African subjects to the superior system of capitalist "free" labor. Free labor ideology was part of "the imagery of freeing Africans from various forms of bondage," essential to construing a righteous colonial project "distinguishing the progressive colonizer of the early twentieth century from the freebooters, bandits, kidnappers, and buyers of human flesh who had for past centuries represented Europe overseas" (Cooper 2000, 111). Like other European countries, France recognized the roots of this barbarity not in Europe—where proponents had elevated the perverse narrative of slavery's civilizing influence—but in Africa, which they characterized as a land of despotism and stateless anarchies, with peoples naturally inclined to enslave one another if not to be themselves enslaved.[7] The promise of free labor and the portrayal of African savagery, in other words, obscured in order to legitimize the violence of Europe.

Abolitionists became some of the most outspoken "propagandizers for expansion" (Cohen, W. 2003, 155). The French abolitionist movement promoted colonialism as not only moral but an economic alternative to the slave economy. The colonial labor force would cultivate the raw materials upon which Europe had come to depend, and colonial populations would provide new markets, thus "fulfilling the laws of humanity and enriching its exchequer" (2003, 164). The major abolitionist constituency, the Société des amis des noirs, founded in 1788, declared that the end of the slave trade would "ope[n] with greater ease the countries until now closed to commerce; then will the domain of European activity spread" (quoted at 165). Similarly, the Institut de l'Afrique, an abolitionist group formed in 1841, promoted three goals: the ending of slavery, the development of European commerce, and the establishment of European settlements (268). Free labor and a money economy was also to produce consumers, Africans to be incorporated into the modern world for the expansion of industry and the enrichment of empire. Under the cover of emancipation, by the 1884 Berlin Conference France and the other European empires had claimed the majority of the continent. On the ground, they evaluated entire populations according to their utility in the pursuit of power and profit. An 1891 article in the daily *Petit Parisien* stated plainly: "Each gunshot opens another outlet for French industry" (quoted in Schneider 1982, 72).

Formally eradicating the practice of slavery in its West African territories in 1905, France envisaged these new colonies as havens of freedom on an unfree continent. Yet its narrow definition and legalistic "evasions and euphemisms" simply transformed "what was once called an 'esclave' into a 'captif,' then a 'non-libre,' then a 'serviteur'" (Cooper 2000, 119).[8] Finally, colonial administrators settled on forced labor. Promoting "civilization through coercion," the administration "insisted that use of force was required to help Africans progress" (Conklin 1997, 212).[9] Until formal abolition of the practice in 1946, the lucrative plantations of Côte d'Ivoire became dual epicenters of forced labor and wage labor in AOF (Cooper 1996). To justify the persistence of forced labor, administration officials extolled its profitability—by the late 1920s Ivoirian export agriculture was boasting the most impressive economic growth in all of AOF, and governors' reports from this decade embellished Côte d'Ivoire with monikers such as "Garden Full of Rich Promises" and "Land of the Future" (Coquery-Vidrovitch 1992, 289, Cooper 1996). Officials also stressed the imperative for cautious withdrawal, to advance "toward freedom but not so fast as to allow forced labor to be replaced by 'barbarism'" (Cooper 1996, 81; quoting a 1937 labor inspector).

Gabriel Louis Angoulvant, governor of Côte d'Ivoire from 1908 to 1916, was an early advocate for the forced cultivation of cocoa; he insisted on the necessity to "completely modify the black mentality" in order for "subjects to be brought

ADRESSE

A L'ASSEMBLÉE NATIONALE,

POUR

L'ABOLITION DE LA TRAITE DES NOIRS.

Par la Société des Amis des Noirs de Paris.

FÉVRIER 1790.

A PARIS. De l'Imp. de L. POTIER DE LILLE ,
Rue Favart , N°. 5. 1790.

605803

FIGURE 2.02. The Société des amis des noirs seal was reproduced from Josiah Wedgwood's 1787 slave medallion, which pled, "Am I not a man and a brother?" These medallions were popular among French, British, and American abolitionists and represented an early instance of the commodification of Black struggle (Eschner 2017). Société des amis des noirs abolitionist pamphlet cover with its seal of an enchained and kneeling slave, reading, *"Ne suis-je pas ton frère?"* (Am I not your brother?) (1790). Reprinted from Wikimedia Commons, Société des amis des noirs, February 1790, User Joost Vandeputte.

to progress against their will" (quoted in Conklin 1997, 215). This attitude, coupled with local conditions—namely, a sparsely populated territory amid a dense forest zone identified as prime for cash crop cultivation, generated a system of forced labor so expansive that it threatened regional demographic decline (Conklin 1997, Cooper 1996). The implementation of an indigenous tax, hailed as necessary for transitioning into modern capitalism, was a crucial tool of labor coercion. Further ensuring the compulsion of the colonial population, in 1910 the administration began refusing payment of taxes in the local currency, and in 1917 it mandated payment solely in French francs (Coquery-Vidrovitch 1992, 113). Even after formally eradicating forced labor, the administration devised provisions for the practice on public works and private enterprise alike, thereby underwriting settlers' investments against the unruly agency of African labor (Conklin 1997).

Neither enslaved nor at liberty to opt out of the new economy, Africans were caught in a purgatory of forced labor that the colonizer rationalized away under the lofty goal of creating capitalist subjects. Driven generally by a spirit of willful misrecognition, European colonizers derided Africans who, on farms, in cities, and in mines, made use of their "mobility, kinship networks, and the ability to move between modes of economic activity to avoid too much dependence on white employers" (Cooper 2014, 21). This charge of indolence interpreted Africans' flexible relationship to the colonial wage economy not as a means to maintain social ties, bodily freedom, or financial autonomy, but as utterly irrational, shortsighted, and premodern. Subsuming their subjects into wage labor regimes, compulsory or otherwise, became the standard by which imperial powers were to establish themselves as "the responsible colonizer" and "to define a progressive mission for themselves in the colonizing of distant peoples" (Cooper 1996, 23). The mission civilisatrice, in short, proclaimed liberation through exploitation.[10]

Mise en valeur

In 1677 Louis Moreau de Chambonneau, explorer and administrator to French Senegal, observed: "The men mostly do nothing, are very lazy and lascivious; as long as they sit in the sun and have something to smoke, some millet and water, they are happier than the princes of France" (quoted in Cohen, W. 2003, 23). Perpetually fearful that they might devolve back into their state of nature, Pierre Tap, in charge of the Inspection du Travail for AOF, expressed similar sentiments about Africans in 1937, a quarter of a millennia later: "But I have the absolute conviction that all these anarchic and naturally enemy races would return to the forest and to their savage life, abandoning fields and shops, if they were not strongly contained by the French" (quoted in Cooper 1996, 84). That progress must be forced, achieved through European domination and African subordination, had become dogma by the twentieth century. What was envisioned was a "close collaboration between European (capital and brains) and native (labor)," as described by one interwar report from AOF headquarters (Conklin 1997, 237).

Mise en valeur was first conceived in the nineteenth century as a mutual benefit for metropole and colony (Schneider 1982). Though colonial officials spoke of "mise en valeur" rather than "'forced labor,' with all the excesses and brutal obligations that this term conjured up," mise en valeur nevertheless entailed "forcibly inculcating a hitherto absent work ethic" (Conklin 1997, 229, 7).[11] Absent this work ethic, they argued, "the free-labor principle could not operate" and moreover, given regular labor shortages, only force "would ensure sufficient manpower for essential civilizing projects" (213). The racial stereotypes upon which the French defended this approach were further entrenched in the 1920s, a period in which demand for colonial commodities was booming and racial theories had gained new prominence in Europe (Conklin 1997). It was in this decade that the administration settled on the principle of mise en valeur as the "rational development . . . of the colonies' natural and human resources" (6).[12] AOF Governor-General Jules Carde explained in a 1924 circular that coercion met the "strictly humanitarian goal of protecting the native against his own nature" and empowered him to "procure the supplementary income to improve his present condition" (quoted at 227). In short, the French charged themselves as moral protectors, with the forced labor regime endowing upon Africans a civilizational gift that they inherently lacked: the value of work. Metropolitan propaganda efforts supported the compulsory efforts of mise en valeur in the colonies. In France government-issued posters belied a pure profit motive as they extolled the economic and business potential of colonization in Africa (Gervereau 1993a). By the economic crisis of the 1930s, and despite reality proving otherwise, "empire was above all presented as a miracle cure" (Ageron 1993, 104). Enforcing mise en valeur upon a subordinate population was indeed core to the founding logic of the mission civilisatrice (Holo 1993).

Mise en valeur intended the dual "production of cash-crop exports and the 'production of men'" (Conklin 1997, 220). When European states began experimenting with the labor conditions to cultivate modern industrial subjects among their own populations and to articulate the parameters of the social contract, they exported variations to their colonies. If, as reasoned by the ideologically progressive, though short-lived, French Popular Front regime (1936–1938), "even a small working class was after all a working class," then it "needed the same kinds, if not the same *level* of protection as one in France" (Cooper 1996, 108; emphasis in original). Foremost in kind was the gendered wage.[13] Its reproduction in the colonies was a projection of the normative European gender order onto negative estimations of African laborers. The effort underscored the fact that stereotypes of lazy Africans were both racialized and gendered. In his essay, "The Natural History of Man," for example, the influential French naturalist Comte de Buffon (Leclerc 1828, 232) philosophized, "Savage nations condemn the women to perpetual labour. They cultivate the ground, and perform every office of drudgery, while the men indolently recline in their hammocks, from which they never think of stirring, unless when they go a hunting or fishing." This oft-repeated depiction, ignoring indigenous divisions of labor in which household provision was a collective responsibility, read normative European gender roles onto African rural, and later urban, economies (Boserup 1970). It moreover decried subsistence agriculture as unproductive, giving cause for the export-oriented plantation enterprise to render bodies and land profitable for the colonial state. Invoked as a moral imperative, this narrative accompanied the transformation of mise

FIGURE 2.03.   Images of laboring Africans aimed to convince French metropolitan populations of the colonies' untapped wealth, to be exploited only with "the happy help" of France (Hugon 1993, 54). Palm oil tapping illustration in advertisement, "Les Colonies Françaises, Côte d'Ivoire," for Édition Spéciale des Produits du Lion Noir, La Grande Marque Française, Paris-Montrouge (n.d.)

en valeur into a post–World War II technocratic project to cultivate an African industrial man.

Race, Culture, and the *mission civilisatrice*

The logic of assimilation posited that once Africans entered a French social category, the universality of French law and French sociology applied to them, but the logic of African society, in French eyes, suggested that few would enter those categories.

—Frederick Cooper, *Decolonization and African Society*

From the moment of imperial conquest, the myth of the lazy African, "indolent and without ambition in the midst of tropical plenty . . . served as an alibi for forced labour and exploitation" (Pieterse 1992, 91). In contrast, a privileged subset of African men gained liberty out of the sun and fields by way of complicity: the closer they approached the colonial state, as "advisors" of indirect rule in British Africa, *assimilado* in Portuguese Africa, or évolué in French and Belgian Africa, the greater their rights and entitlements in the colonies and over their fellow subjects. France in particular prized its form of colonial rule for centering the mission civilisatrice. Adhering to a logic of cultural benevolence, Frenchmen believed that by bequeathing "European political and economic institutions, family structures, laws, and material culture . . . [they] could act as tutors, speeding up the evolutionary process" (Cohen, W. 2003, 176). By governing over all aspects of life, the French aimed to eventually create a local elite loyal to the metropole and "culturally and economically detached from any native social base" (Coquery-Vidrovitch 1992, 29). The colonial school system was core to this project, intended to produce a ruling class to perform the regime's administrative and economic functions while imbuing a duly colonial mentality: "the taste for [its] goods and industry," and a will to propagate French civilization (Cohen, W. 2003, 122, quoting Denise Bouche; Loucou 2012). Imposed as the language of rule, exchange, and cultural worth, in 1817 French became the obligatory language of public education (Coquery-Vidrovitch 1992, 23). Taking pride of place in the imperial imaginary, French colonizers considered their language an especially great gift to their subjects, and its mastery, particularly among Ivoirians, was and remains a crucial proxy for civilizational attainment (Loucou 2012, Touré 1981).

The "republican commitment to the rights of man" inspired Ernest Roume, then-governor-general of AOF, to propose in 1907 the extension of citizenship to "'meritorious' Africans" (Conklin 1997, 103). By the decree of Governor-General

William Ponty this measure was passed in 1912 (Genova 2004). And though the legal premise was that "it was impossible and undesirable to absorb all Africans ... it was accepting the principle that a West African subject could become a French citizen. Skin color alone was no barrier to naturalization, once the requisite acculturation had taken place" (Conklin 1997, 104). Only a miniscule proportion of colonized Africans were ever naturalized as French citizens over the full colonial span.[14] As articulated by one member of the Conseil Supérieur des Colonies (Superior Council of the Colonies) in 1925, "When one scratched the Frenchified surface of an educated African, 'the old [i.e., primitive] man' always reappeared" (quoted at 167).

Material circumstances in the colonies coupled with metropolitan race theories to determine the racial character of French colonial policy, with no strict chronological tendency toward deracialization. When by midcentury the international political climate made explicit references to race impermissible, a discursive shift occurred in which colonial officials made "an argument about culture with the same structure as one they were no longer willing to articulate publicly about race: African culture and African societies were now portrayed as obstacles to the progress toward which all races could now aspire" (Cooper 1996, 17). The link between race and culture, and the affiliated iteration of cultural racism, has remained an entrenched feature of the French racial imaginary.

The Emergence of an *évolué* Constituency

France's colonial foray into the vast territory of sub-Saharan Africa depended on native interlocutors. Hence, brute exploitation could not be its sole strategy. Instead, French administrators encouraged the economic and cultural assimilation of their first colonial subjects in Saint-Louis and Gorée, a policy they replicated in Côte d'Ivoire and across their West African colonies (Cohen, W. 2003, Loucou 2012).[15] This was based on a pragmatic demand for "personnel to fill the federation's growing bureaucratic needs": civil servants to be both loyal to the imperial mission and deeply connected to native society (Genova 2004, 21). These were évolués, "local people that had been instructed in the French language, familiarized with France's legal codes, and integrated into the money economy increasingly dominated by the industrial capitalist societies of Europe and North America" (21). Fulfilling both the instrumental and ideological imperatives of the mission civilisatrice, the successful incorporation of an indigenous elite was "vital to and exemplary of the success of French colonialism" (19).

As a conceptual category, whether subjects or citizens according to the shifting legal codes of a given territory and period, évolués were long ingrained in the

French colonial imaginary to designate an educated elite, a more civilized subset of the native population. Yet évolués' strong ties to indigenous society, essential for the financial and bureaucratic operations of empire, also served to justify their political exclusion from that larger imperial body as French citizens, effectively territorializing their rights within their respective colonial jurisdictions (Genova 2004). Therefore, as it was codified under Governor-General Ponty's 1912 decree, access to French citizenship became an individualized naturalization process that required meeting set criteria. Naturalization, with the exception of decorated military veterans, thereafter obliged the following:

> 1. To have proved devotion to French interests or to have occupied, with merit, for at least ten years, work in a public or private French enterprise. 2. To know how to read and write in French. 3. To demonstrate a stable means of support and to be of good morals and lead a clean life. (Ministère des Colonies 1912, 4918)

Africans who were objectively integrated into the empire by employment and language now faced subjective criteria that could justify their arbitrary exclusion. Accordingly, even évolués were "recast . . . as still fundamentally 'African' and in need of further 'civilization' by France," limiting them to being "regarded as 'half-French'" (Genova 2004, 22). To be naturalized French citizens, they were compelled to fully assume "a French identity defined by colonial authorities" that would extend past their professional commitments to social, cultural, and familial structures (22). They would tread a no-man's land as neither "uncivilized native subjects" nor "assimilated French citizens," and confronted new distinctions between citizen and subject that eroded existing évolué privileges, such as access to certain high-level positions in the colonial administration (Conklin 1997, 152).[16] Until 1923 only three men from Côte d'Ivoire were naturalized under the 1912 decree (Semley 2014, 283). Supplementing these same requirements was a more restricted decree in 1932, with the following conditions:

> 4. To have approached our [French] civilization by one's lifestyle and social habits. 5. If married, to be monogamous, and to have a family that also approaches our civilization by its lifestyle and social habits. 6. To have used the civil status to inscribe his marriage and the birth of his children. 7. To have taught the latter in French education. 8. To have satisfied military obligations. (Urban 2009, 451)

Intending to draw a hard line between citizen and subject, the former rights bearing and the latter not, the 1912 decree was a reaction to an emergent constituency of engaged, potentially mobile, and increasingly politicized Africans in the colonial realm. If Africans were to make claims on France, the administration contended, then they had to prove themselves sufficiently civilized to be worthy (Genova 2004). This imperial estimation of civilizational worth left no room for Africanity.

With this position the French colonial administration also unwittingly formalized "the *évolués*' sense of themselves as a distinct social category" that straddled two worlds (Genova 2004, 21). The contradiction the évolués confronted, having mastered key tenets of French civilization, yet—not quite/not white—still facing persistent barriers to full rights across the empire, heralded a crucial dialectical tension that was to shape the political stance of leading Francophone African independence figures as well as the articulation of the overlapping Négritude movement: the agitation for differential but equal inclusion *within* the French republican imaginary.[17] In both cases, the African évolué elite argued that their intimate knowledge of and commitment to both worlds, over and above metropolitan *colons* (colonists) or African chiefs, best positioned them as Africa's political and cultural vanguard. More immediately, this contradiction ignited effective évolué charges of French universalist hypocrisy and selective and politically motivated concessions of empire. Throughout, however, the évolués' socioeconomic entitlement and claims to cultural distinction above other Africans held constant.

The évolués' links to the metropole demarcated their modalities of living and working, making them a fundamentally urban constituency. So despite persistent rural connections, "what perhaps most distinguished the *évolué* from the rest of West African society was their place of residence": they formed a "new urban elite" (Genova 2004, 22).[18] Settler cities served as the "meeting points between cultures," and its évolué *citadin* (urban resident) within, the "agent of cross-colonization" (22). The confinement of citizen rights to administrative borders in the exemplary case of the Quatre Communes of Senegal explicitly located those rights in urban space. As he "transcended the discursive boundaries of 'Europe' and 'Africa,'" the urban and rural, respectively, the évolué "occupied a separate physical space from that of the native subject, yet only part way between metropolitan and indigenous life" (22).

In short, and despite its political constraints, évolué identity was from the start premised on regime entrenchment and co-constitutive of livelihood and lifestyle: employment for the advance of capitalism and inhabitation of the colonial city, the social identities of work and urbanity as the core indices of proximity to the metropole. And finally, imbricating masculinity with citizenship and civilizational attainment, the gendering of évolué identity was ensured by requirements that privileged men: French education, work in the wage economy, military service. This masculinist colonial modernity was reinforced by the évolués' "embrace" of a homosocial "model of public activity, thus providing the basis for the acceptance and propagation of a patriarchal model of social organization" (Genova 2004, 152).

An ethos of cultural assimilation, with the purported goal of eventually "creating French citizens out of Africans" (Crowder 1964, 203), endured well after formal French assimilation policy gave way to association.[19] The period under Vichy rule was particularly nefarious in its return to forced labor and virulent racism and represented a departure from the official inclusionary stance (Loucou 2012).[20] However, responding to the ascent of an increasingly vocal and politicized post–World War II évolué class in Africa and the metropole, colonial policy shifted back to an overtly assimilationist doctrine and an imperative to impart citizenship to its subjects (Conklin 1997). The resolutions of the 1944 Brazzaville Conference, marking a moment of major reckoning for the future of the French empire, assumed an "assimilationist position . . . promising improved access to positions and increasing levels of political responsibility to those Africans who acquired French forms of knowledge" (Cooper 1996, 178). Recognizing moreover that "deviations from equality of treatment would be evident and galling" between metropolitan and évolué civil servants especially, the late colonial regime passed the Lamine Guèye law in 1950, decreeing equal benefits for all civil servants (Cooper 2015, 185, 1996).[21] By centering sociocultural criteria and professional identity for political inclusion, these measures resolved the post-1912 conflict between évolués and empire while reinforcing "the old sociology of Africa that divided its population into a large group of peasants . . . and a very small number of évolués" (Cooper 1996, 181). Any radical transformation of the labor system remained a point of contention.

Imagining a Wage Laboring Class

While the évolué was from inception set apart, colonialism in its waning years attempted to form a wider subsection of urban, wage-earning Africans in the French image. Still, efforts to demarcate the legitimate worker frequently evoked the évolué ideal. Trade union participation, for example, was until 1952 limited by "evolutionist" criteria to individuals who met certain educational qualifications (Cooper 1996, 97). Family structure was particularly laden with associations that implied a worker's identity and personhood broadly, rendering it a continual flashpoint for assimilationist criteria.[22] Generally accepted as having acquiesced to French civilization, the extension of metropolitan workers' benefits, many of which linked back to family arrangements, were readily extended to évolués without the struggles or contestations that African wage laborers otherwise faced (Cooper 1996).

The introduction of African deputies into the Assemblée Nationale Constituante in 1945 was the decisive factor for eradicating, within one year, systems of
forced labor that the International Labor Organization had since 1930 declared
outside the norms of global civility but without which the French empire had
insisted it was unable to operate (Cooper 1996). In 1946 France approved a ref-
erendum to grant political representation to the colonies, effectively transforming the French empire into the French Union. In other core areas the administration similarly asserted a stance at once enlightened and defensive of its own
legacy, by creating opportunities for native employment, suppressing the *code de
l'indigénat*—which had legislated the inferior status of Ivoirian subjects, legal-
izing professional labor unions, and liberalizing access to education and health
care (Loucou 2012).[23] France perceived its policies to be distinctly progressive
and racially egalitarian, particularly those that granted opportunities to advance
to high levels in the civil service, especially vis-à-vis the "British tendency to the
colour bar" (Crowder 1964, 202).[24]

A prefabricated idea of social citizenship constituted the grander mission
civilisatrice that had envisioned making Africans into Frenchmen.[25] Its core
elements were labor legislation, social welfare, and family promotion policies;
in pushing for their extension beyond the metropole, the colonial administration agonized over "whether the nature of African society made it possible for
Africans to be citizens in a social sense as well as the constitutional one" (Cooper 1996, 281). Reckoning with ideological biases and practical obstacles to
such an expansive project, colonial officials thus resolved to direct their atten-
tions to a substratum of African wage earners. The évolué class, typically high-
level civil servants originating from multiple generations of privileged contact
with Europeans, remained perched at the top. Their negligible size designated
exclusive membership, itself a defining factor for their ability to exist at all.
The more democratic vision of an urban industrial working class, to be produced by the colonial state and reproduced in the Europeanized African family,
marked a significant reorientation from the metropolitan approach to African
labor as expendable. It was a social vision that drew on evolutionary discourse
to argue "that the problem of the African worker could be separated from the
problem of the African" (198). In other words, a "'worker'—who might be entitled to certain rights—was envisioned against the 'mass'—which was dangerous and backward—and against 'traditional society,' whose cultural backwardness necessitated the intervention of colonial powers in the first place" (265).
This vision derived from a set of convictions: that one could neatly define
and demarcate "work" in the capitalist realm, and this work was fundamentally distinct from other sorts of activities; to produce his labor a worker had
certain needs that could be universally defined; these needs encompassed the

worker's domestic situation and familial relations (Cooper 1996). Furthermore, by producing this idealized worker and his requisite lifestyle—habituation to a certain temporality, urban spatiality and economic exchange, a nuclear family, a French education—France would imbue the values of social citizenship. When officials asserted that wage earners were distinct from Africans generally, this "was less to state a fact than to offer a program: to define a class and its life style and to make it identifiable" (284).[26]

Established in 1932 to codify metropolitan labor practices in the colonies, the Inspection du Travail emerged as an "apparatu[s] of surveillance, shape[r] of discourse, [and] define[r] of spaces for legitimate contestation" (Cooper 1996, 16). Steadily formulated over the next decade, in 1945 France drafted the Code du Travail for its overseas territories, only passing it, after sustained debate, in 1952—two years after the Lamine Guèye law for civil servants. Advanced by Léopold Senghor, the Assemblée Nationale formally defined a worker as one "who has engaged himself to put his professional activity at the disposition of another person, physical or moral [i.e., a corporation], public or private, in a manner so as to exercise it for hire under the direction and authority of the latter" (quoted at 294). It was this constituency that was to receive the benefits and entitlements of French social citizenship, including family allowances that were conferred across AOF's African wage laboring population in 1956. In Côte d'Ivoire, by 1958, a midlevel industrial worker with two children was receiving an additional 10 percent or more of his salary in benefits per child, with additional pay for his wife's pregnancy and upon the birth of their child.[27] In exchange, he submitted to state surveillance, registering marriages and births, making regular medical visits, and enrolling his children in school. These benefits were part of his salary and rendered inseparable the institutions of work, family, and the state (Cooper 1996, 459). Racial capitalism in its French West African colonial iteration, refined after nearly a century of practice, was to be heavily reliant on state intervention.

But this experiment was short-lived. Within the space of four years, the colonies of AOF had achieved independence, leaving the burden for such grandiose social protections on the inchoate states themselves. The precursor to independence was the 1956 Loi Cadre. Asserting territorial independence for the colonies, the Loi Cadre was both a step toward political independence and economic autonomy and a means by which the French empire would relieve itself of the financial burden imposed by equality and universality. Once the all-encompassing rights of man were regulated into a set of tangible demands, they had proven far too costly for imperial imperatives (Cooper 1996, 2015).

The compulsion to assert the moral authority of the French empire was especially pronounced in the post–World War II reckoning of the global racial order and the rising tide of anticolonial movements. It was a context in which "universalistic notions of social progress—based on knowledge and capital resources" supplanted "old claims to colonial authority based on superiority of race and civilization" (Cooper 1996, 173).[28] This new context signaled a discursive shift from the language of labor exploitation and resource extraction for the metropole to that of development for the colonies. Mise en valeur was then squarely concentrated within a benevolent logic of colonial social and economic betterment, enacted under a series of modernization plans out of the Ministère de la France d'Outre-mer (Overseas France) and enthusiastically promoted by the state propaganda unit, the Agence de la France d'Outre-mer (Bancel and Mathy 1993). News of major infrastructural projects, factories, airports and ports, colonial buildings, and urban plans thus filtered back to metropolitan populations "with the clear intention to signal that progress in Africa, it is French" (Hugon 1993, 56). In promotional tourist material, scenes of modernizing cities replaced those that invoked exoticism and tradition (Gervereau 1993a). No longer depicting native backwardness, this new iconography offered proof of an emergent African évolué society, care of French technology and culture. Portending a future political economy of Françafrique, the imaginaries of these twilight years of French empire "testify to a utopia: to assimilate African colonies by way of

FIGURE 2.04.   L'Aérogare d'Abidjan-Port-Bouet Cérémonie d'Inauguration (Abidjan Port-Bouet airport inauguration ceremony), Robillard (1953). Archives nationales d'outre-mer.

cultural homogenization" (Bancel and Mathy 1993, 230). In doing so, the regime asserted an "obligation to manufacture an African *homo economicus*" (224).[29]

Ingratiating themselves foremost for imparting on their subjects French citizenship, culture, and way of life, this triad became France's principal justification for colonialism in its final decades of rule and shorthand for its grand narrative of progress. In this evolutionary spirit discrepancies between native norms or institutions and French civilization inevitably subordinated the former to the latter (Conklin 1997, Loucou 2012). In exchange for the fruits of civilization, African colonies, perceived as tributaries to the metropole, were to sacrifice their resources and their bodies (Conklin 1997, Crowder 1964). Thus despite the "suppression of forced labor and an economy of pillage," the logic of racial capitalism persisted in "an exploitative trade economy dependent on foreign support" (Loucou 2012, 154).

The Way Out Is In

For Francophone Africans, the only way out was in—via French institutions and culture. As the colonial project drew to a close, in particular, "the class struggle became more of a racial struggle pitting colonizer against colonized," while the African elite born of colonial tutelage emerged as "the primary actors of social change" (Loucou 2012, 197, 209). These divisions generated an enduring legacy. The class that reigned upon independence represented those who had thoroughly assimilated into French networks and acculturated into French norms and distinguished themselves from the African majority by their level of education, professional trajectory, and lifestyle (Coquery-Vidrovitch 1992). Embedded in postcolonial state power, the évolué inherited the functional equivalent of white privilege, which manifested alongside party affiliation or ethnic or regional identity. In addition to this elite, a somewhat wider net of status and entitlement was cast for those Africans who were subject to the directives of global capital. The tenets of the Code du Travail remained in the postcolonial regimes, as did the legal definition and regulatory status of workers (Cooper 1996). Wage laborers—the *salariat*, in other words, were the only ones who would be defined as real workers. And it was this substratum of the population that was conferred legitimacy as citizens of the modern state.

Translating racial difference into racial inferiority was, in short, a matter of hegemony. With their dominance in the new regime's political economy secured, the évolué embodied the hegemonic order; by conforming to the colonial work ethos and domestic arrangements they ensured its reproduction. The metropolitan worldview was visible in the manifold dimensions of the évolué: in modes of representation, in designated legal rights and entitlements that expanded with proximity to first the colonial and later the postcolonial state and acquiescence to French social and cultural mores, and in all manifestations of individual and collective life oriented around the salary. Having narrowed racial distance to the white *colon* by adopting his economic, social, and cultural practices, the évolué gained visibility and its accompanying worth.

This was one means by which Black humanity acquired social value and asserted agency in racial capitalism. Having examined the production and classi-fication of wage labor in France's West African colonies, in what follows I theorize Blackness vis-à-vis commodification and consumerism and consider the rela-tionship between these three forms of incorporation into the world capitalist economy. Finally, I situate this discussion in late capitalism, a period of prolifer-ating surplus bodies and the creation of idealized market subjects.

PRODUCER, CONSUMER, COMMODITY, SURPLUS

As an origin story racial capitalism made explicit the co-constitution of capitalism and racialization/racism. This involved both capitalism's material enterprise, whereby slavery and colonialism were oft-sidelined protagonists to the story of industrial revolution, and its ideological scaffolding, insisting on innate differences between constructed categories of humanity, already established in European precapitalist societies (Robinson 2000, Singh, N. 2016). Race, as a primary mode of differentiation and intersected with gender, organizes the division of productive and reproductive labor and unequally distributes capitalism's costs and benefits. History has ushered in significant mutations to earlier racial hierarchies, and while some prior distinctions have deracialized, Blackness endures as the abject other.[1] The value of the Black body in the development of capitalism is proportionate to the reification of its difference. Imaginaries of Blackness reflect racial capitalism's dual production of labor and ideology in the past and present.

As a theoretical framework, several components articulate Black masculinity in racial capitalism. First, slavery and colonialism operated as a singular project of racial capitalism that organized and justified the exploitation of Black bodies.[2] This has generated similar albeit distinct manifestations of racial capitalism across the Black Atlantic and situates the Black experience in one location as a familiar representational referent for another.

Second, gender norms are intrinsic to capitalist organization and ideology and intersect with race to establish the parameters of economic participation.

Whereas masculinity identifies the appropriate laboring body and acting subject of capitalism, Black masculinity is a contested terrain, poised at the interstices of patriarchal entitlement and racialized negation. Thus in affirming their Blackness, Black men might assert patriarchal claims to economic dominance. Moreover, promoting a gendered division of labor in which men are the sole family providers clashes against the experiential fact of marginality that disproportionately prevents Black men from enacting those roles. Hence, the failures of Black masculinity prelude late capitalism's breakdown of the social contract between man and state, the feminization of work, and "human-as-waste" (Yates 2011) economies of permanent unemployment and disposability. In so doing, Black masculinity offers a theoretically rich analytic from which to critique capitalism's racial and gendered dimensions.

Third, being initially incorporated into capitalism as a slave or forced laborer created the unique situation whereby the Black body was from the start commodified by the discrete categories of labor and capital, abstracted not only to produce value but also to be property itself.[3] The modifier "black" induced "thingification" (Césaire 2000, 42). As a phenomenological premise, Hegel (2004, 96), for example, contended that the African was by nature a slave who had not yet attained a "consciousness of his freedom, and consequently sinks down to a mere Thing—an object of no value."[4] Presupposing that Africans intrinsically lacked worth or value, this Hegelian logic insisted that "the European alone can and must put a value on it" (Krell 2000, 121).[5] Blackness assumed value as a good to be exchanged while simultaneously justifying the Black body as a subhuman, undervalued laborer, in other words, of greater relative value when exploited by others—a commodity in itself, a passive object, than as free labor power—a commodity for itself, an acting subject. Constituting "a relationship to subjection," Blackness thus produced "a body from which great effort is made to extract maximum profit," a body reduced to an "exploitable object" (Mbembe 2017, 153, 18). In economies of surplus labor, Blackness-as-commodity, a cultural artifact, continues to bestow value even while the Black human is rendered redundant, disembodying Blackness. A commodity subject, Blackness thus imagined is a product of racial capitalism.

Fourth, Blackness acquires value in its potential to produce and consume. In production, the racial penalty extracts additional surplus from the value of Black labor power. But active participation in capitalist relations is also achieved through consumption, and the freedom to consume wants and needs is a measure of both capitalist freedom and agency.[6] In societies structured by colonialism and slavery, Blackness imposes material, social, and legal constraints on consumption capacities. Production and consumption are then sites of Black struggle for equal rights and recognition.

The signification of Blackness and Black masculinity in racial capitalism underscore the ideological organization of systems of production, commodification, and consumption. The slave and colonial legacy elucidate the three-fold manner in which racial capitalism situates the Black man as labor and capital, commodifies Blackness, and distinguishes active consumers from passive commodities. These elements provide the theoretical scaffolding to interrogate tropes of Blackness in racial capitalism.

The Mission Civilisatrice: Perceptions of Blackness in Racial Capitalism's Evolutionary Project
Animal to Human
Feminine to Masculine
Savage to Civilized
Object to Subject
Indigène (Native) to *Citoyen* (Citizen)
Commodity to Consumer

Blackness Commodified

Domination . . . consisted less in the exploitation of the labor of those who had been subjugated than in the transformation of the latter into objects within a general economy of expenditure and sensation, which were both mediated by commodities.

—Achille Mbembe, *Critique of Black Reason*

Capitalism's original commodity fetish was the Africans auctioned here as slaves, whose reduction from subjects to abstracted objects has made them seem larger than life and less than human at the same time. It is for this reason that the Black body, and subsequently Black culture, has become a hungered-after taboo item and a nightmarish bugbear in the badlands of the American racial imagination. Something to be possessed and something to be erased.

—Greg Tate, *Nigs R Us, or How Blackfolk Became Fetish Objects*

Whiteness, "the quintessential property for personhood," commands rights and inheres privileges, preeminent among them, the right to exclude racial others (Harris, C. 1993, 1730). Whiteness, in other words, is "not merely race, but race plus privilege," and "as a theoretical construct evolved for the very purpose of racial exclusion" (1738, 1737). By contrast, the "hyper-exploitation of Black labor was accomplished by treating Black people themselves as objects of property" (1716). The "mixed status . . . as humans and property" in the slave economy made commodification "the critical nature of social relations" (1720). Racial capitalism, the ongoing material expression of social relations predicated on Black objectification, continues to alienate by way of commodification. In this sense racial capitalism is "the process of deriving social and economic value from the racial identity of another" (Leong 2013, 2190). Commodification "dissociates racial identity from the individual," so that "identity may be bought and sold on the market" (2198).

The codification of the body as Black fixed its status as property, or capital. Capital, be it an expression of economic, social, or cultural value, is always realized through relations of exchange. In slavery Blackness was valued as a thing to be exchanged, "a social link of subjection and a *body of extraction*" (Mbembe 2017, 18, emphasis in original). Entrenching this mode of exchange, "capitalism reinforces both the commodification of individual labor and the exploitative social relations made possible by that commodification" (Leong 2013, 2198). The value of Blackness as a commodity is derived from the very devaluation of Black life. It is a core tenet of racial capitalism: the commodity form at the expense of Black agency and Black bodies. This is important for thinking about tropes of Blackness in the absence of Black labor. It is the very commodification of Blackness, a thing in itself, that blurs the distinction between Blackness as it is embodied and Blackness as a cultural artifact.[7]

Commodification constructed a global divide between racialized agency and passivity in capitalism, manifesting in a distinct representational repertoire of Blackness. It was through advertising, for example, that European metropolitan populations were familiarized with their African subjects in the colonies, and this dynamic illustrates the tenuous boundary between the commodity body and commodity object. Consuming colonial goods became a means of "consuming the subjection of the colonized, a process that began with the packaging and marketing of the products," and reflected the "cultural pecking order" of the global economy (Pieterse 1992, 188). Always the objectified other, Black people were depicted as workers, servants, or "decorative elements," but never "as *consumers* of the product" being sold (190, emphasis in original).[8] Visual caricatures accompanied the prohibitions they faced participating in material culture, and both were crucial means of negating Black personhood.

Racial capitalism situates the Black body as capital, commodifying Blackness, and divides some (white) bodies as consuming and others (racially commodified, Black) as those that may be consumed. It demarcates participation in capitalism as an acting subject versus as a passive object. For men, the very distortion by which racial capitalism commodified the Black body elicits a masculine reclamation of agency as capital, a thing for itself—in other words, a performing commodity, a *commodity subject*—even while being denied masculine agency as a free laborer.[9] Commodification, in economies of surplus labor, has the perverse effect of extolling Black masculinity within the very system that objectifies it. The legacy of Blackness inducing "thingification" enables the personification of capitalism via the commodified Black man: the iconic media figure, presented as a trope.[10] Tropes are not merely personifications of a stereotype. As performing commodities they embody extreme expressions of livelihoods—whether celebrity or criminal—that emerged external to the breadwinning social contract. They idealize the market fundamentalism of late capitalism. In doing so, "basic tropes of 'blackness'—black culture, black identity, black institutions—have been distorted, remixed, and undermined by the logic of the current global economy" (Neal 2013a, 556). This Blackness enables a "stake in transnational capitalism"—but at the expense of being "posited and circulated as a buffer against white supremacy . . . and the collusion of racist imaginations and commercial culture" (556).

The marginalized position of Black men in economies of production has long confounded any total reliance on the laboring body to assert value. In the metropole or settler colony, capitalists have characterized free Black workers as unskilled, second-class, or labor of last resort.[11] In the extractive and plantation colonies, their contribution to capitalist enterprise was tallied not as labor at all but as resources and raw materials that laborers of metropolitan industry would eventually transform into goods of value. The prohibition of manufacture in the colonies guaranteed this territorial chain of differentiated value production. Rendered invisible, the picking of cotton or cacao, the tapping of rubber or harvesting of palm oil, all these were reduced to mere inputs. It was by industry that material was to be truly transformed—an active process—by man.[12] Chocolate is thus "made" in Belgium, fine cotton linens "made" in England. The packaging of the finished product recalled remnants of Black labor with compliant, dim-witted, and grinning caricatures, the fixing of Blackness not as active laborer but passive commodity object. The dominant logic that Black bodies were always already external to the labor process, even while compelled to work under the command of the whip, naturalizes the exclusion of those same bodies in economies of surplus labor. Yet commodification imbues value on the trope even when Black bodies are nonproductive. Upon the decline of productive economies and the preeminence of exchange, commodification recovers agency.

The reduction of Blackness into a performing commodity, or trope, originated in the construction of the Black slave as "capitalism's original commodity fetish" (Tate 2003, 4). This is particularly salient for the African American articulation, which, moving through the Black Atlantic, comes to represent hegemonic achievement and counterhegemonic resistance. The historical record bears witness to how, even while subjected to profound social, juridical, and economic inequalities, "the grandsons and daughters of antebellum America's slave commodities have become the masters of the nation's creative profile" (3). This counter/hegemonic commodification of Blackness as capital itself anticipates late capitalism, when Black labor is excluded rather than exploited. It is a legacy that renders Blackness particularly susceptible to disembodied market value: when Black laboring bodies have become in many instances redundant, the social and cultural registers of Blackness remain highly significant. This "'blackness' and an attendant black masculinity" replaces the value of labor with "real capital accumulation [that] comes from the circulation of black 'representations' . . . throughout the globe" (Neal 2013a, 556). This divide, between "the labor of black popular culture" and "the labor of black bodies" (561), belies how Blackness in the interest of capital accumulation transforms "the dreams of Black Power" into "quantifiable assets" (Neal 2013b, 77). Posing "urban black masculine alterity" (Fleetwood 2011, 154) as aestheticized rebellion—a deceptively common sense interpretation of counterhegemony—obscures the trope's entanglement in a social contract underwritten by racial capitalist commodification and accumulation. It produces a caricatured Black masculinity that achieves what is otherwise out of reach for many Black men: to be "at once an ultra-stylish thug and the ultimate American citizen" (154). This contradictory orientation effectively fractures the potential for Blackness to singularly oppose white supremacy and capitalist exploitation, those dual sources of its objectification and the devaluation of Black life.[13]

Struggle and Hegemony in Diasporic Representational Repertoires

Savage people are not consumers, but civilized people are becoming increasingly so.

—Sylvain Meinrad Xavier de Golbéry, *Fragments d'un voyage en Afrique*

All persons shall be entitled to the full and equal enjoyment of the goods, services, facilities, privileges, advantages, and accommodations of any place of public accommodation . . . without discrimination or segregation on the ground of race, color, religion, or national origin.

—(US) Civil Rights Act of 1964

From the start, commodities drove imperial expansion, both as a means to extract raw materials for their production and to expand beyond metropolitan markets. From the triangular trade to integrated colonial economies, Africans were then both sources of labor and markets.

When Europeans introduced manufactured goods to Africa, they sought to make its inhabitants "need them so badly that they cannot be without them, and thus will offer . . . all their labor, their trade and their industry" (eighteenth-century French explorer and clergyman Jean-Baptiste Labat, quoted in Cohen, W. 2003, 173). This search for relationships of dependency galvanized the mission civilisatrice. In the spirit of a "militant geography," France's Société de géographie commerciale, founded in 1876, linked civilizational ideology to trade (266). Repeating the directive of the *Journal des Chambres de Commerce* "to civilize people still barbarous," an 1882 column in the popular French *Petit Journal* advocated empire as a means "to instill in them the wants that are similar to our own in order to sell them our products" (quoted in Schneider 1982, 65).

The market imperative prevented Africans from being conceived, on the African continent, solely as property, and generated an early need and enduring desire to reconcile the commodified Black body with the Black consumer. In postcolonial Côte d'Ivoire, reigning as Francophone West Africa's regional hegemon, consumption of Western culture was the means through which Ivoirians "civilized" themselves in spirit, body, and taste (Touré 1981, chap. 8). Demand for imported goods, perceived as necessities in the elite cultural and material realm, perpetuated a cycle of import-substitution dependency (Touré 1981). Across the full spectrum of contemporary African economies, conspicuously consuming goods from elsewhere persists as the central mode of "participation in planetary exchanges, [especially] if we take into account the collapse or stagnation of its productive activities and the fall in its exports" (Bayart 2007, 220).

Consumption since the colonial encounter provided African men "access to maturity and masculinity" and "demarcate[d] the respective spheres of social success or failure" (Bayart 2007, 220). While wage labor has become the predominant means to access the cash economy and all that it facilitates in modern life, consumer practices also denote the properly évolué subject. The colonial legacy and its postcolonial attachments in the intimate and public spheres provide the "structurally entrenched underpinning of manhood as a performance intrinsically linked to money" (Smith 2017, 4). This expression of African manhood resonates powerfully with imaginaries of Black masculinity from the American hegemon. As both confront proliferating un- and underemployment, the "commodity fetish" supplants "commodity production" (Watts 2005, 188) and obscures the fact that a "truly free people possesses the power to produce, as well as to consume" (Weems 1998, 131).

How does one account for an imaginary whose legacy is embraced by men of disparate histories and whose lives are lived an ocean apart? The initial configuration of continental Africans in a world capitalist economy as labor and markets situated masculinity within a constellation of aspirational worth whereby African men would work and consume in symbiosis. Incorporation into a slave economy, by contrast, entailed a singular focus on laboring value to the point of the laborer's ultimate disposability. In that instance, the denial of consumer citizenship shaped the emergent struggle, as a set of oppositions, contested identities, negations, and affirmations.

The ascent of a hegemonic, diasporic representational repertoire of Black masculinity over the long twentieth century contained the history of its struggle and transcribed its material and ideological tensions onto the familiar terrain of unmet aspiration on the continent. Because Black American representational repertoires imprinted on imaginaries of Blackness in Francophone Africa and indeed globally, in what follows I reconstruct this struggle as a set of oppositions through which particular associations of racial and gender affirmation and economic agency emerged. It is an account that connects commodity object to consumer citizen, related through significant cultural articulations of the political economy of the time: as slaves denied property; as hyperexploited workers and fraught consumers; as dually civil rights propagators and a powerful emergent consumer base; as Black Power ideologues-cum-aesthetic revolutionaries; as media-generated Blaxploitation heroes; and as global consumer icons who are themselves branded, commodity objects. Embedded in these iterations is a dialectical struggle, shifting alignments of Black masculinity vis-à-vis capitalist hegemony. As I explore this struggle, from slave to branded icon, I highlight how negations and affirmations of Black masculinity in and against white supremacy reflect and reinforce Black men's value to be extracted as a laborer, consumer, and commodity. The tension I narrate between laborer on one hand and consumer and commodity on the other, was particular to the diaspora experience. Yet in becoming the hegemonic representational repertoire within the Black Atlantic, it produced a capitalist dialectic of value creation that has become integral to projects of self-making in the postcolonial African city—projects that take center stage in Part III.

The specter of the slave hangs heavily over consumer subjectivity among Black Americans. Initially situated in the national imaginary as property, "desegregating the dollar" (Weems 1998) represented a significant advance for Black social citizenship. Contesting their negative treatment as consumers and the "callous disrespect" from the advertising industry in which racist caricatures of Black people were featured as objects on products—"Nigger Hair" from the American Tobacco Company, "Pickaninny Chocolate" from the Whitman Candy Company, for example—became important aspects of the civil rights movement (1, 60).

In postbellum America the foremost constraint to Black opportunity is the denial of property, itself the liberal premise of the capitalist subject (Ranganathan 2016). Defying the "color-coded mainstream," the pursuit of property with equal fervor as life and liberty reveals "a semi-transgressive desire to join in the carnival of American plenitude as full participants in ways that racism might deny" (Gilroy 2001, 84). In so doing, "consumer citizenship and its brand identities" promote a depoliticized belonging in which "freedom often entails little more than winning a long-denied opportunity to shop on the same terms as other, more privileged citizens further up the wobbly ladder of racial hierarchy" (86). Life and liberty remain, as enduring structural elements of Blackness, deeply precarious.

For Black Americans whose ancestors were property, and Black people worldwide who continue to face formidable barriers to property ownership, the body has assumed unparalleled urgency as a site of struggle.[14] Challenging the strict and often deadly controls over Black bodies, resistance could be expressed as embodied acts of self-gratification. Black diaspora cultures "have used the body—as if it were, and it often was, the only cultural capital we had. We have worked on ourselves as the canvases of representation" (Hall 1993, 109). The labor of Black bodies, moreover, has not only been subject to the "super-exploitations" (Harris, D. 1972) of the capitalist system but also used to deny Black humanity. Work, the locus of Black men's denigration if not outright rejection, could not then be easily located as the site of Black *working*-class struggle (Kelley 1994). For Black men to be adorned in fine clothing, to dine well, in short, "to take back their bodies for their own pleasure rather than another's profit," was to assert their dignity and self-mastery, level status distinctions, and challenge stereotypes about uncivilized Black bodies (45). Finally, "refus[ing] to be good proletarians," such displays of consumer participation were to identify outside the degradations of the Black labor experience (163). Sartorial expression and consumer citizenship have offered alternatives to the public image of white working-class life, enabling Black men to contest racist depictions and affirm their own contested masculinities.

Because the full battle for social citizenship extends beyond work to the full realm of public life, consumer spaces have been critical sites of contestation. Beginning in 1892 with Ida B. Wells's successful call for a boycott of Memphis streetcars in response to the lynchings of three Black businessmen, either refusing

Black custom, in boycotts, or insisting on it, in sit-ins, emerged as important tactics in the American civil rights struggle (Weems 1998). Desegregation of consumer spaces by the mid-twentieth century was not due to any inherent "altruistic white liberalism"; rather, the growing disposable incomes of an urbanizing Black middle class stimulated an "enlightened self-interest," and coupled with effective hits on corporate fortunes as a consequence of Black organizing, pushed through significant representational shifts and increased access to the public sphere (4).[15] Despite pervasive anti-Black vitriol, catering to Black Americans often proved better business sense than not. Attentive to this increasingly important target market, a subgenre of articles emerged in advertising journals to advise companies on how to court the Black consumer, with one exemplary 1961 piece, titled "Know-How Is Key to Selling to the Negro Today," beginning with the observation that "the Negro needs to be recognized as a person" (72–73, quoting *Sponsor*). The article offered the following insight: "Can the Negro identify with your product? Can the Negro identify with the ad that promises 'lovelier, whiter hands with ABC soap'? Because of the Negro's history of suppression his need to be 'invited' to try the product appears to be a strong one indeed." Effective Black political organization and rising purchasing power, in short, spurred positive representations of Blackness.

Civil rights were at times synonymous with consumer rights and the overarching politics of representation. Hence "consumer militancy" and resistance to the "cultural assaults" of the advertising industry were identified as powerful components of the struggle against institutional racism (Weems 1998, 60). It was in this context that Martin Luther King, Jr., would juxtapose the newly achieved independence of former colonial territories with the situation in the American South: "The nations of Asia and Africa are moving with jet-like speed toward gaining political independence, but we still creep at horse-and-buggy pace toward gaining a cup of coffee at a lunch counter" (quoted in Meriwether 2002, 202). Over the course of its existence, the National Association for the Advancement of Colored People (NAACP) has consistently underscored the significance of the "black dollar" and threatened consumer action or negative publicity to corporations in campaigns such as "Black Dollar Days" and the Fair Share program (Austin 1994).

Black populations long ignored by manufacturers have been especially drawn to "the dreamworld of American consumer culture" (Gilroy 2001, 94–95). Capitalizing on their newfound inclusion, corporations charted the political and cultural shifts of their Black consumers. Black media icons reflected these transformations (Weems 1998). In the early 1960s, for example, Sidney Poitier was the face of the "respectable Negro," an assimilable representation of Black masculinity (81). Yet the rising militancy and Black nationalist consciousness of the following years derided what a new generation termed the "Sidney Poitier syndrome" (81). Compared to the "neutered Poitier," National Football League star running back-turned-actor Jim Brown initiated the Blaxploitation film industry of the 1970s to become the "Black Buck Hero of a Separatist Age" (81). Brown and other Blaxploitation heroes embraced stereotypes of a bestial, hypersexualized Black masculinity (Ongiri 2009; Weems 1998). By exalting a "beautiful Black phallocentric masculinity," Blaxploitation offered "an aesthetic revolution befitting the social and political revolutions of the time" to confront and contest oppressive representations of Black men in the mainstream American consciousness (Ongiri 2009, 173, 160).[16] To the cheers and jeers of their predominantly Black male audiences, the racialized and gendered exploits of these protagonists "put Whitey in his place" while relegating Black women to object status as "sexual playthings" (Weems 1998, 83, 125). The genre was serving a new market—Black men—for Hollywood at a time during which competition with television and internal problems had the industry "floundering badly" (Ongiri 2009, 160). Consumer power, in short, provided the incentive to script Black male virility outside the dominant lynching narrative. As such, Blaxploitation emerged from a patriarchal, capitalist dialectic, one whose effects linger in mass-media representations of Black masculinity today.

Showcasing a "very specifically limited masculinist version of Black Power," Blaxploitation was an important cultural form for "establishing and defining hegemonic social consent on the role of African Americans in the post–civil rights era in the United States" (Ongiri 2009, 168, 167). The terms of consent advanced Black men by way of a politics of representation that presupposed male dominance, both in the private and public spheres of Black life and in the mainstream American imaginary. Further securing their commitment to the economic status quo, these representations "stimulated conspicuous consumption as young Black males sought to emulate the lifestyles of these dubious film icons" (Weems 1998, 90). Traveling beyond the nation's borders, the popularity of Blaxploitation was "symptomatic of America's cultural hegemony over the rest of the world, and b[ore] all the negative implications of this imperialism" (Diawara 1998, 252). Yet the films also evinced potent "elements of empowerment and pleasure and the subversive strategies . . . available to people oppressed because of the color of their skin" (252).

The representational politics of Blaxploitation is illustrative of how Black masculinity's aesthetic revolution, occurring against the backdrop of the civil rights movement, collapsed image and ideal to produce a singular common sense imaginary of struggle. This visual messaging was increasingly characteristic of American popular cultural expression during a period of expanding US dominance (Ebron 2008). When the US economy transitioned from a mass producer of things to a producer of mass images, Blackness was thus positioned to be a premier global export. As this Blackness "[took] over the world with oppositional 'style' . . . Black social and political aspirations [could] no longer be separated from corporate globalization itself" (328). Black male celebrities, icons of "cool" and "badness" (326, 327), rose to prominence as consumer citizens and commodity subjects. They offered un- and underemployed men of the Black Atlantic a representational repertoire that unified "commercial potential and oppositional politics" (321).

In *Branded Head*, by artist Hank Willis Thomas, the clean-shaven head of a Black man traces a graceful curve against a plain white background (see figure 3.01). Eyes, nose, and lips, features that might have discerned his identity, are left outside the frame. In their stead, his head is marked by a keloid in the shape of the Nike swoosh. The man is branded. *Branded Head* critiques a visible Blackness, a "branded visibility" (Gilroy 2001, 86) that has embodied the conquest of capital. As the swoosh protrudes from the otherwise anonymized Black man's head, it raises to the surface of the viewer's sensibility the link "between black male legibility and commercial brands" (Neal 2013b, 7). Invoking the tragic continuity of multiple moments in the unfreedoms of racial capitalism, Thomas (2016, 39), reflecting on his portrait, observes how "slaves were branded as a sign of ownership and how today so many of us brand ourselves and increasingly live in a branded society." He (39) elaborates: "African Americans have proven to be a great testing ground and billboard for making things commodifiable. Young African American men especially have been known to pay to become the best advertisers anyone could ask for."

Air Jordans, the love children of Michael Jordan and Nike, are emblematic of such entanglements providing "an avenue for black style to represent the future of capitalism" (Ebron 2008, 330; Andrews 2001; LaFeber 1999).[17] Several generations later, Nike's alliance with Colin Kaepernick reproduced common sense associations between brand(ed) visibility, consumer allegiance, and Black power. In this instance Kaepernick's proselytizing against the violence directed at Black lives lost him a paycheck but earned him a position as a corporate spokesperson. Transforming the terrain of struggle, hegemonic common sense offered brand(ed) recognition as a remedy to the fragility of Black life. Such highly visible expressions of Black masculinity are specious substitutes for revolutionary potential, becoming but selling points for disposable bodies in the market of disposable consumerism.

Black male bodies are "continually recycled to serve the historical fictions of American culture" (Neal 2013b, 4), be it to package rebellion, marginality, or phenomenal economic attainment. As blinged-out Horatio Algers, these expressions of Black masculinity signify both hegemony and counterhegemony in what might more accurately be described as "alternative" rather than "oppositional" (Kelley 1994, 47). Celebrity status enables iconic Black men like Jordan and Kaepernick to sell their images so that the "biggest artists [are] brands themselves" (Chang

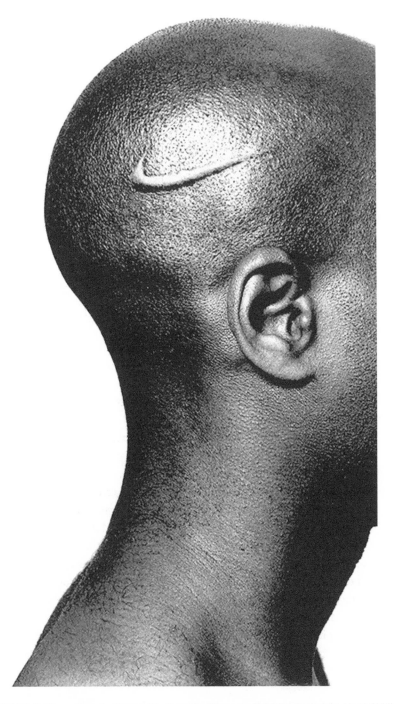

FIGURE 3.01. *Branded Head*, Hank Willis Thomas (2003). Copyright Hank Willis Thomas. Courtesy of the artist and Jack Shainman Gallery, New York.

2005, 447). The familiar performativity of the Black male body doubles as consumerist excess and an entrepreneurial potential whose "taste-making influence makes billions more for every other lifestyle-and-entertainment business under the sun" (Tate 2003, 8). Jay-Z, the first man of hip-hop, nods to these spillover profits when he coolly declares in his 2005 song with Kanye West, "Diamonds from Sierra Leone (Remix)," "I'm not a businessman, I'm a business, man." Jay-Z counts his music sales as a minor portion of enormous profits that otherwise come predominantly from business initiatives; he is himself a "quintessential hip-hop commodity" (Neal 2013b, 43–44; see also Spence 2015). The hypercapitalist successes of men like Jay-Z and Kanye West are inseparable from their Black masculinities. Embodying market principles, this millionaire, and now billionaire, stratum of Black stardom transforms the thingification of Blackness into personifications of capital. In short, as the *media* of complicity commodity subjects reproduce imaginaries that encourage all Black men to participate in capitalism.

The risk of essentializing Blackness is that "we are tempted to use 'black' as sufficient in itself to guarantee the progressive character of the politics we fight under the banner" (Hall 1993, 111). An identity devised by racial capitalism to differentiate and dehumanize, Blackness assumes a common sense location in opposition to capitalist exploitation. It is a logic by which the cause becomes the consequence—you are resistant because you are Black. But that is only its potentiality, and not its unyielding, ontological truth.

To hinge racial equality on "buying in rather than dropping out ... [produces] high-risk strategies where [Black people] accept the link between commodities and identities" (Gilroy 2001, 87). If performing commodities perpetuate structures of racialized subjugation, then "divestment in the performance of 'Blackness' is where true Black liberation must begin" (Tate 2003, 10). Divestment involves an untangling of the co-constitutive racialized and gendered modes of value production that position Black masculinity in racial capitalism. The construction of the Black body as a commodity object uniquely positioned it to critique articulations of Blackness-as-commodity fetish and exchange value. Yet dominant imaginaries of Black masculinity have proven compatible proponents of capital. What might appear a contradiction is in fact indicative of how agency operates within this hegemonic value system. When racialized subjugation makes economic participation prohibitive for Black men, defiance might manifest as either capitalist critique or capitalist incorporation. The gender politics of masculine affirmation favors the latter: using commodification to glorify a "Black" way of being a man overwrites anticapitalist narratives and generates consent to the status quo.

Blaxploitation and the representational repertoires that followed have been "an extremely effective means to more fully incorporate blacks as American consumers"; however, "the millions of dollars blacks spent visiting a fantasy world of African American triumph and achievement" never managed to "effect changes in the real world" (Weems 1998, 90). The structural asymmetry of profit throughout, from Black hands into white-owned corporations, demonstrates that "blaxploitation, in an economic sense, has remained alive and well" (125). On a global scale the consequence is for Blackness to be "reinscribed in the service of commercial reach rather than [its form as a racial type] abolished in the name of human freedom" (Gilroy 2004, xix).

The "patriarchal assumption that equates [male] unemployment with loss of value as well as . . . the materialist assumption that you are what you can buy" (hooks 2004, 31) strikes at the core of the fragile intersection of Blackness and masculinity in racial capitalism. In becoming "the sole measure of the man," money allowed "more black men [to] enter the game" (18). But this game has privileged a white supremacist, patriarchal capitalist system that, at inception, excluded Black men from the breadwinning ideal, even while it was their "brute labor" that "helped build [its] foundation" (19). It was in the context of commodification for the profit of another, unequal access to productive, remunerative labor, and the forceful denial of consumer power that common sense ideas of Black consumerism and branding were established. Suggesting that participation in capitalism, rather than anticapitalist critique, is not only Black resistance but, moreover, Black male empowerment, consumer citizens and commodity subjects obscure racial capitalism's globally entangled processes of exploitation and dispossession. Consumer choice is taken for social justice and branding for Black power. Reaching across the Black Atlantic, where African men similarly use their bodies to "display an aesthetics of selfhood realization as much as [to] counter and subvert dominant paradigms about manhood" (Gondola 2016, 107), consumer choice and branding become redemptive forces amid insecurities concerning masculine value and social worth.

Surplus Bodies as Race-Gender Extralife

There are no more workers as such. . . . If yesterday's drama of the subject was exploitation by capital, the tragedy of the multitude today is that they are unable to be exploited at all.

—Achille Mbembe, *Critique of Black Reason*

Man the hunter becomes a parasite.

—Margrethe Silberschmidt, "Poverty, Male Disempowerment, and Male Sexuality"

Work, however exploitative, is a "unique configuration of social wealth and social relations" that bestows value on the laboring body (Yates 2011, 1688). From capitalism's inception, the stigma of nonwork and its legalized dictum of vagabondage produced a "proto-racialization" that continues to exclude both the unemployed and the racial other from the status of "relational beings," a "capital relation [bound] to the social" out of which respect and self-worth are derived (Melamed 2015, 81). A racial logic thus naturalizing work and the meritorious working subject, race acts as "the final arbiter of waste and wastage" (McIntyre and Nast 2011, 1472). "Race," in other words, "is an instrumentality that makes it possible both to name the surplus and to commit it to waste" (Mbembe 2017, 34–35). This racialized capital relation simultaneously presupposes a male subject. By doing so, it consigns Black men in perpetuity to the interstices of masculine entitlement and racialized disposability. The enduring contradiction of Black masculinity lays bare its long history of crisis in racial capitalism.

Purportedly a slave in his natural state, the mission civilisatrice was to evolve the African man into the salariat so that he might take his place among the community of men. The colonial state having a near monopoly on wage labor, and wage labor clearing the field for a masculinity déraciné (uprooted, detribalized)—and moreover déracialisé (deracialized)—it was through a patriarchal social contract embodied by the civil servant that the metropole planted social and ideological roots. This emphasis on wage labor and state planning reflected an ideal type of capitalism as it was envisioned in the post–World War II global political economy and its extension from metropole to colony the faltering cry of imperial legitimacy (Cooper 1996).

Across African cities hegemonic "discourses on masculinity [offer] models that many of today's young men struggle to emulate" (Lindsay and Miescher 2003, 20). The contraction of the formal economy erodes men's capacities to accumulate and denies them opportunities to marry, without which they cannot assume legitimate fatherhood or adult masculinity (Lindsay and Miescher 2003). They are caught in an eternal youth, a designation for underemployed, unmarried men that marks not a demographic but a social status (Jeffrey 2010; Locke and Te Lintelo 2012; Mains 2012; Newell 2009a). In this sense youth refers to a period of "life on hold" (Diouf 2003, 6), a "waithood" (Honwana 2012).

The disappearance of wage labor, the functional equivalent of an informalizing economy, constitutes a feminization of work in the triple sense that those (remunerative or not) life-sustaining activities not sacrificed to structural adjustment were always outside the purview of the state and the salary and left largely to women; relatedly, forms of socially reproductive labor comprise the bulk of these activities and are incommensurate with the ideological and material demands of masculinity; and men's loss of privileged access to the salary and breadwinner status is inextricable from late capitalism's idealization of women workers—an idealization precisely due to women's dissociation from salaries and breadwinning, thereby legitimating subordinate pay and permanent job insecurity, if not outright disposability (Cooper 1996; Enloe 1989; Radhakrishnan and Solari 2015; Roy 2003; Roy 2012; Standing 1999; Wright, M. 2006). The feminization of work marks the dominant feature of urban Africa's postdebt economies. Proof at once of the malaise of late capitalism and the incomplete conquest of capital (Heller 1999), informality portends a civilization in decline or yet unrealized. Rendering its laborer a lesser man, the stigma of informality is equivalent to the colonial subject-designation of *grand enfant* (big child). Still, the promise of the postwage economy is to be remade in the image of the market—to become a self-made man.

The exclusions that young African men experience mirror the sustained unemployment of Black American men, for whom the "concurrent retrenchment of wage labor and social protection" bound the "black ghetto" to "the jail and prison system" (Wacquant 2000, 384). The latter "serves only to warehouse the precarious and deproletarianized fractions of the black working class" (385). We may extend to men throughout the Black Atlantic Mbembe's (2001, 55) prediction, "If a neo-liberal way out of the crisis has—so far—led to any renewal of growth, it is growth with unemployment.... It is quite reasonable to hypothesize an end to a wage-employed African labor force."

The breadwinning compromise between capital and labor was a social contract, a patriarchal dividend, that incentivized complicity among even racially marginalized men. Posited for much of the twentieth century as a normative reality, this compromise was in fact an aspirational model afforded only to the dominant group within a given social order. In societies constructed around racial cleavages, the failures of this compromise were reinscribed as failures of the racially subordinate subject; for Black men, failure came at the double cost of racial and gender denigration. As the late capitalist regime of nonwork spills over boundaries previously fixed by race and gender, it disrupts the patriarchal and white supremacist compromise of which the family wage had evidenced an advanced civilization and its ascendant middle classes. It is feminized work and the "*Becoming Black of the world*" (Mbembe 2017, 6, emphasis in original). The closure of breadwinning as a world societal vision, in other words, reflects both a contraction of the patriarchal dividend for men whose racial or class identities had previously entitled them and capital's refusal to extend to racially subordinate or feminized labor a social contract predicated on dignity and human security. The expansion of precarious economies indicates the underlying fragility of the gender and racial privileges upon which capitalism is built.

Prior modes of production—and productive potential—foment the conditions for the next mode of production and potentiality, and the racial and gender ideologies that produced the laboring subject have been instrumental for generating consent in the postwork economy. Preempting the proliferation of surplus bodies, Black men are simultaneously marginalized and venerated for engaging in alternative forms of economic participation. Consumer citizens and commodity subjects, exemplified by iconic Black men whose visibility and financial power offer evidence of Black racial progress, promote glamorized tropes over structural change. They provide a hegemonic counternarrative to the long crisis of Black masculinity. As models of economic survival outside the wage laboring, breadwinning social contract, their extralives—lives and livelihoods excess to the formal contours of the capitalist world system—model afterlives of surplus to propose an alternative future for all.

In what follows I explore imaginaries of Blackness, negated and affirmed, within the Black Atlantic and Ivoirian state-sponsored projects of racial capitalism. I outline a lineage of global media icons alongside the geopolitics of Black masculinity in Abidjan. I contend that we read the racialization of the post/colonial city by reading the strategies of the bodies that inhabit it and the spaces they make their own. Abidjan, positioned as a faded regional hegemon with a firmly entrenched political economy of Françafrique, inspires inquiry into the multiple ways that men engage Blackness to generate positive racial identities while still forging identities complicit to capitalism. I examine the expression of Blackness as self and other as it emerges from the interplay of place and social imaginaries, one in which belonging is articulated as powerfully in the sphere of representation as it is in localized political and economic structures.

Part II
BETWEEN PLACE AND IMAGINARIES

Colonial occupation itself was a matter of seizing, delimiting, and asserting control over a physical geographical area—of writing on the ground a new set of social and spatial relations. The writing of new spatial relations (territorialization) was, ultimately, tantamount to the production of boundaries and hierarchies, zones and enclaves; the subversion of existing property arrangements; the classification of people according to different categories; resource extraction; and, finally, the manufacturing of a large reservoir of cultural imaginaries. These imaginaries gave meaning to the enactment of differential rights to differing categories of people for different purposes within the same space; in brief, the exercise of sovereignty.

—Achille Mbembe, "Necropolitics"

We dressed to resemble our black American heroes. We walked tall in packs and pretended we couldn't speak French. We called one another by our American nicknames, and slowly we became aware of race in our daily relations with French people. We began to see racism where others before us would have seen colonialism and class exploitation.

—Manthia Diawara, *In Search of Africa*

4

IMAGINARIES OF NEGATION

The colonial African city was a product of racial capitalism. Born in the sixteenth century out of the colonial imperatives of extraction and exploitation, what began as outposts for the trade of goods and people had by the nineteenth century become permanent European settlements. The geography of these cities revealed their function: cities were strategically positioned along waterways for access to ports (e.g., Abidjan), as railway supply depots (e.g., Nairobi), or adjacent to mines (e.g., Johannesburg). Native populations displaced from their rural livelihoods and those who saw opportunities as interlocutors of the new regimes migrated to cities to become wage laborers, a category restricted to men according to the gendered division of labor at the heart of capitalist domestic organization. Intent on regularizing the sporadic work cycles of temporary migrant laborers, colonial planners envisioned women in the city singularly as wives to reproduce men's—purportedly, their husbands'—labor power, proposing that labor "stabilization" would naturally emerge out of a nuclear family structure (Cooper 1996). What resulted was a racialized and gendered register of inclusion and exclusion to urban life with the salary its foremost organizing principle (Agadjanian 2005; Cooper 1996; Ferguson 1999; Hunter 2010; Lindsay 2003; Silberschmidt 2005; Smith 2017). This legacy lingers in contemporary sensibilities around formal and informal work and the constitution of modern manhood; it constitutes the gendered social architecture of racial capitalism in the postcolonial African city.

The mission civilisatrice justified the pillage of Africa by virtue of an Enlightenment narrative that othered the "Dark Continent" as a savage, unchartered abyss.[1] It employed a terra nullius iconography by which supposedly uninhabited or uncultivated land would enter history through conquest.[2] Geographically, culturally, and economically, the settler city was a manifestation of the colonial project, "exuding an image of whiteness and modernity" (Coquery-Vidrovitch 1992, 8) to the African interior. It was moreover the "direct, privileged link between colonized and colonizer" and the "fruit of colonial administrative coercion" (9, 33). The settler's districts—the city proper—were conceived as oases from which civilized life would expand outwards: a capitalist geography predicated on property and rigid racialized and gendered economic and social relations. "Western notions of property are deeply invested in a colonial geography, a white mythology, in which the racialized figure of the savage plays a central role" (Blomley 2003, 124). The European settler's city stood at the frontier of the worlds of property and a lack thereof, simultaneously conceived as law/lawlessness, history/prehistory, and civilization/savagery.[3] In this way, place was "less . . . a geographic marker than . . . an overdetermined cultural signifier" (Reynolds 2010, 460). Those properly inhabiting cities were entitled to modern rights as citizens, and those outside, subjects (Ferguson 2006; Mamdani 1996).

In Francophone Africa a man was not fully a freely residing, rights-bearing citizen until he had adopted the ways of the colonist, at which point, "evolved," he was designated évolué. While the contours of évolué status shifted over the colonial period, ideologically and practically, the évolué contrasted with the ignoble status of subject and was exempt from otherwise degrading compulsions to forced labor such as *prestations*, or annual labor quotas, and other legislative indignities (Conklin 1997). Évolués constituted the elite of an already discrete category of wage earners entrusted as the receiving population of the mission civilisatrice, an effort articulated as remaking African man in the French universalist image. "Détribalisé" or "déraciné"—uprooted from custom, tradition, and rural homestead, he was to be oriented to the economy and norms of the metropole (Cooper 1996). A renewed vision of African masculinity thus emerged as "a locus of urban modernity" (Gondola 2016, 11).

Outside of the civil service, the colonial project never significantly realized the institutionalization of salaries or benefits to support that parallel ideal of the nuclear family—a patriarchal claim on life's public and private spheres through the novel designation of breadwinner (Cooper 1996). And it was only after prolonged struggle that, by finally "conceding low-level government workers some kind of family allowances, officials were accepting the urban labor force as a complex social entity whose conditions of production and reproduction were crucial to control, order, and productivity" (233–34). For many men, then, direct affiliation with state employment, particularly at the elite levels, became integral to colonial "expectations of domesticity" (Ferguson 1999, chap. 5).[4]

Those not gainfully employed in the interests of colonial enterprise were unwelcome in this urban civilizational project. Colonial administrators initially conceived of the urban proper as exclusive territory for white settlers and those exceptional évolués. Entry into formal city life was therefore rendered conditional upon access and concession to colonial terms of livelihood and lifestyle, subjecting outsiders to nonrecognition, if not derision and degradation. These outsiders included long-term yet "auxiliary" workers on repeated short-term contracts, the laboring populations who built and sustained the city but were always imagined as temporary in the colonial urban plan, and the majority engaged in economic activities not easily captured by the state regulatory machine, including women, whose work was "more often labelled 'customary labor' or the 'informal economy,' with all the insecurities and vulnerabilities that such a status implied" (Cooper 1996, 2). Black French Equatorial Africa governor-general and évolué ideal Félix Eboué described these appropriately urbanized populations as the colony's "socially stable element," while the rest were "unstable," and required "discipline" through mechanisms of social control, including police and social organizations, but primarily via labor (quoted at 157).[5] This was a "sociology of Africa that divided its population into peasants and educated elites and treated everyone else as residual, . . . a 'floating population'" (169). Residing in the interstices of urban citizen and subjected peasant, the auto-constructed slums, or *bidonvilles* that emerged contemporaneously on the edges of the settler city were evidence of the unplanned, and thereby surplus, laborers that have existed since.

As the colonial economy increasingly subsumed indigenous society, carving out a new, modern existence for the African urban man, the wage became a prerequisite to marriage and masculine status. Activities such as food preparation and market trade were left out of new categories of "work" and fell under the woman's domain, designated traditional and feminine—and in the postcolony, informal. Manhood thus at stake, this civilizing logic translated cultural difference into racial deficiency and gendered distinction. The évolué, by contrast, legitimated the notion of colonialism as a project of social betterment. The predominant instrument of colonial social engineering in the African city, the wage was a means by which the African man, in the language of a 1953 French Office des Études Psychotechniques (Office of Psychotechnical Studies) study, would be "profoundly Europeanized, [such] that he has adopted our motivations and accepted our own necessities." The ultimate goal was "that he [retain] nothing African except the color" (quoted in Cooper 1996, 321).

In short, the African city of the colonizer represented the belief in a Western, property-oriented rationality to impart progress on a backward terra nullius and established new class distinctions coalesced around racialized and gendered norms. Demarcating the terrain of exclusion and inclusion, the city mapped limits of permissible and navigable space for African men and women. It divided citizen from subject, but it also promised the possibility of crossing over through acculturation as evolution. To reject (or be excluded from) those terms essentially meant acquiescing to "bare life" (cf. Agamben 1998), stripped of a citizen's rights and entitlements.

The Color of Slavery

From the beginning of the Atlantic trade, the continent became an inexhaustible well of phantasms, the raw material for a massive labor of imagination whose political and economic dimensions we can never underscore enough.

—Achille Mbembe, *Critique of Black Reason*

For enslaved Africans wrenched from their native lands, Blackness similarly denoted negation, the absence of civilization. Well prior to the first European colonial settlement on the African continent, the prerogatives of an emergent global capitalism subordinated the African subject and registered a previously little-known territory in the European consciousness foremost as a place from which to extract slaves.[6] The transatlantic slave trade began parallel to the development of European notions of race, beyond blood or lineage, as a visible fact, determined by a set of physical characteristics through which human groups could be distinguished (Boulle 2003).

The compulsion for economic gain was justified in all manners "from biology to the Bible" (Pieterse 1992, 59). In Enlightenment thinking, more than a sense, "sight . . . was a way of knowing," and European interpretations of Africans' visible difference "combined nefariously . . . with their desire to extract labor and resources" (Camp 2015, 676, 81). Albeit not a new institution, responding in the sixteenth and seventeenth centuries to the significant labor demands of the plantation economy and the political and moral logics of the triangular trade, slavery now "acquired a colour" (Pieterse 1992, 52). Blackness "was the cog that made possible the creation of the plantation—one of the period's most effective forms of wealth accumulation—and accelerated the integration of merchant capitalism with technology and the control of subordinated labor" (Mbembe 2017, 20).[7] Regulating slavery in France's colonies from 1685 to 1848, the Code noir dictated that to be Black was to be a slave and vice versa.[8] The slave trade was called *la traite des noirs* (trade of Blacks), or equivalently, *la traite négrière* or *traite des nègres*. The derogatory term "nègre" defined Black humanity and the institution of slavery as one singularity, a conflation so complete that "nègre" surpassed "esclave" (slave) in popular parlance for plantation labor (Cohen, W.

2003, 132; see also Fleming 2017). "Nègre," in other words, designated "a kind of human thing, or quantifiable merchandise" (Mbembe 2017, 73). The reification of racial difference rationalized subjection "over the bodies and liberties of the person during service as if he were a thing" (Williams 1994, 16). It was the means by which the planter, trader, and others profiting from the slave economy might effectively collapse capital and labor in the Blackness that embodied both.

The Construction of Savages and Lazy Natives

In the same extractive spirit, "Frenchmen viewed black men and their continent as needing a white master to make of Africa the rich and prosperous region that, by the calculations of traders, officials, and publicists, it could and should

FIGURE 4.01. "Being *carried* by natives sums up the symbolism as well as the reality of European hegemony" (Pieterse 1992, 90, emphasis in original). Note the distinction in attire between the men carrying the colon and the one who is armed. Colonie Français, Côte d'Ivoire. Le Chef de Batallion Noguès, commandant la colonne de répression des Abbeys (French Colony; Côte d'Ivoire / Battalion Chief Noguès, commanding the support for the repression of the Abe). From the Collection Étienne Thai Wan Chanh(g). Published by Bauer, Marchet et Cie, Dijon [France]. EEPA Postcard Collection, Côte d'Ivoire, EEPA IV-47–04 Eliot Elisofon Photographic Archives. National Museum of African Art. Smithsonian Institution.

become. The imperialist dream thus coincided with and reinforced the tradition of racial inequality" (Cohen, W. 2003, xxiv–xxv). In an 1885 speech to his chamber of deputies, France's Prime Minister Jules Ferry declared: "The superior races have a right because they have a duty. They have the duty to civilize the inferior races" (quoted in Palermo 2003, 296). Rendering race "at once the currency of exchange and the use value," Blackness in the French empire was "invented to signify exploitation, brutalization, and degradation" (Mbembe 2017, 6, 62). In other words, enslavers and colonizers legitimated their economic incentives under the same mutually reinforcing racist logic.

As iterations of racial capitalism on the African continent and off, slavery and colonialism operated under the shared schema that prized Western economic order and devalued African lives and livelihoods. Thus from the fifteenth century onward, European expansion into Africa and the appropriation of African bodies demanded that the "'Negro,' that is the color black, [signal] both a negation of Africa and a unity of opposition to white," and mandated that "the Negro ha[ve] no civilization, no cultures, no religions, no history, no place, and finally no humanity that might command consideration" (Robinson 2000, 81). Unlike prior terms such as "Ethiope," "Moor," or "African," by collapsing total identity into the color black, the binary negative of the Enlightenment metaphor, European conquerors denied all that was worthy (81; see also Jarosz 1992). This deconstruction of Blackness required negation, the steady, centuries-long erasure of African civilizations from the European consciousness, thereby rendering the African savage (Mudimbe 1994; Robinson 2000). It was a process of layering stereotype upon erasure, the creation of a "colonial library . . . [to establish the] civilizing mission" (Mudimbe 1994, 29).[9]

In 1570 France barred the "loading or exhibition of Black slaves" in metropolitan ports, a "gesture [by which] France announced its will not to know anything about the victims of its racial logic" (Mbembe 2017, 67).[10] The geographic divide between the civilized metropole and terra nullius was "the logical consequence of the distinction between Europeans and savages" (61) and gave carte blanche to Europe's own political and economic savagery. It was in lands destined for conquest that otherwise condemnable sins were permissible, a quarantining of brutality that maintained a conviction of innocence in the popular European racial consciousness. This transatlantic segregating of racial others and the violence enacted upon them instilled a legacy whereby "the relationship between the metropole and the colonies" constituted the definitive feature of "French racial thinking" (Peabody and Stovall 2003, 4). An otherness brought close through relations of domination has thenceforth been deeply embroiled in the French idea of race.

European representations of Africans were an inevitable consequence of intercontinental contact and commenced well before the fifteenth-century transatlantic voyages that brought forth the world capitalist system (see, e.g., Mudimbe 1994). These representations were varied and unstable, reflecting shifting dynamics of power, alliance, and purpose. Imaginaries of negation that typified representations of Africans in racial capitalism were neither inevitable nor ahistorical facts; rather, they were a consequence of the subjugation of Black bodies for economic gain. It was within this constellation of political economy and politics of representation that European travelers to Africa in the "Age of Discovery" made the unknown intelligible to populations back home.

This act of translation required fixing difference through recognizable markers or "producing an image for an unfamiliar subject that evoke[d] a *familiar* body of *conceptual* knowledge" (Strother 1999, 4, emphasis in original). The Khoikhoi (derogatively referred to as "Hottentot") of southern Africa, who Europeans had by the eighteenth century posited to be the "missing link" between human and beast, were emblematic figures in this construction of difference. The earliest European pictorial depiction of the Khoikhoi, a woodcut by Hans Burgkmair in 1508, reproduced Dürer's *Adam and Eve* to evoke a primitive state (Strother 1999). From this point, economic imperatives guided the Khoikhoi's pictorial difference. During the period of colonial exploration, European illustrators represented Khoikhoi eating fresh animal entrails to signal their savagery, thereby justifying conquest. During the period of colonial settlement, European illustrators represented Khoikhoi smoking pipes to signal their indolence, thereby justifying European appropriations of native labor (Strother 1999). In one era, the figure of the savage; in the next, the lazy native.

These two moments of Khoikhoi representation reflected the two major phases of European representations of Africans broadly, from early conquest to established colonies (Pieterse 1992). In the latter stage the "paternalistic aura of the White Man's Burden required subjects who would fill the bill" (88).[11] As popular as the image of the lazy native was the child—or boy—and as late as the mid-twentieth century, French colonial officials diagnosed problems of labor control as "infant diseases" or a "puberty crisis" (Cooper 1996, 198). These representational repertoires, in the interest of European domination over land and labor, exemplified their embeddedness in the emergent world political economy. Colonial representations of the other were crucial in "form[ing] part of the social construction of reality and the negotiation of the future" (Pieterse 1992, 231).

Support for colonization was not initially or consistently strong among the French population and required steady propaganda efforts among its proponents in the private sphere and in the colonial arm of the state. It was through "the idea of the 'mission civilisatrice' that the Parti colonial sought to win over a public little inclined to political and economic arguments alone" (Holo 1993, 58). This colonial doctrine, developed by Jules Ferry in the 1880s, articulated a triad of "economic interest, political ambition, and humanitarian duty" (58). Like his imperialist predecessors, Ferry obliged societies supposing themselves to have attained a "high degree of moral and technological development" to "drive 'inferior peoples' along the path to progress" (59). Embracing the nineteenth century's firm "belief in progress and the conviction of Western superiority," the mission civilisatrice produced a discursive and iconographic canon, the latter a visualization of the former (58). From the moment of imperial expansion toward a capitalist world order, race was the ideological accomplice and emerged the obvious signifier from which all subsequent facts and rationalizations were to derive.

Spectacle, Commerce, and Commodity Racism

With colonialism in full swing in the late nineteenth century, the mission civilisatrice promoted imaginaries of Black primitiveness among their metropolitan populations by showcasing Africans in colonial expositions and commodity advertisements. Here, Black Africanity was portrayed as a deficiency that French economic exploitation promised to remedy. Through these media and others, the imperial project normalized the "thematic of racial difference . . . within mass culture" (Mbembe 2017, 63). In colonial exhibitions Europeans presented natives from their colonial territories enacting pseudotraditional life-cycle rituals in zoo-like environments and classified them according to how evolutionarily progressed they perceived them to be (Hodeir 2002). In 1810, Sara Baartman, the "Hottentot Venus," was the first African to be thus displayed and signaled the transition in public representation from "freak" show to "ethnographic 'type,'" her physiological differences used to exemplify a standard, inferior other (Strother 1999, 29). In 1877 Paris's zoological park, the Jardin d'Acclimatation, began including "exotic" people to complement its array of plants and animals (Ezra 2000, 30; Schneider 1982, 132).[12] Beginning with fourteen Africans whom organizers called "Nubians," these ethnographic exhibits immediately became a "mass phenomenon" with audiences in the hundreds of thousands, providing the French public with its first direct encounter with Africans (Schneider 1982, 128, 8). Ethnographic expositions were reliably lead attractions at world fairs, drawing over ten million visitors to the Paris World's Fair in 1878 and over fifty million to the 1900 Paris Exposition, and they continued well into the twentieth century. From 1889 expositions explicitly advocated empire, with the French government itself exhibiting colonial subjects; the Agence économique des colonies was a prolific supplier of photographs for

FIGURE 4.02. Indigenous representatives of the Pai-Pi-Bri exhibit at the Jardin d'Acclimatation, photo by M. Maurice Bucquet in the September 19 edition of *La Nature* (1893). Collection Radauer: Human Zoos archive.

the public collections that accompanied these expositions (Blanchard and Boëtsch 1993; Schneider 1982).

Under the dual purpose of spectacle and commerce, and guided by a logic of otherness ripe for conquest and exploitation, within "a single cultural event," colonial expositions "concentrated the central themes of colonial rhetoric" (Ezra 2000, 13; Schneider 1982). The Pai-Pi-Bri of Côte d'Ivoire were first exhibited in the Jardin d'Acclimatation in 1893, the year that Côte d'Ivoire became a colony, and the visit by its governor, Gustave Binger "bestowed an air of legitimacy" (Schneider 1982, 141). While other contemporaneously displayed Africans were characterized and duly presented as "bloodthirsty," conquest by treaty rather than violent conflict as well as commercial interests in the colony of Côte d'Ivoire drove depictions of the Pai-Pi-Bri as "peace-loving and industrious" (Wan 1992, 70–71).[13] The program for the Pai-Pi-Bri exhibition (quoted at 71) thus described "an enticing novelty" in the form of a "carefully constructed model factory":

> One could say that this factory, so interesting with its practical and commercial character, is the "highlight" of this exhibition, itself remarkable for its ethnographic merit. . . . Divided into two sections, on one side,

the goods that Europe exports, and, on the other, the exotic products that the native sends. It is the commerce of the black continent taken alive. It is the triumph of free trade between two worlds, a peaceful and lasting bond between two peoples, a link between the races, a mutual pledge of understanding and progress.

This progressive framing of Ivoirian subjects "was not only reiterating a late eighteenth-century liberal view of the benefits to civilisation of free trade but was in fact recalling how France had asserted its control over the Ivory Coast—through commercial treaties" (Wan 1992, 71). And while the metropolitan public's demand for representations of savage Africans endured through the history of colonial expositions, the shift from conquest to a "government desiring the *mise en valeur* of its colonies" compelled representations of pliant populations among whom Europeans could safely settle (72). The Alliance Française exhibit at the 1900 Exposition Universelle, for example, demonstrated Africans "dutifully and obediently learning to speak French" (72).

Because the "leitmotiv of colonial propaganda was economic gain," its two principal themes were commodities and laboring bodies put to use by resourceful Europeans (Pieterse 1992, 91). The first exposition to showcase people alongside commodities, thus laying evidence to the dual wealth to be derived from the colonies, was the 1889 Paris Exposition Universelle (Hall 1997b).[14] At the 1906 Marseilles Colonial Exhibition, whose purpose was above all to promote the economic potential of French possessions, pavilions included, Methods of Colonization, Colonial Buildings and Implements, Special Products Suitable for Export to Colonies, and the Export Palace (Schneider 1982, 180).[15] In these pavilions visitors were relayed information of commercial interest, such as the colonies' natural resources, available land concessions, product samples, and metropolitan goods that might attract colonial markets (Schneider 1982). Organized either by private firms such as the Fraissinet plantations of Côte d'Ivoire or more commonly by the colonial governments, each pavilion highlighted "the commercial and economic viability of the lands" (180). As the colonial project matured, expositions increasingly emphasized the utility of colonial labor, "preview[ing], and thus facilitat[ing], the transition from a colonial to a third world economy, from the exploitation of raw materials to that of human labor" (Ezra 2000, 16). For example, posters for the 1931 Paris Exposition coloniale, amid a moment of fierce colonial propaganda, portrayed laboring natives who "tirelessly and with a smile, bring to France the fruits that their country produce in abundance" (Hodeir, Pierre, and Leprun 1993, 130).[16] Colonial expositions, apparitions of material and human commercial viability, demonstrated "once and for all that the capitalist system had not only created a dominant form of exchange but was also in the process of creating a dominant form of representation" (McClintock 1995, 208).

As commodity spectacle, "advertising translated things into a fantasy visual display of signs and symbols" (Hall 1997b, 240). Reducing Blackness to a commodity placed advertising directly within the schemata of "colonialist bias that could not exist outside of a racialized vision of the universe" (Debost 1993, 101). In the exemplary case of soap, advertising situated the expansion of commodity culture under the civilizational guise of "washing and clothing the savage," thus entangling "racial hygiene and imperial progress" (McClintock 1995, 208, 09).[17] Within this repository of images, caricatured Black children cleaned themselves white. It was a racially diminutive register that associated Black skin with dirt and depicted civilization as the literal washing away of Blackness.[18] Other depictions of Black people in colonial-era advertisements were as commodity objects: goods or bodies to be consumed. In these instances, dark skin signified the quality of dark-colored products like coffee or chocolate, the workers who cultivated the products on the African or Antillean plantation, or those in service to their white consumers (Bachollet et al. 1994; Debost 1993; Hale 2003).

The "representation of 'difference' through the body became the discursive site through which . . . 'racialized knowledge' was produced and circulated" (Hall 1997b, 240). The imperial project adapted racialized knowledge as the iconography of its new commodity capitalism, with "French entrepreneurs and their [trademark] designers depict[ing] Africans . . . in ways that not only corresponded to how they perceived them visually, but also to the roles that they *wanted* them to fill in the empire" (Hale 2003, 131, emphasis in original). Of the 1725 trademarks registered between 1886 and 1940 in Paris and Marseille—the peak of the colonial conquest in France's two centers of colonial and overseas trade—656 depicted sub-Saharan Africans or Blacks (134). Earlier trademarks "evoked the plantation slavery system," which had been operational only a few decades prior (137). Scenes that "showed French planters in tailored, white, three-piece suits surveying their lands, while black workers in loincloths and shifts labored over crops . . . made master and servant roles clear, confirming the inferior position of the black to the consumer" (137–38). Later trademarks drew on the representational repertoire of an exoticized Africa and its domesticated commodities as well as from stereotypes of Black Americans, particularly inspired by performers in Paris. The former aimed to "nourish an image of the Empire's immensity, prosperity, abundance, and adventure," promoting a sense that the "colonies are full of riches—fruits, no doubt, of French efforts to develop lands that were often inhospitable" (Delporte 1993, 162).

FIGURE 4.03. Gus Bofa, Sodex soap advertisement, France (c. 1910). Credit: Ville de Paris / Bibliothèque Forney. Copyright 2021 Artists Rights Society (ARS), New York / ADAGP, Paris.

American caricatures of emasculated Black male servitude that appeared in late nineteenth-century commodity advertisements such as Cream of Wheat's Rastus and Uncle Ben had a significant influence on the racist iconography of European empire (Delporte 1993; Gates 2019; Kern-Foxworth 1994; Pieterse 1992). Sambo, the ultimate stereotypical figure of the Black American man, found his cross-continental equivalence in the French "Bamboula" (Pieterse 1992). The *tirailleurs sénégalais*, a division of soldiers who fought valiantly for France in World War I and out of which many évolués were forged, were from 1915 popularized as advertisements for Banania cereal, their likeness on no fewer than ten trademarks through 1925 (Hale 2003). Black men generally foiled as "commercial buffoons," a representational repertoire that countered "black strengths with comic, infantile images" (140).[19] Representations of Blacks in the metropole, particularly at the height of 1930s imperial fervor, depicted them "desperately trying to reach the level of their masters," clearly communicating that "if they are not obviously entertainers, they have but one role to play in white society: to serve" (Bachollet et al. 1994, 16). Implicit in colonial iconography was acquiescence to white superiority, which declared that "in seeking to imitate him [the white man], the Black can only ape him" (Delporte 1993, 168).

Illustrations used in product branding "document an important aspect of cultural history because they represent images the French encountered in their daily home environment" (Hale 2003, 131). Unlike the elite domain of race science undergirding the ethnological logic of colonial exhibitions, commodity advertising was disseminated across all levels of metropolitan society and was instrumental to codifying mass racism in a set of familiar visual cues (McClintock 1995).[20] Caricatured subjects could at best be understood by the metropolitan population as "inferiors who stood to benefit from the government's 'civilizing' efforts" (Hale 2003, 144). Colonialism thus depicted was a "redemptive" force (Delporte 1993, 168). By contrast, in the post–World War II decolonial and antiracist global discourse, when France was compelled to portray its empire as a project of African incorporation, fewer derogatory images appeared in advertising—although fewer Black people appeared in images at all (Debost 1993). At the moment of African independence, when "the representation of the African, claiming his new freedom, could not reproduce these archetypes," their images in advertisements targeting metropolitan populations nearly disappeared altogether (Bachollet et al. 1994, 15). There was no space in the imperial iconography for powerful, liberated Africans.

Across imperial regimes of racial capitalism, "the commodity had taken its privileged place not only as the fundamental form of a new industrial economy

FIGURE 4.04. "Je déchirerai les rires Banania sur tous les murs de France" (I will tear down the laughs of Banania from all the walls in France) (Léopold Senghor, quoted in Manceron and Debost 1993, 143). Banania cereal poster featuring tirailleur sénégalais (c. 1915). Bibliothèque nationale de France.

but also as the fundamental form of a new cultural system for representing social value" (McClintock 1995, 208). As a signifier of capital, the Black body was productive potential and cultural artifact, in both cases objects to be consumed by white society. To metropolitan audiences, commodified tropes subordinated Black humanity as civilization's binary other.

From Commodity Object to Colonial Subject

In the metropole there was no civilizing mission seeking to incorporate Blackness beyond an object status, and as such Black subjectivity in the capitalist economy was actively erased and repressed. In its stead, "representations of Blacks were made by Whites to promote products manufactured or commercially managed by Whites, for a clientele essentially composed of Whites" (Bachollet et al. 1994, 26).[21] Within this register, Blackness was easily flattened into "spectacles for commodity exhibition" (McClintock 1995, 224). These same repertoires of "stereotypes . . . [or] . . . facile generalizations" informed the earliest French imperial voyages to Africa and "helped build the myth of the 'black man'" (Cohen, W. 2003, 27). They constituted the colonial iconography ubiquitous in the metropolitan social imaginary in every form of popular media, supporting the "racist view that, condemned by their biology to an inferior existence, blacks were suited only to serve whites and to live dependent on them" (284).

Within the African colonies themselves, however, European dependence on Africans for colonial conquest, expansion, and settlement made it difficult to create one-dimensional spectacles of Africans. They were colonial subjects rather than commodity objects. Reimaging Africans as consumers, here advertising imagery evoked the extension of metropolitan capital into colonial markets to evince imperial modernity (Debost 1993). The metaphorical washing away of Blackness occurred through acculturation, bearing the promise of civilization in new modes of production and consumption capacities enabled by the colonial economy. While it was impossible to literally wash away one's Blackness, soap advertisements targeting Black consumers on the African continent whitened them symbolically by depicting them in European clothing and colonial professions. Lifebuoy soap's post–World War II "Successful Man" campaign in the settler colony of Southern Rhodesia (currently Zimbabwe), for example, featured illustrations of "an African man dressed smartly in a suit and tie, sometimes holding a pen, beaming from ear to ear" (Burke 1996, 153).[22]

Imperial dusk compelled a shift from "wanton exploitation" to "social Darwinist policies" (Gondola 2016, 30). The aim was to create the colonial subject in the metropole's image: the évolué. Within this representational lexicon, évolués were many things at once to the French and their African citizen-subjects. As "liberatory ideals," they were both instruments of propaganda for Africans and the purported endpoint of the French colonial project (Landau 2002, 158). Yet the predicament of being forever not quite/not white refracted évolués through the colonial lens as "unsettling figures, leaning to dandyism, mired in opaque tradition, tragic figures, unable to fit in" (158).

Culture Consumers

Representation in systems of production, consumption, and commodification is inextricable from the racial capitalist economy. While producing wage laborers was fundamental to capitalist expansion, the active capacity to consume—both material things and cultural norms—served as a crucial means of refusing the passive status of commodity object and rejecting evolutionary narratives of Black negation. As the apex of the mission civilisatrice, évolués were constantly obliged to demonstrate their exceptionalism and thereby counter their debased Africanity in racial capitalism. A population apart—this was a time when less than 1 percent of the French West African population was engaged in any form of wage labor (Cooper 1996)—the salary was but the entry point to the total, co-constituting and enduring producer-consumer, producer-provider identity.

Thus, in addition to a revolution of employment aspirations, African urban cultural movements appropriated the signs and symbols of the new social order—at times selecting among competing hegemons for local validation. If the "icon of the nineteenth-century savage is determined by *absences*: the absence, or scarcity, of clothing, possessions, attributes of civilization" (Pieterse 1992, 35; emphasis in original), then commodity culture acted as a civilizational proxy, the consumer citizen the African subject of history. In Brazzaville and Kinshasa in the 1910s, male domestics inherited their European masters' discarded clothing or spent handsomely to appropriate their own (Gondola 1999). Clothing became an integral means through which Congolese with access to the wage economy—domestic servants, as well as others—asserted superiority in the urban racial hierarchy as "whites with black skin" (26–27). Developing unique and flamboyant styles, by the 1980s they were calling themselves *sapeurs*, a collective of men who acquired high-end clothing in "adventures" to Brussels or Paris, thereby proving their conquest of

European modernity (Friedman 1991; Gondola 1999).[23] The sapeur dreamed not simply of the journey but also of his return "as an aristocrat of ultimate elegance" (Tamagni 2009). In 1930s southern African mining towns, ballroom dancing raged in social clubs (Ferguson 2006). The phenomenon inspired studies in the 1940s and '50s by anthropologists at Northern Rhodesia's Rhodes-Livingston Institute, who proposed that white society and its cultural forms comprised a "'reference group' against which black status was measured"; Bernard Magubane later charged that these scholars' analyses of "successful urban cultural 'adaptation'" was laden with their own "colonial racism" (157). By contrast, in 1950s Kinshasa, "tropical cowboys" inspired by the Western cinematic genre came into vogue (Gondola 2016). Mostly male adherents formed gangs known as "Bills" or "Yankees" that rejected évolué masculinity to form an alternative variant as the "street elite," one outside the purview of the state (10). Having "parlayed their vision of the Far West from the screen into the street . . . [these youth created] a unique hybrid blend that conflated the Hollywood version of the drifting cowboy with local elements of manhood and fashioned township gangs after frontier posses" (66). Among Bamako's newly independent youth, the style and music of Black American popular culture collapsed into an ideology of revolution to rival *Francité*—a way of speaking, thinking, and being as the former French colonizer (Diawara 1998). Describing a brief exchange with touring American musicians in 1965 and his own experience coming of age at that time, cultural theorist Manthia Diawara (103–4) recounts—

> By being considered as one who spoke English like an American and was able to converse fluently with star musicians, I was acquiring a new and equal type of subjecthood. . . . I was in the vanguard. I was on the front line of the revolution. You see, for me and for many of my friends, to be liberated was to be exposed to more R&B songs and to be up on the latest news about Muhammad Ali, George Jackson, Angela Davis, Malcolm X, and Martin Luther King Jr., all of whom were becoming an alternative source of cultural capital for African youth and were creating within us new structures of feeling, which enabled us to subvert the hegemony of *Francité* after independence.

Innumerable examples that span the continent abound, rejoinders to Black negation in civilizational discourse and assertions of manhood within the integrated world capitalist economy. These movements and so many others that captivated and escaped the ethnographic gaze were born in African cities, the site of contested claims to participation, visibility, and the negation of racialized difference.

Making the Savage Known

"The strength of the imagined place renders *invisible* the reality of the African site" (De Boeck and Plissart 2014, 22; emphasis in original). So immersed in their fictive ideas of Africans' identity and the simple lives they lived, the urban cultural movements described above rarely garnered the attention of metropolitan publics. Their bigotry instead nurtured, and was nurtured by, static images of African backwardness in European commodity culture; as they propagated the social imaginary, these representations both reproduced and were productive of imperial reality. Cultural production was as instrumental to African social revolution as it was to fixing representations from afar.

While fictional depictions of Africans, as seen in the spectacles of colonial expositions and commodity advertisements, obeyed a standard imperial narrative, perhaps most revealing of Europeans' fabrications were those images that purported to depict reality itself. Photography emerged as a tool for cataloging difference, and "'tribal' Africans were measured, prodded and poked during the colonial era to satisfy the ethnographic eye" (Reynolds 2015, 74). The earliest ethnographic films produced at the turn of the twentieth century scripted native roles to conform to a priori Western imaginaries (Landau 2002; Reynolds 2015). Thus filmmakers were tasked with "getting Africans to perform as 'Africans,'" a feat that was often quite difficult (Landau 2002, 158). The command of these imaginaries was such that if reality did not match the preconception, then the filmmakers rejected reality—and not the stereotype (Dunn 2004; see also Reynolds 2010, 475). In short, rather than make the African visible, these imaginaries made the Black savage known.[24] They transformed a stereotype into a truth.

Photography's "seemingly objective visual presence of Africans [and] plangent specificity and realness . . . stabilized 'authenticity' and obscured a world of politics and labor that people in Europe did not wish to see" (Landau 2002, 161). Complementing the legal fiction of Africans frozen in tradition that divided citizen from subject, performances or photographs of the "tribesman" served as the "visual manifestation of the phony stasis of custom" that colonialists professed to be unaltered by their arrival, thus "neatly concealing the dependence of whites on the coerced or semi-coerced labor of Africans" (Landau 2002, 156). A foil for the imperializing white-savior narrative, colonial filmmakers created the recurring theme of an African hero "rewarded for embracing the modernizing project of colonialism, and the villain, whose intransigent traditionalism inevitably brings suffering and hardship to himself and his family" (J. M. Burns quoted in Reynolds 2010, 467). Demonstrating the path to progress, "off and on screen, the white paternal figure was invariably juxtaposed and contrasted with

FIGURE 4.05.   Robinson, Lamour, and the Italian in a bar, still from Jean Rouch's film, *Moi, un noir* (1958). Copyright Les Films de la Pléiade.

the infantilized, feral black figure of the indigène and with the image of his colo-nial avatar, the évolué" (Gondola 2016, 56).

Aiming to counter the tendency of ethnographic films to depict the subjec-tive truths of their European beholders, French filmmaker and anthropolo-gist Jean Rouch set out to produce, in collaboration with his protagonists, an "ethnofiction" that might more closely represent the life-worlds of those men. What resulted was the 1958 film, *Moi, un noir*, exploring the rhythms of day laboring migrants from Niger in the ports of colonial Abidjan. Oumaru Ganda and Petit Touré, two central figures, adopted the pseudonyms and alter egos of Edward G. Robinson and Eddie Constantine, respectively, as they led the viewer on a tour of their imagined lives in Abidjan.[25] A repeated theme in the film was the migrants' lack of money, inhibiting them from living as they believed men did elsewhere. In one poignant scene Robinson sits in a bar with his love inter-est, Dorothy Lamour. An Italian interrupts their soirée, inquiring of Robinson, "Who's that monkey?" as he installs himself at Lamour's side. Robinson's frus-trated monologue commands the foreground while snippets are heard of the

Italian negotiating Lamour's price. Having lost her attention, Robinson, defeated, finally resolves, "You might have Dorothy, but you can't take my beer!" He ends his evening in a drunken stupor, fantasizing about the day he will return home to Lamour waiting for him in nuptial bliss. Not yet sober the next morning, Robinson staggers to her door, and the Italian steps out to greet him with a fistfight. In scripting his own character in Rouch's ethnofiction, Robinson cannot compete with the European, the latter's financial capacities endowing him with a more potent masculinity.

ACCULTURATION AS EVOLUTION

> **Construction sites open, new buildings are erected, gardens are created, urban roads are widened; but it is too much of a quotidian spectacle to be surprised.**
>
> —Antoine Konan Kanga, Mayor of Abidjan (1960–1980), *Abidjan: Perle des Lagunes*

Abidjan, Côte d'Ivoire's economic, cultural, and administrative center, was an appropriate staging ground for Robinson's dream sequence. There the imperial imaginary, casting its long shadow over articulations of African modernity as a sociospatial urban project, was particularly successful. Colonial Abidjan was a physical manifestation of assimilationist privilege and évolué exceptionalism in an otherwise routine context of African exclusion and unmet aspiration, and established the stratifications and differential mobilities that were to constitute city life after independence. As the urban plan and urban neglect separated Abidjan into center and periphery, the built environment reinforced deep distinctions of metropole and colony.

Initially a scattering of villages inhabited by the Ebrié people, Abidjan was founded in 1903 by the French, who identified the location as a suitable rail terminus and deepwater shipping port to facilitate transatlantic trade.[1] In 1921 Abidjan was one of five cities in AOF to receive mixed-commune status, mandating that it be jointly run by Europeans and African évolués and endowed with greater independence than native communes. This was an intermediate status before *communes de plein exercice*, which were granted equivalent privileges as municipalities in metropolitan France (Conklin 1997, 192–93). In 1928 local authorities began enacting strict urban plans, and having been conceived as a place of value in the colonial imaginary, Abidjan was soon known as a "flagship city" with architectural competitions held to design key administrative buildings (Steck 2005, 216). It became the colonial capital in 1934, and the population increased rapidly

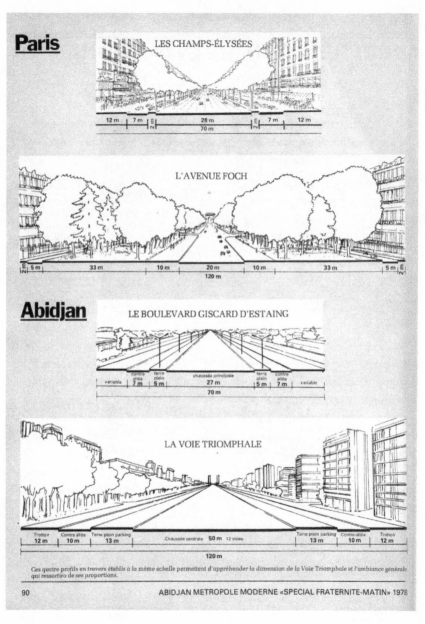

Paris

LES CHAMPS-ÉLYSÉES

| 12 m | 7 m | 28 m / 70 m | 7 m | 12 m |

L'AVENUE FOCH

| 5 m | 33 m | 10 m | 20 m / 120 m | 10 m | 33 m | 5 m |

Abidjan

LE BOULEVARD GISCARD D'ESTAING

| variable | contre allée 7 m | terre plein 5 m | chaussée principale 27 m / 70 m | terre plein 5 m | contre allée 7 m | variable |

LA VOIE TRIOMPHALE

| Trottoir 12 m | Contre allée 10 m | Terre plein parking 13 m | Chaussée centrale 50 m 12 voies | Terre plein parking 13 m | Contre-allée 10 m | Trottoir 12 m |

120 m

Ces quatre profils en travers établis à la même échelle permettent d'appréhender la dimension de la Voie Triomphale et l'ambiance générale qui ressortira de ses proportions.

ABIDJAN MÉTROPOLE MODERNE «SPECIAL FRATERNITE-MATIN» 1978

FIGURE 5.01. Principle avenues in Paris and Abidjan. *Abidjan Métropole Moderne*, Fraternité Matin (1978).

thereafter.[2] The recipient of significant colonial investment, Abidjan served as a "sumptuous prelude . . . to the durability of the post-independence French urban model overseas" (216). During the particularly enthusiastic period of post–World War II economic development in its colonies, France invested in transportation networks within the city and modernized its points of entry and exit (Loucou 2012). Following the construction of the Vridi canal in 1950, Abidjan was transformed from an administrative capital to an industrial and commercial center, and it emerged as a powerhouse of West Africa (Chenal et al. 2009; Freund 2007).

The ambiguities of the mission civilisatrice were manifest in static colonial iconography, however. Côte d'Ivoire's primary function as an agricultural producer limited attention in the French metropole to its urbanization (Loucou 2012). Thus, despite the idealized cityscape that colonial planners were actively constructing in Abidjan, postcards directed at the French public prior to 1950 rarely represented the Ivoirian city, and the colony's population was imagined instead through a lens of rural backwardness (Tirefort 2013–2014). Furthermore, depicting France as the harbinger of native progress, images of évolué Blacks in postcards of the era were incomplete without a white colonist in the center (Tirefort 2013–2014). As a clear statement of their uneven relationship, the "indigenous represented here is the 'black in the service of,' the one who works within the framework of the European economy" (30).

Postcards are but one illustration of how the politics of representation powerfully articulated the social order of racial capitalism in the Ivoirian colonial imaginary. More encompassing was the urban plan and demographic overlay of Abidjan itself; colonial urban planning became a "strategic instrument for determining how European and African political, economic, and social relationships should evolve" (Cohen, M. 1984, 58–59). As such, urban space mirrored colonial social stratification.[3] Notable was Abidjan's "apparent replication of a French provincial city," which, echoing the layout of eastern and southern African settler cities, segregated colonizers and their African subjects by district (Freund 2007, 178). Abidjan's initial geography carved up three districts: Plateau, Treichville, and Adjamé. Plateau was the center of administration and commerce, a marvel of modern architecture and fine boulevards where the French lived, worked, and shopped. It was situated on a "well-ventilated site, conforming to colonial imperatives of good health" (Steck 2005, 216). Treichville and Adjamé, housing the African residential quartiers and industrial districts, were located to the south and north, respectively (Appessika 2003; Steck 2005, 217). The French built Cocody as a European residential quartier adjacent to Plateau. Lagoons facilitated natural divisions between Plateau, "la ville blanche" (the white city), and the African southern quartiers. Colonial planners intentionally left absent bridges to connect them, while the Gallieni and Mangin military camps segregated Plateau from the African northern quartiers (Cohen, M. 1984; Loucou 2012; Steck 2005).

Assimilationist doctrine delivered the ideological cover of integration between city and metropole, évolué elite and French citizenry (Loucou 2012). Évolués, particularly those employed in the administration, were "welded together" through familial unions and membership in voluntary associations, so that as independence approached, they had consolidated status, wealth, and power (203). They also lived together. French officials provided planned housing for Africans according to their work status, overlapping with ethnoregional origin (Cooper 1996; King 2002). Wage earners, who were further demarcated by work in the civil service and skilled labor, received land plots in enviable locations while poorer, auto-constructed settlements emerged adjacent to wealthy neighborhoods to provide ready manual labor (Freund 2007; Loucou 2012). Housing was systematically underplanned, especially for those migrant workers intended as temporary, and their auto-constructed homes never received municipal incorporation or amenities. They became the slums that today encompass the majority of African urban space (Appessika 2003; Chenal et al. 2009; Freund 2007; King 2002).

Travail de ville/Travail des Blancs

Côte d'Ivoire's colonial-era African urban classes were comprised of a bourgeois elite and middle class, a proletariat, and an otherwise marginalized, contingently employed working poor (Loucou 2012, 201–4; for Ivoirian classes generally, see Coquery-Vidrovitch 1992, 302–17). Évolués were counted among the upper and middle classes and had a distinct lifestyle, inhabiting modern homes, forming residential societies, and enjoying European leisure activities, all thanks to "the favorable upward social mobility brought about by political and social changes" (Loucou 2012, 203).

The urban bourgeoisie worked in the highest echelons of the administration and in trade, although the latter were few in number and frequently foreign or métisse. The number and proportion of Ivoirians in elite administrative positions increased steadily in the interwar period, but growth was "somewhat illusory since they were neither in leadership roles, nor did they hold any significant power" (Coquery-Vidrovitch 1992, 315). Bureaucrats and private-sector employees and professionals constituted the bulk of the middle class (Loucou 2012). As was the case elsewhere in Côte d'Ivoire, the French administration and private companies met demands for skilled labor in Abidjan's port and industrial zones by recruiting foreign Africans (Cohen, M. 1984, 61). Consequently, by the end of the colonial period, non-Ivoirians dominated the urban labor market.[4] Upon independence Ivoirians secured their place in the public sector, while a significant foreign population remained in the nation's workforce (Cohen, M. 1984).

French interests subordinated the unskilled urban proletariat and contingent classes into forced labor. These classes encompassed laborers from other colonies, conscripted to construct the wharves, railroads, and other major projects (Coquery-Vidrovitch 1992; Loucou 2012). In the 1930s the colony began to recruit manual laborers in numbers that met demand, a point at which further migration raised concerns of an emergent population of un- or underemployed (Bazin and Gnabéli 1997). Upon the abolition of forced labor in 1946, the distinction between coerced and voluntary labor disappeared, while the salary endured as a criterion for status and opportunity. Extended to lower-tier workers, salaries were to be accorded based on qualification, and the number of salaried workers rose from 70,094 in 1947 to 171,000 in 1957 (Loucou 2012, 204). The social distinction between salaried manual laborers and those employed in office jobs was rigid, however, with the latter admirably designated as those who "*connaissent papier*" (know paper), in other words, the educated classes who had mastered the French language (Bazin and Gnabéli 1997, 699). The nascent industrial sector was predominantly foreign owned and managed and generally affiliated with trading companies, from which emerged a small industrial proletariat (Coquery-Vidrovitch 1992; Loucou 2012). These developments corresponded with greater demands for workers' rights and, in 1952, the implementation of a labor code in France's overseas territories to match its legislative counterpart in the metropole (Bazin and Gnabéli 1997). What later came to be designated informal labor, while a constant in the colonial urban economy, never figured into official plans or assessments. At best, the colonial state perceived these populations as temporary excess in an otherwise modernizing city. Despite persisting as a core contributor to the colonial and postcolonial built environment and political economy, they were thus rendered invisible.[5]

In the early colony salaried laborers were either European settlers or their African administrators, thus situating wage labor exclusively in the domain of the colonial city. This classificatory schema persisted in the postcolony and produced an Ivoirian urban vernacular for this esteemed category: *travail des Blancs* (white people's work), or alternatively, *travail de ville* (city work) (Bazin and Gnabéli 1997). A *travailleur* (worker) inferred a salary and could moreover be distinguished from the phrase *se débrouiller* (to get by, make do, fend for oneself, hustle), the latter describing both informal work and unemployment (Bazin and Gnabéli 1997; Murphy 2015). As a "linguistic peculiarity," the travailleur/se débrouiller distinction "refers to a double anxiety," at once economic and social, the salary pitting the state and the European modern, "seats of power and wealth," against the informal, traditional, peasant, and African (Bazin and Gnabéli 1997, 698–99).

Originating in France's nineteenth-century empire-building military forays, the concept of se débrouiller described "forms of everyday resistance and survival strategies" in the face of "power imbalances, unequal access to resources, or an overbearing state" (Murphy 2015, 353). One proponent wrote approvingly in 1913 that the *débrouillard* was expertly adapted to the "productive instability of modern societies" (quoted at 355). As the term migrated to the informal economies of post-structural-adjustment Francophone Africa, its presumed ingenuities contended with how to approximate the male breadwinner role, most often by drawing on personal "networks of interdependence, solidarity, and social cohesion" (367–68). The travailleur, on the other hand, composed a comfortable totality: he who is gain-fully employed may be supposed to have "an anchor into modernity in addition to a stable income and the possibility of turning to the state for support in times of need" (Bazin and Gnabéli 1997, 699). Travailleurs are "a distinct social category: salaried employment is conferred as an emblem of social status" (699). With the promise of *le travail* but the reality of *la débrouille*, among the metropolises of the region, Abidjan nevertheless acquired a reputation as a hub of job opportunities and relatively high earnings. And tied as they were to the new masculine ideal, the lure of modern work and wages made Abidjan a city of men, compelling a 1.22 male-to-female ratio in the city at early independence (Cohen, M. 1984).

From the start, French colonial rule partitioned land and organized labor in West Africa according to its principles of efficient extraction and perceived ethnic quali-ties of the indigenous population (Banégas 2007; Chauveau and Dozon 1988).[6] In the early twentieth century, the northern region of contemporary Côte d'Ivoire fell within the boundaries of the colony of Upper Volta (present-day Burkina Faso), and the two colonies were joined until 1932. Upper Volta functioned principally as a labor reserve. Northern inhabitants broadly shared common religious, cul-tural, and ethnic identities, and the French favored them as "*bon sauvage*" (good savage(s))—namely, the Dioula, "*bons commerçants*" (good traders, merchants), and the Sénoufo, "*bons travailleurs*" (good workers) and encouraged their south-ward migration to labor on plantations and to man the low-skilled urban workforce (Banégas 2007, 21).[7] Ethnic groups from the eastern region, the Akan generally, but among them the Baoulé in particular, were reputed for their "aristocratic" nature and favored as regime intermediaries. By contrast, the Bété of the west was "a colo-nial creation par excellence . . . constituting the negative ethnosocial figure, the dark Africa" (21). Generally, the colonial regime constructed people from the west as "anarchical," lacking in social structure and political organization (21). France devalued these western populations in proportion to the value they placed on their land—its "agricultural mise en valeur"—noteworthy for rich timber reserves and fertile soil for the cultivation of cocoa, palm oil, and coffee (21).

Oriented toward French imperatives, these ethnic stigmas laid the lasting foundation for the social order of the colonial and independent Ivoirian state, particularly as it was concentrated in Abidjan and expressed in the emerging urban labor ecology. Mostly low status and informal, foreigners and northern migrants found work in the diminutive *petits métiers* (little jobs): domestics, drivers, petty traders and commerçants.[8] They and their progeny were subjected to a heightened degree of exploitation, and citizenship claims were put out of reach—as well as the protections they inhered—upon an autochthonous turn in the 1990s. Abetted by their preferred status in the colonial imaginary, the Baoulé were disproportionately predisposed to become évolué. Finally, the French maintained a consequential presence in the city, with ten thousand expatriate personnel in Abidjan in colonialism's waning years, increasing to fifty thousand in the decades following independence in 1960 (Crook 1989).[9]

Entangled class, labor, and ethnoregional and racial stratifications persisted in the postcolonial social imaginary to designate an individual's evolutionary stage. These were the indicators by which a resident might properly inhabit Abidjan, idealized as the Paris of West Africa, that intermediary site between Africa and Europe. Traveling from across the Atlantic and inward to Africa's hinterland, French colonists were civilizational gatekeepers, Abidjanais civil servants, the évolué not quite/not white in-betweens, and finally, men from the Ivoirian north and immigrants from neighboring countries, backward savages. These hierarchies were so firmly entrenched that in the postcolony, to fully embody an Abidjanais identity was to approximate the alterity of the French colonizer (Newell 2012; Touré 1981).

Le miracle ivoirien

On August 7, 1960, Côte d'Ivoire transitioned into independence peacefully—in fact rather reluctantly, with first President Félix Houphouët-Boigny predisposed to a "French Community" of West African countries.[10] Houphouët-Boigny's personal role in Françafrique ensured French stewardship over Ivoirian independence until his death in 1993, thus securing peace and prosperity with neocolonial military, political, administrative, and financial backing. In particular, the 1961 Defense Accords guaranteed French military support from internal and external threats to the regime, thereby justifying a permanent military base near the Abidjan airport (Boone 1995; Bouquet 2005; Crook 1989; Ridler 1985; Woods 1988). In return, Côte d'Ivoire granted France directorial and financial monopoly control over its treasury, which included the regulation of the Francophone West

FIGURE 5.02.   Named after Maurice Lapalud, governor of Côte d'Ivoire from 1925 to 1930, Place Lapalud was the site of the country's first independence celebrations and renamed Place de la République by a 1961 ministerial decree (Reseaulvoire, n.d.). Place Lapalud (currently Place de la République), Plateau, Abidjan. Photograph by Louis Normand (1960). Copyright Centre Ouest Africain de l'Image (COAI). Courtesy Michel Buitruille, COAI.

African regional currency, the CFA franc (abbreviated for Colonies Françaises d'Afrique until 1958, and thereafter Communauté Financière Africaine), its utilities and natural resources, and a preferential trading partnership (Bouquet 2005; Koulibaly 2005; Mytelka 1984).[11] In his lengthy exposé of Françafrique, François-Xavier Verschave (1998, 130) remarks on the close ties between former metropole and colony, "*Faute de mariage, va pour la concubinage!* [If not marriage, then a mistress!] The 1961 accords in fact included most of the financial and military provisions envisioned by the [French] Community." Monopolies were not restricted to the French state, and private interests, with the majority of profits reaped by the largest colonial-era companies, maintained significant control over Ivoirian natural resources, infrastructure, and real estate (Amin 1967; Verschave 1998). The Presidential Palace, completed on the first anniversary of Ivoirian independence, was itself French-designed, French-financed, and rumored to have been leased by France (Banégas 2017, 295; Gervais 2011; Massire 2018). In what was known as "the most famous tunnel on the continent," from 1962 until Houphouët-Boigny's death in 1993, a hundred-meter-long underground passageway, guarded by the French army, retained an "umbilical link" between the palace and the French embassy (Boisbouvier 2015).

Many scholars hailed Côte d'Ivoire, aligned as it was with the dominant perspectives of global capital, as an African developmental model—one of the continent's few "emerging economic magnets" (Shaw and Grieve 1978, 3). The critical lens of dependency theory attributed Ivoirian success to its "well integrated position in the Northern or world capitalist economy, operating through . . . the cooptation of Ivorian elites into Western economic values and circuits" (Zartman and Delgado 1984, 12). Cushy relations with its former colonizer and the West generally, in addition to regional African dominance, earned Côte d'Ivoire the designation of a "semi-peripheral" state (Mingst 1988), one that Immanuel Wallerstein (1974, 13) characterized as "development by invitation."[12] Others labeled it a "subcenter in the periphery" (Zartman and Delgado 1984, 12), and a "sub-imperial" state that acted as a "regional hegemon" (Shaw and Grieve 1978, 11). In his detailed analysis of the economic marvel of early Ivoirian independence, Samir Amin (1967, 270) observed, with a heavy dose of sarcasm, "We tend to forget the brilliant days of colonization. The Ivoirian experience reminds us that the possibilities of foreign capitalism are not exhausted."[13]

Coupled with success as the world's primary cocoa producer, the economic and political stability secured by neocolonial complicity contributed to a growth rate surpassing 7 percent for the country's first two decades of independence, and the postindependence narrative was one of le miracle ivoirien.[14] Acting as both cause and consequence, Côte d'Ivoire was the undisputed destination for West Africans responding en masse to Houphouët-Boigny's open-door policy welcoming migrant labor and fueling the plantation economy and low-status urban employment, yet also subject to periodic violent xenophobic outbursts (Banégas 2007; Crook 1989; Crook 1997; Newell 2012; Sandbrook and Barker 1985; Zartman and Delgado 1984).[15] On the highly remunerated side of the social divide, the "opening [of Abidjan] to foreign 'experts' provoked the arrival of a population that was rich, white, and resolutely urban" (Chenal et al. 2009, 118). These non-African expatriates, whom the French dominated numerically and socially, were the "principal beneficiaries" of the early independence urban economy, extracting about half the gross nonagricultural income from their share of major businesses and real estate, and as individual traders and salaried executives (Amin 1967, 177).[16] Antiforeigner sentiments in the 1970s generated measures to limit foreign access to salaried employment, replace French managers with Ivoirians, and recruit nationals to fill positions in the public sector (Bazin and Gnabéli 1997). The consequences were significant: according to L'Office National de la Formation Professionnelle (National Office of Vocational Training), between 1971 and 1984 the proportion of Ivoirians making up the salaried workforce rose from 47.8 percent to 68.3 percent (Bazin and Gnabéli 1997, 693). Nonetheless, immigrants from neighboring countries, predominantly Burkina Faso, Mali, Niger, and Guinea, constituted between a quarter and a third of the population during the first decades of Ivoirian independence and made up a quarter of Abidjan's workforce (Nyankawindermera and Zanou 2001, Sandbrook and Barker 1985). At the onset of civil war in 2002, when the question of *ivoirité*, an "authentic" Ivoirianness that favored southern-originated populations, took center stage, migrants (foreign and domestic) still constituted half the city's population (Institut National de la Statistique 2003).

As the formal economy's principal employer, the civil service provided the ultimate modern employment and central path to middle-class, évolué status (Dozon 1997; République de Côte d'Ivoire 2007; Woods 1988).[17] While those connected to French financial capital retained a privileged place in the new economy, state-society relations were the crucial means by which to ascend the independence-era socioevolutionary ladder. The postcolonial political and economic elite constituted an amalgamation of (frequently absentee) plantation owners—a key coalition led by Houphouët-Boigny during the decolonial turn—and top-tier civil servants (Banégas 2007; Cooper 1996; Woods 1988).[18] In addition to the substantial export-oriented agricultural wealth accrued by the planter bourgeoisie, in the urban economy civil servant salaries in 1965 represented 28 percent of total African incomes and 48 percent of all salaried employment (Amin 1967, 278–79).[19] This bureaucratic stratum reproduced itself by restricting access to the civil service for educated and well-connected Ivoirian men (Le Pape and Vidal 1987). Graduates, educated with generous state-funded scholarships, staked their futures in national examinations that placed them, depending on some combination of skill, money, and networks, somewhere in the Ivoirian bureaucracy, where after a lifetime of work they expected to retire with healthy pensions (Crook 1989). The school-to-public-sector pipeline was so entrenched that Côte d'Ivoire was dubbed the "republic of good students" and the "civil servant republic" (216).

"Rarely has a state been so present as in Abidjan after 1960" (Chenal et al. 2009, 127). The spatial manifestation of Houphouët-Boigny's idealized Ivoirian nation, Abidjan's development was a highly centralized undertaking and the privileged recipient of national investment (Couret 1997; Dembele 1997). Thus a vigorous project of state-built housing was foremost an "expression of political power" and designed with elements of European domesticity in mind (Massire 2018, 7). Housing for civil servants, those "cells of the state body," was especially to "display the complete vision of the [Ivoirian] social project" (7). Houphouët-Boigny's urban fantasy thereby articulating the state-society contract, these and other hefty urban subsidies placated the powerful Abidjanais constituency, who came to expect such support (Cohen, M. 1984). Registers of national belonging soon coalesced in Abidjan, conflating *citadin* (urban resident) and *citoyen* (citizen) (Newell 2012, 9).[20] The social effects of this singular urban emphasis were significant. By the 1970s the Paris of West Africa was projecting an image of a cultivated, modernizing nation—one whose elect, by way of state-sponsored acculturation as evolution, had inherited the prestige of the colonial metropole.

In short, the colonial and later postcolonial coupling of employment with a racial and ethnoregional identity shaped the citizenship classifications of the city, endowing some working bodies with more or less civilizational attainment than others (Le Pape and Vidal 1997; Newell 2012). Being truly Abidjanais, then, meant treading an aspired French sociality and a denigrated migrant underclass. Well after the onset of la crise, real work, in the Abidjanais imagination, involved a suit and tie, a chauffeured vehicle, and an air-conditioned office. The civil service offered the surest path.

National Culture, Imported

French colonizers prized linguistic mastery as a mark of true assimilation and met their greatest success in Abidjan, where French became the lingua franca, and for many Abidjanais, the primary language spoken in the bureaucracy, the marketplace, and the home. Through educational institutions and the mass media, the colonial regime further disseminated French language and culture. "The idea was to create an elite class of black French people—*évolués*—who would perpetuate French culture in the colonies" (Land 1995, 440–41).

Like many new states attempting to establish a cohesive nation within arbitrarily drawn colonial borders, Côte d'Ivoire similarly looked to culture (Vogel 1991). For Houphouët-Boigny the solution to overcoming divisive ethnic stratifications fomented under colonial rule and to creating an authentic and prideful Ivoirian identity was through the equally French classification of the évolué. His regime enacted cultural policy via three principal means: a state-controlled media, centralized education, and state financing to prioritize his vision of economic development. Through these avenues markers of French identity, notably the French language, transformed everyday life to shape Ivoirian identity, particularly as it was articulated in Abidjan (Vogel 1991). The slippage between national culture and political economy meant that "the need for development— both economic and political—was invoked by Ivoirien leaders during the postcolonial era to rationalize cultural modernization in the Western image" (Land 1995, 440). The explicit objective of the nationalized Ivoirian television in the

FIGURE 5.03.   Traffic agent, Abidjan (1963). Copyright Roger-Viollet / Roger-Viollet.

first decades of independence was to give the population a lens to the outside world, one that would expose them to preferential models of modernity. This was a means for the state to forge a singular culture that relied heavily on imported content and through which France also maintained its grip on the independent African state's cultural production. Metropole and postcolony therefore not clearly distinct, it was France's broadcasting authority that in 1962 created the public radio-and-television corporation Radiodiffusion Télévision Ivoirienne (RTI), Côte d'Ivoire's primary state broadcasting service. French interests controlled independent Ivoirian broadcasting as well (Land 1995).

Beyond perceiving media as a window "through which a guiding beam [would] light the way toward modernization and economic prosperity," bureaucrats and cultural producers "behave[d] as if that light, which shines brightly from the West, [was] necessary to achieve appropriate cultural identity" (Land

1995, 443). For domestic cultural producers, this resulted in a conviction that they "must take their cultural cues from the West to achieve legitimacy" (443). Research into the 1980s cultural scene thus found that "virtually every encounter between the press and Ivoirien artists establishe[d] the inevitable link between the performer and Western culture" (443).

The *colon*-as-évolué

The Paris of West Africa inextricably bound individual worth to participation in the modern economy. As imaginary, this was no better personified than in the colon statue, an iconic symbol of the Ivoirian colonial era (see figure 5.05). The colon stands erect, as if called to attention by some superior. Past his twilight years, he betrays a slight paunch. His dark skin coupled with full lips and wide nose indicate that he is African, but this bureaucrat dresses as the white man. Traditionally costumed in a crisp suit and pith helmet, his attire and accessories change depending on his profession: sometimes he holds a briefcase or a book, other times a camera or a doctor's stethoscope hangs around his neck; yet all signify that this man embodies one of the new, European trades imported during the French colonial conquest.[21]

In West Africa broadly, colon statues generically describe any statue adorned as a European but depicting either Africans or Europeans. They mark a "rupture between the traditional and modern sculptures of Black Africa" (Werewere-Liking 1987, 5). Variants emerge from local cultural forms and are produced by a wide range of ethnic groups, primarily in Côte d'Ivoire but also in Benin, Burkina Faso, Cameroon, Ghana, Guinea, Guinea-Bissau, Nigeria, and Togo (Girard and Kernel 1993; Werewere-Liking 1987). For example, among the Manjaco in what became the Portuguese colony of Guinea-Bissau, *pitchap*, or posts staked into the earth, acted as the rough equivalent of land titles (Gable 2002). These pitchap "signaled . . . a moment in a life-cycle and a relationship . . . when a young man asserts his right to build a conjugal hut around the courtyard of the corporate house. It marks the moment when a youth becomes a man with domestic responsibilities" (311). Upon colonial contact, the pitchap was transformed from abstract carvings of ancestors into representations of Manjaco interlocutors of the colonial state—or in other words, colon statues. These revealed how Manjaco tradition integrated Portuguese authority, such that it adapted the rights to land that the pitchap once conferred to colonial power. The hybrid reflected a period in which "the ability to manipulate the forms and technologies of bureaucracy became more and more a necessity of political life, a manifestation and instantiation of power. A carved 'portrait' of a Manjaco chief in the guise of a colonial officer makes perfect sense in such a context" (296).

FIGURE 5.04. Baoulé spirit mate. Reprinted from Wikimedia Commons, *Houten beeld van een man op stoel vermoedelijk een waarzegger*, Collectie Tropenmuseum, part of the National Museum of World Cultures.

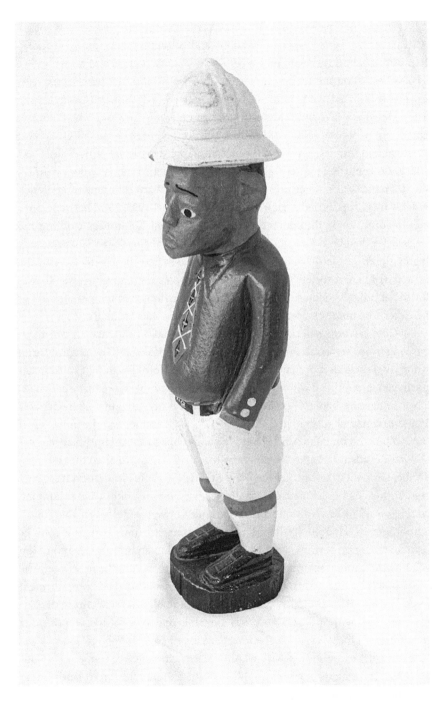

FIGURE 5.05. Colon statue. Author's collection. Credit: Carlos Carmonamedina.

A signifier of cross-continental contact, colon statues can be traced to coastal African contact with European explorers and colonizers and from their inception were domesticated into native beliefs and rituals (Girard and Kernel 1993). The earliest colon statues depicted whites exclusively and later represented Africans who imitated them in dress and comportment (Werewere-Liking 1987). They "designate, first and foremost, a foreign body in Africa, one whose lifestyle and accessories have influenced the customs of an entire continent at its most personal and intimate level" (22). Penetrating the "very heart of traditional art, which, for centuries, has responded to precise aesthetic canons," colons confirm the dramatic "clash of cultures" and an emergent Westward frame of reference, notably by Europeanized Africans (Girard and Kernel 1993, 20). They reflected a cultural diffusion in the bodies they portrayed, in which European clothing and accessories "had become a sign of wealth and social change" (18). Colon statues, highly significant in the iconography of colonial Africa, "bear witness to an era, as well as reveal a society's desires, fantasies, projections, and interests: desires for social progress, fantasies of appearance, projections into the past, future, or hereafter, and interests simultaneously spiritual and mercantile" (132).

In Côte d'Ivoire especially prominent among colon statuary art are those deriving from the Baoulé ethnicity's "spirit mates," ideal mates in the spirit world whom these statues represent (Ravenhill 1980). The proliferation of spirit mates portrayed in dominant colonial professions indicated the desire that one's mate, albeit remaining Baoulé, "exhibit signs of success or status that characterize a White-oriented or -dominated world" (10).[22] They exemplified the influence of the évolué ideal on public and private life and shaped Ivoirian imaginations.

First President Houphouët-Boigny's story brings living form to the colon-as-évolué. His political ascent reflected the colonial African's idealized route to success: both a chief in his native Baoulé village of Yamoussoukro with a thorough command of Akan traditions and a Catholic convert educated in the French school system, Houphouët-Boigny quickly immersed himself in the colonial regime, taking on various posts as doctor, plantation administrator, and union chief before gaining international renown as an African of influence among the most powerful Europeans (Toungara 1990). He founded the Rassemblement Démocratique Africain (RDA), the major African political force during decolonization, and upon independence was a reliable operative for the Françafrique mission across the West African region (Verschave 1998). Houphouët-Boigny was "the kind of African 'évolué' with whom the French wanted to cooperate" (Cooper 1989, 753), a point best exemplified in the abolition of forced labor under what became known as the "loi Houphouët-Boigny" (Houphouët-Boigny law). Being himself from an elite family of former slave owners, Houphouët-Boigny assessed settler colonists' use of forced labor against the métayage system on

African-owned farms. He drew from personal experience with both to convince officials that the latter was not only more amenable to free labor principles, but also significantly more productive (Cooper 1996). In doing so, he and the other deputies who formed the first cohort of Africans within the Assemblée Nationale Constituante (National Constitutional Assembly) deployed colonial ideology to lay bare its hypocrisies, declaring in 1946 the imperative "to abolish the slavery which is still practiced in Black Africa by men, civil servants and civilians, who are traitors to France and her noble civilizing mission" (quoted at 187). In formally proposing the law to the assembly, Houphouët-Boigny (quoted at 188), coopting French universalism by his use of the first-person plural, proclaimed:

> In suppressing forced labor, a unique occasion is offered to us today to prove to the world that the France of the rights of man and of the citizen, the France of the abolition of slavery, remains always true to herself and could not contest or limit the liberty of any of the people living under her flag.

In the years that followed, Houphouët-Boigny and his consortium of cocoa and coffee planters in the Société Agricole Africaine (SAA) demonstrated that the métayage system was indeed more profitable and rendered the white settlers' voices redundant in the political economic arena.[23] They emerged a triumph of France's "post-war development fantasy, . . . the agricultural vanguard of West Africa" (Cooper 1996, 402). André Latrille, then-governor of the colony, wrote in praise that Houphouët-Boigny ran a "model" plantation and that it was "particularly satisfying to note that this situation is the work of an African entirely trained by French Civilization" (quoted at 191). Having mastered the logic of empire, Houphouët-Boigny's personal commitment to socioeconomic ties between polities was made evident as he shaped the independent country into a "bourgeois" regime (7). In exchange he remained a close confidante to France until his death, forging a strong alliance between local elites and the metropole, often at the expense of broader African interests.[24] It was Houphouët-Boigny who first used "France-Afrique," the antecedent of Françafrique, in 1955 "to encapsulate the close and amicable ties" between metropole and colony (Bovcon 2011, 5). The cultural infusion of France into Côte d'Ivoire was for Houphouët-Boigny transcendent, the manifestation of a "mystical Franco-African community" (Zolberg 1967, 464).

President from independence until his death in 1993, Houphouët-Boigny endures as an eminent symbol of the Ivoirian nation. He embodied the ideals of French civilization and upheld the notion that Côte d'Ivoire was a country apart, its evolution far surpassing other African states. Like his legacy, colon statues, national emblems of art and identity, demonstrate how in Côte d'Ivoire the

FIGURE 5.06. From Gouttman, A. 1978. *Il était une fois . . . Félix Houphouët-Boigny*. Paris: Afrique Biblio-Club. Drawings by J. M. Ruffieux. Gifted from Zappin for author's collection. Copyright 2021 Artists Rights Society (ARS), New York / SAIF, Paris) / Bibliothèque nationale de France.

expressive hegemony of racial capitalism was particularly discernable. The colon-as-évolué proved a formative figure in the public and private spheres of modern Abidjanais masculinity, and in so doing, buttressed neocolonial Franco-Ivoirian relations. Elsewhere, however, declarations of Black power and Black beauty signaled resistance to oppressive regimes of racial capitalism.

IMAGINARIES OF AFFIRMATION

In the magazines the Wolf, the Devil, the Evil Spirit, the Bad Man,
the Savage are always symbolized by Negroes or Indians; since there
is always identification with the victor, the little Negro, quite as
easily as the little white boy, becomes an explorer, an adventurer,
a missionary "who faces the danger of being eaten by the wicked
Negroes."

—Frantz Fanon, *Black Skin, White Masks*

Heralding the arrival of European hegemony, the colon statue was a testament to the momentous changes that colonial conquest had compelled upon the Black body, changes material and cultural, public and private. It was but one example of the Black body as the primary site in which the politics of representation responds to economies of dispossession. This body's legacy as property claimed and property denied transforms acts of self-possession, self-expression, and self-adornment into acts of resistance, performing for multiple gazes and inevitably engaging, even while contesting, the referentiality of whiteness. At times these embodied performances are outright rejections of the hegemonic representational repertoire, declarations of Black pride that affirm Black identity and Black sociality to oppose dominant meanings of dignity, respect, and success in the modern world. At times they relish appropriation in order to master the hegemonic representational repertoire.

Like the évolué, who straddled the not quite/not white divide, Black dandies—men who coopted imbricated signs of modernity and whiteness through embodied practice—were liminal figures. The multiple gazes from which they were seen—as self and other, and the diverse contexts in which they have appeared, provide conflicting readings of their performances: liberatory, repressive, "mimicry" (Ferguson 2006). For sapeurs of Brazzaville and Kinshasa, clothing offered material proof of their European conquest to audiences back home against a global backdrop of racialized exclusion. Throughout the Black Atlantic the sartorial refinement of the Black dandy has threatened the racial strictures that rejected Black consumer citizenship. By engaging in conspicuous consumption, Black dandies have participated in capitalist modernity as more than exploitable commodities to dangerously transgress the boundary from passive object to commodity subject. In doing so they have become cultural phenomena. At the 2017 event *Fashion Night: Modern Black Dandies*, the Brooklyn Museum thus rendered homage to "men of color who use fashion to define and inhabit a racially independent public persona, in fashion, film, music and conversation" (Leonhardt 2017).

Yet the story of Black dandyism is also entangled with objectification. The practice in England originated at the confluence of the slave trade and a novel consumer culture, compelling "luxury slaves" to dress and act flamboyantly (Miller 2009). Black dandies appeared as fixtures in the American racial imaginary in the 1880s, when Black northbound migrants began to establish their own centers of entertainment. On New York's "African Broadway" such fashionable denizens participated in a "dress parade," "an impressive, exuberant display of fashionable elegance and dandyism" (Pieterse 1992, 138). These transgressions were not taken lightly. White American society, dubbing the dress parade the "Monkey Parade," responded to those uppity Blacks by creating "Tambo," minstrelsy's urban counterpoint to the rural plantation figure "Sambo" (138). With "his would-be classy clothes and pompous language caricatur[ing] the new figure of the free black," the Tambo caricature "was a way of undermining black emancipation" (134).[1]

Minstrel shows found enthusiastic audiences in France. At the celebrated Folies-Bergère music hall in 1885, the Brothers Bellonini first performed blackface, which they called "Hottentots à l'oeil blanc" (white-eyed Hottentots) (Gervereau 1993b, 34). Representations of Africans in France were generally subjected to the same derisory tropes as their African-descended counterparts in the United States. In addition to monkeys and cannibals, dating from the nineteenth century an assemblage of representational repertoires pronounced "the impossibility for the metropolitan Black to become a civilized being, his taste for sartorial elegance, his speaking '*petit nègre* [Black vernacular],' his incompetence with technical progress" (Bachollet et al. 1994, 18).

The American minstrel figure continued on its Black Atlantic voyage to Africa to project the "loose-limbed cartoon 'native'" (Landau 2002, 150). Here, however, the context and the gaze shifted its interpretation. The mode of recognition mediated reception such that Africans did not unequivocally reject these characters. For example, the Congolese public largely embraced Belgian comic artist Hergé's 1931 *Tintin au Congo*, with its blackface depictions of Africans (Hunt 2002). But the 1950s comic series "Les aventures de Mbumbulu" in the colonial-state-run magazine *Nos Images* was not similarly well received. The series portrayed Mbumbulu, an aspiring évolué, as a "colonial-made, bumbling, minstrel-like *petit nègre* figure," whose poor imitation of Belgian colonial life served as an instrument of "Belgian colonial propaganda" (103). Unlike the supporting roles of Tintin's savage Africans, from which it was easy for an educated Congolese readership to establish distance, Mbumbulu was the protagonist of the series. While in the former instance the Congolese could identify with Tintin, with Mbumbulu their only choice was to play the fool (Hunt 2002).

The "figures of the 'savage' compel recognition" (Mudimbe 1994, 6). Constructing the savage demands a politics of representation whereby visible difference presupposes seer and seen, *self* opposing *other*. Who has the power to recognize whom within a dominant narrative is one-half of the story of conquest and structures the signifier of Black Atlantic subjugation. For much of the history of racial capitalism, visible difference has been the alibi for devalued Black life. In racial capitalist societies, racial recognition, in other words, is regularly "an act of race subordination" (Harris, C. 1993, 1741). Visibility, then, is liberatory only as it vindicates difference. The emergence of the Black Atlantic as a self-referential category has played an important role in vindicating difference outside the register of whiteness. Tasked with subverting the most visible tools of negation, the imaginaries of affirmation explored in this chapter forged connections and borrowed across oceans to reinvent the meaning of Africanity and to transform the reified Black body into an essence of power and beauty—insisting as they did that representation cannot but be a political act.

The Live Dialogue between Affirmation and Negation

> In the club, it was also remarkable that black Americans could be recognized and distinguished from the Africans and others by the way they stood—with their waists cocked as if to show that the lower and upper parts of the body were detachable—and the way they danced and dressed. . . . Even though I was dressed that evening in the best suit I had brought from France, it dawned on me that this was the black style I had been looking for all my life in Bamako and Paris. This was where I had always wanted to be: hairstyles with their own languages, shirts that were symbols of some political struggles, and bodies that were modern enough to rival machines. They looked defiant and rebellious. Just looking at them brought out in me some deep feelings of Africanness that had been repressed by . . . French colonization.

—Manthia Diawara, *We Won't Budge*

> **One cannot resist the stereotype in representation without creating another stereotype. The language of resistance is itself caught up in another form of caricature, symbolism, and pastiche that robs the black person of his or her individual history.**
>
> —Manthia Diawara, "The Blackface Stereotype"

Confronting Blackness as negation and Africa as its source, in the mainstream diaspora consciousness the continent was long one from which to seek distance. The hegemony of whiteness shaped the terms of inclusion for Black, second-class citizens in their new homelands, and until at least the mid-twentieth century, having absorbed "Western ideas of civilization . . . most found themselves viewing contemporary Africans as, on the whole, at least semibarbaric" (Meriwether 2002, 15). And because "negative images of Africa held ramifications that went beyond the cultural sphere," the imaginary of Africa was the primary site of an entangled struggle for global Black consciousness, political autonomy, and economic advancement (172). Pride for Africa was then a counterhegemonic act of the Black diasporic vanguard in their demand for restitution and recognition. Against the civilizational narrative, they derived value out of Blackness by idealizing an African homeland and invoked a solidarity that arose "from a common sense of oppression" as much as from "a shared heritage" (242–43).

The pan-African movement was an early instance in which diaspora Blacks reclaimed the African continent. Trinidadian Henry Sylvester Williams organized the first Pan African Conference in London in 1900, and W.E.B. Du Bois the first Pan African Congress in Paris in 1919. In the 1910s and 1920s, Jamaican activist Marcus Garvey espoused a "populist pan-Africanism," its concrete platform the return to Africa (Meriwether 2002, 21). Garvey's emigration efforts "injected the issue of Africa into Black America's intellectual and political life on a mass scale, forcing African Americans to examine their relationship to Africa" (22).[2]

In France, the Parisian journal *Les Continents* disseminated Garvey's ideas (Genova 2004). In African ports eager audiences awaited editions of Garvey's *Negro World* publication, and for colonized Africans on and off the continent, pan-Africanism offered a powerful alternative modernity that rejected the European civilizing mission (Conklin 1997). Among Francophone Africans, however, the pan-African movement was far from populist, confined rather to "elitist dissent" (Loucou 2012, 235). Privileges of the African few—literacy, travel, and a modern worker's identity buttressed by union membership—nurtured their cosmopolitan consciousness. Moreover, the imperial assimilationist project had created an intellectual vanguard as concerned with integration into the French nation as with African self-determination. This tension characterized the cultural and political expression of Négritude that emerged in the 1930s as the Franco-phone answer to pan-African ideology (Wilder 2003).

"Négritude" was first coined in Europe as a derogatory term, indicating a people of lower civilizational attainment (Touré 1981). Reclaimed by Francophone diaspora and continental Africans, Négritude "constitute[d] a founding moment that made possible a reflection on the Black's being-in-the-world" amid a colonial context in which "the affirmation of a racial identity and identification served as weapons for combat" (Mudimbe-Boyi 2012, 25). It appeared against the backdrop of "the passing of legislation consciously cast in the language of racial degeneration and regeneration" and a general intensification in race consciousness in France and the colonies (Conklin 1997, 165). Aimé Césaire and Léopold Senghor, two of the most prominent Négritude founders, were titans of the Francophone literary tradition, and the movement reflected their centering of culture as the means to advance Blackness in the changing global order. Theirs was an évolué struggle to define the terms and place of authentic Africanity in the French empire and therefore assert legitimate "leadership of the *sujet* [subject] populations" (Genova 2004, 135).[3] After initial alliances with the French Communist Party in the 1920s, by the ripening of the Négritude movement, its évolué founders, accused of "bourgeois nationalism," had largely splintered away (141). Working for elite recognition in the context of empire, Négritude demonstrated the potential for affirmations of Blackness to operate within, even while they contested, the hegemonic order.[4]

Yet many affirmations of Blackness approached racial negation as itself the core of the imperialist project—one that encompassed the indignities of capitalism broadly. Participants of the 1922 Fourth World Congress of the Communist International, for example, adopted "theses describing blacks as a nationality oppressed by worldwide imperial exploitation," and "black workers' struggles were now considered inherently anti-imperialist" (Kelley 1994, 107).[5] In this period, the French Communist Party formally supported the formation of the Ligue de defense de la race nègre (LDRN). With the financial support of the French Communist Party, the LDRN published the newspaper *La Race Nègre*, which they disseminated across France and its West African colonies (Wilder 2003). In the following decade the Union des Travailleurs Nègres (Union of Black Workers), founded by Comintern member Tiemoko Kouyaté, served the Franco-phone world as a "vehicle for Panafrican political organizing" (242).[6] As decolonial and civil rights struggles unfolded and activists identified white supremacy foremost as an expression of capitalist hegemony, they understood Blackness, de facto, as a culture of opposition. Politicizing Blackness became a fundamental mode of affirmation.

FIGURE 6.01.   In a context in which "the capitalism-anticapitalism debate is superimposed on the colonial issue," Gervereau (1993b, 63) explains that the Black subject is made a symbol of revolution or repression. In this anticommunist and xenophobic propaganda poster, a Black man carries the Communist flag, a dagger at his waist. *"Travailleurs français! les meneurs communistes les voilà!"* (French workers! The communist leaders are here!), André Galland (1928). Anticommunist poster depicting Communist leadership as racial others. Copyright 2021 Artists Rights Society (ARS), New York / ADAGP, Paris. Copyright Calland / Collection La Contemporaine.

Black affirmation offered a rejoinder to imaginaries of negation, the latter insisting the Black body enter history by acculturating to whiteness. In doing so, it was a revolutionary act against the established politics of representation. Affirmed, Blackness stood dually as a "symbol of beauty and pride" and "as a sign of radical defiance, a call to revolt, desertion, or insurrection" (Mbembe 2017, 47). This counternarrative of positive difference emerged as a product of the "live dialogue" (cf. Matory 2005) between Africa and its diaspora, while the politics of empire across the Atlantic divide differentially sorted Black bodies along its evolutionary ladder. Just as Africa became an emancipatory idea for diaspora Blacks, descendants of slaves who were renowned intellectuals, performers, athletes, and activists modeled for colonized Africans mastery of the white man's world.

Appearing at the 1900 Paris Exposition was the *American Negro Exhibit*, assembled by W.E.B. Du Bois and Thomas Calloway and featuring a monograph by Booker T. Washington (Bruce 2012). Unlike portrayals of French colonial holdings, this exhibit showcased Black progress. Calloway used the Black American experience to "furnish Europe with such 'evidences' of the Negro's value as a laborer, a producer, and a citizen that the statecraft of the Old World will be wiser in the shaping of its African policies" (214). In a persisting incongruity of the Black experience, France's fascination with African Americans was juxtaposed against the low regard it reserved for its African subjects. "While Africans were being colonized in the name of European civilization, Black entertainers from America found themselves *à la mode* in the European capitals" (Pieterse 1992, 144)—and this was particularly so in Paris. In the Roaring Twenties—that decade in which colonial policy vigorously pursued forced labor under its mise en valeur—Paris was renowned for its hearty reception of African American celebrities, making itself a second home to the Harlem Renaissance (Blake 1999; Stovall 1996). In this way, the "preferential hospitality accorded Black Americans in France served an officially sanctioned discourse proclaiming the absence of race discrimination and negrophobia" (Gondola 2004, 209). Their popularity belied a contradiction: during a period in which French depictions of Africans were limited to caricatures of children or savages, Black Americans were heavily influencing French articulations of modernity.[7] In short, "black American émigrés served as liminal figures"; they were "auxiliaries to create a fiction that race does not matter and that culture is, in essence, what sets subjects apart from citizens" (Gondola 2004, 202; see also Keaton, Sharpley-Whiting, and Stovall 2012, 3). In imperial France an affirmed Blackness was found not in the colonies but in the New World.

Media Star Revolutionaries

The Black Panther Ten Point Program, "What We Want" (1966)

1. We want freedom. We want power to determine the destiny of our Black community.
2. We want full employment for our people.
3. We want an end to the robbery by the capitalists of our Black community.
4. We want decent housing fit for the shelter of human beings.
5. We want education for our people that exposes the true nature of this decadent American society. We want education that teaches us our true history and our role in the present day society.
6. We want all Black men to be exempt from military service.

7. We want an immediate end to police brutality and murder of Black people.
8. We want freedom for all Black men held in federal, state, county, and city prisons and jails.
9. We want all Black people when brought to trial to be tried in court by a jury of their peer group or people from their Black communities, as defined by the constitution of the United States.
10. We want land, bread, housing, education, clothing, justice and peace.

Huey P. Newton, "War against the Panthers:
A Study of Repression in America"

The movements that coalesced around Blackness at the moment of African independence and civil rights struggles frequently contested whiteness as an articulation of capitalist hegemony. Many notable figures emerging from this period identified with Marxist doctrines, explicitly pairing antiracist struggles with critiques of capitalist exploitation and emphasizing that economic subjugation was entrenched in other forms of structural and physical violence. Afro-Marxist regimes were realized for a time in several African states. Yet more pervading than formal political power was its deep impression among Black populations in the politics of representation. As a consequence, the rise of Black Power ideology, itself composed of projects for political self-determination, economic autonomy, and cultural pride, created an enduring Black aesthetic. Representation, in short, was a primary means to contest ongoing political, economic, and cultural domination.

As diaspora Black nationalists defined themselves as internally colonized "victims of capitalist exploitation that resulted in racism and other forms of institutionalized violence," they rendered Black Power "another battle in the struggle against international capitalism that invariably [was] manifested in the resistance to hegemonic dominance by western neo-imperialists" (Singh, S. 2004, 26). Militant groups like the Black Panther Party, founded in 1966, "espoused an ideology of third world revolution" (Stovall 1996, 268). They taught that lifting the yoke of white oppression was inseparable from gaining economic autonomy, thus linking material gain and antiracist struggle. This philosophy was central to the Black Panthers' development of a "vanguardist visual language and iconography" (Ongiri 2009, 193). They built "an especially sophisticated relationship to broadcast and print media" and thus effectively "create[d] a canon of images, slogans, and gestures that codified these symbols into an iconic language of revolution" (50). The Panthers' effective branding of Black revolution exemplified how imaginaries of affirmation responded to the dual oppressions of whiteness and capitalism in racial capitalism.

FIGURE 6.02. Emory Douglas, the Black Panther Party's Minister of Culture, produced images that graphically subverted power hierarchies to contest racial inequality at home and abroad. *Huey P. Newton*, Emory Douglas. Copyright 2021 Emory Douglas / Artists Rights Society (ARS), New York. Photo courtesy of Emory Douglas / Art Resource, NY.

As "media star revolutionaries," the Black Panther Party confronted "ambigui-ties . . . between revolutionary action and revolutionary representation" (Ongiri 2009, 51, 35). The ideational slippage from affirming representations toward a total political economic project enabled a "spectatorial community that had been and was being constituted by the political and cultural configurations of Black Power discourse"—a set of preconditions that produced its own brand of com-modity subjects (168). The Black Panthers' media and communications savvy helped establish the group's notoriety in American popular culture, while also becoming the medium through which it would "disseminate its plan for radical social change" (184). But their remarkable success was a double-edged sword. Their relationship with the media was symbiotic, and the Black Panthers in turn provided a novel and highly marketable revolutionary style (Ongiri 2009).[8] Coopted into the iconography of edgy capitalism, in the popular American con-sciousness the Black Panther's image has since subsumed its message.

Extolling "the Black Man," Black Power movements also projected a mas-culinist aesthetic (Alexander-Floyd 2003; Springer 2006; Wallace 1999). The Black Panther Party portrayed a "highly stylized, hypermasculine, military Black macho," a "valorization of the 'brother on the block'" (Ongiri 2009, 21, 42).[9] It reflected how, even as class politics made space for race, Black male leadership often claimed entitlements that reproduced a hegemonic gender order. The heavy grievance of patriarchy denied emboldened Black men with an intersectional blind spot—if not defensive posturing against a rising Black feminist move-ment—in their critique of capitalist hegemony. In doing so, they cultivated a "black power movement [that] made synonymous black liberation and the effort to create a social structure wherein black men could assert themselves as patri-archs, controlling community, family, and kin" (hooks 1992, 98). Yet to achieve a truly "patriarchal macho [access to money and power] it would have taken black men years to avenge themselves. With the narcissistic macho [access to women] of the Black Movement, the results were immediate" (Wallace 1999, 68–69).

"We shall have our manhood," former Black Panther leader and Minister of Information Eldridge Cleaver declared in reaction to the assassination of Malcolm X (quoted in Alexander-Floyd 2003, 181). Cleaver was an egregious example of misog-ynist and heteronormative Black nationalism. Centering the domination of women, Black and white, and pronouncing Black homosexuality a "'racial death wish' typical of the Black bourgeoisie who have rejected their Blackness, their African heritage," for Cleaver, Black liberation was a hypermasculinized affair (Shin and Judson, 1998, 250). He marketed this ideology with "cock pants," a style he innovated while exiled in Paris. "As a Black Panthers Party leader, Cleaver was a revolutionist in the cause of Black liberation. As a designer of clothes, Cleaver's revolutionary thinking is shown in a male-liberation creation" (*Jet Magazine* 1978, 22).

FIGURE 6.03. Eldridge Cleaver wearing his "cock pants" in Paris. bell hooks (1992, 98) asks, "And what does it say about the future of black liberation struggles if the phrase 'it's a dick thing' is transposed and becomes 'it's a black thing?'" Copyright Rene Burri / Magnum Photos.

The cultural politics of Black power "sought to exploit visuality and negotiate the dominant media's attendant stereotyping in order to create strategies of resistance and empowerment" (Ongiri 2009, 182). The Black Panthers purposed their aesthetic appeal to disseminate their message widely, directly addressing the link between representation and exploitation. Encapsulating this aesthetic of Black power and the rejection of white supremacy was the parallel affirmation of "Black is beautiful." So, while demanding economic and civil rights, Black Americans also "raised political consciousness about cultural expression and popularized exuberant new personal styles and beauty ideals" (Camp 2015, 686). Integral to the antiracist struggle in the United States, Black activists "understood [beauty] to be a taproot of black life, black consciousness, and black politics" (677). To insist on the value of Blackness as it was embodied was a political act; it responded dialectically to its negation, one essentialism countering the other. The insistence on Black beauty was directed both toward mainstream white society and within the Black community itself. It sought out an authentic Blackness apart from hegemonic, white beauty ideals, addressing aesthetic hierarchies that had resulted in colorism, hair straightening, and skin bleaching (Camp 2015;

Pierre 2013). The rallying cry of "Black is beautiful" traveled across the Black Atlantic, informing, for example, the ethos of South Africa's Black Consciousness Movement (Hirschmann 1990).

Synthesis

Black power and Black beauty have distinct lineages that do not immediately align with the anticapitalist struggle. Within the purview of Black capitalism-as-emancipation, buying Black mobilizes the aesthetic appreciation of Black beauty and political consciousness of Black power into potentially transformational acts. So too does Black purchasing power. These commodified affirmations of Blackness, achieved via accumulation and consumption, reject racial negation by upholding capitalist common sense: if money is power, then Black money is Black power. As such, they complicate the politics of Blackness vis-à-vis racial capitalism.

First Black American world heavyweight boxing champion Jack Johnson illustrates such a configuration. From 1908 to 1915, Johnson was renowned for his boxing talent and proclivity for white opponents. In 1910 Johnson defeated Jim Jeffries, the "Great White Hope," for the heavyweight title in what was a highly anticipated match laden with political significance and eugenic overtones. Jeffries's monumental loss ignited race riots, and footage of the fight was banned in the American South and the British colonies in media battles that "not only exposed the growing global influence of U.S. racial culture, but . . . also pushed the instability of Western imperialism to the forefront of public debate" (Runstedtler 2012, 100).

Outside the ring, Johnson was known for his flashy clothing, fancy cars, and marriages to white women (Carrington 2010; Gilroy 2001; Runstedtler 2012). He was also a savvy entrepreneur whose portfolio included lucrative product endorsements and original ownership of New York's Cotton Club (Brundage 2011; Tate 2005).[10] A precursor to the Black musician or athlete as a brand unto himself, "Johnson's skill, style and verbal wit can start one to thinking that late-twentieth-century Black Masculinity as we've come to know it from BET and ESPN was, by and large, a Johnson invention" (Tate 2005).[11] In the midst of Jim Crow America, when racial strictures normalized indignity and ostentatiousness could be met with lynching, Jack Johnson was a victorious global icon of Black manhood. He contested negations of Blackness by becoming the protagonist within capitalism's hegemonic narrative. His defiance was not in rejecting an exploitative economic system, but rather in mastering it, and he exemplified a persistent articulation of the struggle for Black male affirmation.

FIGURE 6.04.   Johnson promotes the White Steam Touring Car in a sardonic jab off his 1910 opponent Jim Jeffries, the "Great White Hope." Jack Johnson, White Steam Touring Car advertisement (c. 1910).

As talent bolstered by commodification, Jack Johnson's rebellion against dominant modes of representation in the early twentieth century reveals that there was a constant tension between the imaginaries of negation and affirmation explored in these pages, the dialectic unfolding in no straight chronological order. Nevertheless, the social, political, and economic climate of the day fomented the conditions for one or another expression to establish a common sense understanding of what Blackness signified in racial capitalism. The world capitalist economy incorporated Blackness as the essence of negation. Through steady contestation, by cultural cooptation, racial solidarity within or against empire, media savvy, profiting off athletic prowess, or otherwise, Black people have shifted the representational repertoire. Whether or not Blackness serves this purpose, these gains in representation have had the specious effect of appearing also to undermine racial capitalist exploitation. Indeed, built into racial capitalism's double oppression by way of whiteness and capitalism is the possibility of conflating the sign (whiteness) with the system (capitalism). In the dialectical struggle of racial capitalism, Blackness, signifier of negation, has countered with affirmation. Emerging as synthesis, commodified forms of Blackness declare victory over white supremacy at the sacrifice of anticapitalist critique.

LA CRISE

In stark contrast to the Black power imaginary emanating from the diaspora, postcolonial Côte d'Ivoire, as the center of Françafrique social, cultural, and economic order, perpetuated the évolué ideal and its erasure of Blackness. It was only in the 1980s, the decade that Ivoirian icon Alpha Blondy debuted on national television embracing a fusion of traditional music and reggae beats, that mainstream Ivoirian popular culture opened "a connection to the past, to Africa and Black identity" (Land 1995, 447).

Alpha Blondy, "the Bob Marley of Africa," was the first major Ivoirian export to the popular cultural realm of the Black Atlantic, and he himself produced from an accumulation of cultural referents. Born Seydou Koné, in his teens he called himself Johnny (after French singer Johnny Halliday), then Elvis, and finally Alpha Blondy. As a "symbolic rite of passage . . . later realized concretely with his jaunts to Paris, New York and Miami," this progression of name changes "rescued him from his traditional Sénoufo context, transported his imagination to France, the United States and Jamaica" (Land 1995, 446). In French, Dioula, and English, Alpha Blondy's songs ranged from local anthems such as "Cocody Rock" (1984) and "Jah Houphouet" (1985) to continental themes and beyond, including his 1985 hit, "Apartheid is Nazism."[1] Alpha Blondy's impact launched Abidjan on the international scene, making it the world's third reggae capital after Kingston and London and making him a veritable political force (Schumann 2015). Just as significant was his success in the domestic market in the context of the state-sponsored and French-supported cultural production that had worked hard to

cultivate a local évolué class. Alpha Blondy's music resonated for this generation once removed from the colonial state, a generation that sought to identify
as cosmopolitan and global, but distinct from the legacy of Françafrique. Thus
heralded a cultural revolution of Anglophone imaginaries.

Ivoirian researcher Aminata Ouattara (1985, 77) described the impact of Black
American cultural production on the national youth and media. "American!" she
declared. "It is a magical word because it is synonymous with great quality." The
United States, the reigning world superpower with its formidable Black population, posed a powerful alternative to the civilizational realm that Françafrique
had demarcated, "exercis[ing] a considerable fascination on many young Ivoirians whose goal [was] to become 'évolués'" (87). Music videos by Black artists
impressed upon Ivoirians new styles in music, dance, dress, and speech, influ-
ences considerable enough to question whether "the Ivoirian song even remains
Ivoirian" (83). When positive stereotypes of Black Americans entered Ivoirian
homes, the ongoing racial struggles of an ocean apart were substantially muted.
Rather, Ouattara's (95) respondents surmised that "the Black American is distinguished from the white only by the color of his skin and his African origins.

FIGURE 7.01. The cover for Alpha Blondy and the Solar System's popular
Revolution album offered a powerful iconography of Abidjan's shifting orientation
to an Anglophone imaginary. Compact disc of Alpha Blondy and the Solar
System's album *Revolution* (1987) and Tiken Jah Fakoly's album *Mangercratie*
(1999) displayed on a table with drinks. Credit: Carlos Carmonamedina.

Otherwise, he lives in the US, is as rich and educated as the white American." One thirty-year-old architect postulated, "When I see the Black American, I imagine that this will be the African of the twenty-first century" (95). She (95) concluded, "Young Ivoirians admire and emulate the Black American because the latter represents all that they want to be: a Black 'évolué.'"

A survey of Ivoirian television viewers in the late 1980s found Alpha Blondy to be the nation's favorite artist, domestic or international, and a general preference for Ivoirian musicians who sung in local dialects and rhythms over Western adaptations (Land 1995). Ivoirians had begun to reclaim their Africanity. It was in this moment, in the twilight of le miracle ivoirien, when the Francophone évolué model was proving structurally untenable, that the phenomenon of Black Atlantic modernity came to rival the Côte d'Ivoire of the colon.

La Rue publique

It has been noted with irony that the principal "industry" of many underdeveloped countries is administration.

—Walter Rodney, *How Europe Underdeveloped Africa*

A reputation for financial integrity, owing not to a fiscally prudent treasury but to the complicity of Françafrique, had generated superficial prosperity well past Côte d'Ivoire's heyday. Yet by the 1980s, its state coffers were severely anemic. Unable to pay a debt that, beholden to runaway interest rates, rose from $4.7 billion in 1970 to $7.5 billion in 1980, global finance institutions compelled Côte d'Ivoire to implement austerity measures in 1981 (Bouquet 2005, 242–43).[2] In 1989 world cocoa prices were 25 percent of their peak value in 1978, and Côte d'Ivoire had the highest per capita debt in sub-Saharan Africa (Crook 1990).[3] In 1993, the year of Houphouët-Boigny's death, Côte d'Ivoire "succeeded in breaking the world record for indebtedness: 240% of its annual production" (Verschave 1998, 132). The following year—once their presidential ally had passed—France inflicted a major currency devaluation that halved the value of Ivoirian exports. Over the next decade global finance institutions imposed three additional, increasingly harsh structural adjustment programs, stripping the Ivoirian government of its substantial public sector and much of its sovereignty (Bouquet 2005). Of the threat that "such a manifestly impossible austerity programme" was sure to have on Ivoirian stability, in 1990 one scholar wondered of the Bretton Woods institutions: "Did they want the whole regime to collapse?" (Crook 1990, 669).

The period of la crise that began in the 1980s and culminated in civil war from 2002 to 2011 was devastating for Côte d'Ivoire according to all major indicators. Between 1988 and 1997 the World Bank changed its classification of Côte d'Ivoire from a middle-income to a low-income country (N'Diaye 2001, 113), and in the first decade of the new century, per capita GDP growth averaged -1.28 percent (World Bank 2018). Whereas the percentage of Ivoirians living below the poverty line of $1.90/day in 1985 was 6.81 percent, by 2008 this figure had soared to 29.02 percent (World Bank Development Research Group 2017a).[4] Côte d'Ivoire's Human Development Index (HDI) was slightly higher than that of sub-Saharan Africa in 1980, but by 1990 its rate of improvement had slowed below the region's average, under the United Nations Development Programme range for "low human development" (United Nations Development Programme 2011, 133–34). This gap continued to widen with the onset of civil war in 2002, and at its conclusion in 2011, Côte d'Ivoire ranked 170 out of 187 countries on the HDI (United Nations Development Programme 2011). In 2010, at the end of Gbagbo's presidency (and despite being among the first six countries to receive debt relief in 1998 under the World Bank and International Monetary Fund's Heavily Indebted Poor Country Initiative), Côte d'Ivoire's public debt represented 63 percent of its GDP, and its external debt was $11.52 billion (CIA World Factbook: Côte d'Ivoire 2012; United States Government Accountability Office 1998).[5]

"In the good times, education, access to the civil service, the move to town, and ultimately Abidjan was the golden road to success, to becoming a real *patron* [boss] to one's friends, family, and ethnic group . . . [but] now the road was virtually cut off" (Freund 2007, 182–83). Even Ivoirians whose familial backgrounds and educational attainment would have privileged them in a prior generation faced uncertain employment prospects (Bouquet 2005; Crook 1990). With the plummet of cocoa prices and the implementation of fiscal and monetary austerity policies, Côte d'Ivoire's government-funded path to évolué status had grown untenable. The contraction in civil service employment was particularly egregious. For three decades the civil service was "the principal purveyor of jobs in the Ivoirian modern sector" (République de Côte d'Ivoire 2007, 177). Yet from 1980 to 2005, the number of civil servants had increased by about half, compared to a population that had nearly tripled (République de Côte d'Ivoire 2007).[6] A 1991 World Bank loan conditionality was particularly brutal, demanding a one-quarter reduction in the civil service (Bouquet 2005, 207). Wages also shrank: by the mid-1990s the salary of civil servants was 28 percent less than their 1985 earnings in real terms (247). Fewer and lower wages significantly influenced men's breadwinning roles. In one longitudinal survey from Abidjan, the proportion of salaried men sampled fell from 57 percent in 1979 to 29 percent in 1992. Over the same period female-headed households increased from 9 to 19 percent (Le Pape 1997, 90).

The formal private sector did not replace the drop in civil service employment. Instead, informal trades, once designated for and denigrated as migrant or women's work, surged. In the new century, the civil servant republic had become the "*Rue publique*" (public street) (Banégas 2007, 46). Data from 2001–2002 indicated that 74.9 percent of Abidjan's working population was involved in the informal economy. By contrast, 17.4 percent of workers were formally employed in the private sector, and 6.6 percent in the public sector (administration and enterprise). Employees in public administration in this period earned the highest average salaries, 221,000 FCFA (US $300) per month; a worker in the formal private sector averaged 146,000 FCFA (US $198); and a worker in the informal economy averaged only 40,000 FCFA (US $54) (Institut National de la Statistique 2003).[7]

The shock of unemployment among the educated elite destabilized faith in the foundational tenets of the mission civilisatrice, "rendering obsolete the equation between the diploma, salaried work, economic affluence and social prestige" (Proteau 1997, 653).[8] Belonging to the "sacrificed generation," the story of the would-be évolué of the new economy roughly paralleled that of his father's generation up through university, after which, despite a once respected degree, no job in government was open to him. Instead, he waited, often a decade or more, for work that did not exist.

In the Francophone évolué model, state employment dominated the formal economy, such that the civil service was the primary source of job security and entitlements. Work being the nexus around which modern life revolved, the forms of sociality and economic dependencies it produced ensured deep state allegiances. The évolué was the colonial and later postcolonial embodiment of the racialized and patriarchal social contract, an iteration of the man-state-capital triad established in the imperial imaginary that posed wage earners as ideal citizens. He stood atop a hierarchy of value, his employment status implying a total identity. Excluded were the informally employed, forsaken outsiders of the global economy, marginalized within Ivoirian norms of urbanity and modern manhood.

TABLE 7.01 Employment characteristics in Abidjan, 2001 to 2002

SECTOR	TOTAL OF WORKERS EMPLOYED (%)	MONTHLY EARNINGS (FCFA)
Public administration	5.5	221,000
Public enterprise	1.1	256,000
Private, formal	17.4	146,000
Private, informal	74.9	40,000
Average earnings	N/A	71,000

Source: Le marché du travail à Abidjan en 2002 (The labor market in Abidjan in 2002). Institut National de la Statistique (2003, 40).

The évolué model did not adapt to the new reality of la crise. And as the path to elite status narrowed, Ivoirians sought to eliminate potential competitors. They did so by restricting what it meant to be Ivoirian. Conflating class and an autochthonous citizenship by reserving for Ivoirians a state-funded path to middle-class life and maintaining an underclass of extranational ethnic others had ensured complicity to both the state and its neocolonial arrangements. When this social contract fell apart, Ivoirians were left to compete with foreigners/northerners for work and dignity in a post-miracle Côte d'Ivoire. Social and economic precariousness prompted a decade-long political-military conflict that divided Côte d'Ivoire between north and south. Beginning with the country's first coup d'état in 1999, divisions reignited in the 2000 elections, when the Supreme Court disqualified Alassane Ouattara, a northerner and a presidential candidate, on the grounds that he was of Burkinabé origin—despite his having served as Houphouët-Boigny's prime minister. Ouattara's exclusion was concurrent with ivoirité, a movement to exclude persons of ambiguously foreign origins, including those of migrant parentage who were born and raised in Côte d'Ivoire.[9] Civil war broke out in 2002, dividing the country into a government-controlled south and a rebel-controlled north. Abidjan's population swelled with migrants from the interior seeking refuge in the stability of the de facto capital, and many expatriate businesses disappeared. The population increase coupled with the loss of jobs intensified un- and underemployment in Abidjan well beyond official tallies.

While much of the civil war passed in a cease-fire stalemate, in 2004 Côte d'Ivoire bombed a French military base in the rebel capital of Bouaké. Nine French soldiers and one American civilian were killed. The Ivoirian command maintained that it had mistaken its target, but France nevertheless retaliated by destroying the entire Ivoirian Air Force fleet. This assault and its affront to Ivoirian sovereignty fit President Gbagbo's persistent narrative that France was covertly funding the northern rebellion, and Ivoirian protestors took to the streets en masse. French troops opened fire, killing twenty protestors by their count and sixty according to Côte d'Ivoire. Emergency evacuations of French and other expatriate populations proceeded in the tense aftermath, and many of the departures were permanent.[10] The international community vilified Côte d'Ivoire, and in 2005 Mercer Human Resources Consulting rated Abidjan second only to Baghdad as the world's most dangerous city for expatriates (Skogseth 2006, 21). The 2006 *West Africa Lonely Planet* (256) warned travelers that the "British Foreign & Commonwealth Office advises against all travel to only two countries: Somalia and Côte d'Ivoire." The basis of le miracle ivoirien: regional migrant labor and the Françafrique pact—had become foci of populist aggression. In turn, global actors portrayed as savage the same country they had long esteemed as an oasis of civility.

Contested elections in 2010 declared Alassane Ouattara the victor. Gbagbo refused to concede, and violent street confrontations left hundreds dead as Ouattara held court in the faded luxury of the Hôtel du Golf. After more than four months of open conflict, a combination of French troops and northern rebels descended into Abidjan and instated Ouattara. The war was over, and a new chapter in Ivoirian history had arrived. The decade of conflict had been both a political and economic interregnum. For Abidjan, the city that exemplified the mission civilisatrice, this period represented the tail end of a narrative arc: the violent finale to an interplay of urban space and social imaginaries that began with the promise of acculturation as evolution and closed, by those same measures, with backward slippage.

La crise revolved around the predicaments of being citizen and civilized, identities inseparable from nation and capital. The story of Abidjan's twenty-first-century man was written with a new plot: no longer was he to contest his exploitation by acculturating to whiteness, an aspiring évolué determined to replace the colon. Excluded from global capitalism and its schema of value production, the urban protagonist was now the *débrouilleur* of the informal economy.

Shifts in the political economy had reshaped the politics of representation. In the economy of la crise, Abidjanais carved out "itineraries of accumulation" beyond education and the civil service, both as survival strategies and forms of sociality (Banégas and Warnier 2001, 6; Kohlhagen 2005–2006). With the évolué model no longer assuring a lifetime of wages or transferable cultural capital, another set of models: "diaspo" figures, athletes, musicians, and entrepreneurs, emerged (Banégas and Warnier 2001, 5, 7). Abidjan, like many cities in sub-Saharan Africa, witnessed a "reorientation . . . from being the center for a modernist elaboration of formal public and private employment to an arena for highly improvised small-scale entrepreneurial initiative," in which the majority of its inhabitants would pursue livelihood strategies fundamentally "survivalist in nature" (Simone 2004a, 168).

Every man newly unable to lay claim to a salary undermined the patriarchal contract at the core of the mission civilisatrice. Rising from its ashes, the "moral economy" of the débrouille encapsulated "the spirit of initiative of the new urban capitalism" (Banégas and Warnier 2001, 8). For those Abidjanais now shut out from the wage economy as a reality or realistic aspiration, the total lifestyle of the évolué—one of career, wife, and viable future—was transformed into an "imaginary of materialism" garnered piecemeal through ephemeral consumer acts and projected onto the body with the same intensity as more enduring status investments (10). Stripped of the civilizational promise of the French colonial évolué, revealed in these feats of petty capitalism was the naked truth that money makes the man.

Colonial compromise fixed the ideological foundation of racial capitalism in the Ivoirian imaginary. As the means to achieve hegemony, the évolué ideal was an expression of white supremacy while also an enabler of African capital accumulation; it involved at its core the negation of Blackness. The celebrity icon status of Black mass-media figures upended and usurped that legacy of negation to posit Blackness as powerful, beautiful, and inherently oppositional. But its materialist premise upheld the legitimacy of a racial capitalist world order that continues to negate the majority of Black populations. Media trope Blackness, dignified for its material potentiality, realizes the promises of capitalist excess to challenge the indignities of racial subordination. Heralding a new era in the politics of representation, the imaginaries that come to the fore are imaginaries commodified.

Distanced from the doubly antiracist and anticapitalist imperatives of prior articulations of Black power, media trope Blackness derives affirmation from thriving inside, rather than rebelling against, systems of economic domination. For Black men whose omission from the patriarchal social contract has been normative, thriving inside is intimately entangled with personal ambition and social entitlement. Black abjection set against the anticipation of male privilege, it is humanizing. Black masculinity thus expressed defies the structural exclusions of global capitalism, and embracing the commodified legacy of Blackness—the very thingness that once assured its negation—asserts value.

Part III
IMAGINARIES IN A CRISIS ABIDJAN

The classes were overcrowded, day and night the pupils went hungry . . . Many children did not make it as far as the *certificat d'études* [primary school completion]. They deserted their desks but refused to go back to the fields—it must be said that African farm work is one of the most backbreaking and thankless tasks of all human activity. They wandered the markets and the streets of the towns, became the first generation of the *bilakoros* (the unschooled), became the first gang members, the first birds to fly.

Many of those who passed the *certificat d'études* could not get a place in secondary school, nor a job as a messenger in the public services. They would hear nothing of going back to the machete, the *daba* [hoe], the fishing line. They preferred to join their friends in the markets and the streets.

Then the crisis came and budgets were cut back. Many of those who passed the *brevet d'études* [secondary school completion] could not get a place in the second cycle nor find jobs as pen-pushers in the civil service. They swelled the numbers of the *bilakoros* in the markets and the streets.

Those with a *baccalauréat* [high school diploma] were given no career guidance and the civil service organized no *concours général* [civil service entry examination] for teaching or administrative positions; they were obliged, forced to take to the streets and the markets.

Those with a bachelor's or a master's degree received no grants for foreign work experience. The École nationale d'administration (ENA) and the École normale supérieure (ENS) offered no entrance exams. And, since their parents could no longer support them, the graduates took to the markets and the streets to lead the *bilakoros*.

The crisis worsened. Belatedly, those who had been tossed into the streets by an ill-conceived educational system were joined by young workers driven out of offices and factories by closures, cut-backs and business restructuring. It was this diverse group, who had learned from bitter experience, from injustice and lies, who—when the bell signaling the leap from dictatorship to democracy tolled—took the reins of the République du Golfe and of ancient Africa, the cradle of mankind.

Ahmadou Kourouma, *Waiting for the Wild Beasts to Vote*

CITOYENS AND CITADINS

The men, for them it is very difficult. The majority of unemployed are men. The women are open to *petit commerce*, they sell *attléké* [ground cassava] and juice, they are open to that, but men do not do that. They need to work in an office, open up a tailor shop or all that. It is more expensive. But women do not need anything big to do their commerce. A little shop of 20,000 [FCFA], 10,000, can be enough to provide them with some money later.

—Boka, Sorbonne orator

I know that here we live like shit, in Burkina [Faso] they live like shit, in Kinshasa they live like shit, even in Brazil, they live like shit. So one must speak of it all, to make it known, see . . . I want that you, you in America, I want that you know me, Zappin here in Abobo or in Yopougon, to know that things are not good . . . Rap, it's universal.

—Zappin, musician and Abobo vendor

Wage labor and the évolué, anchored in the colonial economy by their proximity to whiteness and capital, were deeply embedded in notions of what it meant to be a citoyen and citadin in Abidjan, Côte d'Ivoire. As civilizational criteria, they situated masculinity in a racialized hierarchy of worth to provide an exaggerated example of breadwinning's centrality that filtered through all registers of modern life. The *lumpenproletariat* were, by contrast, evidence of colonialism's incomplete, and the developmental state's failed, project.

State patronage relations forged in the colonial economy were perpetuated in the postcolony, relations in which the salary constituted political subjects, or "clients," such that the "state granted means of livelihood to all it had put under obligation" (Mbembe 2001, 45). By and large, la crise killed the salary, but patronage relations endured informally between members of the Gbagbo regime and its supporters and sustained the évolué ideal. Thus for those outside the state-sanctioned, formal economy, trading political loyalty for financial support represented, in the language of the market, duly earned state "investment." Those who were surplus to these arrangements were subject to the state's predatory whims; economic uplift or social validation were to be acquired elsewhere. It was a familiar division that

FIGURE 8.01.   Still of vendor displaying a briefcase in Adjamé traffic. Author's video, Abidjan (2009).

elucidated the tight entanglement of political allegiance, economic distribution, and institutional violence across eras of racial capitalism. Yet while the évolué configuration offered the surest path to security of life and property, media tropes of Blackness, posited as oppositional identities that survived and at times thrived outside the realm of the state, came to compete for space in the Abidjanais everyman's representational repertoire. Part III examines how the évolué and the media trope manifested as aspirational imaginaries for men in the era of la crise.

Orators and Vendors: A Profile

Orators and vendors, highly visible in Abidjan's public space and social imaginary, were respectively symbols of the political and economic dimensions of la crise.[1] Orators held a privileged relationship in the regime of President Laurent Gbagbo. They were the sons of the postindependence generation's middle class of plantation owners and civil servants, and they assumed public identities as regime henchmen during Côte d'Ivoire's decade-long civil war. In their struggle for recognition, access to material goods, and social status, they adopted "patriotic speech like a veritable trade" (Cutolo and Banégas 2012, 23). Expecting to cash in on a "patriotic debt" (Banégas 2010, 33) of state-financed entrepreneurial initiatives, orators

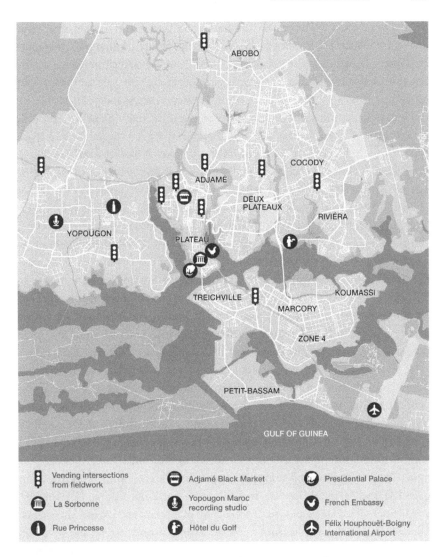

FIGURE 8.02. Map of Abidjan. Credit: Carlos Carmonamedina.

engaged in pro-Gbagbo propaganda efforts.[2] Their vision of the Ivoirian state departed from the French model of a substantial public sector that had marked the regime of President Houphouët-Boigny. Still, the state remained the country's most reliable source of formal employment and the central node through which to find work elsewhere. This was particularly the case during the hiatus in job creation as a consequence of the conflict. Therefore, orators positioned themselves as privileged entrepreneurs in a state whose main role, they argued, was to support a nascent private sector. They called this market-oriented system "Anglophone," and their entrepreneurial aspirations reflected the contemporary hegemonic masculinity of the transnational businessman (Connell 1998). While their oratorical activities generated minimal albeit vital earnings, orators were primarily concerned with using their activities to network among the Ivoirian business and political elite.

Orators spoke and socialized at the Sorbonne, a *parlement du peuple* (people's parliament), self-designated as a "patriotic" public space in Plateau.[3] It was a space where the educated but unemployed, in the process of *"se cherchent"* (seeking a place for themselves in society), found a way to become social actors and public figures (Banégas 2010, 36). Born with the rise of multiparty politics at the end of Houphouët-Boigny's presidency, the Sorbonne became the central venue for street-level propaganda among President Gbagbo's network of Jeunes Patriotes (Young Patriotes) after the 1999 coup d'état and the 2002 civil war. Those highest in the organization had come of age within the national student movement, FESCI (Fédération Estudiantine et Scolaire de Côte d'Ivoire, or the Student Federation of Côte d'Ivoire), or as self-described "militants" with the Jeunes Patriotes. In the context of creeping informality across all aspects of Abidjanais life and livelihood, the Jeunes Patriotes, with the orators as their mouthpieces, filled a power vacuum "to impose themselves . . . as the 'new sovereigns' in urban public space" (Banégas 2007, 46).

At its most basic level the Sorbonne was a place to keep busy, to be seen and heard. From 10 a.m. to 6 p.m. on weekdays, orators pontificated on the social and political. Commuting from their homes in the quartiers populaires to Plateau, the orators' movements reflected the temporal and spatial rhythms of the gainfully employed urban man (Cutolo and Banégas 2012, 44). By midday the seats had filled with men who, irrespective of employment status, were often dressed in business attire. There they conversed among themselves and listened to speeches. It was an open space where admission was free, but patrons paid for seating. Deferentially, young boys shined shoes and women sold cups of espresso and inexpensive snacks. Orators held titular identities such as professor, analyst, ambassador, and governor, and honorifically referred to men who paid for individual seats as *doyens* (deans).[4] They advocated for Ivoirians to embrace a business mentality, sold business start-up pamphlets, and welcomed guest speakers' elaborate money-making schemes. Few women frequented the space as spectators. Speeches always addressed the male subject, and the tone was regularly misogynist. A regular speaker came around lunchtime to rally the crowd in anticipation of the day's main political speech, telling jokes involving a triad of power, politics, and penises. His prop was a large black dildo.

For five months I conducted ethnographic fieldwork with the orators. I attended the Sorbonne for half-day periods two to four times a week between November 2008 and April 2009. On occasion I accompanied orators as they spoke in *parlements* in Abidjan's outlying neighborhoods. Additionally, I socialized with orators in a *maquis* (open-air drinking and eating establishment) adjacent to the Sorbonne and in their neighborhoods, and once I met with an orator and his family at their home. I also conducted in-depth interviews lasting between one and two and a half hours with two ticket takers and eighteen prominent current and former orators, many of whom held leadership positions within their organization, the Sorbonne Solidarité. Among them was the opening speaker for the Jeunes Patriotes leader Blé Goudé and the winner of a national orators' competition organized by Simone Gbagbo, President Gbagbo's wife.[5] The majority of my interviewees had participated in the Sorbonne between five and nine years, and some were among its founding members, having participated for nearly two decades. Most were in their late twenties to mid-thirties. Despite the Sorbonne's autochthonous rhetoric, two respondents described themselves as foreigners, although one had been naturalized. For a contrasting perspective, I interviewed a woman, one of two female orators in the Sorbonne Solidarité's existence. While all of the self-described Ivoirians were unmarried, most had girlfriends and sixteen had children. All but four respondents had some university or alternative higher education; seven had or were in the process of receiving advanced degrees. In addition to a monthly salary of 50,000 FCFA (US $100) provided by the organization and coins tossed at the end of a speech, the orators supported themselves fully or partially through odd jobs from their Sorbonne contacts or received sporadic support from the Sorbonne network.[6] A lucky few had moved on to secure salaried work, predominantly in the civil service, through this network.

Mobile street vendors (vendeurs ambulants) sold their wares in the center of roads, sites that purported no dignity but were just as animated as spaces of sociality and creative hustles. Without a fixed location and little if any capital, their activities were low status and precarious. Vendors were both Ivoirian and migrant, but typecast socially as foreigners and easy victims of state harassment, with the police chasing them away, seizing their goods, or jailing them on the pretext that their activities were illegal. Some had worked the same intersection for a decade, becoming familiar sights to sympathetic clients they called *patrons* or *chefs* (bosses) who drove past regularly and on whom they depended more often for charity than sales.

Vendors circumvented national belonging to emphasize commonality in a borderless Black urban experience. They identified with men in Abidjan and throughout the Black Atlantic, notably the United States, whose performative masculinities had garnered immense success without having adhered to normative accumulation strategies via education or conventional employment. Media outlets transmitted celebrity Black masculinities as tropes that were flattened, glorified, and malleable: as one-dimensional representations of life, experiences of Black men elsewhere were flattened and glorified; representing both global hegemony and counterhegemony, Black Americans were also malleable, and thus doubly suited discourses of success and marginality. In appropriating these tropes of Black Atlantic iconicity, vendors affirmed their denigrated selves. Expressing appreciation for a particular media icon, the vendor's standard line was, "I like his style," or "I like how he does his business." They classified generically as "Anglophone" models of stylized, money-making men to whom they admiringly referred, in English, as "black" and "business." Terms within this representational repertoire also frequently appeared as English words in Nouchi, Abidjan's local slang: "ghetto," "nigga," "job," "VIP," "time is money." Adopting a Black capitalist ethos, aspirational vendors espoused self-styled business identities and adhered to the corporate logic of the entertainment industry and its hyperconsumerist imaginings.

Over the course of the year I conducted ethnographic fieldwork, interviews, and focus groups with thirty-five current and former vendors at work and at play. I made single visits to intersections popular for vending throughout Abidjan and made repeat visits to three. After casual, preliminary discussions, I conducted informal interviews and focus groups lasting between twenty minutes and three hours with vendors at their intersections or in follow-ups at maquis. Of these men, I further socialized with thirteen, going out with them at night, sharing afternoon drinks, watching them play football and rehearse, record, and perform music, visiting their homes and meeting their families, and generally just hanging out.[7]

I sought out vendors in their twenties and thirties. None came from well-off families. Many demurred on stating their educational level or reported minimal schooling, although eight had some university or alternative higher education. Of my respondents, twenty-one were Ivoirian and fourteen were nonnationals, seven of whom were born and raised in Abidjan. All but one, a foreigner, was unmarried, and most did not have girlfriends. Some had children, of whom two were in regular contact. The worst off of these men were removed from female companionship altogether and instead surrounded themselves with other men in music and sport subcultures if they socialized at all. Their possibility of formal work being as distant as the chance of media stardom, the most ambitious vendors endeavored to transform their hobbies into viable professions.

Orators and vendors both explained that they were unmarried by repeating the standard line, "*Je n'ai pas les moyens*" (I lack the means). Distinguishing marriage from cohabitation, orator Koné explained, "It is not prudent to marry. A marriage is a contract. I do not want to be a bad father." Remaining unwed avoided the social repercussions that men otherwise faced once they became legitimate husbands and fathers. Unmarried, financial support was but a benevolent gesture. Married, support was expected, and insufficient or irregular provision signified failure. Yet practically speaking, the precariously employed could not provide steadily with their unsteady earnings. Nevertheless, this situation barred men from the social status accompanying marriage and fatherhood.

TABLE 8.01   Orators and vendors: A comparison

	ORATORS (*N* = 18, + 2 TICKET TAKERS)	VENDORS (*N* = 35)
Imaginaries in racial capitalism	Political imaginaries: entrepreneurial évolués	VIP imaginaries: media tropes
Age sample	25–43 Mean age: 34	19–38 (*N* = 31) Mean age: 26
Age status	*Jeunesse* (youth) to *doyen* (dean)	*Jeunesse* (youth)
Earnings	Sporadic; estimated 5000 FCFA (US \$10)/speaking day or 50,000 FCFA (US \$100)/month	Sporadic; estimated 1500 FCFA (US \$3)/working day
Marital/family status	2 married (1 naturalized ticket taker, 1 foreign orator); 3 engaged; 14 with partners 16 with children	1 married (foreigner); 14 with girlfriends (2 in home country) 9 with children; 1 supporting girlfriend's child from former partner (*N*=28)
Education	4 without university or alternative higher education route; 5 with some university or alternative higher education route; 11 completed university, of whom 7 were receiving or completed advanced degrees	1 with no formal education; 3 with primary school (*école primaire*); 3 with junior high (*collège*); 2 with high school (*lycée*); 2 with *baccalauréat*; 8 with some university or alternative higher education route; 1 with Koranic education (*N* = 20)
Citizenship status	19 citizens (17 orators and 2 ticket takers, 1 of whom was naturalized); 1 foreign (orator)	21 citizens, 14 foreigners, of whom 7 were Abidjan-born and -raised
Relationship to state	State helps	State harms
Self-image	Ivoirian, *patriote*; évolué; entrepreneur; dignified; Sorbonne-based titular identity (professor, governor, doctor, pastor, *conférencier*, president)	Abidjanais if not borderless; media trope: consumerist/ performative identity (football, music: hip-hop, *coupé décalé*, reggae (*rasta*), *zouglou*), stage name (e.g., MC, DJ, Busta Rhymes, Black Poison)

Note: Vendors' reports of age, education, and income were unreliable and should be taken only as general estimates. Over the course of one or several interviews, vendors often provided different answers; in these cases, I reported the highest age or lowest educational level/income, as those responses tended to come after more familiarity and comfort with me. In the case of age, at times men did not know their birth date, or they stated a younger age to compensate, I suspected, for their low educational achievement or employment status. Furthermore, many vendors exhibited clear signs of shame when I asked them these demographic indicators. To respect their dignity I did not insist, nor did I ask them to fill out exit interview survey questionnaires as I did the orators (which, moreover, expected a basic level of literacy that I perceived many to lack). Finally, the vendors in my sample were not representative of the age of Abidjan's vending population. While I commonly saw teenaged or even adolescent vendors, because I was interested in understanding adult masculinity I intentionally approached men who appeared somewhat older.

Suspended in categories that were coded as failure, men remained youths, the unsalaried called themselves students, and fathers denied the responsibility of fatherhood by denying themselves as husbands to the women in their lives. Fleeing such indignities, it was in the realm of the imaginary that orators and vendors asserted their masculinities in the Abidjan of la crise.

Black Vernaculars of Racial Capitalism

Material accumulation at the personal level reinforced faith in le miracle ivoirien and its civilizational narrative. But in the absence of markers like a coveted job in the civil service, disposable income for a new, imported automobile, or the financial ability to support a stay-at-home wife or a pay child's school fees, media imaginaries circulated as cultural artifacts to animate Abidjan's quotidian spaces. These were the counterfeit trademarks of luxury brands, hand-painted portraits of celebrities, and sartorial performances of the commodified Black male body. These artifacts signified a rerouting from the Paris of West Africa to the Black Atlantic.

Chapter 11 highlights the visual terrain of Blackness in Abidjan's quartiers populaires. It was via the branded tokens of a market ethos, on the barbershop signs of Yopougon and Abobo and the gbakas (privately operated minibuses) that traversed these quartiers, and on the bodies of the men working and socializing in them that men appropriated media forms and made visible alternative imaginaries of Black masculinity. Resignifying life on the periphery, these images appropriated global markers of wealth and status to articulate localized renderings of media tropes.

As everyday interpretations by, and improvisations of, the Abidjanais precariat, media tropes conveyed idealized Black masculinities. They offered visual evidence of a vernacular among marginal men that contested narratives of exclusion and claimed masculine agency in Abidjan and the world. Just as Gbagbo's *patriotes* used the Sorbonne, this was a strategy for marginal men to occupy physical and social space. It underscored the politics of representation in racial capitalism, one that drew on Blackness to activate registers of economic participation. In lieu of the productive sphere of wage labor, media tropes inhabited consumer space. As commodities to be seen and consumed, they exemplified commodity subjectivities. And when men participated in the consumer culture-laden realms these tropes had popularized, they were vindicated as consumer subjects.

POLITICAL IMAGINARIES

It is 2008, four years after the French expatriate community had fled Abidjan en masse, fearful of those protestors who took to the streets in anger over the French military's attack on Ivoirian sovereignty and leaving behind a nation with far fewer Europeans than it had seen in its colonial or postcolonial history. Hovering above one of Plateau's major commercial centers is an advertisement for an elite jewelry designer. The viewer faces an elegant, statuesque Black woman in a slinky evening gown. Her long fingers toy with an extraordinary diamond necklace that her beau, rich as he is adoring, places around her neck. He is a handsome white man in a fine tuxedo. The models play as much into the fantasy of the white corporate man seeking more than a business deal on his trip to Africa as of the ambitious young Ivoirian woman who frequents forbiddingly expensive clubs where potential partners with means—often white male clientele—may be found. This imaginary gives no role to the Ivoirian man.

Across the road and down the street, another racialized trope is at play. Situated at the Sorbonne's main entrances, hawkers sell pirated electronic and print media featuring hard-core pornography. On the cover of a VHS cassette a narrowed-in, fishbowl perspective of a large, round, Black derrière in a skimpy thong renders it larger and rounder. Passersby gape at full frontal views of Black penises penetrating platinum-blonde white women. As a "ritual of initiation into 'authentic' manhood" (Fanon 1967, 54), the images avenge the colonial strictures that gave Black men secondary access to Black women's bodies and denied them access altogether to white women's bodies. "Between these white breasts that my wandering hands fondle, white civilization and worthiness become mine" (54).

Like the grating contrast between these shady images and the authoritative billboard whose content replicates a racially hegemonic order, the Sorbonne was in Plateau but not of Plateau. The men who frequented the space insisted on their own centrality despite carrying with them the narratives, tropes, and practices from the periphery as caveats of their tentative belonging.

Spaces that allow men to assert nonproductive yet affirming masculinities have become commonplace in urban Africa, from the concert stage or football field to the street parliament—sites to perform rather than produce.[1] In Abidjan the entangled and disrupted meanings of man, citizen, and modernity came together at the Sorbonne, the street parliament in central Abidjan.[2] Sorbonne activities began with the transition to multiparty politics in the late 1980s but had become decidedly pro-Gbagbo by 2004. Upon the resolution of postelectoral conflict in 2011, the Ouattara regime razed the Sorbonne structure.

This chapter examines the Sorbonne and its orators who contested the crisis narrative and their place in it. Predominantly underemployed spectators and orators filled their otherwise idle time with Sorbonne activity. It was a protected space for Gbagboist autochthons to enact, by embracing the correct rhetoric and appurtenances, a hyperbole of modern manhood. They instrumentalized the legacy of Ivoirian exceptionalism and projected a future of "financed projects" for its patriotes to challenge narratives of exclusion. In their speeches, comportment, and interpersonal relationships, insiders affirmed their value as men in the city and as Ivoirians in the world. Their nationalist and misogynist worldviews remained attached to the évolué identity, even as they sought a new, "Anglophone" means of achieving it.

These were not generalized strategies available to any underemployed man. Rather, underscoring the fundamentally colonial, exclusionary logic of racial capitalism as it was embedded in localized hierarchies of domination, these were political imaginaries accessible only to a subset of the Ivoirian population: President Gbagbo's patriotes. Constituting the intellectual epicenter of his party's Front Populaire Ivoirien (FPI) informal activity, patriotes projected these political imaginaries in the space of the Sorbonne. It was here, and throughout the sociopolitical network it commanded, that patriotic ideology disseminated across Abidjan via speeches, pamphlets, and recordings. Literally and ideologically, Sorbonne orators and spectators moved themselves and their country from the periphery to the urban and global core.

Imagining the Core in the Periphery

The productive society has well imbued Abidjan with its notions of efficiency; in Plateau, it is business that prevails and people come from every part of the city to participate in the grand waltz of the economic boom.

—Fraternité Matin, *Abidjan Métropole Moderne*

Well into la crise, le miracle ivoirien remained tangibly validated in the urban core. Plateau's bygone splendor could be rediscovered in its tree-lined boulevards, haute-couture boutiques, five-star hotels, and headquarters of government bureaus, banks, and international development organizations, all residuals of the political economy of Françafrique and évolué identity. There, informal practices appeared out of place. The citadins who came to Plateau on administrative business were impressed with a vision of modernity that in other African cities had largely been relegated to the past (see e.g., Ferguson 1999). In these ways, Plateau remained the city of the colon, its built environment and spaces of sociality striking juxtapositions to the "others" of le miracle ivoirien—low-level workers, street hustlers, or not-quite-citizens poised to be humbled by a bureaucracy that was never intended to serve their needs.

Already conceived as an extension of the metropole under colonial rule, French planners, architects, and engineers committed Plateau to reflecting newly inaugurated President Houphouët-Boigny's "will to make Côte d'Ivoire a model country and Abidjan its showcase" (Steck 2005, 215). This Franco-Ivoirian alliance was formalized in 1968 under AURA (Atelier d'urbanisme de la région d'Abidjan), whose collective of "French expatriate experts and technicians was tasked primarily with transmitting urban knowledge and standards from the West" (Chenal et al. 2009, 120). Abidjan's preservation of "French urban influence" was to help Houphouët-Boigny demonstrate the "singularity and success" of Côte d'Ivoire across West Africa (Steck 2005, 216). Fastidious state-planned and foreign-advised adherence to a Europeanized national image thus underwrote Plateau's civic and infrastructural vision and later upkeep. In doing so, the official urban plan preserved colonial biases of what was to be within its purview and what was to be ignored, in turn deepening the social divide between those whose livelihoods and residences would be considered, and those which would be excluded (Dembele 1997). The vision for postcolonial Plateau, in short, offered a "striking continuity" with the colonial "techniques and discourses" that segregated the elite from the rest (Steck 2005, 219). It was a "fantasy of Western modernism" that contested the "slums [otherwise] found in cities in the developing world, [and] an 'informal' presence in its streets" that might be charged as the city's "main vector of dysfunction" (219, 223). Only in Plateau, therefore, were lanes designated for municipal buses, while gbakas that transported the lumpenproletariat about the rest of the city were barred (Steck 2005). Its modernist architecture intended to "become not only the expression but also the vehicle, an indisputable means of evolution rather than an artificial projection of a culture in a foreign world" (Fraternité Matin 1978, 66). Plateau's "promotion [was conditioned on] negating everything that might invoke the classic image of a developing—particularly an African—city. The 'pearl of the lagoons' [was to] symbolize to the world, and foremost to its neighbors, Ivoirian exceptionalism" (Steck 2005, 223). While Abidjan was the Paris of West Africa, Plateau, with its tight concentration of tall buildings designed to project the city of the future, had another nickname: "le Petit Manhattan" (Fraternité Matin 1978; Steck 2005).

The Sorbonne

Even as its denizens rejected Françafrique, the Sorbonne had proudly appropriated the appellation of an institution renowned as the apex of French knowledge production. Like its metropolitan namesake, Abidjan's Sorbonne was a site of ideological manufacture and dissemination. For those politically astute men who used its partisan terrain to ascend the social ladder of city, nation, and world, the physical act of coming to Plateau symbolized grander things. Literally and ideologically, they centered themselves.

The insiders involved in making the Sorbonne function were part of a larger network of patriotes who regulated access to the Ivoirian state and constructed the appropriate autochthonous subject. This network provided a means for "social juniors to take power by imposing themselves in the public sphere as a political category in their own right" (Banégas 2006, 545). Orators in turn acted as the Gbagbo regime's loyal propaganda mouthpieces. The Sorbonne embodied both la crise and its exclusionary response, at the heart of which was a contest of imbricated belonging from the quartier to their worldly imagining.

Initially located in a public park in Plateau, the Sorbonne emerged as a free-speech forum amid the decline of one-party rule in the 1980s (Bahi 2003). Men gathered to speak about anything on their minds: society, the economy, religion, politics. As its structure formalized, the Sorbonne began conferring degrees to sanctioned orators whom it denoted "professors." By the turn of the century, the Sorbonne had settled into its permanent space, a city block reclaimed as a market serving a primarily male clientele, at the heart of which stood an abandoned high-rise. Informal vendors bartered in the style of the quartiers populaires, contrasting with Plateau's otherwise regulated and neatly enclosed shops.

FIGURE 9.01.   The Sorbonne, Abidjan (2007). Reprinted from Wikipedia, *Agoraci, Reroupement de jeunes dans un espace de discussion de rue "Parlement" au Plateau*, User Zenman.

All of the merchants, mobile and fixed, paid rents to the Sorbonne Solidarité in what was the organization's primary income stream. Repurposed, the base levels of the abandoned edifice housed the most established businesses, from tailors to copy-and-print services; the Sorbonne leadership's offices were on its upper levels. A brothel was also rumored to operate. Two speaking areas were situated on either side, separated by a gritty market atmosphere. On any given day the Sorbonne attracted dozens to hundreds of clients and spectators, drawing peripheral Abidjanais who had come to Plateau for administrative business, working bureaucrats on their lunch break, students, and a hodgepodge population of the precariously underemployed.

Poverty, Politics, Penises—and the Pursuit of the Patriotic Enterprise

The Sorbonne was at once a discursive construction and a durable strategic enterprise for political and economic advancement. Their themes ranging from the interpersonal to the international, oratorical performances embodied the multiple levels by which the Sorbonne reimagined a local and global political economy that moved man and nation from periphery to center. In prior chapters I demonstrated the profound entanglement between the construction of Ivoirian masculinity and le miracle ivoirien, ideas of evolutionary—évolué—attainment perhaps unsurpassed elsewhere on the continent. Sorbonne sociality and social critique, political positioning and posturing through the registers of nation, leader, and everyday man, and articulations of manhood and sexuality were principal discursive constructions that responded to personal experiences of exclusion and the witnessing of national decline in the context of la crise. In doing so, they nurtured a space for President Gbagbo's patriotes to enact évolué masculinities. And it was through the business of politics: the remunerative strategies and entrepreneurial forays realized through patronage relationships, that oratorical performances translated into tangible strategies for survival and status.

The Sorbonne was a space of sociability and social critique. Even while purporting to be centered as citoyens and citadins, the orators related to their audience with the shared struggles of living on Abidjan's periphery. In these "universities of free time" (Banégas 2010, 38), the orators lamented the chronic unemployment, humorously related stories about life in the quartiers populaires, and hostilely beseeched spectators to contribute to their transportation home. They hustled booklets on business entrepreneurship, collected contributions for sick members in what they referred to as the Sorbonne "community," and proposed strategies for collective investment. To the best of each one's ability, orators and spectators presented themselves as men who belonged in Plateau. Yet despite proclamations of solidarity, hierarchies separated those who authentically belonged—upper-level membership, bureaucrats, and otherwise gainfully employed men, the doyens—from the rest. Rather than create a utopian egalitarianism among patriotes upon whom fortune had frowned, the Sorbonne network produced an informal hierarchy adhering to the status quo. For those of contested belonging, it was a forum for "competition from below for social recognition" (Cutolo and Banégas 2012, 40). Emulating established social structures, Sorbonne rituals gave much credence to respectability and procedure; oratorical legitimacy inferred social and cultural capital and affirmed the revered position of the intellectual (Banégas, Brisset-Foucault, and Cutolo 2012). Moreover, these hierarchies doubled as interpersonal dependency relationships that constituted the normative patronage system of "grands" and "petits" (big and small) (Cutolo and Banégas 2012, 45). It was a means for orators to recover the esteem and mobility to which their qualifications would have entitled them had the crisis not cast them as surplus.

While the orators described the Sorbonne as a space of "free expression," they also spoke openly of its mission to support the state in the context of the northern "rebellion." As a political strategy, the Sorbonne constructed partisan narratives of belonging that determined Gbagboist, Christian, and southern Ivoirians to be the authentic citizenry. It constructed a "we" of "patriotes," "resistors," "brothers," and "friends" powerful by association and united in a struggle to claim the country from "them": inauthentic Ivoirians and a resource-greedy international community with France at its helm. To its public the Sorbonne positioned Côte d'Ivoire and Gbagbo as key players in global affairs. From an insider perspective they portrayed the Sorbonne Solidarité and their spectators as privileged members behind the scenes of breaking news. Purporting to "unveil the truth," the orators affirmed themselves as moral and political subjects, "secular prophets of the Ivoirian nation" (Cutolo and Banégas 2012, 25, 45). They gave men, many of whom had little else to do in their day, a sense of relevance and inclusion in a wider nexus of current events. In this way, the Sorbonne and its affiliates could be seen as "examples of youthful political bluff involving a dozen or so junior political leaders" (Arnaut 2012, 23). Be it performance or reality, through their "privileged insertion in the . . . patriotic galaxy, they act[ed] as authorized interpreters of power and its double" (Cutolo and Banégas 2012, 37).

The Sorbonne was furthermore a men's space. Orators, regulars, shoppers, and gawkers were overwhelmingly male. It was a space where men, in tailored *pagne* shirts, slacks, and briefcases, set about to approximate the businessman in dress and behavior and to inculcate this ideal among junior men.[3] The space valorized national and personal ascension through masculinist articulations of "private enterprise and individual initiative, viewed as a means of emancipation and self-realization" (Banégas 2007, 28). It promoted gendered imaginaries of citizenship associated with risk-taking, intellectual excellence, and respectable self-presentation (Banégas, Brisset-Foucault, and Cutolo 2012, 16–19). In speeches and advertisements the orators and market vendors appealed to the male subject. Nationalist discourse explicitly linked penises and politics, affirming the masculine character of the African state (Mouiche 2008), while also mimicking the "fixation of elite Africans on the 'consumption of women' as a privileged attribute of phallic domination" (Biaya 2001, 77). Such hegemonic-misogynist discourse contested the fact that in reality, the crisis had left these men increasingly incapable of controlling many parts of their lives, including women. In short, where elsewhere in Plateau they might have been dismissed, in the Sorbonne marginal men projected status as public figures, dominant, informed, and formalized.

Nevertheless a great number of women were also present, tending food and drink stalls, squatting over basins of hot oil as they fried fish and plantains, and peddling snacks on platters balanced delicately on their crowns. In the early morning, when the cockroaches retreated to their diurnal crevices and Sorbonne underlings arranged benches around the speaking areas, the Sorbonne belonged to women in pagne wraps. They tied undernourished infants to their backs, and their unschooled children adroitly navigated this second home. During these off hours, the presence and energies of these women were most palpable, yet as the day's activities picked up they slid into the background. Contrasted to Plateau's elite, stiletto-strutting *dames*, their scenes of reproductive labor exposed the Sorbonne's peripheral status, the feminine face of poverty in Abidjan's core.

Finally, seeking to retain pride in the country's regional sphere of influence while rejecting the neocolonial Françafrique upon which it was built, the orators looked to an "Anglophone" model. Disparaging Franco-Ivoirian relations under President Houphouët-Boigny, they were particularly critical of the first postcolonial Ivoirian generation's inheritance of the school-to-public-sector pipeline and bloated civil service, charging that it had proved a failed developmental path with desultory consequences on the characters of man and nation. In its stead they suggested that the state should invest in entrepreneurs. The orators proposed themselves as the primary beneficiaries of such investment, arguing that in return for their commitment to the patriotic cause, the post-conflict Ivoirian state should privilege their business ventures. As a "political economy of common patriotism," mobilization was therefore rendered inextricable from its business component (Cutolo and Banégas 2012, 29). With few other opportunities for upward mobility, "the ultranationalist vein became . . . a powerful vector of economic accumulation and social ascension" (Banégas 2007, 40).

In short, the Sorbonne provided a forum in the urban core for men to perform dominant masculinities despite the marginal social locations of the actors themselves. It was a space to articulate an exclusionary Ivoirian citizenship, even while its members acknowledged their personal struggles and recognized internal hierarchies. Beyond defining what it meant to be Ivoirian in a post–Houphouët-Boigny geopolitical terrain, the orators redefined the path for success, turning away from the civil service ideal and toward the entrepreneurial businessman. They situated themselves in this model as patriotic and privileged entrepreneurs. In doing so, the orators reclaimed their status as the appropriate protagonists in a modern, capitalistic, global, and Anglophone Abidjan.

Poverty: Sorbonne Sociality and Social Critique

Reality and imaginary alternately found expression in Sorbonne rituals. Authentic- and inauthentic-looking businessmen came for hours at a time to listen and socialize. It was a place to be—or at least to look—busy. In their speeches the orators presented the Sorbonne as a well-recognized information platform where national and international media outlets uncovered facts and sought local insights. And though it was unlikely to have been the place where top-level decisions were made, the Sorbonne was a definite feature of the ground-level Ivoirian political scene and the patriotic elite assembled among a generalized consortium of Gbagboists. Irrespective of shared belonging within, however, its hierarchy mirrored distinctions outside.

Lowest on the Sorbonne pecking order were the women vending refreshments and the preteen shoe shiners. Above them were pamphleteers, typically teenagers, who sometimes presented themselves in professional attire but were more often in threadbare shirts and plastic sandals. Ticket takers followed: twenty- and thirty-something men who likewise varied in their sartorial efforts. Finally, the master of ceremonies and the orators treated their activities with the dignified style and comportment of an office job. The orators, though self-described as unemployed and among those everyday Ivoirians with limited opportunities, had nonetheless achieved local renown and boasted of having the numbers of government bureaucrats or company directors saved on their phones. They harbored hopes that their oratorical activities and regime loyalty would launch their careers in the public or, preferably, the private sector. Finally, Sorbonne leadership was composed of men of realizable political ambition who had lunched with ministers. When they appeared among the orators, their high status was obvious, the latter extending verbose salutations, readily offering up their chairs, and exhibiting other signs of deference. Usually, however, these men were seldom seen in the Sorbonne's public spaces.

Like the Sorbonne leadership, political elites made rare appearances in the principal speaking area. They could instead be found holding discrete conversations in the orators' preferred maquis abutting the market or en route to offices in the repurposed edifice. Easily recognizable, others accorded them respect befitting an African "big man."[4] These elites consisted of mid- and upper-level members of Gbagbo's formal and informal patriotic network: political appointees, business leaders, and a generalized consortium of Jeunes Patriotes. The Sorbonne being a liminal space, they held a coveted place apart, representing the potentiality of political affiliation. The most successful orators hoped to cross over, either by ascending the patriotic network or by finding formal employment through its contacts. In the meantime, exposure to these big men allowed the orators to travel between the fictive realm of Sorbonne propaganda and the terrain of formal recognition.

The Sorbonne set its distinctions aside to circumscribe a clear, oppositional "us." The greater Sorbonne community was united not by its commonalities but by the ever-present specter of nefarious outsiders. It posed some of these outsiders as a national threat and others as a national affront, contending that they treated the country and its leader like geopolitical juniors. For example, President Gbagbo had postponed elections since 2006, citing security concerns and general unpreparedness. During this time the United Nations (UN) had remained in the country to monitor the conflict and help facilitate the electoral process, attracting the ire of Gbagbo's patriots. Describing France and the UN as "collaborators," speeches raised alarm at their concerted interference in domestic affairs and argued that the UN was on Ivoirian soil to manipulate, not mitigate, political outcomes. Appropriating the term "évolué," orators asserted that Ivoirians were evolved (*"Nous sommes évolués!"*) and could determine their own fate; they were in no need of international monitors. On an individual level one orator, Zokora, described how President Gbagbo had for years put up with French President Jacques Chirac calling him "Laurent" in lieu of the formal titular respect exchanged between heads of state. Rejecting such infantilizations, the Sorbonne affirmed men's évolué status: informed, relevant, and commanding respect.

Regulars in the audience played the part. Seated with legs crossed, they immersed themselves in the morning paper. Men arrived with briefcases in hand and commissioned adolescents to shine their shoes. The act itself superseded its function so that men with leather, canvas, or rubber shoes commanded the service in equal measure. On one occasion I listened to a man insist that his soles be shined perfectly white. Female vendors paced the speaking area, selling drinks and snacks. One espresso vendor circled the speaking area with a large thermos and dainty blue cups and saucers, stirring her customers' sugar on demand. A vendor of boiled eggs deferentially squatted before her clients to peel their shells while they looked past her, absorbed in conversation or their newspapers.

These exchanges added an air of importance but remained affordable: peanuts and water cost 20 FCFA (US $0.04) each, a shoeshine 100 FCFA (US $0.20). Seating costs were similarly within reach. At the request of doyens or *parents* (parents, used to confer seniority), ticket takers carried out white plastic chairs to the front rows for which they charged 100 FCFA. Less expensive bench seats, where the general public typically sat, cost half that amount, and it was not uncommon for arguments to ensue as loiterers were grudgingly ordered from their places of momentary rest. In the back, free of charge, stood la jeunesse.

The Sorbonne provided a script and an audience before which the orators could contest their emasculations. There, reclaiming worth of man and country, the orators imprinted a masculinized social and political world. Women, enacting subordinate gender roles, were quite literally in their proper place. While shoe shiners or pamphleteers rested periodically in empty seats, rarely did a female vendor take this liberty; in one instance a woman who crossed the open speaking area during a speech was subjected to an onslaught of verbal abuse I had not seen directed at male offenders. In the ritualized misogyny of the Sorbonne, patrons were inculcated with entitled masculinity.

Encouraging a business mentality, the orators peppered their speeches with entrepreneurial rhetoric. Proclaiming that economic independence begins with the individual, they segued into advertisements for how-to, start-up pamphlets sold by the Sorbonne. One such pamphlet began by stating that all Americans want to work in the private sector, echoing a general sentiment whereby the orators contrasted the striving "Anglophone" business mentality with a Francophone lethargy of state dependency. African poverty, the orator Boubacar explained, was due to a poverty of thought and an aversion to financial risk.

Other pamphlets provided contact details for various embassies—Japan, Germany, India, Israel—on the pretext that they would support sound business initiatives and provide information for obtaining visas. Special Sorbonne guests proposed investment opportunities, and the master of ceremonies occasionally advertised properties around Abidjan. During one promotional question-and-answer session for a credit cooperative, an invited speaker, flanked by two intimidating bodyguards and accompanied by a sizable entourage, described a venture he had modeled after the successful collaborations of the Lebanese expatriate community. Captivated audience members paid into his scheme.[5]

Yet bourgeois masquerades and business schemes collided with the recitations of many an orator about the hard-knock life. In his opening salutations Gneki greeted first the higher-ups, next the unemployed. He contrasted the argot of Plateau and Cocody with Yopougon and Abobo: whereas the civilized residents of the former were "nourished" (*nourrir*), the poorer and more primitive residents of the latter simply "eat" (*manger*). He described la crise as an experience of wasting away, a man of twenty at the time of the coup d'état, now but three years from thirty; a man of forty, now almost fifty. In the meantime, these men had been condemned to unproductivity. As he spoke, spectators nodded in solemn agreement. Collapsing narratives of sustained economic crisis with civil conflict, Gneki blamed both on the northern rebels, with the resolution being elections— elections that anticipated Gbagbo's inevitable victory and the enactment of a new economic vision.

In one speech, Zokora concluded that life without money was worthless and only imbeciles were happy and poor. Even in death, he contended, money matters; hence a rich man has a body (*corps*) while a poor man has a cadaver (*cadavre*). When a poor man tries to speak to a woman, Zokora elaborated, he follows her shyly, calling out faintly for her attention. Upon her turning around, fear renders him speechless and resigned; he says only that he had mistaken her for his cousin. A rich man, on the other hand, simply asks a woman to join him for a meal; the thought of food is enough to spark her interest. And a dog in Yopougon or Abobo competes with his hungry owner for dinner, whereas one in Cocody, so confident of a steady meal, sits patiently with food under his nose. In this speech Zokora equated poverty with stupidity, amorous failure and irrelevance, and animality. Mapping out the city's socioeconomic terrain, he established that dogs in the center lived better than men in the quartiers populaires. Amid deep poverty a rich man could appeal to women not by offering to adorn her with luxuries, but simply by feeding her—a feat that a poor man was incapable of doing even for himself.

At the end of the speeches, the spectators demonstrated appreciation as well as relative means by throwing coins to the center. Those with paper notes strode confidently to the front and handed the orator the money directly. Larger donations were graciously acknowledged with a handshake, reference to the giver as a gentleman or a doyen, and the applause of impressed fellow audience members. Men who appeared to have been in Plateau on genuine business were targeted specifically with refrains such as, "I see you are coming from work. God bless you, you must have something to give." But it was mostly 50 FCFA and 100 FCFA coins that trickled in, and contributions petered out altogether as the end of the month approached and the incomes of the employed minority had been exhausted. Then the master of ceremonies might engage in a standoff with the crowd for ten minutes or more, pausing the program until upward of one hundred spectators had collectively relinquished 1000 FCFA for the orator's "taxi ride" home. Frustrated by the poor contribution record, the orators often asked how spectators could afford the 200 FCFA gbaka ride into Plateau but have nothing for them. Some grew irate, emphasizing that "informing" the public was a job for which they also deserved a salary or sarcastically thanking the crowd for the meager donations that were no more than the earnings of a Burkinabé. They framed audience contributions as part of the war effort, so that the more a man gave, the more patriotic he had proved himself.

Politics: Global Nation, Global Leader, and Global Everyday Man

As a site of knowledge production, the Sorbonne generated a world view in its speeches, pamphlets, and electronic media. Be it Israel's bombing of the Gaza strip in 2008, when Ivoirians were reminded of close Israeli-Ivoirian ties since independence, or Pope Benedict's 2009 Africa tour, when his decision not to pass through Côte d'Ivoire was a slight rendered conspiratorial, oratorical accounts implicated the Ivoirian state in every foreign event. Amid the global financial crisis of 2008, pamphlets explained how the Ivoirian civil war had destabilized the former metropole, with the headline of one March 2009 pamphlet declaring, "The Impact of the Ivoirian Crisis in the French Economy: More than 20,000 Workers Fired in the French Administration." The American International Group (AIG) disaster on Wall Street similarly implicated Côte d'Ivoire. A repeated theme was that the virtual economies of the global North had proven unfavorable compared to the raw-material wealth of the Ivoirian economy, such that the former now looked to Côte d'Ivoire to replenish their treasuries. Moreover, the global financial crisis rubbed against the Françafrique arrangement that had pegged the

FCFA to the French franc and later the euro, and the orators charged that this lack of monetary control was dragging Côte d'Ivoire into an economic catastrophe not of its making.

In private interviews the orators echoed their public proclamations, making much of their country's longstanding peace and prosperity as a consequence of its resource wealth and status as a regional hegemon. Yapo opined, "We think someone who lives in Europe and comes to Côte d'Ivoire will not be too disappointed." Yeboah explained that Côte d'Ivoire was "the first place to develop" because of its resources and its port that linked Europe to the African interior. With respect to neighboring states, Côte d'Ivoire, he said, was "like rain in the desert." Tioté called Côte d'Ivoire the "locomotive of West Africa," noting that the country was responsible for over 40 percent of total UEMOA (Union Économique et Monétaire Ouest-Africaine) activity. He explained, "We are currently the majority of the BCEAO [Banque Centrale des États de l'Afrique de l'Ouest] and control the regional economy. This is why the first leaders of the BCEAO were all Ivoirians. We hold the economy of the zone." Neighboring countries, he continued, "have to wait for what we say. This is why we are the older brother."

Positing their country as a gateway to Europe and an intra-African magnet for trade, commerce, and opportunity, the orators maintained the narrative of Ivoirian exceptionalism. Keïta, for example, situated Côte d'Ivoire one step up the developmental ladder, alongside Argentina as an "intermediary" country. Ousmane remarked that the Ivoirian man was associated with his dominant economy. And Sangaré asserted,

> When you consider the region, with all modesty, [Côte d'Ivoire] has a status above all the other countries. So Côte d'Ivoire has a real problem: young Ivoirians, we in Côte d'Ivoire, we do not aspire for a life like in Mali or Benin. . . . But people in Mali or Burkina Faso . . . for them it is a little Paris. For the little Burkinabé: Abidjan. Malians: Abidjan. Because for them, Abidjan has everything.

Lola predicted that Côte d'Ivoire would be "the lungs of hope for Africa's economic plan." But under Gbagbo this would be accomplished free of the fetters of its neocolonial past. He exclaimed,

> This is a very first! To see an African chief of state attacked by a great power and still succeed in paying its bureaucrats. And paying its debts. It has never been seen in Africa. In all of African history you have never seen an African chief of state do what Laurent Gbagbo has done. For us, if he is given the time to direct the economy in Côte d'Ivoire, we will see a real boom.

Like many of Africa's first leaders following independence, Koudou Laurent Gbagbo was an intellectual prior to becoming a politician. A Bété from Gagnoa, a region rich in cocoa, coffee, and timber, Gbagbo received his master's in history at the Sorbonne in Paris in 1970 and his doctorate at the Université Paris Diderot in 1979, becoming a professor at the University of Abidjan and the author of numerous books on ancient Africa as well as on colonialism and Ivoirian democracy. An early open opponent of President Houphouët-Boigny, Gbagbo earned his political credentials as a prisoner, exile, and trade unionist and formed the democratic-socialist FPI during a teachers'-union strike in 1982. Elected FPI secretary general in 1988, he was at its helm when the party, campaigning against the ruling Parti Démocratique de Côte d'Ivoire and twenty-five other opposition parties, gained nine of 185 seats in the National Assembly in the country's first multiparty elections in 1990. In that year Gbagbo also ran for president, officially winning 18.3 percent of the vote, and unofficially—according to Western election observers—as much as 40 percent (Daddieh 2016, Widner 1991).

To the Sorbonne Solidarité intellectuals, many of whom shared Gbagbo's Bété heritage, le miracle ivoirien was experienced personally as a national myth, an unsustainable regional-ethnic extraction that doubled as generational exclusion. They found in Gbagbo an authentic African leader in their likeness and a "David against Goliath" (Piccolino 2011) of the world order who was determined, with an evangelical fervor, to realize the nation's unmet destiny.

The Sorbonne regularly situated President Gbagbo in a global context, where he was highly esteemed.[6] Following the 2008 US presidential election, the orators alleged that Gbagbo and President-Elect Barack Obama were dear friends. They further reported that he was the sole world leader on close terms with both Obama and Venezuelan President Hugo Chavez, the latter's oppositional stance to the West making him an important figure within their sphere of influence. Gbagbo's acclaim was so widespread, they argued, that France was his only genuine foe. To prove his stature, speeches and pamphlets touted Gbagbo's role as "Vice President of the International Follow-up Conference on the Financing of Development" at the 2008 Doha Summit. Titled "Very Important Address of Gbagbo to His Equals," a pamphlet from December 2008 announced, alongside the full reproduction of his speech:

> The President Laurent Gbagbo is currently in Doha, capital of Qatar, to participate in an important meeting on the financing of development. On this occasion, he has delivered an important speech to his equals.
>
> . . .
>
> Satisfied with this distinction which crowns his unbreakable efforts towards the development of states, especially those of the Third World,

he has, in his address to the entire world, at the opening ceremony of this said conference, first recalled some [prior] successes . . . [the pamphlet goes on to chronicle prior international appearances].

Without fail, the Sorbonne boasted a national leader poised at the fore of a global anti-imperial movement, resisting French dominance and demonstrating a leadership model to Africa's weaker regimes. Nelson Mandela, the orators claimed, had in fact singled him out as Africa's next figurehead. Such global admiration for Gbagbo was made true by virtue of the spectators' inability to verify the claims: how their president was received outside the region was not something the average man would know.

Elaborating on his grandeur, in interviews the orators depicted Gbagbo as a renegade on a par with the twentieth century's most notable Black and brown revolutionary leaders.[7] Touré said, "I have appreciated Laurent Gbagbo since my childhood. I appreciated him for his struggle. . . . For me, Gbagbo reflects the image of Martin Luther King, of Marcus Garvey, of Malcolm X. For me, Gbagbo is like a Fidel Castro, a Nelson Mandela."[8] Lola argued that President Gbagbo would no longer concede to France's being their country's "only master." He declared, "Today we play a real leadership role for an Africa reborn, for a new Africa." Boka described Côte d'Ivoire under Gbagbo as the "pride of Africa," tutor and inspiration to other African states: "When you say you are Ivoirian [in Cameroon], people are content because they say, 'Oh, you are an exception. You have confronted the French. You have uprooted the colon. So we want to be like you.'" Boka elaborated that Gabonais students in Côte d'Ivoire return to their country with the Ivoirian fighting spirit, saying to themselves, "The Black can change. The African can change his manner of working. He does not have to keep saying 'Yes, yes' to the colon. He does not have to keep saying 'Yes' to the imperialists." Orators, in short, portrayed Gbagbo's Ivoirians as a people who had become their own masters, instilled with a sense of self-sufficiency, equality, and pride.

As self-described "political analysts," the orators purported to educate the public, combining unsourced facts and behind-the-scenes details of counterstate activities with common truths about Françafrique exploitation. Their insider perspectives recalled events that had shaken the nation, and they described new developments unfolding almost daily. They attributed their information to top men in a shadowy sphere of illicit political influence. And they sensationalized their accounts with religious or spiritual elements, referring to Côte d'Ivoire as the Chosen Nation, a new Israel on the verge of realizing its destiny.[9] In these versions the orators and the audience members with whom they divulged their information became insiders privy to all things classified.

The Sorbonne gave one particularly gripping report of an attempted break-out from Abidjan's main prison, MACA (La Maison d'arrêt et de correction d'Abidjan). The story had been receiving major media coverage, and the orators suggested that the two hundred attempted escapees were covert members of the northern rebellion. In one speech Tioté linked the breakout attempt to a recent UN visit conducted on the pretext of inspecting prison conditions. Indicating where the rebels were hiding, he described their escape route as one might instruct a friend taking a taxi home, citing neighborhood landmarks like pharmacies and gas stations. He warned that this had been too close a call, a serious effort to take Abidjan overnight, and he closed with the ominous warning that the rebels were right there, masquerading as fellow patriotes. The suggestion of UN involvement, the familiar directions, and the entreaty for audience vigilance—these insinuations transformed the Sorbonne and its membership into important players in a conflict that surpassed national borders.

The orators equated the Ivoirian conflict with Angola's twenty-seven-year-long civil war and the ongoing crisis in eastern Congo. They returned frequently to atrocities that had upended Ivoirian stability and underscored the patriotic network's centrality during moments that had come to exemplify Ivoirian resistance to Françafrique. Exemplary were the 2004 anti-French demonstrations, largely initiated by Blé Goudé and the Jeunes Patriotes. Boka recounted a formative moment in 2004 when the French fired on Ivoirian protestors in front of President Gbagbo's house:

> France fired on the population. They made the face of a young Ivoirian explode. He was named XX, his father was XX, Korhogolais, his mother was Baoulé, she was named XX.[10] And this young man who was born of his mother, he is dead, because he defended the Republic. He came as a patriote. The French army shot this man, and exposed his head, the tape is available at the Sorbonne and all over. . . . This shows that this was not an intra-Ivoirian story but a story of colonizer and colonized.

Recalling being "part of the scene," bringing reinforcements of food and water while the French were shooting, Boka concluded, "This event really forged the Ivoirian people. It was evidence that what Gbagbo says is true." In describing the French attack, Boka lamented the loss of a "comrade," a fellow young patriote of full Ivoirian parentage.

Personal involvement in the conflict aggrandized the orators' biographies and buttressed their positions within the patriotic hierarchy. Cissé, the Sorbonne Solidarité president, recounted his political awakening as a loyal FESCI member:

> In 1992 Houphouët-Boigny sent the Ivoirian police and army to the campus, where there was a massacre of Ivoirian students. And the

inquiry showed that it was the Ivoirian army who had committed these actions . . . So all who were students, all who were revolutionaries took to the streets. And when I took to the street, I was living with my big sister and her husband. My sister's husband gave me an ultimatum: to choose between FESCI and staying in his home. And I chose FESCI.

Cissé went on to describe how during his early days as a "FESCI militant" he had slept in campus hallways and made other sacrifices, such as giving up a lucrative tutoring job that had brought in 90,000 FCFA per month after his student had critiqued the organization. Seventeen years later, this narrative justified his status as doyen. And he was convinced that this had been his first step to leading a movement of global significance.

Penises: Of Manliness and Misogyny

At the Sorbonne we talk politics, but politics is about penises. The penis is power. When your wife denies you, it means you have not been elected.

—Cafard, Sorbonne orator and medicines salesman

Interviews with orators disclosed details of their private lives that revealed how inadequately they approximated évolué masculinity. This was particularly the case with their stalled or abandoned romantic partnerships, whereby despite their Sorbonne fame, they had been unable to assume breadwinning roles. For Lola, it meant that his former partner had married a man who was now raising his four year-old child. He contended that marrying her would have created too many problems. Of the outcome, Lola explained,

> Do not create a problem where there is not one. . . . Right now I struggle to meet my needs, to have something to eat. Because in Africa, when you take a wife, it is the wife's family that you must care for, there are all kinds of problems in the family, the wife has needs to which you are obliged to respond financially. I have decided to abstain from all that and then well, wait until I have a social situation [that will allow me to marry].

Lola posed the difficulties of meeting his own immediate needs against the financial expectations of marriage. While remaining single prevented him from achieving the évolué ideal, it also meant that he avoided charges of failure by would-be in-laws and others in his social orbit. In deciding to "abstain," abstinence became not a sexual, but a social imperative.

The orators described the évolué ideal as one achieved by men in other times and places. For Boka this was a comparison of African fatherhood against its European equivalence—

> In Africa, parents do not have the means to open a bank account for their children. But in Europe, when the father provides, he is well paid and can open an account for his children until they are eighteen and then they can take this money and choose to go to school or start a business.

Many orators, moreover, made highly personal comparisons with their own fathers. They had generally grown up in large families; only two had fewer than two siblings, and it was common to have a dozen or more. All but one orator's father had multiple wives. But none had more than two children of their own and only two—both self-described foreigners—had married. Though monogamy and fewer children was also a sign of changing times, the contrast between the orators—themselves incapable of supporting a single wife and child—and their polygamous fathers, was nevertheless remarkable. Keïta, for example, recalled his upbringing in the following manner:

> My father was a planter, mostly of cocoa, with four wives. I am the third child of a family of thirty-five children. [Laughs] I am a student. I received my master's in law last year. Today I am thirty-three years old and counting, very much alive. I am not married; I have two children from the different adventures I have known. Currently I live with a girl but we are not married, we are *concubins*.

Keïta's account directly juxtaposed his father's life to his own. He was unmarried and lived apart from children born out of what he youthfully described as "adventures," while his father had raised and supported thirty-five children through high school. For Koné, proof of his family's middle-class status was that his father had paid for his children's educations. He stated proudly, "The smallest diploma in my family is the *bac* . . . I would not say we were poor. Okay, well now that I do not work, I will say that I am poor." In his personal biography, Koné measured his life as an adult against that of his more privileged upbringing, enabled by his breadwinning father. Yet as with other Sorbonne performances, there was collective pride in enacting the fatherhood ideal. News of a newborn child received hearty congratulations between speeches, and a young boy who occasionally accompanied his father to the Sorbonne was always met with coos and coddles.

Unequal global relations manifested in deficient personal relationships. Boka explained that this was why men remained single, preferring to have girlfriends for ten or twenty years without marrying. The coupling of public and private deficiencies, joblessness and bachelorhood, suspended African men in the temporal dimension of crisis: the immediate present. It bode poorly with the long-term purview of évolué family composition, a core component of the mission civilisatrice. And it blocked them from adult masculinity, the expression of full manhood.

Sorbonne personas provided temporary respite from personal inadequacies, and through them men sought to actualize the businessman's masculinity. The orators' titular status identities implied learnedness or imitated the formal hierarchies of the formal political and business world. They inculcated these values among their younger peers and social juniors, and to the audience's applause, the orators disparaged the youth who wore low-riding pants with their backsides exposed and spent their money on *drogbas*.[11] Higher-ups gave fatherly tips to younger protégés on wearing a suit with dignity and style, demonstrating, for example, how to prevent one's mobile phone from ruining the line of the jacket. Speeches and advertisements professed that a man's role as a patriote required investment in the national economy, both within the Sorbonne Solidarité and in private business ventures.

Yet more often than not, inauthentic businessmen arrived in tethered and ill-fitting suits. At the local maquis, the Sorbonne's house "mystic" could be seen dressed in a red-plaid shirt overlaid with Looney Toons cartoon characters. Another regular wore a cowboy hat and an oversized suit with pants that sat high on his waist, leaving the behind to sag awkwardly. He completed the look with a toothpick perpetually protruding from his mouth. Still another wore a tattered green Mao suit; its open buttons exposed only a near-transparent white undershirt.

Every day around noon, the roster of speakers paused for traditional medicine advertisements from vendors who surrounded the speaking area and offered a range of concoctions. One woman peddled a soap to regenerate self-esteem and financial well-being, promising that after washing, job seekers would be job finders; she reported that she herself had amassed three million FCFA (US $6000). Some sold cures for AIDS and other chronic maladies. Attesting to the credibility of his potions and pomades, one vendor boasted that a Brit and an Irishman were among his clientele. To the crowd's delight, vendors acted out what would happen after taking pills that promised to increase sexual potency or sperm count or creams to augment the penis, breasts, or behind. One vendor guaranteed that her medicine would "break the bed." Another brought a satisfied customer to the stage; as he approached the vendor remarked on how much space the client now needed in his pants to accommodate his enhanced member.

The Sorbonne's most popular speaker also sold medicines on the side. He held the coveted lunchtime spot, drawing spectators and riling them up before the main, midafternoon political speech. Nicknamed Cafard (Cockroach), he carried with him a large black dildo. To the amusement of those assembled, any woman within sight was a potential target for his act and was subjected to verbal and nonverbal prods that indicated what he or an audience member could and would do to her. In one speech Cafard recounted having penetrated a woman who had implored him for sex when he realized he needed to urinate. So he urinated inside her. Impersonating his chosen target in speech and walk, Cafard would raise his voice to a shrill while hobbling wide-legged, supposedly in postcoital agony. Reversing the typical narrative of men's struggles to find a mate, Cafard's humor involved women desiring and begging. The male protagonist, in turn, left her degraded or in pain.

Cafard's punch lines commonly involved a nexus of penis, power, and race. He frequently assumed the character of a white, usually French, woman, one who pretended to hate or fear the Black man but always succumbed to his penis with giggles and moans. White women, he explained knowingly to eager audiences, might not like Black men. But they loved Black penises. Cafard adopted storylines familiar to the crowd, such as making a trip to the French embassy. The secretary inquires as to his plans in Paris and his profession in Abidjan. On cue, he pulls out the dildo and responds that this is his job. Similarly, Cafard congratulated regulars returning from a noticeable absence, stating that they had taken an "adventure" to France and returned with a French lover. Among Cafard's favorite themes was then–President Sarkozy's inadequate penis—he cited this as the reason his first wife left him—measured up against President Gbagbo's robust member. He suggested that Gbagbo's political rivals, Henri Konan Bédié and Alassane Ouattara, were equally incompetent.

Picking a man from the crowd as the purported protagonist, Cafard created narratives of the wife and children he supported and his mistress on the side. Bemoaning the burdens of breadwinning, he remarked that what made life difficult was how expensive women were. And when the man was at work, it was not him, but his penis that she missed. Cafard detailed that when mounting the maid, he should calmly explain that she has just received a raise. In these ways Cafard constructed an image of the financially and sexually potent Ivoirian man.

Cafard hated condoms. He warned that condoms caught HIV in the penis and their extended use led to impotence. Worse still was *coco,* a little-known side effect of condoms that left men blind and made their penises fall off. Worst of all, condoms wasted sperm otherwise destined for implantation in a woman's egg. Ejaculation, Cafard insisted, marked the moment that proved one's manhood, for God created women to carry a man's sperm and eventually his children. Presumably, this left men to engage in business and politics.

The Business of Politics

> The readiness of the Young Patriotes to embrace careers in the public administration, the *"corps habillés"* or the partisan life thereby indicates that the old models of social ascension have conserved their salience, albeit in a State that . . . is becoming more and more informalized.
>
> —Richard Banégas, "La politique du 'gbonhi'"

Public declarations of mistresses and maids gave way to frustrated accounts of entrenched joblessness and stalled relationships in private interviews. Despite his advanced degree and prior work in accounting and information technology, Koné explained that he "no longer even has the means to have a normal life." For Koné, "normal" consisted of a wife, a car, and a house. He continued, "I will not say that I need to have a car and a house before I marry. I will say that I should have a telephone at home, internet—all the rights of a man to exist." As table 9.01 shows, such "rights" were indeed tied to formal, and particularly state, employment. By becoming patriotic entrepreneurs, the orators positioned themselves as the natural recipients of the shrunken economic pie. Far from new, this close alliance between politics and business was in fact an extension of the colonial state of affairs and underscored the interdependence between the state and the foundational principle of racial capitalism: that despite the market's inherent promise of freedom, the entitlements it unequally bestowed and which the political order maintained and exacerbated presupposed inherently greater and lesser men. The orators encoded the racial-economic order onto the register of citizenship, so that even as they rejected Françafrique in fiercely anticolonial terms, they reinscribed a hierarchy of merit and exclusion premised on the imperial imaginary of a civilized and savage divide.

TABLE 9.01 Modern amenities in Abidjan households by employment sector, 2001–2002

AMENITY	% PUBLIC	% PRIVATE, FORMAL	% PRIVATE, INFORMAL
Car	21.1	13.0	3.8
Refrigerator	77.5	43.7	22.9
Home phone	38.2	18.5	4.8
Mobile phone	75.8	52.4	31.2
House	12.6	7.2	4.0

Source: Tableau 7.2. Institut National de la Statistique (2003, 33)

avec **Electrolux** la vie est belle...
même par les plus fortes chaleurs

Vous pouvez toujours compter sur votre
Electrolux L 20 même si la chaleur est accablante

- Electrolux L 20 fonctionne au pétrole, au gaz
ou à l'électricité, n'importe où, impeccablement

- Electrolux L 20 est parfaitement
étanche ; porte à fermeture magnétique
et une nouveauté : une serrure vous permet
de fermer à clé votre Electrolux.

- Electrolux L 20 est spacieux
grâce à la capacité véritable de 60 litres.

Ah ! ... le plaisir de boire toujours frais
avec Electrolux, le réfrigérateur de qualité.

Demandez à voir la gamme Electrolux
de 60 litres à 320 litres

L 20 (ci-dessous) L 77, LC 43, L 54, L 76, L 115.

Electrolux vous offre le choix et une vraie
garantie de cinq ans sur l'unité
réfrigérante de chaque Electrolux

⊠ **Electrolux**

CONCESSIONNAIRE : **C.F.C.I. Abidjan**

FIGURE 9.02. Imagining a future past: "All the rights of a man to exist" (Koné, orator). Electrolux refrigerator advertisement in *Fraternité Matin* (1964). Copyright Electrolux.

Systematic exploitation was at the root of the Franco-Ivoirian relationship. Lola explained,

> The Belgians pillage the Congo, the Congolese become more and more impoverished, and Brussels becomes prettier and prettier. France pillages Côte d'Ivoire, Mali, Burkina, and other countries, and France is well developed. Even their unemployed are paid while we suffer here, and they say they are rich. The Europeans and Westerners, they say they are rich, but the minerals come from us, but all that they produce they sell back to us; everything they sell to us comes from us. They say they are the best-equipped countries, that they are big powers, that they are rich. But they are rich with our wealth, and we are poor with their poverty.

Here Lola assessed that colonial inequality went well beyond resource extraction and captive markets. He observed that through those devices it had redistributed personal wealth and poverty, a particularly painful experience for those at the bottom. It was in this spirit that Koné asked,

> How can we develop if our value, the work of our citizens, must go to another country to permit those people to live? . . . A student like me who has an MBA in France, the French state gives him a certain [monthly] amount that is equivalent to 250,000 FCFA over a period of three years while he is looking for work. In other words, they have raised the social standards in France with the value of our work.

France, in other words, doled out unemployment benefits like a salary—a salary that was moreover formidable in Côte d'Ivoire. For a man like Koné: thirty-four, single with one child, and chronically unemployed, the French welfare state was indeed a bitter contrast to life in Côte d'Ivoire. Adding insult to injury, it functioned off the expropriation of African labor. The solution then was not to incorporate a social safety net in Côte d'Ivoire, but to trim French largesse.

The orators suggested that the early support that France had extended to Côte d'Ivoire produced a form of dependency as erroneous as its welfare state. For example, Zokora accepted that France had managed critical Ivoirian affairs—but at the expense of Ivoirian development and self-determination. He explained, "It was France that did everything for us, but in return, we gained nothing. We could not construct schools, we could not provide jobs, we could not pay our workers a good salary. All that was France. . . . The current crisis is of sovereignty, a war of liberation." Incomplete independence had, in other words, perpetuated an infantile state incapable of providing for its citizens. Finally ridding themselves of their neocolonial tethers, the orators wanted not to become like the colon, but to replace him by redefining the terms of évolué identity. Yet they themselves represented the social strata that, in better times, had been poised to follow the Francophone route, from schooling to a lifetime career in the civil service. Reconciling their labor market failures and envisioning a new, entrepreneurial "Anglophone" model for Côte d'Ivoire, the orators argued that Houphouët-Boigny's bloated public sector had been a misguided French inheritance.

Ousmane explained that Houphouët-Boigny had cultivated an Ivoirian mentality trained to follow a singular path: "I go to school. I get out. I take my exams. I work in an office." Étienne contended that for an Ivoirian "to put his hands in the sand, in the mud, to fish, this is disgusting, disorganized, it is dirty. He cannot do these jobs." Boubacar contended that real work should facilitate the provider role, "a system of payment that permits you to feed yourself, save a little, take care of yourself and your family." He concluded that informal activities were not "jobs for us."

Paradoxically, the orators argued that these same beliefs had thwarted Ivoirians from seeing past a narrow conception of work that would have prepared them for the liberalized economy. Lola noted that foreigners had amassed fortunes in business, formal and informal, while Ivoirians preoccupied themselves with status markers like suits, air-conditioned interiors, and office jobs. This betrayed a "mental prejudice" for which the colonizer was to blame. Continuing to confer prestige despite the real sources of wealth accumulation, Étienne complained,

> If you are not a *fonctionnaire* [civil servant], your village will say that you did not succeed. . . . If you are a businessman, you have a bar, sell things, have a store, you could make 10 million, 15 million [FCFA] a month, but an Ivoirian will not see you as someone who has money. The moment they hear you are a civil servant they will say, "Oh, he has money."

Orators proposed that Ivoirians make a fundamental aspirational shift.[12] Koné stated, "If you go to my village, everyone wants me to be a minister, but I prefer to be an entrepreneur."

Business, the orators had resolved, was the Anglophone way—and far superior to Francophone colonialism. Speaking favorably of Ghana as West Africa's ascendant, entrepreneurial nation, Étienne argued, "The French system made it such that none of the Francophone countries produces businessmen. Ghana, the Anglophone countries, they have business systems, *le marketing*." Keïta elaborated, "When you take the Anglophone countries, colonized by the English, they are not in the same place. We were colonized by France. It is clearly different. We were formed in the civil service, but when you go to Ghana, it is *le business*. It is *le fifty-fifty*."

The root of the crisis was, in short, the ongoing material and ideological colonialism of Françafrique. Recovery of Ivoirian grandeur was to be found by pivot-
ing away from that pact. This involved ridding Côte d'Ivoire not only of French
interference in its decision-making processes, economy, and resources, but also
by rejecting its social inheritance. The future was Anglophone. Likening Côte
d'Ivoire to Africa's America, the orators presented the United States as the righteous trajectory for Ivoirian development. With this intention, Faé described a
conversation he had overheard between two extranationals. One had called the
other "wild . . . from the bush." The other replied, "You see me this way because
you are coming from Abidjan." Faé explained:

> That is to say, he came from a milieu more civilized than his friend. It is
> like in Côte d'Ivoire . . . someone will say, "He is an Ivoirian but he lived
> in the United States." You see that people will receive him with respect
> right away because he has lived in the United States. So he is civilized.
> He has les moyens.

From this interaction, Faé had constructed a hierarchy of man that ascended
from the African interior to Abidjan and, finally, to the United States. It was a
construction repeated in speeches when the orators derided the northerners and
migrants whom they perceived as lesser African men. They mocked the food they
ate (like *garba*—fish served with attiéké) as being unsanitary and caricatured
them packed in rickety buses to the rebel stronghold of Bouaké—twenty-two
in seats, and an equal number in the luggage space, as one orator described. The
man who travels like this, he concluded, is the same who will rob you at night.

A repeated theme of political speeches was that an emergent national consciousness had evoked French retribution in the form of covert rebel support.
Thus conceived, the civil war was a proxy war between colonizer and colonized.
Their major point of contention being the 1961 Defense Accords, the orators
called not for isolation from the West but to replace unilateral trade relations and
French monopoly control over economic and administrative affairs with diversi-
fied business and trading partnerships. Refusing the conventional neocolonial
narrative, the orators attributed le miracle ivoirien to entrepreneurial activity,
and argued that the state should support the inchoate business sector and attract
foreign investment. Sangaré reasoned, "If the country is liberated, investors will
come. If the investors arrive, unemployment will decline." And though the orators lamented the high presence of foreign workers in Côte d'Ivoire, many drew
parallels between that nation and the United States as lands of opportunity and,
in Yapo's words, "free market principles." Gneki described Côte d'Ivoire as a country where "business is easy." According to Zokora, the main national attribute was
abundant business opportunities, offering incredible potential to make money

and be successful. All anyone required was a creative spirit, imagination, and a viable project. In fact, the only thing lacking was start-up capital. He elaborated: "Americans have their way of life, it is liberty. And here it is liberty. Everyone is free. When a foreigner comes from his country, even if he has no money to eat and it is night, by tomorrow he will have something to eat." In this laissez-faire vision of liberty, freedom was an economic good.

Predicting a positive economic turn, Sangaré reflected enthusiastically that Gbagbo was pleasing the "Bretton Woods institutions." This new market-oriented economy, the orators insisted, offered a path out of la crise for the new Ivoirian man. By adopting this perspective, the orators put a market spin on cronyism to argue that the state should direct public monies toward the cultivation of private business initiatives—and specifically to them, as patriotic entrepreneurs. Hence Yapo's solution to the crisis: "Us, the organization of orators, . . . we have projects. Finance these projects!" Touré would know that Africa had succeeded when it had produced its own Bill Gates. To do so, he proposed that each country finance a robust banking network to loan money to its "youth." When Africa's Bill Gates arrived, Touré believed, he would use his wealth to generate employment. These remarks demonstrate that despite the FPI's official status as a socialist party, the orators did not articulate socialist stances, such as advocating for publicly owned enterprises, strengthened unions, firmer regulations, or income redistribution. As Keïta opined, "The public sector does not create jobs! It is the private sector that creates jobs." The role of the state, he went on, was to create healthy fiscal policies.

Étienne described three stages in life: first, you work for another; then you work for yourself; and finally, others work for you. But today, he said, "the one business that works is politics." So the orators stressed the profit potential of their political connections. Zokora explained that his daily Sorbonne activities in themselves offered no financial return. "But," Zokora continued, "the advantage, it is the relations. The relations that I have in politics, it is this which permits me to live." He regularly sought support from various patrons to pay his daughter's school fees and would ask for small amounts of money—500 FCFA here, 1000 FCFA there—when he was particularly desperate. In a country without a social safety net, this served as an important buffer. Yapo, who had been orating since 2000, received as much as 15,000 FCFA from the occasional speaking gig, but he was still waiting for something more stable. Cynically he remarked, "If I was given a job, every day I would go to work. I prefer work over going to parlements and speaking about Gbagbo, speaking about the country, speaking about all that. Today we are prisoners, we are obliged to be there." Although Sorbonne involvement conferred local status and covered basic needs, the orators viewed it foremost as an investment in an uncertain future, for as Sagbo reasoned, being "made in the political milieu . . . it is normal that men with power will find something for us to do." He reported, "I approach a good number of authorities in the country. I enter into places that before I would not have had access." He concluded, "Even if I do not have much money, for the moment it is okay." Despite his struggles, Sagbo navigated a world of people and spaces that had been previously closed to him, and he confidently recounted that others predicted he would become a big man in politics.

Expectations of "delayed remuneration" fit into an Ivoirian "moral economy of social debt and a patriotic political imaginary of generational emancipation" (Banégas 2010, 26). Within the Sorbonne network the orators made frequent contact with the Ivoirian political and business elite, who, as with Yapo, booked them to speak at conferences, rallies, and other political gatherings around the country. Zokora explained that leading figures could not come to the Sorbonne directly, but they would call him to discuss politics in private. Bamba, with five years of Sorbonne involvement, traveled widely and said of the leading figures he had met, "I have their numbers, they have mine. I approach people, I associate with these people. . . . Two or three years after the crisis, I can do something with this." Regime affiliation moreover entitled the orators to relative immunity from informal state extraction, a major incentive in a country where bribes were rampant. Faé, for example, explained that his Sorbonne renown had kept his nephew out of jail after the boy had stolen a 293,000 FCFA (US $586) mobile phone. Walking into the police station, Faé was instantly greeted with the honorific "Patriote Faé," and his nephew's charge was eventually dismissed.

Although the orators espoused entrepreneurial ideals, ultimately they hoped to become évolué by any means possible. Like Koné and Faé, these were identities beyond work, encompassing roles as heads of household and as elders within their extended families and villages. They also included positions within the patriotic hierarchy, and the more successful among them in this regard transformed their political affairs into returns elsewhere in their lives. Lola, a Sorbonne "ambassador," was singularly focused on a political career and believed he was already on course to achieve this goal.

> I am among the orators who have succeeded, who have put out into the market CDs with information and analyses of the Ivoirian crisis. I am currently on the fourth CD . . . so today they are in Belgium, France, Benin, and other countries. People who do not know me over there have my CD, and they call me and congratulate and encourage me.

Koulibaly said that in addition to higher-up political personalities, "when I walk down the street, youth, children, congratulate me." Alternatively, Zokora, whose residence of Abobo was an opposition stronghold, claimed infamy: "Often my photo appears in the opposition newspaper. This means that people know me, so I must take precautions. I can no longer walk down the street like I used to."

As Sorbonne president, Cissé was the big man among orators as well as in the physical space of the speakers' corners and adjacent market, a microcosm further composed of audience members, vendors, and patrons. His office, situated on an upper level of the central high-rise, was reached by climbing a dingy, urine-reeking staircase. Queuing up those stairs was a long line of members of the public: men in suits with heads held high, tired-looking female vendors, nervous teenagers. Some came to resolve disputes, others to discuss some pressing private matter, to present a case for financial support or to make a plea for work. Several smartly dressed men, all from the loyal inner circle of patriotes, sat on couches in the waiting room before Cissé's office. Cissé himself could be found poised regally behind his desk, with an entourage of insiders. For what he insisted was transparency's sake, the door always open. Self-designating with the French "royal we" (*nous*), he said, "Our objective it to lead a commune one day, to be in politics and development. We want to become the mayor of Plateau." In progressing toward this goal, he was "already there." Cissé elaborated:

> You see when you are at this *stade* [stadium, e.g., the Sorbonne speaking area] here, you have many people around you. And so to win political elections, it is the people who transform a candidate into an elected leader. If in my little stade where I am, I do social work, I take care of people, then they will not think that when I am mayor I will not do this. That is the reality.

Of his renown, Cissé declared, "My reputation has already passed Ivoirian borders. Modestly speaking, the media knows me. In Abidjan I am known, in Plateau I am very well known, in the interior I am known. There is not a place where I can go where at least someone does not know me." He explained that his relations with the Sorbonne public had forged an influential political persona. Cissé now had a ready constituency consisting of thousands of regular audience members, many of whom had made personal appeals to him, and he led a group of men who would publicly advocate for him.

Finally, despite their rhetorical opposition to the public sector, opportunities for a secure livelihood and, as Koné described, the "rights of a man to exist" remained entrenched with state employment. So too, then, did évolué identity. Koulibaly, former Sorbonne Solidarité vice president, had converted his political networks first into financing his *concours* (national examinations), and then into civil service employment as a tax collector. This successful transition had earned him great respect among the orators, and he maintained a "consultative" role within the Sorbonne that included helping patrons to find work and to travel.

Koulibaly earned 120,000 FCFA a month in his job. At the Sorbonne he continued to receive a daily "*prime*" (fee, bonus, tip) of 2500 FCFA for transport regardless of whether he attended—an added 50,000 FCFA to his monthly income.[13]
Now that he was on the other end of the patronage network, he also reported
dispensing a minimum of 10,000 FCFA per week in responding to the appeals of
Sorbonne constituents. While he had not yet married the mother of his child, he
was a provider within his social and political network.

Évolué Aspirations: The Changing Same

Blé Goudé: *Nous étions enfant hier, mais aujourd'hui nous avons . . .*
[Yesterday we were children, but today we have . . .]
Crowd: *Grandi* [Grown up]

—Quoted in Richard Banégas, "Côte d'Ivoire: Les jeunes 'se lèvent en hommes'"

In a 2003 *New Yorker* article, "Gangsta War," journalist George Packer described a
rally held in January of that year in which Blé Goudé, leader of the Jeunes Patriotes,
had riled up tens of thousands of supporters. "The iconography of those demonstrations," Packer observed, "was virulently anti-French and desperately pro-
American." He elaborated: "Blé Goudé waved an American flag and delighted the
crowd by refusing to speak French. 'Are you ready for English?' he yelled, and the
crowd roared as he spoke a few clumsy sentences in the tongue of the superpower,
which, in Ivory Coast, is the language of youthful resistance." Attending another
rally some months later, Packer likened these Jeunes Patriotes, the street fighters
of the patriotic movement, to "American hip-hop singers" in "gold chains, track-
suits, floppy hats," who between speeches gave one another fist pumps "like an
N.B.A. star returning to the bench."[14] Goudé, dressed in this "imitation-gangsta
style," had with a force and persuasion beyond that of the other orators "made [the
crowd] feel that the future was theirs" (Packer 2003). Summarizing the shift that
Goudé and the Jeunes Patriotes embodied, Packer (2003) wrote:

> The Young Patriots represent a new kind of African success story.
> They're celebrated by many young people in Abidjan for beating and
> cheating a system gone rancid. With the corrupt "old fathers" refusing to
> get out of the way, and with all the old channels to success—emigration,
> foreign study, state employment, family connections—blocked, the new
> hero is a young trickster with a talent for self-promotion. The model is
> no longer the formal bureaucratic style of the French colonizer; it's the
> loud, unrestrained style that everyone in Ivory Coast calls American.

Just as President Houphouët-Boigny embodied the Francophone évolué and personified the freshly independent nation, the citadins of the informalized regime identified as a new ideal this Anglophile minister of the street. Known as the "street general" (le général de la rue) (Ford 2014), Blé Goudé began his political journey as a budding anticolonial intellectual and FESCI agitator while majoring in English at the University of Cocody (Trial International 2016). Remaining a leading figure in FESCI after his studies, Goudé was imprisoned eight times for his role in student trade union struggles, and became the movement's secretary general in 1998. He studied briefly in the United Kingdom before repatriating amid rumblings of civil war, and in 2001 he founded the Jeunes Patriotes and the Congrès panafricain pour la justice et l'égalité des peuples. As head of the Jeunes Patriotes, he was a leading presence during critical standoffs vis-à-vis the international community. Yet Ivoirian opposition to the international was selective, and Goudé used his Anglophone connections to reinforce a national orientation toward the United States as a desirable and, in fact, resistant alternative hegemon (Ford 2014; Trial International 2016).

Goudé's intense public following attracted the highest echelons of the state, and in addition to presidential aspirations of his own, he was drawn into President Gbagbo's inner circle to become one of his most fervent propagandists. Known informally for years not only as le général de la rue, but also le général de la jeunesse, in 2010, Goudé was inducted as Gbagbo's minister of youth and sports. When Gbagbo lost the election, Goudé recruited a militia to defend the freshly ousted president (Trial International 2016). After the postelectoral conflict ended in President Ouattara's favor, Goudé fled Côte d'Ivoire, spending several years evading an International Criminal Court charge of crimes against humanity. He was arrested in Accra in 2013 and, after a three-year-long trial, acquitted in 2019.

As le général de la rue, Blé Goudé marked the pinnacle of the patriotic dream. His ascent was not through the concours route, which was closed in any case; rather, he had explicitly rejected Françafrique to excel in the Anglophone academy. He met political success via calculating entrepreneurial acumen and adherence to a street protest that violently disdained the colon. His fall represented the high stakes of the business of politics.

For the average Abidjanais man, contemporary urbanity is experienced as survival etched in crisis. At the Sorbonne masculinity and citizenship converged to underscore the particular geopolitics of le miracle ivoirien and its demise. As a means of being in the world and of being a man of the world, the Sorbonne provided social status, limited financial security, and hope. It was an arena for men to contest their physical and social marginalization. And it was by constructing a

TABLE 9.02   Registers of worth in the Sorbonne political imaginary

	MASCULINITY	CITIZENSHIP
Center and periphery	Civilized évolué with privileged access to city and country	Discourse of Ivoirian exceptionalism positioning Côte d'Ivoire as a regional hegemon, distinct from other Africans
Work and the informal economy	Formal economy is masculine	Localized stereotypes that Ivoirians work in offices, migrants in informal "trades"
Breakdown of le miracle, la crise	Feminization of work, joblessness and loss of breadwinner role	Produces contested citizenship identity and demarcates between who deserves/destroyed the miracle

Sorbonne imaginary that these patriotes gained legitimacy from an identity that excluded regional migrants and bore a stated contempt for the former colon. But by upholding narratives of évolué masculinity and its impossible realization in la crise, for all but the most elite orators, dominance was confined to the fantasized realm of Sorbonne sociality.

Adhering to the évolué ideal by way of briefcases and newspapers, shoe-shines and espressos, the men who frequented the Sorbonne asserted that they were protagonists on a global stage. Orators and audience members presented themselves as informed, politicized, and global, while social juniors and women stood in the background as servile or sexual objects. These men, in short, conflated an anticolonial struggle with a movement that privileged "patriotic" citizens over northerners and regional migrants and upheld their masculinities on the backs of women. It was no coincidence that the stigma of the wrong kind of job was associated with migrants and women. In denigrating them, the orators denied their legitimacy as political or economic actors and therefore confined future entitlements to a subset of Abidjan's citadins. But the fact of their joblessness remained, rendering incomplete what were, in essence, évolué impersonations.

Challenging the powerlessness of the Ivoirian citoyen/Abidjanais citadin amid la crise, the orators seized public space and political discourse as their own. In their political imaginaries they articulated a new kind of évolué man in their city and a newly constituted Côte d'Ivoire in the world. These imaginaries called into question neither the normative "expectations of modernity" (Ferguson 1999) that had undermined their own masculine worth nor a system of rule predicated on the supremacy of the citizen-évolué. Rather, succumbing to hegemonic imaginaries of a market economy, they aspired to become entrepreneurial évolués. Though in a reinterpreted form, the évolué trope had survived unscathed. With it endured the underlying ethos of racial capitalism, whereby the prime requisite for manhood was consent to the capitalist status quo, one predicated on intrinsic registers of belonging and exclusion.

VIP IMAGINARIES

> **Travelers, good day. Allow me to introduce you to my super perfume, the perfume of respected men and respectable men, the perfume of the VIP class. This perfume launched internationally in Casablanca. Endorsed by the Queen of England, this is the exclusive perfume of Air Afrique's VIP lounge, the one-and-the-same of travelers to Manhattan, Baghdad, Toulouse, and Tokyo. It is produced in a laboratory in Paris, precisely in the 5th arrondissement, No. 65, Avenue Henri de Chiffon. Liverpool, Marseille, or Rome, this is the perfume distributed, the perfume they choose. Clients pay 8500 [FCFA]. I will let you have a smell for free.**
>
> —Guillaume, Yopougon vendor

At the Gesco corridor, the police checkpoint in Yopougon that opens Abidjan to the country's interior, a collective of eight mobile street vendors had learned to hustle a very Abidjanais global imaginary.[1] Appealing to men "respected and respectable" and invoking a circuit of cities in far-flung locations and the elite transit space of the airline lounge, they sold the "perfume of the VIP class."[2] The imaginaries they peddled converted the buyer's status as traveler to those who jet-set between metropolitan centers.

These savvy vendors had met while attending the University of Abidjan's Yopougon campus. The political instability that interrupted the studies of the Ivoirian youth soon forced them to drop out. In 2005 they came together to vend, distributing their earnings among members on a *tontine* basis (weekly rotating) and setting aside a little for emergencies. Each man aimed to contribute either 15,000 FCFA per week or 3000 FCFA daily. Their emergency fund entailed an additional daily contribution of 300 FCFA, which if unused at the end of the month, was spent on a group social activity. This distribution system sought to provide each man with a salary as high as 120,000 FCFA every two months. It collectivized accountability for the vendors' work habits and encouraged saving.[3]

The Gesco vendors were practicing a system long standard among market women, and it afforded some financial stability in a climate of otherwise chronic insecurity. Despite its benefits, these were the only men I encountered during my fieldwork who used this collective savings system. It was a telling indication of the stigma of street vending that the men were generally desperate to escape. Gesco vendor Samuel explained that their strategy typically "belonged to petit commerce, especially in the markets, in the women's markets. . . . Generally men work alone, and when they have money, perhaps they put it in a bank account. And generally men, they do not do the petit commerce that women do." This feminized—and feminizing—narrative of market work was sufficiently damning as to prevent male vendors, irrespective of their reality, from perceiving a work regime beyond the day to day.[4] Hence while peer networks certainly formed on busy corners, where tenure and mutual, albeit marginal, support could act as a last defense against hunger, homelessness, or illness, the men rarely pursued strategies that shifted from the atomized to the collective or envisioned work beyond a daily struggle (see also Bayat 2000).

The Gesco vendors stood apart in other ways. They always dressed in business attire. Confident and well mannered, they presented themselves as professional salesmen dealing in global luxury commodities. They socially embedded themselves among the bus drivers, police, and other vendors, and the networks they forged gave them preferential treatment selling to bus passengers, buffered them against the harassment common to vendor-police encounters, and acted as additional eyes and hands to help with transactions, to watch their goods, and at times to contribute to their savings pool. Engaging in friendly banter, they sprayed samples on passengers and market women who laughingly implored them to direct a little to their armpits as they adjusted large trays of food on their heads. Bus drivers and police regularly received complimentary bottles in exchange for unfettered and monopoly access to vend inside the buses. Customers who made large purchases were also gifted bonus packs. These acts guaranteed their continued presence at the Gesco corridor, effectively allowing them to become semi-installed. Between sales they gathered to rest on a bench they had set up, an umbrella sheltering them from the sun. They would tell their clients that they could always be found there, in their "air-conditioned" office.

And they all repeated a variation of the introductory script in the buses that they mounted, two at a time, to sell their perfumes and colognes. This was a story of international origins and repute: theirs was a *foreign* product worn by *foreign* customers. Changing brands periodically to keep things fresh, the scent of the moment was called, "Débutant: For Men." The label read "Paris," and promoted itself in French and English as an "eau de toilette" and "natural spray." The men's scripts variously referenced the queen of England or the king of Belgium. Though the back label read clearly, "Made in Abidjan," they gave the precise address of the lab that manufactured their cologne and described another lab in Manhattan. Explaining that it sold for 8500 FCFA on international airlines, they would offer to these lucky travelers a discount price of 500 FCFA each. Gesco vendor

FIGURE 10.01.   Fabrice, a Gesco vendor, with his colognes for sale. Author's photo, Abidjan (2009).

Guy explained, "The Ivoirian loves everything that comes from abroad, from the United States, from the Occident. So there you go, quickly he takes it."

Guy's observation acknowledged that in Abidjan, "elsewhere" was a reference point from which to establish hierarchies of status and worth. "Elsewhere" was omnipresent in imaginaries that played out at every level of interaction, from the individual to the state. Just as the Gesco vendors relied on narratives of "elsewhere" to peddle their perfumes, from the moment of independence, President

Houphouët-Boigny and his planners took to Abidjan as a physical manifestation of the state-directed vision of a modern elsewhere.

The Devolution of the Urban Plan

Together, the disparate characteristics of central Abidjan and the quartiers populaires reflected the "cultural feeling" of the city's "*maquis*-restaurants and cuisine, its distinctive French argot and its cosmopolitan character" (Freund 2007, 180). These were qualities that existed side by side for a half century without appearing to have much to do with one another. Officials and citadins alike were optimistic that Plateau, Abidjan's centerpiece to the world, would be a model that expanded outward, with planners anticipating new manufacturing zones and suburban developments to complement the dense urban core. In particular, metropolitan growth from the 1970s prompted new axes of urban sociality in the sprawling quartiers populaires, namely Abobo in the north and Yopougon in the west (Haeringer 2000).

In the Abidjan of the twenty-first century, the periphery constituted the bulk of urban space and populations. Here, the typical cityscape consisted not of skyscrapers but vegetable and food prep stands, plywood and corrugated-metal structures for hair salons and barbershops, maquis, carpenters, tailors, and repair shops, secondhand clothing boutiques, small household goods shops, bakeries, internet cafes that doubled as international calling stations, mobile phone *cabines* (credit recharge stations), copy-and-print services, an array of privately operated public transportation vehicles, churches, "Lebanese shops" (small- to mid-sized marts often owned by Lebanese ethnics), banks, and Western Unions. Mixed with petty modes of corporate extraction, Abidjan's informal activities and precarious livelihoods tacitly conceded to the "deviation of the city from the Western model" and "the end of le miracle" (Steck 2005, 225).

A palimpsest of one future imagined but another actualized was Yopougon. Symbol of le miracle and la crise, Yopougon was as prescient as Plateau in the postcolonial Abidjanais imaginary. Similar to the 1965 Delouvrier plan of Paris, Yopougon was constructed as a satellite city that, extending Abidjan proper, was to be an independent source of jobs and housing. Facing northward, the quartier was intended to link Abidjan to the interior, to "the conquest of continental markets" (Steck 2005, 219). It was conceived in the model of mid-twentieth-century, middle-class suburbia, a controlled sprawl of single-unit dwellings and automobile dependence (Steck 2008). Mixing public and private modes of investment, the state set aside housing for the disproportionately civil servant constituency of wage laborers that was to be purchased with private bank loans. Employment was to follow, with plans for a major northern port and commercial centers (Steck 2008).

This vision could not withstand Côte d'Ivoire's economic demise. By the late 1970s, individual homeowners and the state on which they relied for their incomes were unable to realize an imported suburban lifestyle reliant on mortgages and private automobiles. Infrastructural services likewise failed to fully connect Yopougon with the rest of Abidjan, leaving residents dependent on informal transportation networks to navigate congested and poorly maintained roads (Steck 2008). Nor did the manufacturing sector or other local employment arrive. At the turn of the new century, Yopougon provided one-eighth of the city's formal jobs while housing one-quarter of the urban population; this compared to the southern quartiers that provided half of Abidjan's formal employment, and as much as three-quarters when including Plateau and Adjamé (235).

In all the ways the planners fell short, in Abidjan, as throughout Africa's austerity-devastated cities, the informal economy took hold. By the 2000s sub-Saharan Africa had experienced the fastest growth of informal street vending in the world (Lyons and Snoxell 2005). For residents of Yopougon, the informal economy was "no longer a means of entering the city"; rather, it was "a means of maintaining oneself there" (Steck 2008, 236). Rather than assimilating to the urban center, in the classic model of the neglected bidonvilles on the edges of the colonial settler city, the quartier's economy marked a recourse to base survival and left Yopougon largely segregated from the rest of Abidjan: in 2008, Steck reported that 95 percent of commerçants were also residents, compared to 78 percent in the city as a whole. Fifty-eight percent of capital came from the commune compared to 51 percent as a whole, and 80 percent of clients were locals, compared to 63 percent for Abidjan generally. A remarkably high proportion of daily purchases—98 percent—stayed in the commune (236).

Yet as Abidjan's largest and most populous quartier, Yopougon signaled that despite never achieving its promise, "its residents [were] deeply attached to their status as citadins" (Steck 2008, 236). They forged a strong local identity and, replacing the "long hegemony" of the first African quartier of Treichville, Yopougon emerged as the new locus of the "real culture" of Côte d'Ivoire (Konaté 2002, 779). Furthermore, cultural production had moved from well-heeled Plateau, still the core for the popular imaginary, to the periphery, such that "Abidjan was no longer in Abidjan" (779). The Abidjan for Abidjanais, Yopougon authenticity has been memorialized in Ivoirian Marguerite Abouet's *Aya de Yopougon* comic books, which chronicle life in the peripheral metropolis. In the Abidjan of la crise, Yopougon had become the "reference" for city and country, if not for West Africa generally (Steck 2008, 237).

The Yopougon of 2008 and 2009 interspersed a scattering of multistory office towers and intersecting paved roads among unsigned, unnumbered commercial structures and shanties. Its younger residents found inspiration in "Black American culture and the discourse of 'Black Power' . . . [as well as] the culture of the French banlieues—references . . . to American inner cities and an urban periphery" (Steck 2008, 239). As a burgeoning site of cultural offerings, Yopougon's rue Princesse hosted a dizzying array of neon signs, food stalls, and maquis blasting coupé décalé, zouglou, and hip-hop. On weekends throngs of Ivoirian party-seekers in their evening finest turned this thoroughfare into a pedestrianized space. In all of Côte d'Ivoire, the rue Princesse, with over two thousand maquis, "shine[d] the most with beer, grilled fish, chicken, and sex" (Konaté 2002, 780).[5]

While Yopougon represented the nucleus of the post-miracle Abidjanais culture, Abobo symbolized the depth of its poverty. Whereas Yopougon was a plan unrealized, Abobo was the quintessentially unplanned. Abobo emerged in 1962 as a resettlement for evictees (Fraternité Matin 1978). Over the next decade state-built housing estates were interspersed with what were predominantly informal constructions. In *Abidjan Métropole Moderne*, a 1978 publication of the nation's daily newspaper, *Fraternité Matin*, that otherwise lauded the "dazzling, phenomenal, fantastic" city of Abidjan, Abobo was described as a quartier in which "150,000 people have thus far lived . . . totally devoid of road infrastructure, sanitation, or at most, with a few water and electricity connections" (Fraternité Matin 1978, 19, 37). It moreover offered no employment opportunities besides "*activités artisanales*" (crafts) (119). Located "exterior to the urban perimeter," the daily (1978, 37) concluded that Abobo "cannot take advantage of the enormous means put in place in the capital city." Yet its authors (37) stated with optimism that "the Authorities have decided to intervene . . . so that Abobo becomes a quartier worthy of Abidjan."

Abobo figured as the target of derisory jokes about hard-knock Ivoirian urbanity. Mapping Abidjan's imaginary of cultural evolution and metropolitan sociality, it articulated the space of the nonmodern (Thomann 2016). Its many makeshift settlements made it the most undercounted, and thus unaccounted for, quartier. Roundabouts on Abobo's main road served as densely used public spaces, where rotting fruit and mosquito larvae marinated in iridescent puddles of petroleum-laced urine within paces of women squatted low on footstools selling baskets of wilted vegetables or tightly stacked pagne wraps, men selling secondhand T-shirts or sneakers displayed on muddy tarps, and chickens pecking liberally at whatever nutritious refuse they came across. Beyond the central paved roads—escapes out—dusty dirt roads extended for miles. Large segments of Abobo were beyond Abidjan's official parameters and thus unapologetically lacked basic amenities like electricity, potable water, and sanitation services that were otherwise associated with big-city life. Characteristic of profound "ethnic, social, and economic marginality" (Steck 2008, 243), Abobo was a stronghold of immigrants and unentitled nationals, while clashes between them only added noise to the many complaints that went unheard on these outer edges.

Profiles of the *débrouille*

> When you practice a trade, this has nothing to do with someone who is a fonctionnaire. A fonctionnaire, either one of the state or of a private business, has nothing to do with those who se *débrouillent* [get by]. Because they receive a monthly salary. He who gets by, it is daily; today he makes something, maybe tomorrow, two days, three days later, he will have nothing. . . . He who gets by, as they say in Africa, he lives day to day. . . . So for the moment, I am *un chômeur* [unemployed].
>
> —Romaric, Treichville vendor

> They say they have given six billion to clean Abidjan, that the guys at the mayor's office have given six billion [FCFA]. To clean Abidjan, that means to chase away all those who sell along the road, to clean it, to get rid of the dirty, the garbage.
>
> —Danon, Adjamé vendor

For the vendors whose words I recount in this section, Yopougon and Abobo constituted the Abidjan they knew and lived. Though they peddled their wares throughout the city, it was in these quartiers where the majority resided and etched out identities against the quotidian erasures of the periphery. Among peers and in popular social spaces, vendors, like all débrouilleurs, cultivated their extracurricular selves with care. It was a far cry from the dressed-down if not unkempt manner in which they commonly presented themselves at intersections, what Abidjan-born Burkinabé vendor Prospère called the "vagabond" look (further setting the Gesco vendors apart from the norm). I witnessed this marked contrast when, on a social outing with the Gesco vendors, they introduced me to a man locally praised as a well-respected zouglou artist. He was familiar, and for some minutes I struggled to place him. The realization threw me. Dignified, polite, and smooth in a crisp, white, button-down shirt, clean jeans, flashy watch, and several bracelets, he was the same man in torn and soiled clothing whom I had seen on my first visit to the Gesco corridor, jostling passengers into buses for a few FCFA a pop. I remembered him well because I had witnessed him exact a silent revenge upon a passenger's rejection of his custom: he had picked his nose and wiped the booger on the back of the man's shirt. But here he was—a popular and respected musician by night.

The more aggressive practices of hustling people onto buses or charging to watch parked cars with an underlying threat of vehicular damage for refusal represented a menacing informality into which mobile street vendors complained of being injudiciously grouped. Vendors described the indignity they felt when drivers rolled up their windows and locked their doors on their approach, and they regularly faced accusations that their activities dirtied Abidjan's streets and brought shame upon the state. Regular targets of police harassment, which served to not only "disrupt commerce but also publicly humiliate" (Agadjanian 2005, 265), the vendors compared their experiences against local drug dealers with whom the police were in cahoots. Jaurès, one of a community of migrants from Niger vending along the main thoroughfare of a rough area known as "Vietnam" in Adjamé, protested, "You must imagine: you, a vendor, trying to get by, and you are taken for a criminal, someone who killed a man, who raped. You are put with them, and how would that make you feel?" His compatriot Souma despaired, "The junkies live better than us, among the sellers at the traffic light. . . . We who get by looking for something to eat, it is us with the problem." Even Robert, one of the more self-respecting Gesco vendors, lamented, "When you see us on the side of the road running to sell perfumes, you have no respect for us. You take us as thieves, as street children, abandoned children, children like parasites who never went to school, unconscientious children who never wanted to go to school and who spend their time running in the streets . . . vendeurs ambulants." Few then found it worthwhile to counter the stigma and poorly remunerated character of their débrouille in efforts at personal appearance or comportment. They defended themselves instead as the moral poor, doing what they could to survive when their sole alternative was crime.

Inadequate substitutions for the *bureaux climatisées* (air-conditioned offices) of the Abidjanais imaginary, streets of commerce were "arenas for a protracted struggle over the legitimacy of self-employment and of the right to survive in the city" (Simone 2004a, 169). As "symbols of decline" (Lyons and Snoxell 2005, 1078), vendors' livelihood strategies threatened the postcolonial grand narrative that, by imagining what Abidjan was, remained firm about what it was not: that messy informality of other African cities. Relegated to the exterior of le miracle ivoirien, informality was associated with the double illegality of economic activity and immigrant status. In these ways, street vending "challenge[d] the notions of order, the modern city, and urban governance espoused by Third World political elites" (Bayat 2004, 91). They marked the "quiet encroachment" of the periphery into the center (Bayat 2000; Bayat 2004).

Mobile street vendors, in short, personified the devolution of the urban plan. Thierry, an Ivoirian from the north, contended, "If you say that man has évolué, it is because he has les moyens." After years of mobile vending, Thierry now sold shoes in a permanent market stall, but this was still not good enough. He explained, "I know that if I have money, I will create a business." Any *real* business upheld tangible requirements of the évolué ideal: for example, being seated in a swivel office chair with the cool vents of the climate-controlled workspace creating an ambient buzz, not standing under the hot sun at a cacophonous intersection. By extension, the money earned in a débrouille was not to be taken seriously. Thierry designated it "weekend money." He observed, "What we make is not enough to live. Because often what you make, that is only enough for you and your friends to amuse themselves." The pecking order of vending therefore involved, over the negligent earnings themselves, how closely activities aligned with an image of entrepreneurial worth. In equal measures this image encapsulated signals of social status and, if not access, at least allusions to capital.

Mobile street vending was a diverse practice. At the lowest tier water sachets sold for 50 FCFA and newspapers for 200 FCFA, from which vendors took home profits of 15 FCFA and 20 FCFA per sale, respectively. Earning a pittance in such activities demanded long days on the streets while inhaling dust and heavy vehicular exhaust. For a newspaper vendor to earn 2000 FCFA, he would have to sell one hundred newspapers, a feat made more difficult by the other newspaper vendors who invariably congregated in the same area. Vendors who sold more expensive items—and were more inclined to dress the part—achieved only sporadic success. Arnaud, an Ivoirian from the north, sold what he described as goods "of worth"—he might have purchased a product for 1000 FCFA and sold it to clients for 1500 FCFA—but explained that his daily earnings "depend on luck." At the time his goods included a Blackberry phone. I asked whether he ever sold water, to which he retorted, "Nooo, I do not sell water. I am above that. Money from water, I have had enough of that. I prefer to put it into big merchandise." Linking his vending profile to a "cybernetic modernity" (Schilling and Dembele 2019), Arnaud was articulating a common sentiment among vendors: that personal worth was affiliated with the most sophisticated and potentially lucrative sales. Although he was unlikely to meet a customer interested in a Blackberry on the street, the product elevated Arnaud above the men selling water sachets. In short, potentiality was prestige. It required a display of capital and bestowed higher status even when the vendor took home less at the end of a month—or nothing at all at the end of a day. Hence when reporting their earnings, vendors readily referenced the value of what they sold rather than what they had made. Vendors' goods were an alternative lexicon of worth through which they measured one another as social beings. Designating the kind of women whom he could not approach, Arnaud thus said, "If I see a girl selling in a shop of value, she sells things worth 20,000 FCFA [US $40], and I am just getting by like this, I try to get with her and she will surely reject me. . . . So you know your categories."

At the elite end of the street vending spectrum was Guëï. A Guinean who arrived in Abidjan in 1999 and stated an age far too young for his life story, Guëï

FIGURE 10.02. Modeste, a mobile street vendor, displays his goods. Author's photo, Abidjan (2009).

was adorned in a necklace that he reported had set him back 20,000 FCFA for the chain and 45,000 FCFA for the pendant. Selling phones in the elite residential quartier of Deux Plateaux, Gueï purchased most of his goods from Adjamé's "Black" or on one of his regular trips to Ghana.[6] But his best custom, he said, was on demand, selling Armani suits to clients à domicile, in their private homes and offices, and he explained that his street vending was simply a base to attract a regular clientele.[7] Gueï cut costs on his daily commute—a significant drain for many vendors—by giving gbaka drivers discounts in exchange for free rides. Proudly describing himself as a businessman, he reported having established, in ten years of vending, a clientele of movers and shakers who bought his imported suits at the discounted price of 50,000 to 100,000 FCFA. Refusing to be recorded and never fully trusting me, he declined to say where he came across these designer threads. But his self-presentation and vending strategy indeed suggested that he was a cut above the typical vendor. Reality following imaginary, such a "display of success" was "a key way of building the social networks that formed the principal means of support and accumulation" (Newell 2009b, 163). Gueï's ability to look the part, in other words, was itself a sort of credential. Both his appearance and what he sold presented the image of a real businessman.

At the other end of the spectrum, constant demand generated somewhat predictable earnings for men who sold smaller items like newspapers, for which they could expect to make between 1000 to 3000 FCFA a day. By contrast, vendors of "big merchandise" reported going a month without a single sale, surviving instead—like many a débrouilleur—on borrowed money or the generosity of their social networks. Sixty days of sales data from a water-and-juice distributor at an intersection known as "Kuwait" in Yopougon revealed a wide range of outcomes. The most successful and consistent vendors rivaled the highest earnings of any mobile street vendor I encountered, and even that of the orators' 50,000 FCFA stipend. For example, after paying the distributor, the highest earner made 93,125 FCFA (US $186) working forty-three days, and the second highest earner made 87,300 FCFA (US $175) in twenty-nine days. The highest day's profits during that period, 8925 FCFA (US $18), required selling 266 water or juice sachets while competing with six other vendors at the same intersection. But these vendors' earnings were highly irregular and called for Herculean—if not Sisyphean—efforts. And in general, the one constant among the vendors I met was inconsistency and impermanence. Any given man's débrouille varied according to season, week, or day. Among the thirty-five water vendors who sold at the Kuwait intersection over the two-month period I examined, only nine put in twenty or more days. Sixteen put in at least five days. Eleven sold only once.[8]

The next step up from mobile street vending was to have a fixed location, which even in its most meager instance inferred some social embeddedness and the regular payment of rent. For example, Tino and MC, my research assistants, met with little success selling perfume at Adjamé market on what could be best described as a stool that they carried to and from the market daily. Yet when I remarked that they might learn something from the fastidious Gesco vendors, they shook their heads and replied with the slow, annunciated speech reserved for stupid foreigners, "But Jordanna, we are installed."

Like the Sorbonne orators, the vendors imagined future entrepreneurial "projects." Instead of drawing on political connections, however, they hoped to convert their street skills into viable businesses. Romaric, who sold mobile phones, wanted a phone accessories shop, and Samuel, selling perfumes, aspired to be a perfume merchant. The biggest dreamers envisioned global (albeit nebulous) enterprises: for Stephane and Zappin, imports and exports; for Erick, a joint venture company with foreign partners. Serge said, "I want to stay in commerce but at least *grandir* [grow up], be in *grand commerce* [big commerce], you know?" Here, Serge was differentiating "little" informal trades from work in the "big" and adult formal economy. Generally, "commerce," "sales," or the catch-all term "business" resonated with an entrepreneurial ideal that men located in the Anglophone world. Thus Rodrigue believed his experiences hustling petty goods had prepared him exceptionally well to work in the United States, "the El Dorado for us, the African youth." He said, "I already know the American system, I am already adapted to the American system because in America over there, it is *le business*, it is *le boulot* [job]." He explained that he knew all about this because he had watched "*Black* films, American films." Boyz and Germain explained that the United States offered ample opportunities for business because there was less paperwork. This notion of easily facilitated enterprise contrasted sharply with the stifling bureaucracy of the Francophone system, particularly for men who lacked access to "papers." Caught up in arbitrary bureaucracies, deregulation felt indeed like freedom.[9]

Instead of anticipating moves up or away, though, most vendors managed occupational stasis via common scripts that reinterpreted or obscured their daily activities. Much of Abidjan's mobile vending population denied or embellished their débrouille among their social networks. Usually silent about their activities when away from their intersections, if asked they responded vaguely that they "kept themselves busy" or "got by" (*je m'occupe/je me débrouille*): code among the urban informal population to ask no further. Romaric described how he navigated this identity with a romantic partner:

> In the morning you go to work, and you tell her you are going to work. . . . You return at night and you are together, she asks what you do, you

tell her, "Je me débrouille." Je me débrouille, this is more than enough for a girl asking you what you do. Je me débrouille, what is essential is that when she asks me for something, I give it to her. So it is not good to go deeper, because what she asks, really that is what I do.

But there were limits to this ambiguity. As Josué, a born-and-raised Abidjanais Burkinabé, observed, "It is not easy to have a woman and keep her. We are not fonctionnaires." And if you love her, set her free. Samuel recalled a girlfriend who had begun dating an army lieutenant. He had been with her to "build something together, to have a future together." When this better opportunity came her way, chivalrously, he stepped aside:

> Estimating that I was not against her, I wanted what she wanted. I told her that if this guy wanted to marry her, if he could take care of her, then she could go. Because in fact, she came from a poor family. . . . I said, "Well me, I am no big thing you know." Often if I had 1000 FCFA I would give it to her, I could give her 2000 FCFA.

Temporary liaisons, by comparison, kept things simple, and Guillaume explained that if he only wanted sex with a woman, he would tell her he was a police officer. Guy explained that he was "obliged to hide" if he saw an ex-girlfriend on one of the buses where he was selling perfume.

Even among his friends, Romaric said, "no one knows I am here." Despite the cost of daily gbaka rides cutting significantly into earnings, vendors commonly traveled to another quartier to avoid being seen by anyone they knew. Noting how people took vending as an indication of poor character, Arnaud explained, "A garçon must not speak too much about what he does to others.[10] Because there are those who say it is fine, but the day you have a small argument, he will say 'What does he do? He is a vagabond, he sells on the bridge.'" Like Romaric's evasive "Je me débrouille," some vendors limited themselves to the vaguely affirmative description of their "business" without elucidating what this entailed. For example, in addition to contesting his "vagabond" status with the potential profits of his "big merchandise," Arnaud told people he was a commerçant. "You ask me what market I sell in," he elaborated. "I may say in the Treichville market. Because you know, at the intersection where you saw me the other day, there is a market below."

Disputing the entrenched link between work and identity in the Abidjanais imaginary, Romaric asserted, "Your trade, that has nothing to do with who you are." In the crisis economy, men had outlined the contours of selfhood by other means. For example, year-long school stoppages known as années blanches (white years) and the national examination system of concours that, until passed, impeded graduation, permitted out-of-school men to extend to themselves the label of "student." They were simply "waiting to pass the concours." Men who played football for neighborhood teams could say, "I am an aspiring footballer waiting to be selected by a *centre de formation* [training center]." A musician could describe this as a period before his CD hit the market. These imaginaries became alter egos to replace their working identities. "Never in my life," Guy said, would he directly tell a woman what he did. "First, I give her my title of student. . . . After that, I am in business." When Guillaume met a prospective girlfriend at a maquis, he told her he was a footballer—not untrue, as he played for his neighborhood team. If she questioned this, he would describe himself as a "commercial agent."

Remunerative activities were, in short, anonymous pursuits, "public secret[s]" (Newell 2009a, 385) to be replaced by hobbies and aspirations. Work, the vendors asserted, did not define them. The legitimation they found in alternative identities had already been well established: media tropes vindicated marginalized Black masculinity across the Atlantic and deep into Abidjan's periphery.

FIGURE 10.03. Football team in Abobo. Author's photo, Abidjan (2009).

The Social World of the Media Trope

Echoing a popular sentiment among vendors, Fidel, an Ivoirian from the interior, explained that vending had been "imposed" on him. He stated: *"C'est pas pour vivre mais pour survivre"* (It is not to live but to survive). Marc, also Ivoirian from the interior, concurred, elaborating that beyond not being a real job, "It makes us look ridiculous." Jaurès explained that he vended because he had "no solution," and Romaric reasoned that vendors were "obliged to go backwards. You may end up with white hair and still you have not made it." Frustrated with my questions, "Do you have a girlfriend, do you have a mobile phone, do you go out on weekends," Danon stated simply, "All of that depends on les moyens." And Fabrice explained that girlfriends and leisure activities were barred to those who were "not there yet." As vendors, they were only at "the introduction."

Josué, Prospère, and Rodrigue, all Abidjan born and raised, of Burkinabé origins, had been selling newspapers at a prime intersection near the Plateau and Adjamé market for over a decade. They were desperately poor. Josué owned the sole mobile phone among them, but he had not bought new clothes in three years. Only Prospère reported going out on weekends. Their beverage of choice was a caustic 100 FCFA sachet liquor shot that they passed among themselves over the course of our interview. In the same neighborhood lived Patrick, an ex-vendor, footballer, and local pride. Patrick belonged to one of Abidjan's centres de formation, where aspiring footballers went to improve their skills, and ultimately hoped to be selected onto a professional team. A remarkable success story, Patrick had played for a club in Togo before his ailing father drew him back. He had stopped vending or seeking other work years ago, when football had become his primary focus. Although his three-and-a-half-hour daily training regime ended before midday, he explained that he was too tired to do anything else. Unlike Josué, Prospère, and Rodrigue, Patrick depended entirely on family and neighborhood elders to meet his basic needs and for extras like training gear and equipment. Throwing their support behind him, Patrick's community believed that one day he would make them all proud. If he did, it might also mean a handsome return on their investment. Though Patrick inhabited the same spaces and for a time vended alongside Josué, Prospère, and Rodrigue, his potential for iconicity translated into social currency and had significantly enabled him to tap scarce neighborhood resources.

For the typical mobile street vendor, vending was part remunerative activity and part charity, and many fondly recounted the good times when clients, calling them their *bons petits* (good little ones), would slip them some money or check up on them if they were ill. They referred to these clients as *patron* (boss), big brother, or uncle. In these subordinate roles vendors were positioned far from the neighborhood personalities and big men. Still, they were no less susceptible to the human longing to be someone of worth. And in this register, *being* was directly associated with *having*. Exasperated, Thierry declared, "At thirty-two years old . . . I have nothing to say, 'Look, I have worked.' At my age I have nothing of worth." He went on, "It is when you have something you are respected. You have nothing, you have no respect." The social burden of precariousness ranked as high as its financial penalty, and embeddedness in peer networks, either within or external to vending activities, doubly buffered against homelessness or even starvation. But given the few avenues to derive status against the backdrop of highly stigmatized and poorly remunerated débrouilles, and long shut out from opportunities for formal work, vendors sought to distinguish themselves through identities imagined over those realized. Hovering over their hobby-based alter egos was the vague promise of stardom. Imaginary met the pixelated reality of the media trope, invoking observations like those of Modeste about Tupac and R. Kelly: "When I see their music videos, I see the way they live, and that does something for me. It touches my heart."

For men, whose identities are intricately linked to labor and the public sphere, alternative public personas are vital to constructing a dignified self in the absence of a dignified job. The football field and the hip-hop stage were privileged sites for vendors to embody their alter egos. In these worlds of play, they could assert themselves as men of worth, even if this meant performing only for men with equally unmet aspirations.

In neighborhoods poorly connected to main thoroughfares, in dirt fields studded with broken glass and jutting cement and overwhelmed by pools of fetid water in the rainy season, amateur football leagues trained and competed. Players in flimsy sandals kicked footballs on these hazardous surfaces, while wandering goats and manual laborers pushing heavy carts across the field unceremoniously arrested their play. These neighborhood teams represented the lowest tier of a vertical organization of Abidjan's football clubs. As feeder clubs, they bumped their best up to higher-division leagues, but the vast majority could expect to remain at this base level indefinitely.

Only in the elite divisions did team membership entail paid uniforms, paid transport, and facilities. Otherwise, it was up to the captain or coach to garner local sponsors to cover a portion of these costs. In lieu of uniforms, players competed in those of their favorite professional teams, UNICEF jerseys with the Barcelona emblem, Samsung jerseys with the Chelsea emblem. They rented this apparel for 2500 FCFA per match, or 200 FCFA per player. At home matches players purchased their own water and paid a gendarme 500 to 1000 FCFA to lease the field. For away matches each player contributed 1000 FCFA for transportation, water, and uniforms, with any leftover money going toward drinks afterward. The neighborhood community heavily supported these activities.

FIGURE 10.04.   Gesco vendors play a weekend match of football in Yopougon. Author's photo, Abidjan (2009).

FIGURE 10.05.   Workers interrupt the football match. Author's photo, Abidjan (2009).

Better-endowed upper-division clubs organized tournaments for which they selected two of the best neighborhood team players and perhaps five additional men from winning teams to train at their camp. These men hoped to be selected to the national league. Scouts could also approach promising young talent, but more often determined men attended annual tryouts hoping to impress a centre de formation and affiliate with a top-tier league. Tryouts were unpaid, and players hustled to cover basic expenses.

As with professional sports the world over, hope—to make it into the Ivoirian or another West African league, perhaps even a European team—eclipsed reality. Men in the lowest-division teams were often in their late twenties and early thirties, their moment long passed. But hope sprang eternal. With anticipatory logic Patrick reasoned, "Normally in football, experts say that at thirty years old you can no longer play. But you never know when your chance will come. One sees people at thirty, thirty-one years old—that is when they signed their professional contract. So we play, we train." He described the legendary Koutouan, a friend who had sold newspapers and went on to play professionally in the United Arab Emirates, insisting, "It is not rare." For others, local status was a sufficient reward. The entire neighborhood knew these players, and local big men watched the matches. Women knew who they were too, and friends recalled with obvious pride the year that so-and-so made it to the annual training tryouts. Within their social networks, they had already joined football lore.

Maquis sociability emphasized distinction.[11] Revelers came dressed in their finest attire. Fancier maquis featured large mirrors on the dance floor so men—there were always more men than women—could watch themselves dance, practice their expressions, and admire their style. Talented young men approached tables and danced for money. Fashionable men danced the *logobi,* a performance of showing off the logos on one's clothing, for which the audience rewarded him as a travailleur—with money (Newell 2012, 4). DJs interrupted songs to give paid shout-outs or to advertise that they gave paid shout-outs. There were myriad other opportunities to demonstrate *being* through *having.* Bottles accumulated on the table over the course of the night as the display of a party's wealth, and servers knew to never clear a table until the group had departed. Patrons' mobile phones were displayed next to the empty bottles. Those with the least to spend left their 100 FCFA packets of *lotus* (Lotus brand facial tissues) on the table. In the roped-off VIP sections, elite clients reclined on leather sofas with their drinks, usually Heinekens chilled in ice buckets. Here, the standard one-liter drogbas and other local beers were not available for purchase. In every party the man with the greatest means picked up the tab. As the group's big man, he was referred to honorifically as a travailleur or *responsable* (authority figure).

On special occasions collectives of artists rented maquis for live-music shows, with the majority of spectators also musicians themselves. There, men evinced their artist personas, wearing, for coupé décalé, fitted pants, polo shirts, and fine leather shoes, and for hip-hop, oversized shirts, sagging pants, and sneakers. The Abidjan Rap Tour on Yopougon's rue Princesse was the largest annual hip-hop show, attracting sixty groups in 2009. Musicians regularly put on smaller shows in their neighborhood maquis or, less frequently, in concert halls. At one hip-hop show put on by Bizness Productions, the organizers decorated the space with English phrases, money insignia, and homages to Blackness. A large dollar bill hung center stage, flanked on one side by painted likenesses of Barack Obama, Tupac, and a generic Black man in a Lakers jersey with the caption "City Boy"; on the other side, Bob Marley and Haile Selassie. The MC called himself Black Poison. At another show put on by Ghetto Productions, the MC wore a shirt adorned with diamonds and dollar signs. Performers interspersed English words in their rap and flashed gang signs to audience cheers. Groups recycled the same song for years, their verses long familiar to the other aspiring talents who sang the wittiest refrains in unison. When not performing themselves, members of the audience crowded onto the stage as back-up dancers. And few women were in sight. This was a circumscribed, homosocial space where male peers constituted a "most important audience" (Smith 2017, 16). Among the hip-hop artists, one woman made the performance circuit, and at shows I observed a five-to-one ratio of male to female audience members. At the Abidjan Rap Tour, the crowd of approximately two hundred drew eight women. These were garçons performing for garçons.

FIGURE 10.06. Abidjan Rap Tour, Yopougon. Author's photo, Abidjan (2009).

Nearing the end of my fieldwork, I recorded a song with my research assistants, Tino and MC, and Busta, a former vendor. MC rapped in French, and Tino rapped in French and the Gouro dialect from his natal village in western Côte d'Ivoire. Busta spoke some English so I wrote a few lines for him to rap, followed by my own part. Busta had given up vending for the more lucrative trade of pirating music with his brother, and my lyrics were based around the contradiction of pirating while also producing:

> BUSTA: I rob the high seas of the music industry.
> GROUP: *He's a pirate!*
> BUSTA: See the hypocrisy of what I'm trying to be.
> GROUP: *He's a pirate!*
> BUSTA: All these artists like me, we're drowning in the seas.
> GROUP: *He's a pirate!*
> JORDANNA: With one hand he's trying to make it / But the other's gotta take it / It's a rat race that he's playing / Gives all he got so he can stay in / But he's barely even hanging / That's the reason why he's singing.
> GROUP: *I'm a pirate!*
> JORDANNA: He don't wanna be no thief / He don't wanna be no pirate / He just wanna make his music / And he wants you all to buy it.
> GROUP: *I'm a pirate!*
> JORDANNA: But there's a reason and a rhyme / To his nasty little crime / What'll make him do his time / Is his struggle to survive.
> GROUP: *I'm a pirate!*[12]

In homage to the precarious informal activities they had been helping me document, we called the song "Je me bat pour mon avenir" (I fight for my future). Doug MC, a clothing vendor with a permanent stall near Plateau and a successful local musician who had taken Tino and MC under his wing, introduced us to a nondescript studio in Yopougon's "Maroc" neighborhood. The studio had recorded an impressive number of Abidjan's reggae talent, and the dingy walls were arrayed with signed photographs of esteemed homegrown artists. We recorded this and another song at 10,000 FCFA each. It was a one-night rush job that the studio's two-man team nonetheless completed with talent and a sound melodic ear. In the month leading up to recording, we had met perhaps five times to rehearse.

I had not thought much of the experience; in my opinion we had put in minimal effort and for a professional recording it all happened very quickly, with few stylistic or directional interventions. But it was a major accomplishment for them. Near tears, Busta repeated several times that he was finally seeing his efforts realized. Here was a man who had come to expect failure in his life: familial abandonment after his mother's death, an aborted education after fleeing the rebel capital of Bouaké at the start of civil war, a sporadic and unfulfilling work history, and always total state neglect. Tino and MC were similarly inflated with pride, and when a police officer stopped our taxi late in the night as they chaperoned me home, MC reported with confidence, "We just came from a recording. We are artists. Now we are going to Cocody." For men like Tino, MC, and Busta, this was a fantastical sequence of statements. While police encounters tended to cause trouble for Tino and MC, this one ended with the officer's eagerly asking for a shout-out at their next show. That night they had become their alter egos. For weeks after they spoke incessantly about dropping off our CD at Radio Télévision Ivoirienne, confident that they would be Abidjan's newest sensation.

Having a CD with their voices on it gained Tino, MC, and Busta entrée into the world of the media trope. Here they had commodifiable talent. Moreover, they had left a literal and metaphorical record of their existence in the otherwise mundane anonymity of which lack—of identification papers, of attention, of recognition—was standard.

To my question, "Why do you like hip-hop?" Yves responded, "Because I like what Americans do. . . . It is *le business*, you see." For twenty-three-year-old barber, vendor, and popular Abobo musician Commandant Zappin, who as a young boy seeing that rappers were Black like him and resolving, "We were the same," hip-hop and business were indeed mutually reinforcing.

In the late 1990s Zappin founded the Academy Rap Revolution in an area of Abobo that surrounded the 51/52 SOTRA bus terminus.[13] A forty-three-member, majority-male organization, the academy put on rap shows while also teaching trades, providing job placement, educating neighborhood youths in basic writing and sex and health education, disbursing business loans, providing emergency funds, and implementing public works. The academy's sphere of influence included a maquis where they held performances, a recording studio, a road rehabilitation project, and designated class time in the local school. As president, Zappin, along with eight "counselors," ran the academy. He referred to the academy's inner circle as "VIP." Members met regularly and paid monthly dues. Most were in their mid-twenties and ranged in age from late teens to thirties. All were unmarried, and a few had children. Fifteen commerçants, including mobile street vendors, were formally affiliated with the academy and returned five percent of their earnings to the association. Three barbershops were academy-owned and fully reinvested their profits into the academy and its businesses; affiliate barbershops paid out 30 percent of their earnings. Affiliate mechanics contributed 15 percent of their earnings.

They calculated these levies according to the profitability of the trade. Academy loans typically amounted to 60,000 FCFA for equipment or 100,000 FCFA for rent. Finally, music was also a money-making endeavor. In addition to the profits generated at academy-sponsored shows, its leadership doubled as managers, booking musicians for local functions for which performers returned 40 percent of the earnings. Zappin boasted that the academy model had been taken up in a number of neighborhoods in Abidjan and even in the Ivoirian interior.

On a typical workday Zappin cut hair from 6 to 9 a.m., vended from 10 a.m. to 6 p.m., and then returned to his barbershop until 10 p.m. His popularity supported his business activities, with fellow musicians doubling as clients and people in the neighborhood exclusively patronizing academy shops. Because he knew his clients socially, he trusted selling to them on credit and was therefore able to generate a somewhat steady income. He explained, "When I rap, people come to buy. It is a network. My friends, my fans come to see me, to buy things from me, they come to cut their hair at my barbershop. So with my music, I gain." The academy had even begun negotiations to vend in front of the Abobo mayor's office. This move, if successful, would have challenged charges of illegality in mobile street vending.

Zappin's three-man hip-hop group Eastwave, all academy members, vended along Abobo's main thoroughfare. Two at a time, one band member walked along the highway medium, beckoning clients with a loudspeaker and sample merchandise while another manned the stock they had set out on a tarp. They purchased shirts in bulk from Ghana and sold them for a "negotiable 1500 FCFA." The band brought in enough to make monthly 50,000 FCFA contributions, with which they had purchased a small recording studio with a computer, recording equipment, and a soundproofing room.

By supporting local musicians, creating neighborhood entrepreneurial ventures, and providing services to the community, Zappin had made himself a neighborhood big man. He gave free haircuts, otherwise 200 FCFA, to friends and young neighborhood men. Having "adopted" two younger boys whom he regularly fed and clothed, Zappin explained, "Here in my home, my neighborhood, I have a little family that I take care of." Zappin dreamed of becoming a famous musician abroad and returning to build houses and orphanages in Africa like Ivoirian reggae star Tiken Jah Fakoly.

In contrast to the denigrated terrain of the débrouille, football fields, maquis, hip-hop stages, and recording studios emerged as pathways to self-worth and an imagined elsewhere. They constituted a *"prestige economy, which stabilizes youth and offers new currencies to trade accomplishment, success, personhood and social adulthood"* (Fuh 2012, 504, emphasis in

FIGURE 10.07.   Zappin at his Prestige Coiffure. Author's photo, Abidjan (2009).

original). Talent on these platforms provided local renown and promises well beyond. But only some vendors inhabited these spaces. Many more scoffed at the idea of having the time or money for such revelries. In exceptional cases like Zappin's, worlds of play buttressed their earnings potential. More frequently, however, it led to a deficit, with the investment that men put into these ephemeral performances constituting a resolve that their earnings were just weekend money.

Weekend Money

Vendors, as Thierry stated previously, described their limited earnings as weekend money, only enough to entertain themselves. In other words, if they did not have what they considered real work, then what they took home was not real money. And play money could not make of them real men: husbands supporting their wives and children. The difference demarcated the boundary between a wife and a girlfriend, as Samuel explained:

> No, ha! To marry you must have les moyens, in fact it is for this reason that a man searches for a better tomorrow. . . . Because imagine, currently I have a problem paying rent. I marry a woman, I have children and daily expenses, maybe per day it is 2000 FCFA for food so at the end of the month it is how much, 60,000 FCFA. Well, then you have to pay the house, the power and the water. For all that you must at least have a monthly income. . . . You must make at least 150,000 FCFA, at least 160,000 or even 200,000 FCFA and then on top of that you have insurance, you have social security, if your child is sick, yeah, you can go with him to a hospital or at present, take your social contract card to get a discount.

But I probed, "You already have a daughter?" He acknowledged that he did. "It is not the same thing?" I inquired. He insisted unequivocally that it was not:

> No, it is not the same thing. It is not. If it was the same thing, I would be happy with that, huh? I say no, in every way it is not the same thing, it is not the same thing even. It is very, very different. It is very, very different. Because me, I see what I have accomplished. The reality is there. . . . I want it different, I want to have a family like we think about families: you are in your home, the children are there, your wife is there.

Samuel was emphatic that his life circumstances prohibited him from achieving an otherwise normative husband-breadwinner role. Informal workers, in short, begot illegitimate children. In the absence of women and at the expense of the children they had, the vendors strengthened ties among themselves and others in homosocial networks via daily practices of consumer citizenship.

These were investments in sociality that, operating within an unreliable and insufficient informal economy, provided an important safety net (Newell 2012). Conspicuous consumption could moreover regenerate men's business endeavors as "the operations of markets, commerce, and entrepreneurship depend more on the management of social relationships than they do on the specificities of goods and services" (Simone 2010, 228–29). The blurring of work and play, earning and spending, produced an Abidjanais lexicon designating such efforts at conspicuous consumption as "travail" unto itself (Kohlhagen 2005–2006, 98).

Having determined that their earnings were superfluous, the vendors reported spending superfluously even when they could not make rent. Yves, who had migrated to Abidjan from the Ivoirian interior as a small child, explained that it was "obligatory" in Abidjan for a man to look good on a night out. His remarks were representative of how vendors rationed (and rationalized) their expenses.

> JORDANNA: How much do you pay in rent each month?
> YVES: 10,000 [FCFA].
> JORDANNA: And your food expenses?
> YVES: Well, the expenses are too much for me. Often I cannot even pay rent and I have to explain to the landlord ...
> JORDANNA: You buy clothes?
> YVES: Yes, yes, that is normal. It is normal, because when you are a man ... you must be comfortable, you must be well dressed, you know?
> JORDANNA: How much do you spend on clothes each month?
> YVES: Me, well, it is every two months, around. Two or three months, I may spend 20,000 FCFA on clothes.

Each year, Guillaume bought one pair of fashionable shoes for about 50,000 FCFA and several other wardrobe pieces worth approximately 20,000 FCFA. He split his 35,000 FCFA rent with Samuel, but often they were unable to pay until the end of the month, living as they did "day to day." Regardless, Samuel argued that as men they had "biological, sentimental, and social needs" that they "must fulfill." He continued, "Everyone enjoys a little pleasure. I, for example, have a Sony Ericsson mobile phone." Jaurès, who had not paid his rent for some months, had in the past two years saved enough to purchase a 45,000 FCFA television and a 65,000 FCFA mobile phone. When I asked, "What is the nicest thing you have in your closet at home?" he replied incredulously, "At home, in my closet? Ha! A sack. I have no closet, I have a sack."

In the Black section of the Adjamé market for used and stolen mobile phones, hundreds of men lined up single file on either side of the principal thoroughfare, flashing phones at passersby. Some whispered, hissed, or called out; some gestured with silent appeals; and others trailed a few paces, preemptively bargaining down their starting price. These phone hawkers ranged in age and dress, from barely teens with grubby tees and anxious eyes to handsomely dressed, self-aware twenty- and thirty-somethings to tired-looking men past their prime dressed in respectable pagne shirts and trousers. With prices typically starting at 5000 FCFA, they offered relics alongside bona fide smartphones equipped with the latest technology. If supply indicated anything about demand, Abidjan's market for mobile phones was ringing off the hook.

When I met Calice, a hard-up juice vendor from the interior, the headphones in his ears resembled an iPhone advertisement. It was only a look: his device had been out of commission for some time and he could not afford a new one. The accessory, however, had cost him 27,000 FCFA up front, and he was paying the rest of its 40,000 FCFA cost in installments. Particularly popular expenditures in the Abidjanais budget, the ubiquity and variety of mobile phones were commensurate with their place along the urban status hierarchy. Jaurès explained, "I love expensive phones, you know, serious phones. Because once you have this, people respect you." Of whether he wanted to upgrade his 5000 FCFA mobile phone, Erick, from the interior, remarked, "Of course I want to change. I am a human being. Every person is ambitious." Across the city billboards for the largest phone companies imitated music video stills, featuring hip men accessorized by doting divas—and a phone. On Abidjan's dating circuit, it was standard practice for men to buy their girlfriend a phone and keep it topped up with credit.[14]

Sold at a full range of prices, mobile phones were generally accessible, even among deeply peripheral populations whose use was more symbolic than functional. Phones defined the realm of attainable consumerism for poor men; on only three occasions did I come across vendors without them. And the more the better: there was nothing strange about carrying around two or three phones.[15] Even cheap phones with limited capabilities could offer the veneer of bling, a fact not lost on marketers who embellished basic models with shiny metallic faceplates and other eye-catching features.

Mobile phones countered the anonymity of peripheral life. A name and phone number, and sometimes only a phone number, made for common graffiti around Abidjan and could be found scrawled on street-side stalls, in the backs of taxis and on maquis tables, all with the distant hope that someone, somewhere, was looking for a good time. Phone numbers were one of the few forms of documentation for populations whose lives were lived informally: unregistered, undocumented, unseen. Furthermore, one's contacts nodded to local and distant networks. Boasting about his friendship with an Ivoirian artist whose New York City performance was featured in a magazine he was showing me, for example, Doug MC evidenced his connection by pulling up the man's US number on his phone.

While phones made fine decoration, as a device to listen to music, and to receive calls—receiving calls was free—downtrodden Abidjanais seldom used their phones to make calls. Instead, they used cabines, credit recharge stands comprised of a small wooden bench and table and typically manned by a young man or woman with a mobile phone and bulk credit from all the networks.[16] Credit was available for up to 100,000 FCFA, and the more that was purchased at once, the more *bonus*, or free credit, the buyer received. If needing to speak but unwilling or unable to pay for the call, it was common to either ring and immediately hang up, or to "beep" someone: send a free automatic text call-back request. Credit could also be sent from cabines. The politics of who called whom betrayed the hierarchy between caller and called, the former asserting over the latter dominance and a social debt.

Thinking themselves "losers in a world of winners," marginal men in Abidjan "changed camp through appearance" (De Latour 2001, 154). Ultimately, however, weekend money was a self-fulfilling prophecy. Vendors typically spent 500 to 1000 FCFA on food a day, and their rents ranged between 7500 to 15,000 FCFA. Yet only two reported spending less than 5000 FCFA on a phone, and only the most destitute vendors described paying less than 3000 FCFA for an article of clothing. Much more was at stake in their consumer practices, however: inward-facing, they risked personal dignity; outward-facing, they contended for positions in social networks whose returns were more lasting than a meal and more meaningful than a timely rent payment.

For those bound to a crisis Abidjan, consumption was a "partial migration," and located modernity "in places, objects, and people, rather than a state of development" (Newell 2012, 178). Consumer identities approximated mass-media icons and signaled participation in the global economy. They embodied a "material culture of success" that drew on cultural resources such as music videos, with their "abundant references to money, appearance, and extravagance" (Kohlhagen 2005–2006, 92, 95). In doing so, consumer identities situated peripheral Abidjanais men within the transnational Black urban imaginary.

Vendors imagined themselves not as recuperated évolués in a postcrisis Abidjan, but as global Black men in the extraterritorial space of the media trope. Embodied and performative, expressions of Blackness supplanted narratives of breadwinning while remaining firmly committed to a manhood premised on money. Clinging to flattened, glorified, and malleable tropes in the likenesses of men who had themselves risen above the crowd, the vendors sought recognition among their downtrodden equals in a maquis or on the football field. These imaginaries were at once global and wholly Abidjanais. Through them, men reclaimed and affirmed their otherness within the hegemonic counternarrative of racial capitalism.

THE VISUAL TERRAIN OF BLACKNESS

In figure 11.01, a bare-chested Tupac Shakur, peering from the open door of Salon VIP (VIP Barbershop), beckons passersby in for a haircut. No more than a shack, the designation "VIP" might appear bold. Yet it typified the way Abidjanais appropriated what it meant to be a "very important person." Initially signaling exclusive membership, the expression grew popular in hip-hop parlance before finding its way to Abidjan's streets. There, far from denoting elite perks, a select clientele, or high-end services, the widely used claim to be VIP could refer to a circle of friends, a hole-in-the-wall maquis, or as seen here, a barbershop.

Tupac, like the acronym "VIP," registered as a visual vernacular in the public spaces of the urban periphery. Just as a barbershop shack proclaimed itself VIP, Tupac was simultaneously outstanding and symbolized the Black everyman. Fame and an early death transformed the short life of this American rapper from a generation whose moment had since passed into an icon traversing time and space. In Abidjan, where crisis resulted in social death for men who lacked the means to call themselves men, Tupac's literal death at the age of twenty-five located him in the shared space of their eternal youth. He now inhabited the realm of representation, one in which the beholder revived him with meaning. As a Black man whose promise was cut short, Tupac evoked a tragic recognition.

In the realm of representations, where identities are empty vessels until projected with meaning, Tupac signified the contradictory potential of Black popular culture: in coming to represent "the dominant form of global culture, so it is at the same time the scene, par excellence, of commodification" (Hall 1993, 108).

FIGURE 11.01.   "Salon VIP" barbershop. Author's photo, Abidjan (2009).

Thus captured, Tupac's image-life entered "circuits of power and capital . . . where control over narratives and representations passes into the hands of established cultural bureaucracies" (108). The social protest he invoked in his music and life were relegated to one of several possible meanings, to be used or discarded at will.[1] On the façade of the barbershop in figure 11.02, the combination of "2Pac" and American flags squarely associates Tupac with global hegemony. On the sign of the barbershop "Garba 50" (figure 11.03), Tupac's image is rendered with garba, a popular local dish of fish served with attiéké, commonly ridiculed as cheap, unclean, and fit for a migrant underclass.

Representations were narrative devices that allowed marginal Abidjanais men to renegotiate the established meanings that otherwise defined them. In the postcolony, the category of youth, or la jeunesse, placed marginal men, unemployed and unmarriageable, into "a social category and a problematic condition" (Weiss 2009, 237). In the context of la crise, la jeunesse was an extended purgatory encompassing the bulk of a man's life. Subverting the colonial order that designated an African man a garçon (boy), Abidjanais vernacular appropriated "garçon" to imply mastery of the street. To say admiringly "garçon" was to assert a counternarrative for men unable to assume established notions of adulthood,

FIGURE 11.02. 2pac and the American flag on a barbershop. Author's photo, Abidjan (2009).

FIGURE 11.03. Depiction of Tupac on "Garba 50" barbershop sign. Author's photo, Abidjan (2009).

elder, or big-man status within their networks. A garçon achieved social success absent the credentials of évolué masculinity.

Media tropes and their consumer worlds risked becoming another "poignant measure of the distance between dream and fulfillment, between desire and impossibility, between centres of great wealth and peripheries of crushing poverty" (Comaroff and Comaroff 2005, 27). But by way of their shared Blackness, Abidjanais men embraced these tropes as representations of likeness. In doing so, they blurred the space between dream and fulfillment, periphery and center, and boys and men. In this cosmology of meaning, the realm of representation emboldened "youthful imaginations" (27), transforming marginal men into active global agents: a bottom billion consumer class. In the ever-present context of crushing poverty, it predicated dignity on visible consumerism rather than the roles and responsibilities attributed to productive identities, thereby reframing the expression of manhood in the global economy. Indicators of masculine worth moved from productive identities to consumer acts of possession and transaction.

"Jeunesse Coiffure" in figure 11.04 depicts American musician Usher. Claiming Usher as a fellow youth established an oppositional space, apropos the

FIGURE 11.04. Usher, an American R&B musician, on a sign for the "Jeunesse Coiffure" barbershop. Author's photo, Abidjan (2009).

colonial paradigm. Shared Blackness resignified manhood and made it accessible for those who, within the dominant socioeconomic purview, remained boys.

Global, Black, and Male

As expressions of "hip-hop cosmopolitanism," media tropes were "undergirded by desires for physical, social, and economic mobility" (Neal 2013b, 37). The qualities of being global, Black, and male packaged as means and ends, media tropes imagined the "homeboy" as mobility personified, a fundamental "shift of the stereotype of black maleness from the margin to the center" (Diawara 1998, 244). Exhibiting livelihoods and lifestyles that contested the breadwinning man, tropes were models of globally successful Black men who had defined their own terms of belonging. In the barbershop sign in figure 11.05, this homeboy is "international" and "heading for the top."

The colonial project left deep connections between identities and rights in the city (Ferguson 2006). For Black men, expressions of citizenship, manhood, and "what it means to be a full human being" were "deeply intertwined" (Morrell and Ouzgane 2005, 12). Asserting that the categories of "native" and "man" were fundamentally incompatible (Brown, C. 2003, 157), the colonial lexicon defined évolué identity as a fundamental standard of worth, and this standard has persisted in

FIGURE 11.05.   A homeboy. Author's photo, Abidjan (2009).

postcolonial Abidjan. Media tropes depicting Black men as full participants in the global economy with alternative approaches to an urban lifestyle were responding to ongoing expressions of racial capitalist hegemony. The celebration of Blackness elsewhere was also a celebration of Abidjanais men's self-worth.

Rejecting indigenous masculinities that might call to mind "traditional" or village ways, an oft-repeated theme in Abidjan was that a man was measured by his suit, air-conditioned office, and chauffeured vehicle. While never a reality for the majority, Abidjanais juxtaposed this gendered ideal of work to the women and migrants who dominated the informal economy and were caricatured as poor adaptations to urban social mores. The public presence of media tropes responded to these stereotypes, recovering the masculine worth of the débrouilleur. They connected marginal men to a center of global Black popular culture, through which manhood was expressed as a set of consumer choices.

The world of the media trope enlivened the everyday mundanity of the urban periphery, when business hours or late-night trysts did not fill otherwise empty time. They encoded spaces and practices as masculine and provided visibility and purpose to men without work or wives. These meanings configured the status hierarchies of marginal Abidjanais men, three of which I explore in this chapter. In the first, the body was a critical site of representation, and sartorial performances were used to navigate social hierarchies and VIP imaginaries. In the next, distinctly Abidjanais iterations of the Italian fashion brand Dolce & Gabbana entangled with coupé décalé legend Douk Saga to symbolize wealth and visibility. Finally, media tropes of global celebrities and local boys made good adorned barbershop signs and gbakas as constant invocations of the alter egos of marginal men.

Embodied Terrains

> The wearing of the uniform of the "nigga" conveys an authenticity to the act of consuming said "nigga" that simply listening to *his* music would never convey.
>
> —Mark Anthony Neal, *Looking for Leroy*

When Thierry boasted to me that an "Anglophone" had once confused him for an American because of his hip-hop attire, he was engaging a popular strategy that, by "wearing U.S. clothing, urban Ivoirians transformed themselves into more potent social beings" (Newell 2012, 178). The body in particular figured among sparse terrain for Abidjanais men to contest their marginalization, and in the absence of dignifying work, commodity subjectivities doubled as markers of manhood. Minimal consumption capacities—a beer here, a pair of secondhand sneakers there—signaled economic agency and membership in a world imagined by mass-advertising campaigns. Thus embodied, these collective forms of "aspirational consumption and [their] attendant politics of appearances [could] be grasped as part of a wider problem of participation" (Weiss 2009, 169). Homegrown and imported, they became self-referential devices, making visible men in Abidjan as throughout the Black Atlantic. Embodiment, in short, transformed commodified representations of Blackness into registers of belonging. In figure 11.06, Busta poses in his maquis best: a secondhand Michael Jordan sweatsuit.

FIGURE 11.06. Busta with Michael Jordan sweatsuit. Author's photo, Abidjan (2009).

On an evening out on Yopougon's rue Princesse, Guillaume modeled for our party what he described as his "designer Cacoste" pants, pointing to a small alligator just below the misspelled brand. Shortly thereafter, a man from an adjacent table spilled beer on them. As he disappeared to the toilets to rinse out the stain, Guillaume complained furiously that his "suit" had been ruined. Guillaume's pants were a poor Lacoste imitation, but the nod to luxury insignia accorded value to an otherwise unremarkable article of clothing. Along with European counterfeit labels, designs that featured English-language inscriptions, US currency, and Americana figured prominently in local tastes to the point that they commanded higher prices on the secondhand market. Value to be worn and sold, Thierry explained, "What is sure is that when you sell American things, it works."

FIGURE 11.07.   Kelly in Money House Rich shirt. Author's photo, Abidjan (2009).

Attention to fashion was one of few ways for a man to distinguish himself in a crowd of débrouilleurs. Gueï, the best-dressed vendor at an intersection in Riviéra, boasted, "People in my neighborhood, they know me, they appreciate me, because I have style." And Stephane stated, "Man is defined by his person, yeah? When you saw me just now, what did you take with you? It was my style." Dressing beyond the limitations of remunerative activities was a matter of self-respect and elaborately managed in the public performance of the "bluff" (Newell 2012). Aiming to level a profoundly unequal social landscape, these counterfeit identities demanded "symbolic mastery of a culture from which [the *bluffeur* was] excluded, a proof of potential membership" (Newell 2009a, 163). Romaric explained, "Even if you are a shoe shiner, if you wash cars, you are whatever, when you go out at night you are well dressed, you are appreciated by the girls." In figure 11.08, Kelly, a shoe vendor in Adjamé's Black, holds up his favorite sneaker covered in dollar signs. He proudly declared, "Each shoe has its value."

Looking the part is the next best thing to being it. Consumerism is "the invisible hand, or the Gucci-gloved fist, that animates the political impulses, the material imperatives, and the social forms" of contemporary capitalism (Comaroff and Comaroff 2001, 4). The embodied and consuming terrain of Blackness was a redemptive force for men who lacked productive capacities and raised to the surface deep layers of signification in the long crisis induced by racial capitalism. The initial

FIGURE 11.08.   Kelly holding up dollar bills shoe. Author's photo, Abidjan (2009).

promise of wage labor among young African men was unprecedented autonomy from their elders as agential subjects of the cash economy. Yet remaining out of reach, the mediating role of the wage in social life condemns this demographic of youth to stasis. Becoming "actors-through-consumption," marginal Abidjanais men reframed the wage labor paradigm, buying "into mainstream interests at the same time as they contested them" (Comaroff and Comaroff 2005, 25). They articulated a "politics of style" that marked "the predicament" of men throughout the Black Atlantic, men who were "would-be subversaries in advanced capitalist contexts [struggling] to seize control of commodified signs and practices" (25).

For Tino and MC, seizing control of the commodity form provided distinction in their neighborhood, and they used this to their advantage as vendors

FIGURE 11.09. MC Black wearing a Black Power jersey and ring. Author's photo, Abidjan (2009).

and musicians. For example, their local reputations as the "hip-hop" vendors singled them out among potential customers, a slight advantage to counter the anonymizing prevalence of petty street trade. As musicians, their complementary jerseys and baggy pants were recognizable markers of belonging within Abidjan's community of aspiring hip-hop artists. Tino and MC variously played with references to the United States, Jamaica, and Brazil as key sites in the global lexicon of Blackness, unapologetically remixing rebellion with consumer excess.

At once personal and public, the body adorned is a terrain of representation. The repudiation of Black bodily autonomy in its incorporation in racial capitalism amplified the public nature and political significance of the body as a representational site. In the economy of la crise, bodily autonomy is secured while the means to nourish or embellish that body remains precarious. Reacting to these palimpsests of racialized dispossession, denigration, and denial, representation is a political act. As representational repertoires unfolded in a dialectical struggle of negation and affirmation, the generative potential of consumer citizenship and commodity subjectivity rendered Blackness a site of ambiguous alterity.

Who the Hell Is D&G?

While civil war erupted in Côte d'Ivoire, Douk Saga and his collective of Ivoirian DJs known as La Jet Set ivoirienne were creating the music and dance style of coupé décalé in Parisian nightclubs. An exemplary commodity subject, "President" Douk Saga literally performed money. In what became known as *travaillement* (working), he globalized the local practice of audiences tossing money at artists on stage to express their admiration, and he in turn threw money at his fans (Kohlhagen 2005–2006, Newell 2019). In the music video for perhaps his biggest hit, "Sagacité," Douk Saga distributes 100€ notes to porters and white women at the Prince de Galles Hotel off the Champs-Élysées. Shots of him on a shopping spree at Versace and Dolce & Gabbana are interspersed with dancing in clubs and in front of the Eiffel Tower. Douk Saga's white patrons and his consumption of elite French spaces are taunting reversals of the global order (see also Kohlhagen 2005–2006).

After triumphing in the Parisian circuit, coupé décalé returned to Abidjan and spread across West and Central Africa.[2] It is an art that insists, in its origins and message, on the essential integration of Paris and Abidjan (Kohlhagen 2005–2006). Mobility being both the vehicle and the measure of success, the transcontinental passage and the wealth it accrued enabled the coupé décalé artist to overcome otherwise crushing social constraints (98).

FIGURE 11.10.   Douk Saga gbaka. Author's photo, Abidjan (2009).

His journey implied mastery not only of *ailleurs* (elsewhere), but also within Abidjan's social networks, where he established his superiority through lavish displays and redistributed fortunes (102). Coupé décalé reflected the slippage between work and consumption as it was performed and lived (Kohlhagen 2005–2006).

Success for Douk Saga and his fellow Ivoirian musicians signaled an African conquest of the metropole that used no diaspora referent to mediate its cultural flow.[3] Coupé décalé thus demonstrated that representational repertoires matter for their visibility and validation far more than for their point of origin—as signifiers of power over place, even as the two are frequently fused. Indeed, homegrown media icons have achieved a level of pride and intimacy among their Ivoirian publics that surpasses the glorified yet flattened diaspora tropes circulating through the Black Atlantic. The latter's ubiquity was a consequence of being seen and recognized on a global platform, operating within the metropole/colony history that negated French West Africans while extolling Black Americans. It was not, however, definitive.

FIGURE 11.11.   Who the hell is D&G? Author's photo, Abidjan (2009).

Italian designer Dolce & Gabbana was reportedly Douk Saga's favorite brand, an association that made the label a pervasive sighting on Abidjan's streets. D&G counterfeits appeared on under- and outerwear, footwear, and jewelry, and as a motif on traditional fabric. It figured in the names of shops, bars, clubs, and gbakas, prompting the question on this man's shirt (figure 11.11), "Who the hell is D&G?"

L'hommage à l'homme: Barbershops and Gbakas

> *Moi, j'habite en la banlieue* [Me, I live on the outskirts]
> *Je suis aux Six Plateaux* [I am in Six Plateau]
> *Tous les gens de là-bas* [Everyone from there]

Se déplacent en gbaka [Travels in the gbaka]
Les gbakas d'Abidjan [The gbakas of Abidjan]
Arrangent bien des gens [Help people out a lot]
En tout cas moi, Daouda [In any case me, Daouda]
Je prends souvent le gbaka [I often take the gbaka]

—Daouda le Sentimental, "Les gbakas d'Abidjan"[4]

In the busy intersections of the quartiers populaires, traffic-congesting blunders are met with a chorus of passersby posing the facetious question, *Tu connais pas Abidjan?* (Don't you know Abidjan?). Knowing Abidjan is knowing how to navigate those spaces excluded from the city of the colon, where rules are not written in clear signage but understood collectively through the trials and errors of time and experience earned on the streets. The gbaka is what only those who really *know* Abidjan would hazard driving.

In a mix of French and Nouchi, Ivoirian musician Daouda le Sentimental's popular 1976 song "Les gbakas d'Abidjan" doubles as a social map of the quartiers populaires—"Adjamé marché, Abobo la guerre [war], Yopougon la bagarre [fight]." Beginning by invoking "Six Plateaux," a parodic contrast to the elite neighborhoods of Plateau and Deux Plateaux, "Les gbakas d'Abidjan" pays homage to a practice that emerged, essential, yet in perpetual shadow to what constituted the Paris of West Africa. On the album cover Daouda drives a gbaka with one hand on the wheel and the other hanging his guitar out the window. Legs and arms with no identifiable owner protrude from the vehicle's rear doors. A passenger rides on the roof atop luggage and baskets of food. The windshield is cracked, and smoke rises from the engine. Exaggerating the unruly nature of gbaka transportation, this is a depiction of Daouda, singer and driver, coolly taking charge.

Daouda le Sentimental's "Les gbakas d'Abidjan" fêted a symbol of Abidjan that the state was working hard to erase. Celebrating this democratic form of transportation, the song came a year before the city (ineffectively) banned gbakas in favor of a fleet of "*taxis-bagages*" administered by the public transportation company SOTRA (Fraternité Matin 1978). In *Abidjan Métropole Moderne*, the 1978 special issue of Abidjan's daily newspaper, the authors relayed, "Of the abolition of Gbakas, all of Abidjan is in a fuss because these small, rickety buses, ragged looking, lacking suspensions and often lacking insurance, crumbling under the weight of luggage and passengers, rendered proud services" (102). Yet, they surmise, "Abidjan chose progress and modernism, and to replace the 300 folkloric gbakas who rolled day and night in the capital" (102). These dueling portrayals underscored a constant tension for Abidjan's débrouilleurs, lauded as fixtures of the city as it was, even as they were shunned by the formal gaze and left out of future urban imagining.

Professions like gbaka driving garnered high esteem among Abidjan's débrouilleurs. The work required dedicated apprenticeships, documentation, and savings and thus inferred time, skills, connections, and money—all rarities in the informal economy. Vendors were similarly evaluated by indicators of capital, fixity, and savoir faire: a booth or a stall was better than nothing, but a shop was ideal; permanent, sheltered shops commanded the most respect, followed by semipermanent sidewalk stalls. Negated altogether was mobile vending. The goods sold were further measures of social rank. Necessitating the minimum of a mirror and razor, low costs of entry enabled a proliferation of barbershops. A shop of secondhand shoes required substantially more start-up capital, and neither compared to an electronics shop. The paperwork for a driving license, the money for a stationary business—these were status markers among men whom the citadins of Plateau and Deux Plateaux roundly devalued. Of the city's débrouilleurs, gbaka drivers and barbers were in particular simultaneously aspirational somebodies and ubiquities of the periphery, predominately twenty- and thirty-something men whose biographies could be read as the "juxtaposition of expansive potential and declining opportunities" (Weiss 2009, 115–16). And it was in their worksites where hand-painted portraits of iconic Black men were most popular.

Barbering was a common trade. It was accessible to those with moderate savings while providing a way for men to be bosses of their own, petty dominions, to showcase personal styles and cultural predispositions, to be the epicenter of a peer group, or even to become a neighborhood big man. Barbershops were moreover quintessentially male spaces. There, men engaged in masculine rituals and storytelling while styling their bodies. The barbershop sign accrued symbols of manhood associated with the barbershop itself.

Rapid and informalized urban expansion generated vast peripheries that residents struggled to connect across; in filling this need, gbakas figured as crucial nodes in the urban economy. Reflecting the denigrated spaces and populations they served, gbaka transportation, like its counterparts around the continent, contended with "a history of illegitimacy, marginality, and ultimately, survival" (Wa-Mungai 2010, 118). Gbaka drivers were master navigators of the periphery and formidable commanders of public space, yet they remained firmly within the lexicon of urban marginality. Drivers rarely owned but instead rented their vehicles, which still demanded significant savings. In lieu of wages they were paid from passengers' fares. Fixtures in urban lore, drivers were at once respected for their skills, needed for their essential services, and despised for their recklessness. As they traversed the city, painted gbakas became mobile expressions of a street art that spoke an Abidjanais and Black vernacular.

FIGURE 11.12.   MC looks at a barbershop sign. Author's photo, Abidjan (2009).

Together, the portraits that adorned gbakas and barbershops expressed a particular iteration of Black manhood, one in which marginal men could identify as protagonists of the Black urban streetscape. In doing so, they venerated deviations from the évolué ideal.[5] As with the vendors in the previous chapter, the gbaka and barbershop signs examined here took inspiration from Black men who had achieved fame well beyond territorial borders to appeal to Abidjanais men's own performative alter egos. Thus, unlike women's hairdressing salons, which featured elaborately coiffed but anonymous models, barbershop portraits overwhelmingly depicted celebrities. The gendered tendency to look to mass-media icons reflected the fact that it was masculinity that la crise had left wanting. For male barbers and clients, drivers and passengers, the particular combination of American signifiers and Black media tropes called to mind "dreams of fame, glitz and money. This category of representation [could] be explained as a coping mechanism, if not outright escapism, for those youths whose daily encounters with poverty, joblessness and crime, among other dreary realities, ma[de] them desire some relief, however temporary" (Wa-Mungai 2010, 120).

As glorified images of media icons adorned by global symbols of wealth—dollar signs, the American flag, the Nike swoosh, the Lacoste crocodile, to name a few—became familiar presences on barbershop storefronts and gbaka doors, men made claims on public space. These summoned up worlds far from where they bartered over the 200 FCFA price of a haircut or a journey costing between 200 and 350 FCFA. They were dreamworlds of Black protagonists, men like them who had converted racial alterity into a currency of conquest. On the barbershop sign in figure 11.13, American hip-hop musician Fat Joe is blinged out in gold grillz teeth, hoop earrings, and a large gold chain necklace.

Positioned at the axis of imaginary and reality, homegrown celebrities exemplified everyman potentiality. Among musicians, the genres they mastered—be their origins local like coupé décalé and zouglou, or from elsewhere, like reggae—conjured "identities based on similar experiences of urban exclusion [that were] globally recognized and experienced in the musically disseminated terms of ghettoization" (Jaffe 2012, 684). The quartiers populaires marked the epicenter of this ghettoized representational repertoire. Celebrating the hard-knock life, the forging of global connections presupposed a shared experience of marginality.

Tiken Jah Fakoly financed the production of his first reggae album as a *balanceur*: the young man who hangs from the passenger side of gbakas soliciting

FIGURE 11.13.   Barbershop mural depiction of Fat Joe, American rap artist. Author's photo, Abidjan (2009).

passengers (Vermeil, Auzias, and Labourdette 2008). After years as a successful singer domestically, Fakoly entered the European stage in the late 1990s by way of Paris. He is an outspoken proponent of African uplift in his songs, a philanthropist, and an activist. "*Réveillez-vous!*" (Wake up) Fakoly cries at the start of his song "Françafrique."[6] After chronicling instances of continental division and theft, the refrain goes, "*La politique France Afrique, c'est du blaguer, tuer*" (The politics of France Africa, it is to lie, to kill). The refrain then replaces *France Afrique* with *Amerique Afrique*. Still, in his song "Ça va faire mal" (It will hurt), Fakoly prophesizes a moment "*Quand nous serons unis . . . comme les États-Unis . . . comme la Royaume-Uni*" (When we will be united like the United States and the United Kingdom). Elaborating on the qualities of these Anglophone countries, he sings:

> *On pourra contrôler* [We will have control]
> *On sera respecté* [We will be respected]
> *On pourra dialoguer* [We will be able to converse]
> *On pourra s'imposer* [We will be able to prevail]
> *Ca va les étonner* [It will shock them]
> *De nous voir évoluer* [To see us evolve]

FIGURE 11.14.   Gbaka depiction of Tiken Jah Fakoly, Ivoirian reggae musician. Author's photo, Abidjan (2009).

Seated in Adjamé's Maquis Mondial (Global Maquis), above the intersection where gbakas deposited their Plateau-bound passengers, I spoke with vendors Christophe, Roland, and Fabio. To my question of where they were from Roland and Fabio quickly conceded their foreigner status, explaining that they were Burkinabé—despite having been born and raised in Abidjan. It was an irony of citizenship that unlike many Ivoirians whose periodic returns for weddings and funerals retained village ties, these Abidjanais "foreigners" knew nowhere else but the city. Zouglou musicians Yodé et Siro captured this purgatory of nonbelonging in "Quel est mon pays" (What is my country), which came on soon after.[7] The song opened with the sorrowful lyrics, "*De père ou de mère, tu es ivoirien / Trop de frustrations à son égard*" (Of the father or the mother, you are Ivoirian / Too many frustrations in this regard). The artists continued,

> *Erico est né à Abidjan oh* [Erico is born in Abidjan oh]
> *Sa mère est ivoirienne* [His mother is Ivoirian]
> *C'est l'enfant de Kaboré* [He is a child of Kaboré]
> *Kaboré qui est burkinabais* [Kaboré, who is Burkinabé]

The refrain implored, "*Quel est mon pays? / Le pays du métis?*" (What is my country? / The country of the mixed-race?), and I remarked that these lyrics must pique. The vendors brushed it off, but as the song went on they both fell silent, eyes downcast, and began to hum along, swaying rhythmically to the melody.

Though recognized throughout Francophone Africa, zouglou is most acclaimed in Côte d'Ivoire. Developed in the late 1990s, it encapsulates la crise to take inspiration from an uncertain future, an ambiguity shared by would-be future elites and those long excluded from the formal system (Konaté 2002, 778). Zouglou created a new set of common referents in Ivoirian popular culture, and mastery of its performative vernacular constituted a "rite of integration" for an entire generation of youth (793). The barbershop sign in figure 11.15 features zouglou singer Yodé, popular in Côte d'Ivoire and France.

While footballers from the African diaspora in Europe and Latin America have made enormous strides, African nationals have only recently become serious contenders on the world stage. Men on Abidjan's streets have taken notice, approaching football as a means to escape poverty and a path to international stardom "on and off the field of play" (Simiyu Njororai 2014, 762). The first Ivoirian to realize this dream was Didier Drogba, captain and all-time high scorer of the national team Les Éléphants. Drogba remains one of the most lauded African footballers in history, and the Ivoirian populace has embraced him as a veritable local legend (Simiyu Njororai 2014). Departing Abidjan at the age of five, Drogba was raised in the Parisian banlieues. He played professionally first in France and then in the English Premier League, signing a £24 million contract with Chelsea to earn the

FIGURE 11.15. Barbershop sign depiction of Yodé, Ivoirian zouglou musician. Author's photo, Abidjan (2009).

status of most expensive Ivoirian player ever. His tenure with Chelsea from 2004 until 2012 achieved stunning success, after which he wore the jersey of the Turkish League team Galatasaray and China's Shanghai Shenhua (Simiyu Njororai 2014).

In his "omnipresence," Drogba surpassed the realm of football to become an icon "to emulate, above all for male youth hungry for social recognition amid unemployment and economic uncertainty" (Künzler and Poli 2012, 213). He personified the "material culture of success" and maintained a social life that oscillated between all-night clubbing and dining with African heads of state (213–14). When appearing in poster form, Drogba's likeness was on average three times larger than other players from his Ivoirian national team (Künzler and Poli 2012, 211–12). As a "key shaper of the imaginary" (208), Drogba inspired the dance "Drogbacité," and popular one-liter Bock Solibra–brand beers, frequently shared among maquis patrons, were called "drogbas." Not long after their beers received this moniker, Solibra enlisted Drogba for their beer advertisements. As an elite athlete and commodity subject, Drogba is firmly positioned at the princely tier of sports figures who are "cultural symbols of the global-local nexus as well as global marketing resources possessing resonant identities with local sports

FIGURE 11.16.   Gbaka depiction of Didier Drogba, Ivoirian footballer. Author's photo, Abidjan (2009).

fans" (Simiyu Njororai 2014, 764). In Nouchi, Drogba has become shorthand for "strong," and "the hero, the celebrity and the superstar" (Künzler and Poli 2012, 209). He is a model of Ivoirian "national identity . . . and by extension, [the African] continent" (Simiyu Njororai 2014, 764), permeating Abidjan's representational repertoire and well beyond.

Fame being the great equalizer, many barbershops portrayed global celebrities on one side of the sign and those with local origins on the other. In figures 11.17 and 11.18, internationally acclaimed Brazilian football legend Ronaldo shares a sign with Djibril Cissé, a French footballer of Ivoirian descent, who played for the French national team.

Odes to American Blackness held a privileged place in Abidjan. In fieldwork that Aminata Ouattara conducted in the 1980s, she observed that media exposure to Black Americans had instilled in Abidjanais youth

> the idea for Black Americans to come to Côte d'Ivoire, not only to help us develop our country culturally thanks to their great talents . . . but also to help us technologically, commercially and financially, because they have lived a long time alongside white people and have learned from them. And as they are the same race as us, it would be better if they came and replaced our European technical advisors. They would understand us better. (Ouattara 1985, 93)

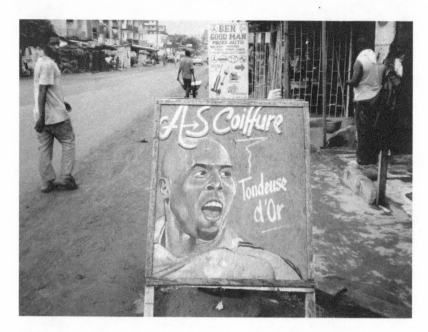

FIGURE 11.17. Barbershop sign depiction of Ronaldo, Brazilian footballer. Author's photo, Abidjan (2009).

FIGURE 11.18. Barbershop sign depiction of Djibril Cissé, French footballer of Ivoirian descent. Author's photo, Abidjan (2009).

The United States, with its muted colonial legacy and as the premier global producer of commodified Blackness, rivaled France and its production of an aspirational évolué. Transatlantic exposure being limited to media icons for whom the full consequences of subalternity did not apply, it was easy for Abidjanais to generalize Black Americans as more integrated, and indeed thriving, members of the world order. Their proximity to wealth and power inferred access for all. It was therefore frequently from the vantage point of the African-descended American that men in Abidjan located affirmative African identities. Of note in figure 11.19, then, is that the barber wrote neither the French "Afrique," nor the pan-Africanist "Afrika." The English word extols the continent through an English, and ostensibly Black American, lens.

"The use of the word *black* in contemporary parlance, rather than *noir*, aligns those described by it with America rather than the region referred to as *l'Afrique noire*" (McCarren 2004, 163). Among Parisians and Abidjanais of the Black Atlantic alike, American Blackness assumed a "third-party role" within the common lineage of slavery and colonization (Bazenguissa-Ganga 2012, 166). Through this "shared singularity," Blackness was a means for marginal men to "activate and

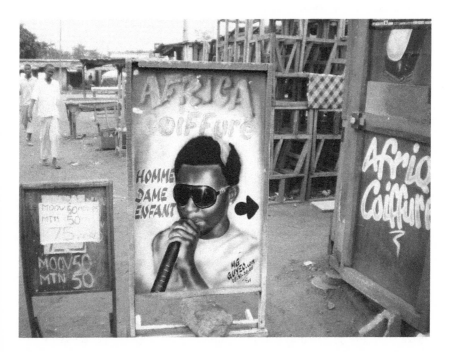

FIGURE 11.19. Barbershop sign depiction of Abidjan DJ Chechevara on "Africa Coiffure." Author's photo, Abidjan (2009).

FIGURE 11.20. Barbershop sign depiction of Le Patron, Ivoirian zouglou musician, on "Black Coiffure." Author's photo, Abidjan (2009).

intensify contacts with figures with whom they [had] only a virtual relationship" (166). For successive generations of Abidjanais, Black popular culture legitimized experiences outside the French colonial imaginary (De Latour 2001, Newell 2012, Ouattara 1985).

At times, Abidjanais broadened the boundaries of Blackness to include other formerly colonized subjects, particularly when these figures expressed their subalternity through similar tropes. The gbaka portrait in figure 11.21 features a Desi hip-hop artist with the Union Jack on his shirt. Desi draws on Black American cultural forms to position the South Asian diaspora, predominantly in Britain and North America (Drissel 2011).

Excluded as productive citizens, Abidjan's débrouilleurs promoted media tropes to construct a counternarrative of belonging. These tropes venerated Black men who had fashioned careers out of their own hypervisibility. Barbershop and gbaka portraits operated as hybrid signifiers, employing a local vernacular to reference the Black Atlantic, a global realm in which men imagined themselves as full participants. By imposing their vision of Black manhood on Abidjan's

FIGURE 11.21.   Gbaka depiction of Dezy [*sic*] artist with the Union Jack. Author's photo, Abidjan (2009).

visual terrain, they engaged in performative displays for publics in urban space and in the Black Atlantic imaginary. Doing so attested that belonging in the city was the necessary precondition to belonging, as Black men, in the world. These were territorial acts. Redressing colonialism's attempt to paint Black men white, they asserted their place as citadins in Abidjan, while insisting also on their status as global citoyens.

The real men behind media tropes were extraordinary. They gained prominence not through salaried office work but by determining the rules of the capitalist game as free agents. Their victories were celebrated by Black men everywhere, and as they embodied media iconicity they became role models of Black masculine alterity. These were commodity subjects whose value creation was a function of entrepreneurial savvy and successful branding. Still, those branded precedents of early capitalist expansion echoed the calls of the auction block.

The normative association of man and citizen with a certain type of Abidjanais subject compelled those who deviated from this ideal to look elsewhere for affirmation. Imaginaries of affirmation responded to marginal men's lived experiences of negation by asserting the embodied, aestheticized value of Blackness.

Yet embodied Black value was itself the precondition of commodification and negated personhood. Contemporary commodifications of Blackness may be articulated as an ordering of things: places, language, style, brands, all potentially transferable to any other body, if not disembodied altogether. Black bodies that cannot transfer this value may be reduced to surplus. The reward for mastering the representational repertoire in everyday life is the reclamation of bodily and social value; for Black men whose devaluation is the normative operation of racial capitalism, everyday survival is a performance.

Racial capitalism linked manhood to the modern, the public, and the productive. And so it was Black masculinity at stake in the politics of representation. Conceived by and for men, these portraits portrayed idealized masculinities in a man's world. The barber in figure 11.22 stands before his own likeness. Thus

FIGURE 11.22.   Barber posing before self-portrait. Author's photo, Abidjan (2009).

imagined, he finds redemption in his own potentiality. Fanon (1967, 112) put in plainly: "All I wanted was to be a man among other men."

Articulations of Race in Space: The Black Urban Imaginary

Because black urban residents have had to maneuver their residency across incessantly shifting lines of inclusion and exclusion, overregulation and autonomy, their experiences provide an incisive platform for coming to grips with the combination of possibility and precariousness that seems to be at the forefront of urban life.

—AbdouMaliq Simone, *City Life from Jakarta to Dakar*

Bronx-Barbès, Éliane de Latour's 2000 ethnofiction inspired by her fieldwork with Abidjan's "ghettomen," opens with protagonists Toussaint and Nixon vying among a jostling crowd for work on the ports. Sending them away with the demoralized majority, the manager declares, "*Il n'y a plus de travail*" (There is no more work). Toussaint and Nixon's fruitless efforts evoke Edward G. Robinson and Eddy Constantine in Jean Rouch's film, *Moi, un noir*, a half century prior. For those men, day labor on the ports had them imagining their more glorious selves elsewhere. De Latour's characters faced a different challenge altogether: Il n'y a plus de travail. This was no longer an economy of exploitation but one of exclusion.

A subsequent maquis scene similarly recalls when, in *Moi, un noir*, an Italian beds Robinson's love interest, Dorothy Lamour. In the 2000 version Toussaint attempts to speak to a woman but is rebuffed—this time by a fellow Ivoirian, a ghettoman. But Toussaint's bravado catches the eye of the gang leader, Tyson, who incorporates him and Nixon into the lucrative criminal underworld of the "Bronx" gang. Toussaint adopts the name "Solo du Grand B," and Nixon, "Scarface." As they supplant the indignities of day labor for the business of fast money and rural signifiers for city smarts, so do they discard their traditional dress for baseball caps and sneakers. Gazing approvingly at his new self in the mirror of a fashionable clothing shop, Solo marks his metamorphosis by clothing size. Unfolding in a fantasy sequence, he pictures himself in various cinematic genres: a war film, a martial-arts film, a Western. Once "S," he tells himself, he has passed through "M" and "L," and is now "XL." "One day they will talk about you," Solo resolves. "That day you will be XXL."

Now a gang elder, Solo adopts a protégé named Simpliste. In an almost bucolic scene with social junior and elder seated at the bank of the lagoon, sheltered from Abidjan's urban bustle and the masculine posturing of the gang, Simpliste, addressing Solo by the honorific *vieux père* (old father), asks him why he quit his studies. "If you had continued, you would not be unemployed," Simpliste offers. Solo replies, "I am not unemployed. It is the *diplômés* [graduates] who are unemployed. I am not looking for work. I am not a slave. I am a fighter." Here Solo has rejected the évolué path to fulfillment, one he associates with subjugation and failed aspirations. He is a fighter, his own boss, a self-made man chasing a new dawn.[8] *Bronx-Barbès* ends with Solo's clandestine emigration abroad, perhaps to return one day as an XXL. Hidden in the hull of a ship, his journey into the unknown resignifies the transatlantic passage as one of hope and possibility.

"Good things and good times," as responses to racial oppression and as crucial features of Black liberation, have shaped cultures of consumer resistance that are "about pleasure, performance, and participation in prosperity" (Austin 1994, 238, 235). These cultures have emerged in circumscribed spaces—ghettoes, banlieues, quartiers populaires—where Blackness acts as a conduit for belonging and enjoyment. Yet full and unbounded integration into city life, not through acculturating to whiteness but via autonomous presence, has been the profound promise of liberation, of the Black citoyen-citadin. It is made possible only when anchored in sovereign cultural, economic, and political space. For Black Power revolutionaries of a generation prior, Black liberation thus necessitated "the appropriation of space" as it was both imagined and inhabited (Tyner 2007, 219). This holistic appropriation was articulated as a struggle against the violence that racial capitalism and state collusion enact on Black communities, particularly as this violence manifests in disparate institutions and resources denied to Black residents in the city. Because Black subjugation is inseparable from capitalism, incorporation without contesting structural impediments would simply "placate a racist and classist hegemony" (227).

In the Abidjan of la crise, visible and experiential urban decline have created a palpable tension between the city as it was and as its citadins idealized it to be. Although Plateau dignified a city of colons and évolués, the quotidian urban experience was decidedly oriented around the quartiers populaires, where the vast majority of the population lived and worked. In these spaces, the state-society contract that supported évolué aspirations had never existed; its populations were always surplus to the formal plan. They reflected the Black Atlantic experience at large, where collectively the margins have become "highly productive spaces" (Weiss 2009, 32) for alternative imaginaries. It was here that men cultivated alter egos in the likeness of media tropes, resignifying success from the diploma to the basketball hoop (figure 11.23).

Blackness identifies both within and across situated communities. Men of the African diaspora have looked to Africa, and Africans to the diaspora,

FIGURE 11.23.   Dollar sign and basketball gbaka. Author's photo, Abidjan (2008).

to vindicate themselves such that Blackness offers alliances, sensibilities, and shared imaginaries. By refusing the model of urban citizenship established under colonial rule, Blackness navigates urbanity through difference as a category of reference and a strategy for action (Simone 2010). "Blackness as a device embodies a conceptual solidarity," and just as it has stood in for exclusion "from certain norms and rights to the city," it also "implies the existence of undocumented worlds of limited visibility thought to haunt the city's modernity or posit radically different ways of being in the city" (285). This Blackness marks not absence but alterity and reverberates back to shape the center. As performances of Black authenticity and urbanity circulate and vie for hegemony, there is the constant possibility of their reduction to commodity form, "invocations . . . [that] may become trite commercial mantras that reinforce rather than contest urban immobility and inequality" (Jaffe 2012, 684). Blackness thus articulated is rooted in and makes claims on space in a dance of consent and contestation, equally ripe for espousing counterhegemonic or hegemonic counternarratives of Blackness.

This is the story of Blackness as an urban condition. Like coupé décalé and Douk Saga, Paris and Abidjan, the expression of Blackness in the city is a focal narrative device for transforming a circumscribed citadin to full citoyen. It is a story of survival and status through and against movement and blockage. Hence the segregation of northern Black American urbanites on the tail of the Great Migration stoked the Harlem Renaissance, thrusting Blackness to the forefront of modern American art, literature, and music. Continuing abroad in their search for unrestrained mobility, the artists and intelligentsia of the Harlem Renaissance met a welcome reception in Paris to initiate the redemptive mystique of the city in the Black Atlantic imaginary—even while it relentlessly cast out those within its colonial orbit. Douk Saga's popularity cannot be fully grasped without attending to this Parisian legacy of conditional Blackness, translating his performance as a reverse conquest of colony-to-metropole. The ghettomen in de Latour's *Bronx-Barbès*, vendors, gbaka drivers, barbers, all looked beyond the metropole, to the Blackness of the "ghetto imaginary"—Harlem, the Bronx, perhaps Kingston or Rio de Janeiro—"to claim the right to the city and to urban and social mobility" (Jaffe 2012, 684). The ghetto imaginary speaks "simultaneously to a sense of harshly bordered immobility

FIGURE 11.24.   American flag and Statue of Liberty on barbershop. Author's photo, Abidjan (2009).

and isolation, and to a border-crossing cosmopolitan transnationalism" (682). It attests to the contradictions of a post-miracle Abidjan that has reworked its geography of center and periphery.

The Long Crisis of Black Masculinity in Racial Capitalism

Crisis "implies a certain telos" (Roitman 2012). Contiguous with the colonial mode of othering, "crisis" assumes an evolutionary narrative in which the city and its citadins ought to have evolved in the metropolitan image. In French West Africa and throughout the Black Atlantic, Blackness was a negated state of being that produced a deficit in the livelihood opportunities and lifestyle choices of colonized Black manhood. Affirmation and inclusion were to be gained by way of economic and social transformation: by becoming the évolué in the settler town or the metropole proper. Here was complicity to racial capitalism expressed through the Françafrique pact, "the expansion of French capitalism at the expense of Black bodies (yet to the advantage of some), Black body politics, Black culture and identity . . . a rhizome with deep roots into politics, the economy, and culture" (Gondola, feedback notes, June 18, 2019).

The postindependence generation proudly perceived Abidjan "to be in a cultural transition . . . fueled by the value judgments of a colonial anthropology" (Touré 1981, 59). In this context true Abidjanais identity was to be located in Plateau, where aesthetic achievements doubled as assertions of global belonging and inscribed onto the bodies of its citoyens as a set of hegemonic economic behaviors and social mores (Touré 1981). The quartiers populaires, their inhabitants and informal practices, by contrast, signaled a "déclassement" (downgrading) (Steck 2008, 236) of the city. Men who lived and worked on the periphery redeemed themselves in a borderless Black Atlantic imaginary, a "territory for the free play of the imagination" through which they acquired new "places of socialization and new sociabilities" that contest received geographies of center and periphery (Diouf 2003, 6, 5).

The initial incorporation of Black men into the racial capitalist world economy initiated a long crisis. Signifying exploitation and the undervalued body, Blackness denoted the minor term of racial binary oppositions and denied male entitlement. Affirmations of Black beauty and masculinist expressions of Black power accompanied decolonial and antiracist struggles to contest these denigrated representations and exploitative political economies within a singular critique. Instruments of both repression and redemption, media tropes signify the danger and hope inherent in Black masculinity in crisis. These multiple Blacknesses, united under the "mark of difference" vis-à-vis hegemonic whiteness and devalued manhood, and equally "threatened by incorporation and exclusion" (Hall 1993, 110), form the contours of common sense, the politics of representation in the construction of and struggle against racial capitalism.

WITH EVERY GRACE AND CUFF LINK

Afro-pessimism is a good alibi for the recolonization of Africa through consumerism.

—Manthia Diawara, *In Search of Africa*

Life imitating art, the sartorial elegance of the Congolese sapeurs had by the twenty-first century transcended Brazzaville and Kinshasa and the field of cultural anthropology to achieve global celebrity status. Sapeurs have become the subjects of theses and special-interest documentaries, evocative characters to adorn coffee tables in Daniele Tamagni's 2009 book, *Gentlemen of Bacongo*, and vibrant human backdrops for the music video to Solange Knowles's 2012 hit, "Losing You." Their performances promote a liberatory consumerism, all the more exaggerated when staged against the refuse of the periphery (Gondola, feedback notes from author, June 18, 2019).

Thus was the state of their art in 2014, when Guinness featured sapeurs in its Made of More campaign. Launched in 2006, Made of More took inspiration from the new economic realities and aspirations of Africa's informally employed. It signaled a significant shift from their prior and equally successful Michael Power campaign. Dubbed the James Bond of Africa, from 1998 to 2003 the fictive character of journalist Michael Power appeared across the African continent in short films and one feature film, idealizing a professional, jet-setting masculinity outfitted in fine suits, a master of technological gadgets, and a conqueror of women's hearts. The imaginaries of the Guinness Made of More campaign, on the other hand, captured new idealized masculinities with new models of accumulation in Africa's urban economy: gritty stories of real men who were pulling themselves up by their own bootstraps.

FIGURE 12.01. "La sape is a movement of contradictions and paradoxes. It juxtaposes symbols of excess and conspicuous consumption amidst some of the most agonizing scenes of urban poverty" (Goodwin 2009). *Mayembo* (Bacongo sapeur), Daniele Tamagni. Copyright Daniele Tamagni. Courtesy Giordano Tamagni.

The Guinness sapeur advertisement opens with snapshots of labor performed under a hot sun; one man burns peri-urban brush, another carts blocks of ice through a pulsing city street. Narrating is the baritone voice of an ambiguously African man: "In life, you cannot always choose what you do. / But you can always choose who you are." On cue, transformation: standing in an old, outdoor bathtub with a dramatic view of mountainside shanties, the ice porter washes himself. The viewer is made privy to several men whose simple drawers and closets brim with bowties, sunglasses, dress shoes, and shirts. Exiting their modest dwellings, we see a Panama hat and fedora, a sunshine-yellow umbrella to match a yellow suit, an elegant cane, sapeurs painting a brilliant contrast to their dusty settlements. These are fashionable gentlemen, colorful blooms against the gray-scale backdrop of dirt road meeting carbon sky. Their thankless remunerative tasks fade from view, and by way of embodiment, they resurrect choice from their lives. Convened in a bar, these stylish men perform their sartorial elegance to the raucous cheers of adoring onlookers. As fuel for the merrymaking, Guinness beer flows freely.

A nod to "Invictus," the William Henley poem that served as a regular inspiration for Nelson Mandela during his long years in prison, the narrator concludes,

> We are the Sapeurs: The Society of Elegant Persons of the Congo.
> You see my friends,
> With every grace and every cuff link
> We say,
> "I am the master of my fate.
> I am the captain of my soul."

From their personalized cufflinks and the graceful line of a coat worn well, they declare that the freedom for which Mandela famously fought has been achieved. Masters of their fate, the future is theirs.

In an accompanying text Guinness describes sapeurs as "everyday heroes . . . whose way of life is a testament to the belief of putting more in, to get more out." The brewery continues: "Their life is not defined by occupation or wealth, but by respect, a moral code and an inspirational display of flair and creativity. This is demonstrated through their love of stylish dressing; but it is not the fabric or cost of the suit that counts, it is the worth of the man inside it." While sapeur identity, tightly linked to the griffe, or label (see Gondola 1999), most certainly derives worth from the fabric and cost of the clothes, Guinness has nevertheless captured the notion that meaning may be made external to occupations and objective measures of wealth. This society of elegant men has forged hierarchies in the absence of opportunities that might otherwise have facilitated an esteemed modern manhood. Yet what sapeurs put in to get out, the moral code from which they derive respect, remains fundamentally material. It is the primary measure of "what makes a good man," as sung by Black British band *The Heavy* while the sapeurs undergo their sartorial transformations.

The latest of a succession of marketing coups, Made of More followed the Guinness Greatness campaign, featured in the billboard described in the first pages of this book. Commissioned to produce the Greatness campaign, the behemoth global communications and advertising agency Saatchi & Saatchi sent its team, dubbed "Xplorers," out to experience the *real* Africa. Silent on distinctions of privilege or differences in national fortune, they discovered that although "life in Africa was invariably tough," its people maintained "an insatiable optimism in Africa and an unwavering belief that success could be around any corner" (Sheehan 2013, 31). The observation led the marketers to conclude that "there is 'greatness' inherent in Africa, in general, and within African men in particular. The greatness and quality of black men parallels the greatness and quality of the world's most famous black beer" (31). Enter Guinness: "For Africa and its men to succeed, they needed to 'believe' in their greatness" (29). Hence the campaign encouraged the African man to "Reach for Greatness," with one brand analyst concluding, "It may even be reasonably suggested that the Guinness brand has actually helped inspire the men of Africa to better lives" (29). In short, this glorification of structural exclusion as entrepreneurial striving turns the trickled-down droplets of late capitalism's promise into a mighty "Drop of Greatness in Every Man" (31).

These Guinness campaigns have broadly captured scripts of informality and consumer politics in late capitalism's African urban man. In doing so, the brewery directly contests the social designation of "youth" in which these men are trapped, asserting for them the manhood denied by financial instability while also making claims on their minimal disposable incomes: Guinness approached a 20 percent increase in sales on the continent in the first year of the Greatness campaign alone (see Connolly n.d). Tapping into imaginaries commodified, this highly successful appeal to a new generation of African male consumers provided a case study of multinational marketing in bottom billion capitalism.

Guinness advertising's registers of consumer power and entrepreneurial glory as common sense modes of being are ensconced in the twenty-first-century narrative of Africa Rising. An upbeat pivot from the African "crisis" literature, Africa Rising is a celebration of economic growth, observing an emerging middle class and African economies consistently positioned among the world's fastest growing.[1] Denouncing decades of intellectual and investor pessimism, as a pragmatic slogan Africa Rising declares that Africa is open for business—and obscures the fact that Africa was never closed—the profits simply flowed outward in dramatic relief to continental neglect. While in the initial (neo/)postcolonial decades, extranational extraction was orchestrated by and fed back into the private coffers of almost exclusively state actors, the joint venture structure of a globetrotting entrepreneurial class is evident in the uneven spaces of the contemporary African city, the state-sanctioned violence of burned-down informal markets and shanties making space for corporate developments in the form of exclusive malls and securitized mansions.

It was never about the dignity of working men. It was always about capital flows. The world over, market-fundamentalism-as-economic-strategy continues to be the default for heads of state despite the predictable outcome of elite wealth concentration at the expense of national immiseration. The story I have told of racial capitalism in Côte d'Ivoire began at colonial conquest and ended in la crise, when economic decline erupted finally into civil war, thus marking the end of a narrative arc. The election in 2010 of President Alassane Ouattara, a former International Monetary Fund economist of Dioula origin, signaled a new era of capital accumulation. At once hero to the northern migrant and champion of the international status quo, Ouattara's victory drew no simple ideological line between global haves and local have-nots. Gbagboists have decried a return to a political economy of Françafrique, with restored bilateral agreements and more visible ties punctuating Abidjan's cityscape in the form of new French retailers and major development projects contracted out to French construction companies (Mitter 2015).[2] But unlike Houphouët-Boigny's fidelity to Franco-Ivoirian exchange, Ouattara beckoned investment from a wide range of countries and corporations, and for the 2013/14 cycle, the World Bank listed Côte d'Ivoire among its top ten "improvers" for "Doing Business" (Mitter 2015, World Bank Group 2014, 5). A half decade into Ouattara's presidency, Côte d'Ivoire was the world's second-fastest-growing economy, boasting 8.5 percent GDP growth (Myers 2016). But this growth did not reflect broad improvement of livelihoods and well-being. In the three years after the return to a peacetime economy, earnings from informal trade—still the vast majority of remunerative activities—had declined 15 percent (Morisset 2015).[3] In 2015 Côte d'Ivoire was among the most unequal nations in the world, with a Gini coefficient of 41.5, an HDI ranking of 171 of 187 countries, and with 79 percent of its workers in vulnerable employment (United Nations Development Programme 2016). From 2012 to 2016, Côte d'Ivoire's GDP grew 50 percent, but new jobs were predominantly restricted to self-employment and household enterprise and "unlikely to provide decent incomes on a sustainable basis" (Morisset 2015). As an indication of what was to come, among Ouattara's first acts upon taking power was to raze not only the Sorbonne, beloved site of the Jeunes Patriotes, but also the informal stalls in the Adjamé market and Yopougon's famed rue Princesse, destructions all justified by the modernist planning logic of infrastructural integrity and beautification (Coulibaly 2011). Thus within two years of my fieldwork, the principal nodes where orators and vendors sought survival and status were gone.

The Narrative Arc of Black Masculinity in Racial Capitalism

Exclusion from the wage economy is a familiar condition of Black masculinity in racial capitalism. Performative masculinities that engage consumer citizenship and commodity subjectivities endure as alternative scripts for asserting economic agency and preempt a world of proliferating contingency, if not outright disposability. In these pages I have explored how racial capitalism produces imaginaries of the Black male body through these three imbricated roles: as undervalued labor power, as commodity object, and as consumer, and I have considered what these relationships to racial capitalism mean in contemporary economies of exclusion. I contend that Blackness has been symbolically positioned against white supremacy as a project of capitalist hegemony, locating the terrain of Black struggle in the arenas of representation and in the political economy.

Establishing this theoretical premise, I explored place—the postcolonial city, and imaginaries of the Black Atlantic, to tell one particular story of racial capitalism— that of the underemployed Abidjanais man. I followed two distinct threads. First, I traced aspirational labor narratives in Abidjan from colonial conquest to la crise, underscoring the enduring role of Francophone culture and political economy in structuring the idealized man-worker, citoyen-citadin. Second, I interrogated the construction of Blackness as a racial imaginary circulating from metropole to col- ony and across the diaspora in distinct yet related discourses that asserted power over Black male subjects in a racial capitalist world order. These Black Atlantic itera- tions were variably expressed as imaginaries of negation and imaginaries of affirma- tion. As ever-present ideological constructions rather than fixed temporal moments, affirmation and negation alternatively came to express prevailing hegemonic nar- ratives contingent on the openings and closures in the political economy and the concordant social struggles of the time. By juxtaposing place and imaginary, I estab- lished how racialized conceptions of the ideal man shifted in response to changing capitalist regimes: the interplay between the ideological and the material forces of capitalism. I suggested that the double commodification of Blackness, as productive (im/potent)ial and cultural artifact, together define this project of racial capitalism. Its synthesis is located in commodified imaginaries of Blackness and reflects the fractured unity of Black struggle against white supremacy and capitalist hegemony.

The ideological sweep I presented comprised a narrative arc of racial capital- ism whose protagonists were évolués and media icons. Having arrived at la crise, I explored the lives and imaginations of would-have-been évolués and aspirational débrouilleurs. My ethnography of the Sorbonne and its orators illuminated the role that political connectedness played in sustaining the livelihood strategies and expectations of otherwise marginal men, demonstrating how the state-society con- tract that originated in colonial capitalism found new articulations for the entre- preneurial man of la crise. My ethnography with mobile street vendors provided a window into their everyday débrouille and the activities and occasions that gave meaning to their lives. I showed that these men contested anonymity and indig- nity through VIP imaginaries, sometimes in their pursuit of earnings but mostly through their alter egos—media tropes of commodifiable iconicity and aspiring consumerism—that they cultivated in spaces of sociality on Abidjan's periphery. For both orators and vendors, these were not contestations of the exclusionary world political economy but strivings for insertion within it. Finally, I used pho- tographs from the field to interrogate the visual terrain of Blackness on Abidjan's cityscape. This terrain encompassed the built environment as well as embodied practice to illuminate the cultural sites and social lexicons that had imprinted alter- native imaginaries of being Abidjanais across the city. Imaginaries of Black mas- culinity, commodified in racial capitalism, deeply inflected this visual vernacular.

What Is at Stake

Tempted and tormented by images and words from elsewhere, trapped in a money economy with nothing to sell, they have no ready way of realizing their desires. But they can't go back. . . . The struggle in Ivory Coast, and perhaps in other parts of Africa, is recognizable as the unlovely effort of individuals to find an identity and a place in a world that has no use for them.

—George Packer, "Letter from Ivory Coast: Gangsta War"

Frustrated to be in his fifth year of vending along Abidjan's roads, Samuel remarked, "The years pass so fast. You find you are still at point A, and you aspire for a better tomorrow to find yourself at point B, but you are suspended always at point A." Confronting an abandoned path, Étienne lamented, "We go far to succeed. Someone who has his Master's, but operates a cabine. . . . This is not because this trade pleases him. This is not because he wants this to be his future." For these men the free market amounted to a permanent state of unfreedom, calculated by the sum total of unrealizable ambitions and denied life chances. The horizon was dark: normative measures of manhood as money to enable marriage and finally, children—"the sin [*sic*] qua non of full personhood" (Smith 2017, 17)—effectively sentenced the formal record of their familial lines to oblivion. Prospère explained, "Here in Africa, here the vision of each human being is to have a child, a child to keep the name of his father. . . . If you have no children you are forgotten."

Tasked with demonstrating a dignified Black manhood when shut out from the breadwinner ideal, alternative possibilities exalt the creative present. The performative body actively asserts worth by styling and posing, consuming drinks and shoes and Black popular culture and the capitalist ethos at large. Like the sapeurs, the Sorbonne orators, and the aspiring musicians and footballers across Abidjan's periphery, the growing multitudes of humanity rendered surplus will continue to innovate themselves and to practice forms of sociality that make meaning in and of their lives. Sometimes these practices will double as livelihood strategies. At the intersection of "possibility and precariousness" (Simone 2010, 281), deprivation will compel ingenuity and tribulation will inspire beauty. By and through the struggle of the débrouille there "remains a surplus value . . . that comes from the exercise of the imagination and from the assertion of one's unique individuality in the face of a system that threatens one's very personhood" (Murphy 2015, 360). If only as temporary fixes, that "excess," those uncaptured "life-times of surplus people," endure and with them the full spectrum of "diverse bodily, perceptual, affective, and imaginative capacities and practices of life making under conditions of unauthorized, foreclosed, and prohibited being" (Tadiar 2012, 795). These are facts of the human spirit. In this book I have probed the ways that capitalism becomes embedded within such forms of sociality and meaning-making, just as it becomes the very condition of survival. When economic agency is made a baseline measure of human worth, it marks the totality: lives that are productive and those that are surplus. For the profit of the former, the latter experience diminished opportunity, diminished quality of life, and diminished life itself. The question is then not *whether* life goes on, but of, qualitatively, *how*. What is at stake are the sudden catastrophes and the slow, immiserated deaths of the bottom billion, lives that pay the price without ever having reaped the rewards of the capitalocene.[4] Life goes on, but in ever more degraded form.

Crisis is the permanent condition of Blackness in racial capitalism. The theory of racial capitalism establishes the constitutive role of race in the formation and operation of the capitalist system and is, with gender, its core organizing principle. It acknowledges the systemic compulsion to naturalize difference and thereby legitimize exploitation, inequality, and dispossession. Vis-à-vis constructions of whiteness, racial otherness—and Blackness as the abject other—provides this role. Subjected to thingification, Blackness is positioned as the symbolic oppositional identity and the site of hegemonic struggle. Within the framework of racialized economic exploitation, Blackness thus opposes white supremacy as a primary manifestation of capitalist exploitation. Yet patriarchal entitlement intersects with the penalty of Blackness, positioning Black masculinity precariously between privilege and exclusion. To borrow from Marx, when Black men make history, they do so under circumstances existing already, given and transmitted from the past. Within histories of exploitation and exclusion, these structuring conditions are as devalued laborers, fraught consumers, and commodity objects. The initial prohibitions to living wages and lavish displays of wealth have made Black masculine resistance a precursor to the late capitalist ethos of the entrepreneurial, consumer citizen.

At the core of the freedoms of making and spending is imperialism's formative vision: an ever-expanding market whose distant atrocities are unfettered by state accountability or social guilt, a profit-and-pain geography of "us" and "them." Infinite growth was premised on the conviction that resources in carved-up territories would provide infinite bounty. The folly of that premise is now an existential threat; an ecosystem overwhelmed by rising waters and choking in toxic waste damns the status quo in a way that worker uprisings never have. *The hour is late and we are pressed for time.*[5] If the baseline measure of human worth remains fixed to some manner of having as being, the cycle of disposable humans on a disposable planet will go unchallenged. Blackness would be a tragic ally in a system built on naturalized inequality and concluding in ecological destruction.

REFLECTIONS ON INTERSECTIONS/
INFRASTRUCTURE

I had just met up with my research assistants, Tino and MC Black, in Adjamé, and we were navigating the market's main thoroughfare to catch a gbaka to Yopougon. They were matching in Timberland boots, low-riding pants, and oversized basketball jerseys, a far cry from the respectable anonymity of the surrounding vendors and their clients. Tino and I were engaged in conversation when we noticed that MC was no longer with us. MC often ran into trouble with authority figures, so it was not surprising to find that a police officer had stopped him. As usual, the hassling became official when the dog-eared identification card that MC produced at the officer's request was barely legible. But this was all he had, and identification cards were difficult to replace. MC was at the officer's mercy: he could demand a bribe, seize his identification, or even take him to jail. I stepped in, confident that my foreignness—my light skin, American accent, and obvious sense of entitlement—would avert the unfolding disaster. The officer looked at me. Then he looked me up and down. He smiled. Knowingly, and in fact respectfully, he asked MC, "*Ahh bon … donc tu t'as trouvé une correspondante?*" or, "So then, you've found yourself a correspondent?" Within moments they were doing complicated handshakes, and MC was explaining that he was an *artist*. The do-rag and dark sunglasses, the hip-hop attire: these no longer signaled rebellion but access to a world elsewhere, one that entailed women—*foreign* women, *white* women. MC was *the man*. After a few more chuckles with MC and hungry looks at me, he sent us off with the best of wishes.

Over the course of my fieldwork, I consistently encountered the phenomenon of the Ivoirian man in search of a *correspondante*. The happily-ever-after version of this story ended with a marriage visa. But even without that prize there were abundant kudos in being seen coupling with a "metropolitan" woman, to use the language of colony/metropole from the French colonial conquest. As such, I became positioned through the desire(s)—not just sexual desire, but generally the desire to experience an *elsewhere*—of the men I studied, a positioning that also contributed to my theoretical framework (see Kulick 1995). Nearly every man I met within my generational cohort on some occasion waxed lyrical—and pointedly—about his fantasy to have a metropolitan if not an American woman.

The oft-repeated urban legend began with a correspondence: preceded by a virtual acquaintanceship or a chance meeting while she holidayed in Abidjan, for a period they might phone one another, email, or write letters. Eventually they meet/reunite. She transports this lucky Ivoirian to her home, far from Africa. His eroticized Black masculinity offers a particular appeal to foreign tastes. And her attraction to him as a potential lover and husband makes a man out of him in ways that the women of his country cannot: because of her financial independence (if not abundance), she sees beyond his otherwise emasculating earnings and deems him marriageable. Her transcending/transgressing desire redeems, legitimates him. Herself being an "exotic object of prestige" (Bourgois 1995, 41), the simple fact of their association assures him status despite everything that, independently, Abidjan has denied him. The ultimate prize of a marriage visa affords him unbounded opportunities to remake himself with work, money, and all that glistens in the global North.

I had expected the officer to be intimidated by the authority of my otherness. It was a privilege I used liberally to help friends and research subjects in our frequent run-ins with the police. But I had not expected him to back off out of a boyish respect—the assumption that I was MC's score. Issues of gendered and racialized difference came up repeatedly over the course of my fieldwork in Abidjan. I expected this as a light-skinned, highly educated African American woman studying marginal African men, and a significant concern for my research and social life was how to handle these situations in the moments they arose. My identity and the relationships I could and did forge ultimately influenced my findings and analysis.

Reflecting on my fieldwork experiences with Abidjanais men, in what follows I consider how my identity as an African American woman entailed for them a direct encounter with elsewhere: an imagined global conceived simultaneously as a space of creativity, possibility, and disillusionment. As a figure in men's lives, I transmitted economic capabilities and possibilities for social and cultural crossover. Yet I also illuminated the deficits that set apart the imagined elsewhere from everyday reality. Each meeting forged a new dynamic, and aspects of my identity were contingent on circumstance and made malleable by my subjects. The *friction* of the ethnographic encounter (Tsing 2005) demonstrates how the *inter-sectionalities* (Crenshaw 1989) of my race (or more precisely, the distinct facets of diaspora and color), gender, class, and nationality at times collaborated and at times opposed one another, creating varied situational power equilibria between me and the subjects of my study.

Racial capitalism and the political economy of patriarchy collapsed the crisis of work into a crisis of masculinity, while state neglect and exclusion from the global economy left *people* as the *infrastructure* (Simone 2004b) with which to navigate the city. Everyday hustles replaced the nonremunerative identities that rendered marginal Abidjanais men personae non gratae as social actors, yet reliant on impoverished networks, these hustles too frequently arrived at dead ends.

As observer and observed, my ethnographic encounter gave tangible form and texture to an intersection at opposite ends of the global divide. It was an intersection of disparate realities and a shared Black Atlantic imaginary, the crossing unevenly patrolled by the stop-go-yield traffic signals of our media age. Thus during my time in Abidjan I too was infrastructure, a point of contact in the search for a better life as well as an instrument of men's imagined connections. Our intersections/interactions obeyed neither stiff colonial order nor scripted media exchange. At different moments my identity as a Black American became more or less useful than that of a light-enough-to-be-white foreigner, shifting me forward and backward along the us–them divide. My womanhood could elevate or diminish my male companions. And sometimes I became the object to be observed. While paying special attention to how my subjects used me, I made use of the situations and alliances that my identities generated.

La crise manifested in my personal relationships. Chronic un- and underemployment had left my age cohort in want of a place in the world. My Ivoirian friends whose families remained solidly middle class still lived with their parents and searched ceaselessly for career opportunities. In people's houses I was always graciously offered a home-cooked meal, but except for a few special occasions organized in advance the bill was inevitably mine to pay when we went out; my friends simply had no money. With acquaintances this was more explicit. Those who have spent time in Francophone West Africa may be familiar with the expression, "*Où est mon cadeau?*" (Where is my present?)—less a request than a demand. "Où est mon cadeau?" was boldly articulated by dancers at the school where I traded capoeira classes for drum lessons, the secretary of a language institute with whom I had had minimal contact, vendors I approached on the street, and a host of fleeting encounters. Many expatriates expressed disgruntlement over the lopsided economy of local-foreigner friendships and, with a deeply colonial air, preferred to restrict contact to Ivoirians who provided them with some form of service. I could rationalize that the foreigner's transience and geopolitical privilege—no matter the circumstances of her arrival, the simple fact of being there, across an ocean, was an irrefutable sign of privilege—exacerbated the functional and disposable nature of her companionship. But I doubted that the reliance on the foreigner to pay the tab, fifty years after independence, dignified Ivoirians or failed to generate resentment. This was a lopsided economy indeed, and the African big man's lunch is not free: the favors he dispenses secure his superior status within a hierarchical relationship. That a foreigner—and a woman—was assuming this role was an imperialist and gendered challenge, a threat to "national honor and masculinity" (Ebron 1997, 227). It was a matter of having or not—and ultimately, of power.

Men who cultivated Black Atlantic media identities found in me an authentic Black American to report on the lived experience of elsewhere. Proud demonstrations of dance moves they had mastered and tutorials on West and Central African popular cultural flows accompanied animated questions about everything Black in America during afternoons passed watching music videos in living rooms or on nights out in maquis. For Tino and MC I was a source of income and patronage but also a status symbol and, above all, a means for them to incorporate native English into their music. Our song, "Je me bat pour mon avenir," quickly became the focus of their attention. They entered it in several hip-hop shows, and I danced onstage with them. It was enduring proof of their connection with elsewhere.

If I had not taken my subjects out for the occasional drink, I might have written an ethnography of waiting (e.g., Jeffrey 2010; Mains 2012; Ralph 2008) or one about wealthier men. So I profited from seeing what happened when I did, well aware that the deeper I involved them in my ethnography, the more my role as infrastructure shifted how they navigated their terrain. The consequences of our intersections became ethnographic truths among many potential actions and reactions. I certainly circumscribed this universe of possibilities. A man, someone with darker or lighter skin, an Ivoirian, or a French woman would have written different ethnographies, each elucidating elements of the composite reality of contemporary life in Abidjan. My control of the purse strings likely exaggerated the social fact of my subjects' inaccessibility to me as a prospective partner, for as Arnaud remarked in chapter 10, "You know your categories." They likely combatted this inadequacy through the bluff or alternative sources of validation. Revealed were the strategies that men without women practice to be someone in Abidjan—and in the world.

That I, an African-descended woman of the global North, was the ideal audience for the scripts and smokescreens with which men revealed their Black Atlantic alter egos, was useful to highlight those very processes. When I set up a meeting with vendors who sold along my stretch of the prestigious Riviéra neighborhood,

FIGURE 13.01. Band portrait of Frères de Zayon (Brothers of Zayon, aka Zion) from album cover photo shoot. Left to right: MC Black, Busta, Jordanna, Tino Black. Abidjan (2009), Author's collection.

I proposed a time directly after rush hour so as not to cut into their vending. I was ashamed to find that they had left their intersections at midday to change out of their dusty work clothes before returning to see me in their evening best, losing a half day's work and paying double their gbaka fare in the commute. From then on when

I met a vendor at a maquis, I presumed he was dressed as he would on a romantic date. When on first contact a vendor lied to me about his earnings (as most did), how far his reporting stretched belied his financial horizon. And when I stood silent as a vendor haggled aggressively with a taxi driver to shave a few cents off my fare home—although alone I frequently, and willingly, paid much more—I did so not only to blend in but also to respect that this small difference might comprise that man's daily wage. I found it instructive that a senior member of the Sorbonne Solidarité chose to be interviewed in one of Abidjan's select shopping malls, impressing upon me an image of climate-controlled sophistication rather than the popular market atmosphere of the Allocodrome, so celebrated among foreigners for encapsulating the Ivoirian spirit.[1] I noted that when I met an orator for a drink after President Obama's 2008 electoral victory, he was utterly giddy over "our" great achievement; at the Sorbonne the next week, however, I listened as he sternly urged caution to his fellow countrymen about too hasty an embrace of this agent of empire.

I took my initial trip to the Sorbonne during a preliminary fieldwork visit to Côte d'Ivoire in 2006. Coulibaly, the first man I interviewed, later became Sorbonne Solidarité's vice president; with patriarchal affection those who remembered me from then referred to me as his wife, "Madame Coulibaly." I suspected that the openness insiders showed me despite my appearing out of place in this "patriotic" space largely resulted from a combination of my being American—when asked to clarify, an *Americaine noire* (Black American)—and (inferring powerlessness) a woman.

For Cafard, the comedian with the dildo, however, his acts were at my expense. Because I embodied the white, French (though I was not), feminine *other*, increasingly over the course of my fieldwork he incorporated me into his gendered and racialized anti-imperial scripts. In the first few months he threw the offhand remark, congratulating my research assistant, a young Ivoirian man, on picking up a *correspondante* on an "adventure" to Paris, or stroking the dildo while pronouncing that I was clearly happy in Abidjan. Eventually I became Cafard's main plotline, as he described in detail, for example, how some lucky protagonist from the crowd had taken me around the corner and satisfied me. His act revealed both of our politics of positionality. In my white plastic chair, reserved at 100 FCFA for the Sorbonne's doyens, I sat through his degradations and the raucous laughter of my fellow spectators. I hid my churning stomach and the taste of vomit behind a stoic façade, telling myself, "This is my data. I will publish this." I swallowed it. But I intended neither to translate his truth in a way he might have validated had I shown him my notes nor to empathize with him as an ethnographic "object"—indeed he did not need or seek my understanding.[2] My task was rather to explain, to a peer-reviewed audience, my "object" as those relationalities of power, those constructions of difference and shifting objectifications, structural and interpersonal, that situated him and me in this ethnographic encounter. These relationalities unearthed histories of métis sons in Africa who had facilitated imperial accumulation, sons whose lighter skin signified complicity to and domination through empire even while their fathers kept their "legitimate," property-inheriting children in Europe—histories that fractured the boundaries of race and racial privilege differently on the continent and off. These relationalities also brought into sharp relief patriarchy demanded and patriarchy denied, an embrace of a weaponized virility as a means to enforce imperial power as well as to contest the disempowerments of empire's afterlife.

Those aspects of my personhood that had otherwise cemented relationships in the field were thus erased in favor of a clichéd narrative of Black male lust and white feminine desirability. Absent his microphone, Cafard made no effort to approach me and risk destroying his illusion of who I was and what I represented for his act. Having located and then fixed me in place, our interaction hinged on objectification and opposition, his power conditional upon taking mine away. It demonstrated another configuration of the encounter with elsewhere: autochthonous angst and the misogynist resentment of colonial emasculation.

Far from the fluid negotiations that regularly positioned me as infrastructure in my subjects' lives, Cafard's fantasy maintained unyielding categories. It showed that my welcome was tenuous at best, contingent upon what those whom I needed for my research wanted me to be. But this exception underscored the norm: unlike the rigid allocation of identities within a colonial order, my race (diaspora/color), class, gender, and nationality were relational negotiations, hierarchies that could and did shift. Within this shared space men most often aimed to establish linkages, not distance. I close with a brief review of the effects that my identity(/ies) had on my ethnographic encounter.

As an American, I opened a path beyond men's temporal and spatial limitations. My presence in their lives affirmed them and afforded a much sought-after local visibility. For the duration of my fieldwork, I offered abbreviated escapes from the worlds they inhabited: status and material resources to move about Abidjan with relative ease, without sacrificing a meal or rent to do so. I was moreover an outlet to a more permanent elsewhere. A few hours into a meeting, the topic inevitably turned toward the good life that was America—"El Dorado," near-mythical accounts of distant acquaintances who had journeyed over, and earnest inquiries into the "contacts" I might have at the American embassy. As a member of the African diaspora, while not one of them, I was the next best thing. I was an accessory, a rare commodity that distinguished the men who kept me in their company and legitimated their alter egos. And I was a source, a live node through which to fact-check their *mediated* knowledge against reality.

As a métisse I could be white or Black as the situation demanded. The first question the Sorbonne Solidarité president asked me was whether I was Americaine noire. His satisfaction at my affirmative response (which included the remark that Black American women were the most beautiful in the world) indicated that my presence was acceptable. Upon frequent shouts of "*la blanche!*" (The white woman!) at the Sorbonne, my principal informant would quickly qualify that I was both American (to be American was better than being French) and métisse, doubly suggesting that I was on their side, part of their struggle. When my white American father visited, this same informant deemed the Sorbonne's central speaking area off-limits. But he strutted with pride in his quartier populaire when my white American friend and I met him for a drink, and he asked after her for months. With mobile street vendors, whom I frequently met in their neighborhoods, the prideful strut was familiar, as were approving shout-outs to them and cries of "la blanche!" to me. But they also accepted me unequivocally as an artifact and an expert of American Blackness. In short, my race shifted by convenience. And while the label "white" fit in the Ivoirian context, my métissage enabled a subaltern solidarity in a way that whiteness would not have; the distance between me and my subjects was undisputed, but we still shared the Black Atlantic connection.

And lastly, as a woman I figured into the emerging fantasy of accessing elsewhere through a marriage visa, a gendered reversal of the mail-order bride. Men boldly shared their desire to find a correspondante—if not me, my friends would do. Yet the attraction of my privilege also put me in charge, threatening emasculation. As a producer and consumer, I held power. Whatever material assistance I offered simultaneously underscored the uncomfortable fact that I did for these men what they would have liked to have done for the women they did not have.

Thus the dark shadow of their exclusion remained cast over our encounter. My time with them was transient, as was the social prestige and material benefits I imparted. Though our exchange was to propel me onto greater things, their futures were riddled with insecurity and uncertainty. Despite our shared membership in the Black Atlantic, they stayed eternal youths, incapable of providing for me as men elsewhere certainly could. All things aside, in this heteronormative, patriarchal universe in which imaginaries of value and worth circulated, I was still a woman and they were still men. Hence the question directed back to me: "Would you ever marry an Ivoirian?"

My closest informants were Tino and MC. Beyond paying them a small salary I stored their music online, produced, and performed with them. Their rising repute nevertheless faded when I left Abidjan. For some years after they would call, asking for money or just to reminisce about the good old days. The last time we spoke, the pauses grown long from a poor connection and lack of news, Tino said to me, "Jordanna, life in Abidjan is very hard."

Notes

INTRODUCTION: GREATNESS IN EACH MAN

1. Literally "popular quarter," *quartier populaire* refers to those districts "peripheral" to the center both physically and in the urban imaginary (see Simone 2010).

2. For example, Plateau's Avenue Noguès owes its name to Commandant Noguès, the colonial official being carried in a hammock who is pictured in figure 4.01. An instance of a name change is Place Lapalud to Place de la République (see figure 5.02).

3. Generally, *Françafrique* refers to France's "sphere of influence" in its former sub-Saharan African colonies with a paternalistic approach that regards them as its own "'*pré carré*' (backyard)" (Bovcon 2011, 6). In its allusion to the "specificity of the Franco-African relationship," Françafrique acknowledges the heavy, if not always visible, French hand in the postcolonial states' supposedly independent affairs (5). An enduring and crucial feature of Françafrique was the informal, "personalized, family-like relations between the French and African political leaders and the parallel networks of economic and political elites" who were the de facto decision makers and major beneficiaries of the postcolonial African states (11). For a thorough account of the realpolitik of Françafrique, see Verschave (1998). Mincing no words, Verschave (175, quoting *France-Cameroun. Croisement dangereux* 1996, 8–9, my translation) omits Bovcon's diplomacy in his preferred definition of Françafrique:

> *Françafrique* refers to a nebulous array of economic, political and military actors in France and Africa, organized in networks and lobbies, and focused on the grabbing of two rents: raw materials and public development aid. The logic of this penetration is to prohibit any initiative outside the circle of initiates. It is a self-degrading system that reproduces itself through criminalization. It is naturally hostile to democracy. The term also evokes confusion, a domestic familiarity squinting at privacy.

4. Still, Ivory Coast is commonly used and appears in direct quotations in these pages. Relatedly, I designate the people of Côte d'Ivoire "Ivoirian." Other authors write "Ivo-rian," a derivative of the English usage. Still others write "Ivoirien," which derives from the French spelling of the term.

5. *Bourses du travail* emerged in France at the inception of the industrial economy to formally match employers with laborers, a kind of public employment office. They mani-fested in the colonies largely as labor union headquarters.

6. Solibra, for Société de Limonaderies et Brasseries d'Afrique, is owned by Groupe Castel, a French beverage company.

7. *La crise* was the appellation for the extended economic stasis following the "Ivoirian miracle" (le miracle ivoirien) which was then punctuated by political-military conflict. See also Mbembe and Roitman (1995).

8. "Paris of West Africa" was a postcolonial designation. In the colonial era the French bestowed the title "Paris of Africa" upon Dakar.

9. I thank Chandan Reddy for this formulation.

10. I use wage labor as a concept that is roughly interchangeable with formal, sala-ried, and contractual work and juxtaposed to day labor, petty trade, and other informal

activities, even when they may also receive wages. This distinction reflects the notions of remunerative work that were articulated by the men in my fieldwork.

11. For Gilroy, the "Black Atlantic" refers to the African diaspora populations as one singularity, while I extend the Black Atlantic to Africa. For a thorough overview of the concept of the African diaspora, see Patterson and Kelley (2000). For the debate regarding whether "diaspora" should include the African continent, see Pierre (2013, 207–16).

12. Yet as Robinson (2000) demonstrates, protoracialist classifications and their corresponding dispossessions predated mercantilist capitalist expansion, organizing labor relations among populations in feudal Europe.

13. Such was epitomized by the Haitian Revolution, which abolitionists perceived as "anarchical, absolute freedom" (Shilliam 2018, 17).

14. In the case of Somersett, an American slave who arrived with his master on English soil in 1772, Shilliam (2018, 14) exposes the "twist of legal fiction" that Blackstone maneuvered to distinguish between servitude, with origins in English common law, and slavery, which originated in commercial law and applied to colonial territories. Common law legitimated servitude because it facilitated a "patriarchal relation" (14). The system of African slavery disrupted "common law's delicate compact between liberty, property, and patriarchy," and was thus "despotic" (13, 14). Shilliam (15) goes on to demonstrate how "the dangerous logics of slave abolition, which targeted commercial law, implicated the problem of 'masterless men,' which referenced common law." In doing so, "the distinction between the deserving and undeserving poor began to be racialized by analogy to the Black slave" (15).

15. When these strategies fall outside the realm of the state and into the illicit economy, Black men confront potentially punitive consequences: the regime of property is entered into at the risk of returning to the state of unfreedom.

16. I refer to neoliberalism as an economic system and ideology that emerged in the 1980s under the Reagan and Thatcher administrations, and that espoused an unfettered free market economy, the privatization of the public, and the casualization of work. The neoliberal state is punitive rather than welfare oriented, and supportive of capital instead of labor (Harvey 2005). Exemplifying neoliberalism, in urban Africa global finance institutions imposed conditionalities, or structural adjustment, on debt-stricken states, prompting a crisis that included the implosion of work regimes and the proliferation of informal economies. This roughly coincided with postindustrialization in the United States. Neoliberal ideology socially classifies people according to their market identities (Comaroff and Comaroff 2001). I refer to this ideology as a market ethos. Neoliberal freedom refers to the freedom to buy or to sell, positioning the ideal subject as a consumer or entrepreneur (Hall and Lamont 2013).

17. See Cohen (2003, chap. 4). Highly dependent on the local population for trade, navigation, and rule, Senegal, as France's first African colony, experienced more "liberal race relations" compared to the "racial exclusivism" of the West Indies (Cohen, W. 2003, 100). The rigid association between Blackness and slavery also did not transfer to the African continent, influencing the fate of mixed-race children as well as the status of Blacks generally (125). Nevertheless, although whites "considered it essential to give enough rights and privileges to nonwhites to ensure their loyalty to the French regime . . . it was felt that a certain amount of white superiority should be asserted, in order to retain some control over the nonwhite population" (127).

18. Connell's masculinities theory encompasses four categories: hegemonic, complicit, marginalized, and subordinate masculinities. In this discussion I address the first three; the final, subordinate, refers to sexually nonnormative masculinities and is outside the frame of my analysis. However, see Matlon (2016).

19. In close conversation, outlining how gender operates as a fundamental structural axis in the racialized coloniality of power and modernity, Lugones (2007, 190) explains that "biological dimorphism, the patriarchal and heterosexual organizations of relations"

are features "crucial to an understanding of the differential gender arrangements along 'racial' lines." Under the coloniality of power, Lugones (191) observes, "wage labor has been reserved almost exclusively for white Europeans."

20. hooks (2004, 25) writes that capitalism itself is "gangsta culture" and contends that "patriarchal manhood was the theory and gangsta culture was its ultimate practice."

21. For research on Abidjan that disrupts the binary heteronormative framework, see Matthew Thomann (e.g., Thomann 2016, Thomann and Corey-Boulet 2017, and Thomann and Currier 2019).

22. Above and beyond its illegality, Black male slaves did not cross the racial sexual boundary because of the prohibitions of white male dominance and at the threat of death; just the idea of this transgression has long served as the singular alibi for lynching in the white imaginary. Racial reproduction and the penalties of interracial sex were gendered, and this is true across contexts. Particularly in slave economies, ascribed Blackness (and enslavement) was matrilineal. Like race generally, permissiveness toward, and more frequently censuring of, interracial couplings functioned to varying degrees by political and economic imperative. Enforcement could be de jure or de facto.

1. TROPES OF BLACK MASCULINITY

1. Indeed, the exploitative compulsions to labor in early industrial capitalism represented freedom only in contrast to the slave's total subjugation. According to Engels (2010, 343–44), "The slave is sold once and for all; the proletarian must sell himself daily and hourly." Classic Marxist analysis narrowly insists on the wage transaction, which simultaneously alienates labor power and incorporates the laborer as a consumer into an ever-expanding industrial economy, and has been loath to include slavery as a capitalist mode of production. Rather, the proletarian "belongs to a higher stage of social development" than the slave. Thus the "slave frees himself when, of all the relations of private property, he abolishes only the relation of slavery and thereby becomes a proletarian; the proletarian can free himself only by abolishing private property in general" (344). In this construction, the slave-as-property takes preeminence over the slave-as-laborer. For a concise discussion of the Eurocentric view of labor relations as determinate of capitalism, see Johnson (2013, 252–54).

2. "For it to operate as affect, impulse, and speculum, race must become image, form, surface, figure, and—especially—a structure of the imagination" (Mbembe 2017, 32).

3. Of the colonial project's permanent oscillation between a "politics of inclusion" and a "politics of exclusion," Ezra (2000, 6) explains: "Colonial administrators were unable to choose between asserting the assimilability of the colonial possessions and proclaiming their irreducible alterity because they needed to do both." Therefore, while

> assimilation was predicated on the eventual eradication of distinctions among groups, the disappearance of these distinctions was implicitly feared and rejected. . . . French cultural texts reiterated this paradox, on the one hand, there was much talk of assimilation, but on the other, there was much talk about the supposedly inherent differences between colonizers and colonized. As cultures were brought together through commerce, colonial settlement, and immigration, their differences from one another were magnified, while differences among members of the dominated culture were minimized or denied altogether. (Ezra 2000, 6, 7)

The contradictory ideological and material imperatives of the mission civilisatrice (civilizing mission) was particularly manifest among évolués. French imperialism needed évolués as interlocutors, Africans integrated into French norms while also moving fluidly within native society. This "contributed to the articulation of *évolué* self-identity as belonging to both 'French' and 'African' cultures, and necessarily precluded the delineation of neatly separated categories of citizen and subject" (Genova 2004, 22). Needing the évolué's native knowledge, yet compelling him to "renounce those personal and historical connections to their cultures of origin" (22), was to set up a powerful opposition between colonizer and colonized that I discuss in chapter 2.

4. Encompassing Côte d'Ivoire, the imperial administrative body of Afrique Occidentale Française (AOF) was created in 1895. When discussing this political-administrative unit, I use the designation AOF.

5. In Black-majority countries, color stratification mimics racial stratification, with lighter-skinned populations experiencing easier access to economic opportunities.

2. THE EVOLUTION OF THE WAGE LABOR IDEAL

1. Original epigraph texts in French. All translations from French editions of texts are my own unless otherwise stated.

2. King Louis XIII legalized French participation in the transatlantic slave trade in 1642. Prior to that, it was a private affair, and French sailors frequently kidnapped slaves from ships sailing under foreign flags (Régent n.d.).

3. Assinie is written also as "Issiny."

4. Then–Côte d'Or was initially a territory limited to Assinie and Grand Bassam, the colonial capital a half century later. First Governor Louis-Gustave Binger renamed the colony to distinguish it from the British Gold Coast, the word "or" meaning "gold" in French (Atger 1960). Édouard Bouët-Willaumez, a marine officer charged with enacting treaties with regional chiefs in 1839, first used "Côte d'Ivoire" to describe the territory between Assinie and Cap des Palmes to the far west, bordering current-day Liberia (Coquery-Vidrovitch 1992). Colonization of Côte d'Ivoire occurred in two phases—as "peaceful penetration" from 1893–1908 and as "forced policy" from 1908–1920 (Loucou 2012, 65).

5. While the aforementioned French-African treaty later clarified that Africans were permitted to continue trading with the British, in 1850 an arbitrary punishment against the king of Grand Bassam for ill-treating his slave stripped them of this right, and it was a continual point of contention. In 1868 France opened trade in Côte d'Or to other foreigners, imposing a flat duty of 4 percent on all imports and exports (Atger 1960).

6. Reeling from military losses and trailing other European powers amid a moment of global expansionism, the French embraced colonial conquest as an Enlightenment project, an assertion of both might and ideological supremacy.

7. This argument denied the historical fact that transatlantic slavery and the world commodity market expanded and severely exacerbated preexisting African forms.

8. The terms translate as "slave," "captive," "unfree," and "servant."

9. It was not until the 1920s that forced labor in West Africa even became subject to debate and formal regulation in the French colonial administration. "The only innovation," Conklin (1997, 223) writes, "was that the need to inculcate in Africans [what Governor-General Carde called] 'the universal law of labor' now became an articulated tenet of French civilizational ideology in West Africa." The labor debate was initiated not out of ethical concern but rather to maximize returns, an "attempt to satisfy the metropole's sudden demand for raw materials, without ruining the labor resources necessary for subsequent *mise en valeur*" (229). In a 1932 report critiquing existing labor practices in AOF, Inspector Bernard Sol wrote, "The moral right to use coercion [is] the automatic corollary to the idea of colonization. . . . Colonial rule rests upon an act of violence. Its only justification lies in the intention to substitute a more enlightened authority for the one in place, one capable of conducting the conquered peoples to a better existence" (quoted at 231). "In the grand scheme of things," Conklin (244) concludes, "'learning to work' was considered too universal a perquisite of civilization to be withheld from Africans, while the racist belief that Africans were inherently lazy and unable to think for themselves was too ingrained to ever make free labor the only option."

10. The mission civilisatrice being the official ideology of the Third Republic, France transitioned in 1895 from the conquest of West Africa to what Conklin (1997, 11) describes as a policy of "constructive exploitation." Underneath the semantic alibis, when the mission civilisatrice moved from ideology to action, its commitments to the universal rights of man gave way to pragmatic approaches to labor and resource extraction. There was moreover an unyielding racial anxiety around how to handle acculturated Africans and their agitations for full inclusion in French society (Conklin 1997).

11. The term "obligatory public labor" emerged in 1930 and mandated the French government's legal forms of forced labor until its abolition (Conklin 1997, 234–35). The reference to "obligatory public labor" was preferred over "forced labor" because, while the latter "evoked the horrors of the slave trade," the former "underscored progress" (320). And although obligatory public labor "officially forbade the administration's direct engagement in recruiting labor for private gain," in 1930 conditions of just such government recruitment prompted one colonial inspector of Côte d'Ivoire to suggest that it was the "excesses" he witnessed that had prompted the International Labor Organization to "organize an international treaty condemning forced labor generally" (242, 241). Indeed, in 1928 estimates for government recruitment of forced labor for settler colonists in Côte d'Ivoire reached 10 percent of the male population (Cooper 1996, 35). In general, forced labor "went hand in hand with economic development and became key to the system." While formally, forced labor was "always excluded from French legislation, it existed in actuality for both public works and private enterprise" (Coquery-Vidrovitch 1992, 116).

12. Pierre Leroy-Beaulieu, a leading nineteenth-century French economist and public intellectual who examined, among other things, labor conditions in the metropole and the colonies, was a vocal early proponent of mise en valeur (see Holo 1993). In his 1874 essay, *De la colonisation chez les peuples modernes*, Leroy-Beaulieu advanced many of the arguments that were to be used a half century later.

13. The consequences of this gendered vision were significant: a French administrative survey in 1954 found that 1 percent of West Africa's emerging wage labor force, public or private, was female (Cooper 1996, 463). The labor question in all its forms was so thoroughly gendered in the European imagination that even slavery "was considered a male problem," while women in the same conditions were simply "assimilated into the category of marriage" (Cooper 2000, 119).

14. See Coquery-Vidrovitch (2001) for the complex, variable, and often contradictory legal distinctions between citizen and subject, political and civic rights, and citizenship versus French nationality—"used for the purposes of indirect segregation" (304)—among colonial inhabitants of French West Africa.

15. These efforts were often in patchwork and to varying degrees, depending on the esteem French colonial administrators held for the native populations and the political strength and mobilization of shifting blocs of African elites. The Quatre Communes of Senegal, France's oldest West African colonial territory consisting of Saint-Louis, Dakar, Gorée, and Rufisque, was the most entrenched center of French colonial tradition and its inhabitants were, until independence, esteemed as more evolved. The abolition of slavery in France's Caribbean colonies in 1848 extended citizenship to their African-descended populations, and this was granted in a parallel move to the Senegalese *originaires*, those privileged African and métis residents of the Quatre Communes distinguished from "natives," or *indigènes*. Their rights would be periodically revoked and reinstated until the next century, when citizenship to all originaires of the Quatres Communes and their descendants was reaffirmed by the 1916 "Blaise Diagne" laws—a direct outcome of the agitation following Ponty's restrictive 1912 decree (see in-text discussion)—after which nearly two decades of more relaxed citizenship regulations followed (Cooper 2015; Genova 2004; Semley 2014; Urban 2009). Thus for different categories of Senegalese subjects, citizenship was over time

inconsistently legislated in and against their favor. It was, however, consistently bestowed in higher proportion than elsewhere in French West Africa.

16. The nevertheless powerful and entitled évolué class, positioned against an increasingly racialized French stance on granting citizenship (and one that viewed the métis with similar derision), persistently agitated for full inclusion in Senegal—of which the Blaise Diagne citizenship laws were a resounding victory—and throughout French West Africa. Though never passed, this debate sparked a 1927 proposal to create an even finer distinction, an intermediate legal class between citizen and subject for the majority of évolués: that of *indigène d'élite* (Conklin 1997). As elaborated below, the évolués finally achieved full rights amid the negotiated concessions of France's fading empire (Cooper 1996; Cooper 2015).

17. For a careful examination of how, in the post–World War II empire, France and its African colonies articulated, contested, and finally drew boundaries around citizenship in a conflict of equality and exclusion, see Cooper (2015).

18. Further indicative of the territorialization of colonized Africans' rights, citizenship eligibility in the 1912 decree also required having lived in the commune for at least three years (Opoku 1974, 142).

19. This shift occurred in a series of policy changes after World War I (for discussion of this transition and the tenets of French association policy, see Conklin 1997, 174–211). In particular, the imperative to curb évolué power motivated the move from assimilation to association. Association proposed "a counterdoctrine to the *évolué* ideology of assimilation. This justified giving but a small part of French sovereignty to the new elite, instead of the full equality they demanded," thus enabling France to maintain its authority which the évolués were increasingly challenging "without appearing as die-hard racists before world or metropolitan opinion" (Conklin 1997, 203). Lost "in the realm of native policy which civilization through association represented . . . was a certain commitment to the idea of universal man" (211). Yet in a span of "thirty years—rather than the centuries [that the AOF governor-general in] Dakar had originally imagined—the federal authorities would have to accept *évolués* as equals and turn power over to them altogether" (203). At the closure of World War II, the administration of AOF had already "abandoned the policy of *évolué* association for the doctrine of political assimilation for all educated Africans" (204).

20. Nevertheless, Cooper (1996) details the continuity between the Popular Front and Vichy in their actual approach to labor practices, the latter simply being more transparent. Further, Vichy economists' vision of mise en valeur did not shy away from advocating for benefits and improved working conditions amenable to increased productivity, even while they resorted in practice to "a more vigorous and more overt recruitment of forced labor" (142).

21. This was the second Lamine Guèye law. The first, passed in 1946, extended citizenship to all French African subjects.

22. Signaling a major victory from the post–World War II period through independence was the extension of French citizenship rights across religious affiliation and to polygamous families (Cooper 2015). This was especially significant given that Ponty's exclusionary 1912 decree had the greatest impact on the heavy concentration of majority-Muslim évolués in the Quatres Communes of Senegal (Genova 2004).

23. French education, particularly at the highest levels, was only ever experienced by a select few. At the dawn of independence in 1957, fewer than one thousand Ivoirians had been educated in French universities. These graduates later comprised the postindependence political elite (Coquery-Vidrovitch 1992, 335–36).

24. In reality, "Africans were not put in a separate racial classification as much as shunted into positions in lower levels of an intricate hierarchy" and while a few reached the top, proportionately, minority representation was insignificant (Cooper 1996, 103). In Senegal, the colony with the most évolués, as late as 1957 average salaries for metropolitan French were 4.2 times higher than that of Black Senegalese (460). Cooper (168) notes moreover that the

"French administration had long shrunk before the implications of its assimilationist tendencies and balanced it with a neotraditional view of colonial societies quite comparable to that of British authorities." Throughout the colonial era the "myth of the backward African coexisted with the myth of the universal worker in considerable tension" (267).

25. Cooper (1996) demonstrates how the question of social citizenship sounded the death knell of assimilationist ideology and provided the opening for African independence. He (425) explains: "Assimilation, as articulated at Brazzaville for example, had been a doctrine of politics and culture. The social question had entered through the back door." The willing dissolution of the French Union reflects the fact that France "could [not] prevent their formalistic notion of citizenship generalized throughout the empire in 1946 from opening questions of material equality" (469).

26. Upon enacting labor legislation, officials maintained that their program had succeeded in generating a new kind of subject with new needs. The "urban detribalized wage earner" thus "encounters special difficulties from the necessity of maintaining a family notably when, having attained a certain level of social evolution and stabilization as a worker, he tends to base his living conditions on those of the European worker" (Cooper 1996, 316, quoting Pierre Pélission, former head of the Inspectorate of AOF in 1954).

27. This compensation covered two months' salary and was limited to three children (Cooper 1996).

28. Cooper (1996, 268; emphasis added) nevertheless observes:

> The depiction of African cultural backwardness had long been a part of racial ideologies, and remained part of official thinking even when colonial governments formally repudiated racial discrimination and looked increasingly toward the incorporation of Africans into a world of wage labor, economic rationality, generalized education, and citizenship. The fact that *"capital," whatever it was in theory, generally came with white skins, as did the people who constituted the "state,"* was still an important fact. The commonality of language, social connections, and participation in metropolitan politics underscored the racial division that derived from conquest itself.

29. Yet, to eliminate the threat of competition and maintain dependency on the metropole, industrialization projects were extremely limited (Bancel and Mathy 1993). The "pacte colonial" inferred a "state-controlled division of labor between an industrial metropole and colonies devoted to primary products" (Cooper 1996, 73).

3. PRODUCER, CONSUMER, COMMODITY, SURPLUS

1. Whether race is simply a mutation of class as opposed to its own discreet category is of continuous debate. To argue that racialism occurred with the formation of capitalism, but that this was ultimately an expression of class identity and no more is not the same as asserting—as Robinson (2000) would—that racialization, however it may have been conceived, is integral to the construction and legitimation of difference, without which capitalism could not function. Hall (1996, 55) has explained that race and racism have "a practical as well as theoretical centrality to all the relations which affect black labour. The constitution of this fraction as a class, and the class relations which ascribe it, function as race relations. Race is thus, also, the modality in which class is 'lived,' the medium through which class relations are experienced, the form in which it is appropriated and 'fought through.'"

2. The emphasis on the body also obscured other manifold and vital contributions of Black people in slavery and colonialism, ranging broadly from feminine emotional labor to agricultural knowledge (e.g., Kaplan 2009; Carney 2009).

3. "From the perspective of mercantilist reason, the Black slave is at once object, body, and merchandise. It has form as a body-object or an object-body. . . . In this view the Black

Man is material energy. This is the first door through which he enters into the process of exchange" (Mbembe 2017, 79).

4. Similar to Shilliam's (2018) aforementioned "patriarchal servitude" imagined by Adam Smith and William Blackstone, within Hegel's "teleology of freedom," property achieved through labor, as an active command and production of things, was the precondition by which "individual man establishes his relation to family through marriage," such that "property, marriage, and family were . . . the means through which the individual will was brought consciously into identity with the universal will, expressing the realization of true 'freedom,' rather than mere duty or servitude" (Lowe 2015, 28, 29).

5. Hegel believed that European enslavement bode favorably compared to the African condition, "since there a slavery quite as absolute exists" (Hegel 2004, 96). This reasoning reflected a dominant strand of eighteenth-century thought whereby despotism, or political slavery, was posited as the ultimate unfreedom. Popular belief held that Africa was a despotic continent, hence "Africans were predisposed to be slaves" (Cohen, W. 2003, 146). The slave trade would enable Africans to "leave a despot who has the right to strangle them for a master who has the right to make them work" (Pierre Victor Malouet quoted at 147).

6. The interdependence of labor and consumption was essential to Marx, for whom free wage labor constituted a necessary relation in which wages enabled consumption, which in turn furthered capitalist industry; the breakdown of this cyclical relation generated crisis. Slaves were precluded from this relation and hence Marx theorized them not as agents of history in capitalism but as primitive accumulation.

7. Thus, while Leong (2013, 2204–5) distinguishes the commodification of Black bodies from Black culture ("cultural appropriation"), I find this distinction tenuous at best.

8. The *tirailleurs sénégalais* in the French Banania advertisements discussed in chapter 4 are an exception.

9. Pieterse (1992, 141) observes: "The black entrée into the musical world was a form of emancipation, but it took place within the confines of the existing imagery, of black segregation and of the roles allocated to blacks. Black entertainers were decorative and not necessarily emancipatory figures. . . . Entertainment is a kind of service too. Entertainers were not a threat to the status quo." Of the global dissemination of race and racial stereotypes, Auslander and Holt (2003, 162) look to longstanding "minstrel stereotypes" of singing and dancing, or the naturally gifted Black athlete. "Minstrelsy," they write, "was not only a founding moment in that play historically, but it also gave form and expression to a process that since its inception has unfolded globally, although with specific local variations." Drawing on Taussig's analysis of mimesis-as-commodity fetishism, they (163) write that in the process of minstrelsy, "the whole of black life and character was colonized, that is, blacks became *only* song, dance, and sexuality." They nevertheless also assumed "the flip side of what [whites] desired—the dangerous, the lustful, the bestial."

10. The Black male body in American popular culture has achieved iconic object status. See Hopkinson and Moore (2006) for a detailed discussion of Black masculinity in popular culture.

11. For example, artisan slave laborers were highly sought after in the antebellum United States, but after manumission they were barred from practicing their trades. Not only did this erase the legacy of skilled Black labor, but it also prevented competition with whites as well as Black self-employment, thereby ensuring dependency on white employers (Gatewood 1974, 25). In another instance, excluded from factory work and blocked from union membership, Black men who became strikebreakers were situated not as potential equals but as enemies of the labor movement.

12. Jean-Paul Sartre (1964–65, 39), in his celebration of Négritude, declares: "Techniques have contaminated the white peasant, but the black peasant remains the great male of the earth, the world's sperm."

13. The fixation with Black masculinity moreover exacerbates a politics of Black patriarchy. Commodification "makes phallocentric black masculinity marketable" and "reward[s] black people materially for reactionary thinking about gender" (hooks 1992, 109).

14. Parallels ran across slave societies. In the French Antillean slave economy, for example, even freedmen were prohibited from dressing as whites so as not to muddle the racial gulf that was imperfectly maintained by juridical status (Cohen, W. 2003, 53).

15. Weems (1998, 68–69) explains: "As study after study revealed the growing importance of African American consumers to the U.S. economy, U.S. companies actively sought to befriend, rather than antagonize, Black shoppers. In fact, as the June 20, 1964, issue of *Business Week* noted, businessmen played an important role in smoothing the passage and the acceptance by whites of the monumental Civil Rights Act of 1964." "Minimizing the central role of African American economic retribution erroneously suggests that civil rights legislation resulted from white 'moral transformation,' rather than from the skillful use of African Americans' growing economic clout" (56).

16. "This emphasis on sexuality and sexual display, however, positioned the 'buck' character as a spectacle, thus fulfilling the function of *to-be-looked-at-ness*, a function usually assigned by Hollywood to women" (Ongiri 2009, 180, emphasis in original). Hence Blaxploitation had enormous crossover appeal that "inscribed the look and the gaze to function in the service of dominant culture" (169).

17. Ever focused on his bottom line, Jordan was calculatingly apolitical. When he refused to endorse Black candidate Harvey Gantt against white supremacist Jesse Helms in the 1990 North Carolina senate race, fellow National Basketball Association legend Kareem Abdul-Jabbar determined that Jordan had chosen "commerce over conscience" (Martin 2015).

4. IMAGINARIES OF NEGATION

1. Of the metaphor of Africa as the "Dark Continent," Jarosz (1992, 106) writes:

> In addition to the historical, material, social, and ecological forces which construct, shape, and destroy space and place, language wields similar, although figurative, power through particular linguistic devices such as metaphor and symbol. By fusing two objects or concepts in a relation of identity through metaphor, we are able to comprehend or perceive a particular process, object, or concept in a particular way. Thus, we "see" Africa as Dark, and we "know" by means of this particular fusion.

In so doing, "African places and peoples appear as quintessential objects, ahistorically frozen within a web of dualities such as light/dark, found/lost, life/death, civilized/savage, known/mysterious, tame/wild, and so on." Similarly, of the "myth of the Dark Continent," Pieterse (1992, 64) explains that "the journeys of exploration did not simply produce 'knowledge,' they were also large-scale operations in myth-making, and they unfolded in a kind of western 'tunnel vision' that was to culminate in European colonialism."

2. Indices of civilization, such as the existence of precolonial African cities, conflicted with these depictions, and rarely appeared in images of Africa that reached Europe (Landau 2002; Pieterse 1992). Static, pastoral imagery further cemented the notion that the city was not only the heart of African modernity, but also the advent of the colonizer, who could thus rightfully assert his material claims and cultural hegemony.

3. Mbembe (2017, 59) writes, "The world order was divided into spheres that separated interior and exterior." It was in this interior sphere, "governed by law and justice . . . that all ideas of property, payment for work, and the rights of people were developed. It was here that cities, empires, and commerce—in short, human civilization—were built." The rest, the exterior, was "open to free competition and free exploitation."

4. Passage of the French metropolitan Code du Travail initiated a six-year-long debate over colonial labor legislation in Overseas France. Finally legislated in AOF after a successful territory-wide strike in 1952, the Code extended only to workers fully absorbed into the wage economy. Entitlements included requisite limits to the working week (forty hours), paid vacations, benefits, and family allowances for those whose social reproduction matched European expectations of the nuclear family and who subjected themselves to the surveillance of the colonial state (e.g., hospitals, schools, and other modern bureaucratic institutions). The Code first applied to high-ranking civil servants, but with time all civil servants gained these entitlements. While it formally extended to all wage labor, the question of implementation in the private sector was never resolved (Cooper 1989).

5. Félix Eboué was the first Black Frenchman to be appointed governor of a colony, of Guadeloupe in 1936. While governor of Sudan he advocated the creation of a status between citizen and subject that he considered calling noir évolué (Weinstein 1978).

6. Because the French populace's primary knowledge of Africa was as the source of slaves, the "social context of slavery dictated to an important degree how Frenchmen viewed blacks; slavery further debased the image of blacks" and came to inform ideas of the continent at large (Cohen, W. 2003, 35).

7. Boulle (2003, 19) observes that the "growing popularity [of polygenetic concepts] in the second half of the seventeenth century coincides with the generalization of black slavery, linked to the contemporary spread of the sugar plantation system."

8. Legislating away the humanity of the enslaved, "the code noir had declared them to be property" (Cohen, W. 2003, 58).

9. "Through a process of dissemination but especially of inculcation . . . this massive coating of nonsense, lies, and fantasies has become a kind of exterior envelope whose function has since then been to stand as substitute for the being, the life, the work, and the language of Blacks." Therefore, "to say 'Africa' always consists in constructing figures and legends—it matters little which ones—on top of an emptiness" (Mbembe 2017, 39, 52).

10. "The French maxim . . . that 'there are no slaves in France' . . . is a potent element of the French national ideology [that fosters] a romanticized view of racial egalitarianism in French society" (Chatman 2000, 144). Since "it was not just the entry of slaves but of any person of color that the metropolitan authorities opposed," Cohen, W. (2003, 111) contends that it was not simply France's strong belief in itself as a land of freedom that prohibited slavery in the metropole, but also "the racist fears of being 'contaminated' by blacks." Moreover, at the same time that France claimed to be forerunner in the liberty of man, its brutal slave system was extracting some of the highest rates of production among its European peers: absent the latter's equivalent technological advances, in the late 1700s Saint-Domingue (Haiti) was yielding 25 percent more sugar per acre than British Jamaica (56).

11. For the French case in particular, the image of the "bon noir" or "grand enfant" replaced that of the savage after World War I, when demonstrated military qualities of African soldiers proved too unsettling (Holo 1993, 64). The caricatured tirailleur sénégalais described in the following section is an example of such tamed, emasculated representation.

12. "French logic of race from the beginning has operated on the basis of the annexation of the racial Other and its cleansing through the triple wash of exoticism, frivolity, and entertainment" (Mbembe 2017, 68).

13. The desire for spectacle nevertheless rivaling that for commerce, Schneider (1982, 142; see also Wan 1992, 65) notes that even though the Pai-Pi-Bris "had always traded peacefully with the French . . . their exhibition also included a mock attack on [a] model village . . . in order to give visitors the excitement they expected." Such contradictions evidenced how far from aiming for ethnographic accuracy, these displays had entered "the realm . . . of sideshow" (Schneider 1982, 136).

14. The first colonial exposition was at Rouen in 1896.

15. A review of the 1906 Marseilles Colonial Exhibition described the West African pavilion as "accurately reflecting" the region as "a tabula rasa" that, with "no cities, no roads, a rudimentary political and social organization" and "good negro peoples . . . who are made faithful subjects simply by treating them well," they held "magnificent hopes of its economic growth" and instilled in colonial administrators "a deep joy of creation" (Réné Pinon quoted in Schneider 1982, 195).

16. Silent was any reference to forced labor in the equation. Contradicting the sanitized formal narrative, in 1925 communists and surrealists mounted a counterexposition called "The Truth of the Colonies" that relayed the nationalist struggle amid photographs of brutal colonial violence (Hodeir, Pierre, and Leprun 1993, 132).

17. Of colonial exchange, Bayart (2007, 217) notes: "Foreign objects often entered the countries earlier than did foreigners themselves" so that early commodities trade, in transforming what Fernand Braudel called "'material civilization' . . . [was] at the heart of processes of subjectivation, for example by giving rise to new forms of social life, by arousing furious moral polemics or by modifying the representations and practices of relations between genders."

18. The imaginary of the contaminated Black body persisted in the "sanitation syndrome," a biopolitics that would later legitimize the segregation of the African city (Swanson 1977).

19. The tirailleur sénégalais was exceptional because it was he who consumed the product (Hale 2003). Nevertheless, his "trademark figure, emblazoned on every box of an immensely popular breakfast food, simultaneously brought the heroic Senegalese soldier into almost every home, making him the familiar of all small French children, and ridiculed him" (Auslander and Holt 2003, 168). Calling him the "'unknown soldier' *par excellence*," Mbembe (1993, 135) remarks: "Once the war ended, these men [tirailleurs sénégalais] returned home. They were promised everything, and everything was taken from them: the medals, the trinkets they brought back, and in some cases, their pensions." Catherine Hodeir (2002, 237) identifies the iconic Banania tirailleur as Bakary Diallo.

20. This logic found its apex in ethnographic museums, a bourgeois medium that greatly influenced colonial exhibitions. The elite domain of race "science" and the popular culture of the commodity reinforced one another so as to constitute a singular project.

21. Bachollet et al. (1994, 26–27) observe that by the 1980s, "the only shift in this triad concerned the last aspect: the metropolitan Black was now a consumer target. The rest had not changed. Advertising remains for the moment the business of Whites in which the Black only plays a secondary role. The progress is thus: from a century of utilitarian contempt for the other to an interested consideration."

22. Yet Southern Rhodesia's apartheid society further compelled white corporations to modify the image of the African man to fit the occupational and social restrictions facing Black Africans (Burke 1996).

23. The movement, known as *la sape*, is an acronym for "Société des Ambianceurs et des Personnes Élégantes."

24. "*Knowing* the colonized is one of the fundamental forms of control and possession. One application of this knowledge is that the subject peoples are turned into visual objects. The knowledge circulates by means of images—the availability of ethnological images in scientific, aesthetic or popular form is a basic feature of imperial cultures" (Pieterse 1992, 94, emphasis in original).

25. Ganda and Touré borrowed the names Robinson and Constantine from popular Hollywood and French actors of the era, both of whom were white.

5. ACCULTURATION AS EVOLUTION

1. Grand Bassam, founded along with Assinie in 1843, became the colony's first capital in 1893, but it was vacated after a yellow-fever epidemic. Between 1893 and 1903 the capital was Bingerville.

2. President Houphouët-Boigny changed the capital to Yamoussoukro in 1983, although Abidjan remains the de facto capital with all government functions remaining in the city.

3. "The colonial order was founded on the idea that humanity was divided into species and subspecies that could be differentiated, separated, and classed hierarchically. Both from the point of view of the law and in terms of spatial arrangements, species and subspecies had to be kept at a distance from one another" (Mbembe 2017, 66).

4. As discussed in note 15, a strong xenophobic impulse formed a countertendency to this trend.

5. Keith Hart coined the term "informal economy" in his 1973 article "Informal Income Opportunities and Urban Employment in Ghana," after which the phenomena, so discovered, became a crucial component of urban planning and policy making. The informal reside in the city as a "peripheral" population in terms of their spatial settlements, livelihood strategies, and position in the planner's lens (Simone 2010).

6. Moreover, the French believed that their sustained contact imparted civilization. The influential explorer Jean-Baptiste Labat described people from Issiny (Assinie), where the French established their first port in Côte d'Ivoire, as being "quite civilized" and contrasted them to a "more savage" people from the interior "which sees only Negroes and rarely Whites" (quoted in Cohen, W. 2003, 176).

7. Dioula is a generic designation for "itinerant trader" and is closely associated with Islamic identity (Finley 2009, 204).

8. However, a small minority of this population accrued immense wealth and emerged as a veritable commercial and trading elite of independent Côte d'Ivoire (Amin 1967).

9. At independence in 1960, Abidjan's total population was 180,000. It grew to 341,000 in 1965 and 948,000 in 1975 (Appessika 2003; Freund 2007).

10. Houphouët-Boigny was the sole African head of state to defend the creation of the short-lived French Community, formed in 1958, while opposing autonomous intra-African links (Cooper 2015).

11. Adding f for "franc," my respondents referred to the currency as FCFA. The CFA became the eco in 2019, but as with the CFA, it remains pegged to the euro.

12. Wallerstein's doctoral dissertation, completed in 1959 at Columbia University, was titled "The Emergence of Two West African Nations: Ghana and the Ivory Coast."

13. Assessing the first years of Ivoirian industrialization and its overwhelming reliance on foreign capital, demand, and expertise, Amin (1967, 192) minced no words, declaring that it would produce, "on the social and political level . . . a local society that is totally disharmonious, dependent, exercising no economic responsibility, and benefiting only marginally from the effects of development."

14. Cocoa cultivation had already enabled Côte d'Ivoire to achieve massive economic growth in the decade leading to independence: cocoa comprised 38 percent of AOF's exports, while the colony made up 11 percent of its population (Coquery-Vidrovitch 1992, 99).

15. Antagonism toward so-called foreigners preceded Ivoirian independence. In 1958 the Ligue des originaires de la Côte d'Ivoire (League of Original Inhabitants of Côte d'Ivoire), charging that migrants from France's other colonial territories were "invaders" taking enviable jobs in Abidjan's public and private sectors, rioted against some eight thousand Togolese and Dahomeans (Cooper 2015, 353), and local authorities expelled twenty thousand Africans from the country (Cohen, M. 1984). Nonetheless, regional interconnections were standard order, and the early Houphouët-Boigny presidency spoke frequently of creating special dual-citizenship status, especially for Burkinabés.

16. The next largest non-African constituency in Côte d'Ivoire were the Lebanese.

17. The emerging middle class never constituted the bulk of African postcolonial society. Though they were not the elite, they were among the relatively privileged.

18. Upon independence, Houphouët-Boigny declared agricultural land ownership by usufruct, although he gave local authorities power of enforcement. While the politically integrated authochthons retained a dominant formal if not physical presence, in the colonial and postcolonial period, migrants, including extranationals, were principal cultivators, with shares of the crop often paid out in lieu of wages (Boone 1995). The proportion of immigrants in the plantation zones increased from 15 percent in 1950 to 45 percent in 1965 (Amin 1967, 99). By the 1970s many of these allochthons had acquired their own land (Woods 1999). Moreover, absentee plantation ownership was common. Even the supposedly "rural" elite largely resided in Abidjan, with significant income streams in commerce and the civil service (Hecht 1983). Their extended absences complicated questions of land title when, upon the contraction of the urban labor market, disgruntled sons returned to find their land effectively taken (Woods 1999). This land conflict was a major flashpoint of the civil war.

19. In 1965 Europeans procured approximately 40 percent of all salaries in the productive economy (Amin 1967, 278). With the bulk of African earnings coming from foreign capital and the Ivoirian state, a residual 2 percent of incomes derived from African capitalist enterprises (185).

20. For example, the national anthem (while also a nod to the French Republic's *La Marseillaise*) is called *L'Abidjanaise*.

21. Rather than the white colon's pants, however, he frequently wears shorts. This modified uniform reflects the colonial penchant to have infantilized even their own African interlocutors.

22. Spirit mates depicted as women, however, remained mostly the same in the colonial period. Depicted nude as their male counterparts had previously, the features emphasized were those aspects of female anatomy that the Baoulé considered most desirable, such as a long neck (Ravenhill 1980). While not as frequent, female colon statues have nevertheless also been depicted since the colonial period (for examples, see Girard and Kernel 1993).

23. The SAA became the ruling political party, the Parti Démocratique de Côte d'Ivoire (PDCI).

24. A 1957 UGTAN (Union Générale des Travailleurs de l'Afrique Noire) resolution proposed to battle both "white colonialism [and] Africans who exploit their racial brothers, like the planters of the Ivory Coast" (David Soumah, quoted in Cooper 1996, 417).

6. IMAGINARIES OF AFFIRMATION

1. Paradoxically, Mbembe (2017, 87) observes that "the essence of the politics of assimilation consisted in desubstantializing and aestheticizing difference, at least for the subset of natives co-opted into the space of modernity by being 'converted' or 'cultivated,' made apt for citizenship and the enjoyment of civil rights."

2. Yet Garvey "certainly did not view Africans as equals," and among the "stated UNIA [Universal Negro Improvement Association] objectives and aims were 'to assist in civilizing the backward tribes of Africa'" (Meriwether 2002, 22).

3. Emphasizing culture as the key tenet of African selfhood, one faction of Négritude thinkers, using the journal *La Dépêche Africaine* as their platform, upheld a vision of a "fundamental" and "autonomous" precolonial African unity that had birthed a particularly African collectivism that it was their duty to revive (Genova 2004, 138). They rejected the hypothesis that "racial unity was forged out of shared oppression" from colonial conquest, associating this framework with a Eurocentric Communist perspective that situated the origins of human civilization as well as the nature of class struggle outside Africa (137). For them, Marxism was thus another alien ideology to reject (Genova 2004).

4. Proclaiming Négritude's yet unrealized destiny to lead the proletarian revolution, Sartre (1964–65, 47) wrote that the Black man "establishes his right to life on [a mission that,] like the proletariat's, comes to him from his historic position: because he has

suffered from capitalistic exploitation more than all the others, he has acquired a sense of revolt and a love of liberty more than all the others."

5. In the nineteenth century, however, the conviction that Europeans were bearers of a necessary and inevitable industrial progress aligned socialists and communists with the colonial cause—what Marx considered the necessary "primitive accumulation." France's Socialist Party, whose leadership overlapped with the short-lived reign of the Popular Front in the 1930s, advocated the mission civilisatrice, albeit with socialist characteristics—particularly concerning progressive labor policies (see Cooper 1996, 73–103). Moreover, the Communist Party would soon move away from asserting Blackness's unique positionality and toward insisting on the primacy and singularity of class struggle.

6. Kouyaté and the LDRN had a peppered relationship with the French Communist Party. Among the évolués accused of being a bourgeois nationalist, Kouyaté was expelled from the party in 1933 (Genova 2004). Generally, Wilder (2003) notes that due to a number of external and organizational factors, the alliance between the Communist Party and pan-Africanists in France was ultimately unsustainable. He (249) argues that those same tensions are perhaps "why the informal and cultural Panafricanism formulated by the negritude students proved to be more stable and enduring—if politically moderate—than the more organized and revolutionary Panafricanism of their politicized elders." To further complicate the politics of French Panafricanism, Wilder (249; emphasis in original) observes that its proponents "used transnational forms of racial identification in order to secure a place *within* French *national* society, even as they were identifying with a diasporic community that contained its own political possibilities." Nevertheless, "in an imperial nation-state . . . nation-centered politics may themselves be transnational" (249).

7. Further, Dayal (2004, 38) proposes that there was a "dynamic of deliberate misrecognition (*méconnaissance*) of the African American as representative of 'the African'—onto whom ambivalent modernist fantasy as well as colonial guilt could be cathected." Gondola (2004, 205) concurs, positing that Black Americans provided French people with a "vicarious, 'sanitized' African experience," one "affording engagement with so-called 'African primitive culture' without that uncomfortable intimacy."

8. Ongiri (2009, 35) argues that the Black Panther's "emphasis on the heuristic and the performative would end up creating revolution as a highly visible and visual affair." "Revolution," she (35) explains, "is theater in the streets. . . . The Panther uniform—beret, black leather jacket, gun—helps create the Panther legend." She (34–35) concludes that "it would be the Black Panther Party's interventions into the realm of symbolic, rather than military, culture that would have the most lasting effect in helping to define and position post-1965 African American culture as hypervisible, radically defiant, and the site of a contradictory empowerment and disempowerment." In doing so, "these symbols created an iconography whose power lay much more in its translatability to commodity culture than in its distance from it" (52).

9. Characterizations of the Black Panthers as a masculinist if not misogynist organization have been challenged, and indeed from 1974 to 1977 Elaine Brown served as the movement's chairwoman. The artwork of Emory Douglas consistently depicted Black women, strong and armed, alongside Black men. For a discussion of Black Panther womanhood, see e.g., Lumsden 2009; Farmer 2017; and Spencer 2016.

10. At the time it was called Café de Luxe; it became the Cotton Club when Johnson sold it (Tate 2005).

11. The tragic irony of Johnson's death was not lost on Tate (2005): "Johnson's real fall to earth occurred one day in 1946, when he became enraged at being forced to dine in the back of a segregated Raleigh, North Carolina, restaurant and then fatally drove himself into a telephone pole. After so many dazzlingly decadent years defying and flying above the racial fray, Johnson's long-deferred Black Rage flared up in the heart of Dixie over not being able to share a dining room with crackers."

7. LA CRISE

1. This was during a period that Côte d'Ivoire stood out among African nations for its willing reception of the South African apartheid regime. In a 1989 visit to Côte d'Ivoire, South African president F. W. de Klerk "was accorded the full ceremonial honors of a state visit, including a red carpet and a 21-gun salute. . . . It was the first time in recent memory that a South African President was received in black Africa with the full diplomatic protocol given a visiting head of state" (Wren 1989).

2. French aid was moreover conditioned upon structural adjustment under the 1993 Balladur doctrine (Bovcon 2011).

3. The historic peak for world cocoa prices was, to be exact, July 1977 (Trading Economics n.d.).

4. These figures are based on the Poverty Headcount Ratio at $1.90 a day (2011 PPP). Using the Poverty Headcount Ratio at $3.10 a day (2011 PPP), the figures are 18.28 percent and 55.14 percent for 1985 and 2008, respectively (World Bank Development Research Group 2017b). In a prior publication (Matlon 2016), I reported these figures to be 10.1 percent and 42.7 percent for 1985 and 2008, respectively. I drew these figures from 2015 World Bank data online that is no longer accessible. I hypothesize that the measures have changed since my earlier publication.

5. The Heavily Indebted Poor Country Initiative was launched in 1996 (United States Government Accountability Office 1998). Debt relief did not, however, prevent new austerity measures from being implemented.

6. In real numbers, the number of civil servants increased from almost 74,000 in 1980 to almost 105,000 in 2005 (République de Côte d'Ivoire 2007, 177).

7. The conversion rate on December 31, 2001 was 736 FCFA to US $1 (Bureau of the Fiscal Service 2015). In the following chapters I adjust the conversion rate to 500 FCFA to US $1, its approximate value at the time of my research from 2008 to 2009.

8. The overproduction of advanced degrees proved disastrous for the inchoate Ivoirian economy, generating expectations far beyond what was structurally viable. In the economy of la crise, the unemployed—and not the informally or underemployed—hailed from a social strata that could rely on familial networks while holding out for something better, and in the meantime refusing to engage in work below their status level.

9. Henri Konan Bédié, the second President of Côte d'Ivoire, developed the concept of ivoirité.

10. Despite Gbagbo's hostility to neocolonial Franco-Ivoirian relations and the worsening political situation, "French multinationals . . . showed themselves to be resilient in securing their economic interests" such that "the case of French big business [indicated] that the Ivorian government [under Gbagbo] played an active role in protecting the French economic presence" (Bovcon 2011, 18).

8. CITOYENS AND CITADINS

1. To protect my respondents' anonymity, I use pseudonyms for all respondents except when they assumed public personas under stage names. When these respondents engaged in or described their performative or otherwise public activities, I did not anonymize this information.

2. For a theoretical statement on the merging of politics and business within the informal logic of daily life, see Utas (2012).

3. The Sorbonne was the centerpiece of a larger network of agoras and parlements that appeared predominantly in Abidjan's outlying quartiers. These other peripheral sites operated in the evenings, presumably when men had returned from work to their respective quartiers. From my experience, these venues espoused more explicitly radical

nationalist stances—perhaps because, fully at home and potentially further out of the spotlight of the international media, they were not autocensoring. This network referred to itself as FENAPCI, or Fédération Nationale des Agoras et Parlements de Côte d'Ivoire (National Federation of Agoras and Parliaments of Côte d'Ivoire).

4. Indicative of the delicate balance between authentic and inauthentic displays of dominance at play at the Sorbonne was the quickness with which the master of ceremonies distinguished a guest speaker who was a "real" professor, or doctor, or pastor.

5. The speaker won a trip to South Africa for a continental meeting of aspiring political talent.

6. At the time of my research from 2008 to 2009, the conversion rate was approximately 500 FCFA to US $1.

7. Following international standards, I refer to soccer as football.

9. POLITICAL IMAGINARIES

1. On the phenomenon of street parliaments, see the 2012 edition of *Politique Africaine*, "Parlements de la rue: Espaces publics de la parole et pratiques de la citoyenneté en Afrique."

2. Detailed analyses of the Sorbonne and its affiliated parliaments across Abidjan include Bahi (2003, 2013), Banégas (2006, 2010), Cutolo and Banégas (2012), and Théroux-Bénoni (2009).

3. Pagne is a popular African wax-print fabric introduced by European merchants in imperial circuits and absorbed into traditional clothing styles (see e.g., Sylvanus 2007).

4. For more on informal networks and African "bigmanity," see Arnaut (2012).

5. Some weeks later it was revealed that this man had run off with people's money. The Sorbonne president made an exceptional appearance to share his anger with the crowd and to promise that this would never happen again.

6. Bayart (2000) describes how African leaders have drawn on an external gaze to detract from attention to—and thereby blame for—internal problems.

7. Perhaps not wanting to denigrate the outsized legacy of Houphouët-Boigny, the orators were overwhelmingly silent as to making comparisons between him and Gbagbo or mentioning him at all. When critiquing the earlier decades of Françafrique, they instead focused on French predation.

8. Rarely did orators make ideological distinctions among foreign figures. Notoriety and racial otherness were themselves sufficient.

9. The religious zeal of geopolitical narratives was part of the larger evangelization of Africa and in particular reflected the Pentecostal fervor of the president and his wife Simone Gbagbo. Talk of the crisis frequently contained a significant spiritual dimension. For how experiential incredulity bordered on the mystical amid la crise, see Mbembe and Roitman (1995).

10. I use XX to designate that I was unable to hear these names clearly in Boka's account.

11. One-liter Bock Solibra beers named after Ivoirian football hero Didier Drogba.

12. Roubaud and Torelli (2013, 76) found that "although fewer than 10,000 civil service jobs were filled in Abidjan in 2001–02, 140,000 young people aspired to secure one."

13. Calculating a pay of five days per week multiplied by four weeks.

14. Unlike the front line of Jeunes Patriotes, the Sorbonne orators were the movement's intelligentsia and represented an in-between of old and new. They were more inclined to respect the generational hierarchy and the signs of the old évolué ideal: the briefcase, dress shoes, trousers, and tailored shirt, albeit from pagne fabric. Yet they embraced the same pro-Anglophone, entrepreneurial aspirations for man and country.

10. VIP IMAGINARIES

1. The Gesco corridor was an ideal location: all vehicles stopped here on their way in and out of Abidjan, providing a captive audience of potential clientele.

2. Note however that Air Afrique shut down in 2002.

3. These target contributions were high, and the vendors acknowledged that they could not regularly meet them. A vendor's typical daily earnings in fact fell between 2000–3000 FCFA, and there were days when they did not take home 500 FCFA. So while the system they established was a vital source of social support and a good way to minimize unpredictability and guarantee savings, they frequently encountered the same struggles to meet basic needs as less organized vendors elsewhere in Abidjan. In effect they had transferred the stress of precarious work to their collective dues instead of removing it altogether.

4. One survey of market and street vendors in Abidjan over this period found that over 70 percent of traders were women (Adiko and Anoh Kouassi 2003).

5. In 2011 President Ouattara cleared the rue Princesse, being as it was composed predominantly of informal settlements that he took as a symbol of urban decay.

6. The "Black" was a section of the Adjamé market renowned for goods of dubious origin.

7. I cannot confirm that these were authentic Armani suits. For a discussion of the art of the *griffe*, or label, see Gondola (1999). For a perspective on authentic name brands in Abidjan, see Newell (2012).

8. This data indicated sales at a particular *place* rather than for a particular *vendor*'s earnings. Vendors may have been working at multiple locations or in other trades.

9. Migration to the United States was decidedly situated in the realm of the imaginary, particularly compared to France, the former colonizer. Data from 2000 (the most recent data prior to my fieldwork) indicated that of the approximately 175,000 Ivoirians who had emigrated abroad, 26 percent had departed for France (the country with the largest pull) compared to 6 percent to the United States (Migration Profiles Project 2009).

10. *Garçon* means "boy." However, Abidjanais have appropriated the term to bestow praise, to denote that one is a real man (see chapter 11).

11. Maquis were one of several popular social establishments. While also prominent, *bars climatisés* and *discothèques* were more expensive and thus less frequented among Abidjan's vending population.

12. Link to song: https://archive.org/details/JeMeBattePourMonAvenir.

13. SOTRA, or Société des transports Abidjanais, is Abidjan's public-transport company.

14. Not simply a free phone, this practice aimed to impress while also keeping tabs on a woman, coming as it did with the expectation that she would answer his call at all times.

15. A common justification for multiple phones was that each phone corresponded to a different network, so one could make calls using the cheapest rate per network.

16. See Schilling and Dembele (2019) for a discussion of cabine operators and their embeddedness within circuits of global capital.

11. THE VISUAL TERRAIN OF BLACKNESS

1. See Weiss (2009, 105–8) for an alternative discussion of Tupac's significance for African men.

2. For an extended account of coupé décalé, see Boka (2013).

3. Newell (2019, 119) remarks that Douk Saga, enriched from his time in Europe, "turned up the wattage on [Abidjan's] preexisting performative street style, moving from secondhand American streetwear to designer labels."

4. The song can be heard on YouTube as "Gbaka roulé": https://youtu.be/EYfld70llYw.

5. To identify the men on the signs, I first asked the barber (if he was present when I took the photo) and later, regardless of the barber's identification, I asked fourteen of my Abidjanais friends and research subjects. At times they disagreed on poorly replicated likenesses; in those cases, I went with the majority opinion. All the men were certain that these barbershop representations were of media icons. Because I took photos of the gbaka signs while in transit, I did not have the opportunity to first ask the drivers to identify the portraits.

6. "Françafrique" can be heard on YouTube: https://youtu.be/VaIDu74HR-s.

7. "Quel est mon pays" can be heard on YouTube: https://youtu.be/C8mcyNgvNYM.

8. Still, the distance between ghettomen and évolués remains impenetrable. In a prior scene Solo and his friends are caught touching the car of an important minister's son, who berates them as "*enfants du cour commun*" (children of the public courtyard). Knowing their limits, the ghettomen retreat.

CONCLUSION: WITH EVERY GRACE AND CUFF LINK

1. A closer look at Africa's expanding middle class—"a fraught, even political expression"—reveals a classification of incomes that begin at a lowly US $2 (Kulish 2014).

2. Ouattara's cooperation has also led to debt forgiveness and a major coup for the "patriotic" cause: the joint announcement in 2019 between Ouattara and French President Emmanuel Macron to end the CFA currency.

3. The formal-informal work imbalance was severe: in 2012 approximately 300,000 workers were formally employed in Côte d'Ivoire, out of a working population of over 10 million (Christiaensen and Premand 2017).

4. Black humanity came into this system against its will, condemned to labor until the surplus that could be exhausted from the body finally exhausted the body itself. Critiquing and building on prior scholarship from the Anthropocene to the Plantationocene, Davis et al. (2019) describe how the reduction of humans to exploitable bodies on the plantation, a commodification and disposability of Black life that mirrored the commodification and disposability of nature, also produced the liberatory space of the plot where the enslaved grew their own food, performed acts of care, and fostered solidarity to produce modalities of living distinct from the logic of the plantation economy. The plot thus became "a site for nurturing an oppositional mode of Black life" (7). "Plotting within and against the plantation," they (3) contend, "is a practice of cultivating life and kin that challenges the intertwined death dealing logics of racism and ecocide."

5. "The hour is late and I am pressed for time" (Wright, R. 1956, 347). With these words, Richard Wright opened "Tradition and Industrialization" at the 1956 Paris Congress of Negro Writers and Artists (*Le Ier Congrès International des Écrivains et Artistes Noirs*). This was a call to the African vanguard to join a European-idealized vision of modernity, led by the Enlightenment promises of science, rationality, and individual freedom, and against African tradition. I invoke Wright here to invert his appeal. The hindsight of enduring racial devaluation accompanied by climatic devastation has confirmed the foresight of convergent lineages of indigenous wisdom: that the world created in the image of Enlightenment reason is no more universal than the African religions and customs that Wright decried in his polemic that late evening—and certainly no less destructive.

POSTSCRIPT. REFLECTIONS ON INTERSECTIONS/INFRASTRUCTURE

1. The Allocodrome was a large, open-air food and drink market served by several maquis-like stalls. There was one in Cocody and several in the quartiers populaires. *Alloco* are fried plantains.

2. See "A Note on the Narrative and Rethinking the Ethnographic 'Object'" in my introduction.

References

Adiko, A., and Paul Anoh Kouassi. 2003. "Activities and Organisations of Traders on the Markets and Streets of Ivory Coast: A Case Study of Cocody, Treichville, Yopougon Communities and Some Streets in Abidjan." Paper Commissioned by Women in Informal Employment: Globalising and Organising. Abidjan: University of Cocody.

Agadjanian, Victor. 2005. "Men Doing 'Women's Work': Masculinity and Gender Relations among Street Vendors in Maputo, Mozambique." In *African Masculinities: Men in Africa from the Late Nineteenth Century to the Present*, edited by L. Ouzgane and R. Morrell, 257–69. New York: Palgrave Macmillan.

Agamben, Giorgio. 1998. *Homo Sacer: Sovereign Power and Bare Life*. Stanford, CA: Stanford University Press.

Ageron, Charles-Robert. 1993. "L'empire et ses mythes." In *Images et colonies: Iconographie et propagande coloniale sur l'Afrique française de 1880 à 1962*, edited by N. Bancel, P. Blanchard, and L. Gervereau, 98–110. Paris: BDIC-ACHAC.

Alexander-Floyd, Nikol G. 2003. "'We Shall Have Our Manhood': Black Macho, Black Nationalism, and the Million Man March." *Meridians: feminism, race, transnationalism* 3 (2):171–203.

Amin, Samir. 1967. *Le Développement du capitalisme en Côte d'Ivoire*. Paris: Les Éditions de Minuit.

Andrews, David L., ed. 2001. *Michael Jordan, Inc.: Corporate Sport, Media Culture, and Late Modern America*. Albany: State University of New York Press.

Appessika, Kouamé. 2003. "Urban Slums Reports: The Case of Abidjan, Ivory Coast." Abidjan: Bureau national d'études techniques et de développement (BNETD).

Arnaut, Karel. 2012. "Social Mobility in Times of Crisis: Militant Youth and the Politics of Impersonation in Côte d'Ivoire (2002–2011)." MICROCON Research Working Paper 58:1–30.

Atger, Paul. 1960. "Les comptoirs fortifiés de la Côte d'Ivoire (1843–1871)." *Revue française d'histoire d'outre-mer* 47 (168):427–74.

Auslander, Leora, and Thomas C. Holt. 2003. "Sambo in Paris: Race and Racism in the Iconography." In *The Color of Liberty: Histories of Race in France*, edited by S. Peabody and T. E. Stovall, 147–84. Durham, NC: Duke University Press.

Austin, Regina. 1994. "'A Nation of Thieves': Consumption, Commerce, and the Black Public Sphere." *Public Culture* 7:225–48.

Bachollet, Raymond, Jean-Barthélemi Debost, Anne-Claude Lelieur, and Marie-Christine Peyrière. (1992) 1994. *Négripub: L'Image des noirs dans la publicité*. Paris: Somogy.

Bahi, Aghi. 2003. "La 'Sorbonne' d'Abidjan: Rêve de démocratie ou naissance d'un espace public?" *Revue africaine de sociologie* 7 (1):1–17.

Bahi, Aghi. 2013. *L'ivoirité mouvementée*. Makon, Bamenda: Langaa Research & Publishing CIG.

Bancel, Nicolas, and Ghislaine Mathy. 1993. "La propagande économique." In *Images et colonies: Iconographie et propagande coloniale sur l'Afrique française de 1880 à 1962*, edited by N. Bancel, P. Blanchard, and L. Gervereau, 221–31. Paris: BDIC-ACHAC.

Banégas, Richard. 2006. "Côte d'Ivoire: Patriotism, Ethnonationalism and Other African Modes of Self-Writing." *African Affairs* 105 (421):535–52.

Banégas, Richard. 2007. "Côte d'Ivoire: Les jeunes 'se lèvent en hommes'. Anticolonialisme et ultranationalisme chez les Jeunes patriotes d'Abidjan." *Les Études du CERI* 137:1–52.

Banégas, Richard. 2010. "La politique du 'gbonhi'. Mobilisations patriotiques, violence milicienne et carrières militantes en Côte d'Ivoire." *Genèses* 81 (4):25–44.

Banégas, Richard. 2017. "La politique d'intervention de la France en Afrique vue d'en bas: Réflexions à partir du cas de la Côte d'Ivoire." *Les temps modernes* 2–3 (693–694):288–310.

Banégas, Richard, Florence Brisset-Foucault, and Armando Cutolo. 2012. "Espaces publics de la parole et pratiques de la citoyenneté en Afrique." *Politique africaine* 127:5–20.

Banégas, Richard, and Jean-Pierre Warnier. 2001. "Nouvelles figures de la réussite et du pouvoir." *Politique africaine* 82:5–21.

Bayart, Jean-François. 2000. "Africa in the World: A History of Extraversion." *African Affairs* 99:217–67.

Bayart, Jean-François. (2004) 2007. *Global Subjects: A Political Critique of Globalization.* Translated by A. Brown. Malden, MA: Polity Press.

Bayat, Asef. 2000. "From 'Dangerous Classes' to 'Quiet Rebels': Politics of the Urban Subaltern in the Global South." *International Sociology* 15 (3):533–57.

Bayat, Asef. 2004. "Globalization and the Politics of the Informals in the Global South." In *Urban Informality: Transnational Perspectives from the Middle East, Latin America, and South Asia*, edited by A. Roy and N. AlSayyad, 79–102. Lanham, MD: Lexington Books.

Bazenguissa-Ganga, Rémy. 2012. "Paint It 'Black': How Africans and Afro-Caribbeans Became 'Black' in France." In *Black France/France Noire: The History and Politics of Blackness*, edited by T. D. Keaton, T. D. Sharpley-Whiting and T. E. Stovall, 145–72. Durham, NC: Duke University Press.

Bazin, Laurent, and Roch Yao Gnabéli. 1997. "Le travail salarié, un modèle en décomposition?" In *Le modèle ivoirien en questions: Crises, ajustements, recompositions (Hommes et sociétés)*, edited by B. Contamin and H. Memel-Fotê, 689–705. Paris: Karthala et Orstom.

Bhabha, Homi K. 1994. *The Location of Culture.* New York: Routledge.

Biaya, Tshikala Kayembe. 2001. "Les plaisirs de la ville: Masculinité, sexualité et féminité à Dakar (1997–2000)." *African Studies Review* 44 (2):71–85.

Blake, Jody. 1999. *Le Tumulte Noir: Modernist Art and Popular Entertainment in Jazz-Age Paris, 1900–1930.* University Park: Pennsylvania State Press.

Blanchard, Pascal, and Gilles Boëtsch. 1993. "La révolution impériale : Apothéose coloniale et idéologie raciale." In *Images et colonies : Iconographie et propagande coloniale sur l'Afrique française de 1880 à 1962*, edited by N. Bancel, P. Blanchard, and L. Gervereau, 186–215. Paris: BDIC-ACHAC.

Blomley, Nicholas. 2003. "Law, Property, and the Geography of Violence: The Frontier, the Survey, and the Grid." *Annals of the Association of American Geographers* 93 (1):121–41.

Boisbouvier, Christophe. 2015. "Palais présidentiels: en Côte d'Ivoire, Houphouët et le cordon colonial." *Jeune Afrique*, August 13. https://www.jeuneafrique.com/mag/255343/politique/palais-presidentiels-en-cote-divoire-le-cordon-colonial/.

Boka, Anicet. 2013. *Coupé décalé: Le sens d'un genre musical en Afrique.* Paris: L'Harmattan.

Boone, Catherine. 1995. "The Social Origins of Ivoirian Exceptionalism: Rural Society and State Formation." *Comparative Politics* 27 (4):445–63.

Boserup, Ester. 1970. *Woman's Role in Economic Development*. London: Earthscan.

Boulle, Pierre H. 2003. "François Bernier and the Origins of the Modern Concept of Race." In *The Color of Liberty: Histories of Race in France*, edited by S. Peabody and T. E. Stovall, 11–27. Durham, NC: Duke University Press.

Bouquet, Christian. 2005. *Géopolitique de la Côte d'Ivoire: Le désespoir de Kourouma*. Paris: Armand Colin.

Bourgois, Phillipe. 1995. *In Search of Respect: Selling Crack in El Barrio*. New York: Cambridge University Press.

Bovcon, Maja. 2011. "Françafrique and Regime Theory." *European Journal of International Relations* 19 (1):5–26.

Brown, Carolyn A. 2003. "A 'Man' in the Village is a 'Boy' in the Workplace: Colonial Racism, Worker Militance, and Igbo Notions of Masculinity in the Nigerian Coal Industry, 1930–1945." In *Men and Masculinities in Modern Africa, Social History of Africa*, edited by L. A. Lindsay and S. F. Miescher, 156–74. Portsmouth, NH: Heinemann.

Brown, Wendy. 1995. *States of Injury: Power and Freedom in Late Modernity*. Princeton, NJ: Princeton University Press.

Bruce, Marcus. 2012. "The New Negro in Paris: Booker T. Washington, the New Negro, and the Paris Exposition of 1900." In *Black France/France Noire: The History and Politics of Blackness*, edited by T. D. Keaton, T. D. Sharpley-Whiting and T. E. Stovall, 207–20. Durham, NC: Duke University Press.

Brundage, W. Fitzhugh. 2011. "Working in the 'Kingdom of Culture': African Americans and American Popular Culture, 1890–1930." In *Beyond Blackface: African Americans and the Creation of American Popular Culture, 1890–1930*, edited by W. Fitzhugh Brundage, 1–42. Chapel Hill: University of North Carolina Press.

Bureau of the Fiscal Service. 2015. "Treasury Reporting Rates of Exchange: Historical Rates: December 31, 2001." April 29. https://www.fiscal.treasury.gov/files/reports-statements/treasury-reporting-rates-exchange/1201.pdf.

Burke, Timothy. 1996. *Lifebuoy Men, Lux Women: Commodification, Consumption, and Cleanliness in Modern Zimbabwe*. Durham, NC: Duke University Press.

Burton, Orisanmi. 2021. "Captivity, Kinship, and Black Masculine Care Work under Domestic Warfare." *American Anthropologist*. doi.org/10.1111/aman.13619.

Camp, Stephanie M. H. 2015. "Black Is Beautiful: An American History." *Journal of Southern History* 81 (3):675–90.

Carney, Judith Ann. 2009. *Black Rice: The African Origins of Rice Cultivation in the Americas*. Cambridge, MA: Harvard University Press.

Carrington, Ben. 2010. *Race, Sport and Politics: The Sporting Black Diaspora*. Washington, DC: Sage.

Cassilly, Thomas Alexander. 1975. *The Anticolonial Tradition in France: The Eighteenth Century to the Fifth Republic*. New York: Columbia University, ProQuest Dissertations Publishing.

Césaire, Aimé. (1955) 2000. *Discourse on Colonialism*. Translated by J. Pinkham. New York: Monthly Review Press.

Chang, Jeff. 2005. *Can't Stop, Won't Stop: A History of the Hip-Hop Generation*. New York: St. Martin's Press.

Chatman, Samuel L. 2000. "'There Are No Slaves in France': A Re-Examination of Slave Laws in Eighteenth Century France." *Journal of Negro History* 85 (3):144–53.

Chauveau, Jean-Pierre, and Jean-Pierre Dozon. 1988. "Ethnies et état en Côte d'Ivoire." *Revue française de science politique* 38 (5): 732–47.

Chenal, Jérôme, Yves Pedrazzini, Guéladio Cissé, and Vincent Kaufmann. 2009. "Abidjan, la métropole." In *Quelques rues d'Afrique: Observation et gestion de l'espace public à Abidjan, Dakar et Nouakchott*, edited by J. Chenal, 114–28. Lausanne: Les éditions du LASUR.

Christiaensen, Luc, and Patrick Premand. 2017. "Côte d'Ivoire Jobs Diagnostic: Employment, Productivity, and Inclusion for Poverty Reduction." Washington, DC: World Bank. https://openknowledge.worldbank.org/handle/10986/26384.

CIA World Factbook. 2012. "The World Factbook: Côte d'Ivoire." http://www.cia.gov/library/publications/the-world-factbook/geos/iv.html.

Civil Rights Act of 1964. 1964. United States Public Laws. 88th Cong., 2nd sess., Pub. L. 88–352, 78 Stat. 241. ProQuest Congressional.

Cohen, Michael. 1984. "Urban Policy and Development Strategy." In *The Political Economy of Ivory Coast*, edited by I. W. Zartman and C. L. Delgado, 57–75. New York: Praeger.

Cohen, William B. (1980) 2003. *The French Encounter with Africans: White Response to Blacks, 1530–1880*. Bloomington: Indiana University Press.

Collier, Paul. 2007. *The Bottom Billion: Why the Poorest Countries Are Failing and What Can Be Done about It*. New York: Oxford University Press.

Comaroff, Jean, and John L. Comaroff. 2001. "Millennial Capitalism: First Thoughts on a Second Coming." In *Millennial Capitalism and the Culture of Neoliberalism*, edited by J. Comaroff and J. L. Comaroff, 1–56. Durham, NC: Duke University Press.

Comaroff, Jean, and John L. Comaroff. 2005. "Reflections of Youth: From the Past to the Postcolony." In *Makers and Breakers: Children and Youth in Postcolonial Africa*, edited by A. Honwana and F. De Boeck, 19–30. Trenton, NJ: Africa World Press.

Conklin, Alice L. 1997. *A Mission to Civilize: The Republican Idea of Empire in France and West Africa, 1895–1930*. Palo Alto, CA: Stanford University Press.

Connell, R. W. (1995) 2005. *Masculinities*. Berkeley: University of California Press.

Connell, R. W. 1998. "Masculinities and Globalization." *Men and Masculinities* 1 (1):3–23.

Connell, R.W., and James W. Messerschmidt. 2005. "Hegemonic Masculinity: Rethinking the Concept." *Gender and Society* 19 (6):829–59.

Connolly, Brian. n.d. "Guinness-Greatness. There is a Drop of Greatness in Every Man." Accessed September 10, 2019. http://www.brianconnollywork.com/guinness.

Cooper, Frederick. 1989. "From Free Labor to Family Allowances: Labor and African Society in Colonial Discourse." *American Ethnologist* 16 (4):745–65.

Cooper, Frederick. 1996. *Decolonization and African Society: The Labor Question in French and British Africa*. New York: Cambridge University Press.

Cooper, Frederick. 2000. "Conditions Analogous to Slavery: Imperialism and Free Labor Ideology in Africa." In *Beyond Slavery: Explorations of Race, Labor, and Citizenship in Postemancipation Societies*, edited by F. Cooper, T. C. Holt, and R. J. Scott, 107–49. Chapel Hill: University of North Carolina Press.

Cooper, Frederick. 2014. *Africa in the World*. Cambridge, MA: Harvard University Press.

Cooper, Frederick. 2015. *Citizenship between Empire and Nation: Remaking France and French Africa, 1945–1960*. Princeton, NJ: Princeton University Press.

Coquery-Vidrovitch, Catherine. 1992. *L'Afrique occidentale au temps des Français, colonisateurs et colonisés (c. 1860–1960)*. Paris: Éditions la Découverte.

Coquery-Vidrovitch, Catherine. 2001. "Nationalité et citoyenneté en Afrique occidentale français: Originaires et citoyens dans le Sénégal colonial." *Journal of African History* 42 (2):285–305.

Coulibaly, Loucoumane. 2011. "Anger as Ivory Coast Destroys Illegal Settlements." *Reuters*, August 15. https://www.reuters.com/article/us-ivorycoast-settlements/anger-as-ivory-coast-destroys-illegal-settlements-idUSTRE77E3D120110815.

Couret, Dominique. 1997. "Territoires urbains et espace public à Abidjan: quand gestion urbaine et revendications citadines composent . . ." In *Le modèle ivoirien en questions: Crises, ajustements, recompositions (Hommes et sociétés)*, edited by B. Contamin and H. Memel-Fotê, 429–58. Paris: Karthala et Orstom.

Crenshaw, Kimberlé. 1989. "Demarginalizing the Intersection of Race and Sex: A Black Feminist Critique of Antidiscrimination Doctrine, Feminist Theory and Antiracist Politics." *University of Chicago Legal Forum* 139:139–67.

Crook, Richard C. 1989. "Patrimonialism, Administrative Effectiveness and Economic Development in Côte d'Ivoire." *African Affairs* 88 (351):205–28.

Crook, Richard C. 1990. "Politics, the Cocoa Crisis, and Administration in Côte d'Ivoire." *Journal of Modern African Studies* 28 (4):649–69.

Crook, Richard C. 1997. "Winning Coalitions and Ethno-Regional Politics: The Failure of the Opposition in the 1990 and 1995 Elections in Côte d'Ivoire." *African Affairs* 96 (383):215–42.

Crowder, Michael. 1964. "Indirect Rule: French and British Style." *Africa: Journal of the International African Institute* 34 (3):197–205.

Cutolo, Armando, and Richard Banégas. 2012. "Gouverner par la parole: Parlements de la rue, pratiques oratoires et subjectivation politique en Côte d'Ivoire." *Politique africaine* 127:21–48.

Daddieh, Cyril K. (1987) 2016. *Historical Dictionary of Côte d'Ivoire (the Ivory Coast)*. Lanham, MD: Rowman & Littlefield.

Davis, Jane, Alex A. Moulton, Levi Van Sant, and Brian Williams. 2019. "Anthropocene, Capitalocene, . . . Plantationocene?: A Manifesto for Ecological Justice in an Age of Global Crises." *Geography Compass* 13:1–15.

Dayal, Samir. 2004. "Blackness as Symptom: Josephine Baker and European Identity." In *Blackening Europe: The African American Presence*, edited by H. Raphael-Hernandez, 157–70. New York: Routledge.

De Boeck, Filip, and Marie-Françoise Plissart. 2014. *Kinshasa: Tales of the Invisible City*. Leuven, Belgium: Leuven University Press.

Debost, Jean-Barthélemi. 1993. "La publicité lave plus blanc." In *Images et colonies*, edited by P. Blanchard and A. Chatelier, 97–102. Paris: Syros Achac.

De Gobineau, Arthur. 1854. *Essai sur l'inégalité des races humaines*. Dans le cadre de Bibliothèque Paul-Émile-Boulet. La collection: "Les classiques des sciences sociales." Chicoutimi: l'Université du Québec. https://nacaomestica.org/blog4/wp-content/uploads/2017/02/essai_inegalite_races_1.pdf.

De Golbéry, Sylvain Meinrad Xavier. 1802. *Fragments d'un voyage en Afrique: Fait pendant les années 1785, 1786 et 1787, dans les contrées occidentales de ce continent, comprises entre le cap Blanc de Barbarie et le cap de Palmes*. Paris: Treuttel et Würtz.

De Latour, Éliane. 2001. "Métaphores sociales dans les ghettos de Côte d'Ivoire." *Autrepart* 18:151–67.

Delporte, Christian. 1993. "L'Afrique dans l'affiche, la publicité, le dessin de presse." In *Images et colonies: Iconographie et propagande coloniale sur l'Afrique française de 1880 à 1962*, edited by N. Bancel, P. Blanchard, and L. Gervereau, 161–69. Paris: BDIC-ACHAC.

Dembele, Ousmane. 1997. "Le modèle d'urbanisme Ivoirien face à la crise économique: observations à propos de l'habitat métropolitain." In *Le modèle ivoirien en questions: Crises, ajustements, recompositions (Hommes et sociétés)*, edited by B. Contamin and H. Memel-Fotê, 483–513. Paris: Karthala et Orstom.

Diawara, Manthia. 1998. *In Search of Africa*. Cambridge, MA: Harvard University Press.

Diawara, Manthia. 1999. "The Blackface Stereotype." In *Blackface*, by D. Levinthal, 7–17. Santa Fe, NM: Arena Editions.

Diawara, Manthia. 2003. *We Won't Budge*. New York: Basic Civitas Books.

Diouf, Mamadou. 2003. "Engaging Postcolonial Cultures: African Youth and Public Space." *African Studies Review* 46 (2):1–12.

Donaldson, Mike. 1993. "What Is Hegemonic Masculinity?" *Theory and Society* 22 (5):643–57.

Dozon, Jean-Pierre. 1997. "L'étranger et l'allochtone en Côte d'Ivoire." In *Le modèle ivoirien en questions: Crises, ajustements, recompositions (Hommes et sociétés)*, edited by B. Contamin and H. Memel-Fotê, 779–98. Paris: Karthala et Orstom.

Drissel, David. 2011. "Hybridizing Hip-Hop in Diaspora: Young British South Asian Men Negotiating Black-Inflected Identities." *International Journal of Diversity in Organizations, Communities and Nations* 10 (5):199–222.

Dunn, Kevin C. 2004. "Fear of a Black Planet: Anarchy Anxieties and Postcolonial Travel to Africa." *Third World Quarterly* 25 (3):483–99.

Ebron, Paulla A. 1997. "Traffic in Men." In *Gendered Encounters: Challenging Cultural Boundaries and Social Hierarchies in Africa*, edited by M. Grosz-Ngate and O. H. Kokole, 223–44. New York: Routledge.

Ebron, Paulla A. 2008. "Strike a Pose: Capitalism's Black Identity." In *Recharting the Black Atlantic: Modern Cultures, Local Communities, Global Connections*, edited by A. Oboe and A. Scacchi, 319–36. New York: Routledge.

Edin, Kathryn, and Timothy J. Nelson. 2013. *Doing the Best I Can: Fatherhood in the Inner City*. Berkeley: University of California Press.

Enderstein, A. M., and F. Boonzaier. 2012. "Narratives of Young South African Fathers: Redefining Masculinity through Fatherhood." *Journal of Gender Studies* 24 (5):512–527.

Engels, Friedrich. [1847] 2010. "The Principles of Communism." In *Marx and Engels Collected Works*, vol. 6. London: Lawrence & Wishart.

Enloe, Cynthia. 1989. *Bananas, Beaches and Bases: Making Feminist Sense of International Politics*. Berkeley: University of California Press.

Eschner, Kat. 2017. "This Anti-Slavery Jewelry Shows the Social Concerns (and the Technology) of Its Time." *Smithsonian Magazine*, July 12. https://www.smithsonianmag.com/smart-news/anti-slavery-jewelry-shows-social-concerns-and-technology-its-time-180963975/.

Ezra, Elizabeth. 2000. *The Colonial Unconscious: Race and Culture in Interwar France*. Ithaca, NY: Cornell University Press.

Fanon, Frantz. (1952) 1967. *Black Skin, White Masks*. Translated by C. L. Markmann. New York: Grove Press.

Fanon, Frantz. (1961) 1963. *The Wretched of the Earth*. Translated by C. Farrington. New York: Grove Press.

Farmer, Ashley D. 2017. *Remaking Black Power: How Black Women Transformed an Era*. Chapel Hill: University of North Carolina Press.

Ferguson, James. 1999. *Expectations of Modernity: Myths and Meanings of Urban Life on the Zambian Copperbelt*. Berkeley: University of California Press.

Ferguson, James. 2006. *Global Shadows: Africa in the Neoliberal World Order*. Durham, NC: Duke University Press.

Ferguson, James. 2015. *Give a Man a Fish: Reflections on the New Politics of Distribution*. Durham, NC: Duke University Press.

Finley, Stephen C. 2009. "Dioula." In *Encyclopedia of African Religion*, edited by M. K. Asante and A. Mazama, 204–5. Washington, DC: Sage.

Fleetwood, Nicole R. 2011. *Troubling Vision: Performance, Visuality, and Blackness.* Chicago: University of Chicago Press.

Fleming, Crystal Marie. 2017. *Resurrecting Slavery: Racial Legacies and White Supremacy in France.* Philadelphia: Temple University Press.

Ford, Tamasin. 2014. "Charles Ble Goude: Ivory Coast's 'Street General'." BBC News, Abidjan, March 27. https://www.bbc.com/news/world-africa-26757787.

France-Cameroun. Croisement dangereux. 1996. Paris: Agir ici et Survie/L'Harmattan.

Fraternité Matin. 1978. *Abidjan Métropole Moderne.* Abidjan : Société de presse et d'édition de la Côte d'Ivoire.

Freund, Bill. 2007. *The African City: A History.* Cambridge: Cambridge University Press.

Friedman, Jonathan. 1991. "Consuming Desires: Strategies of Selfhood and Appropriation." *Cultural Anthropology* 6 (2):154–63.

Fuh, Divine. 2012. "The Prestige Economy: Veteran Clubs and Youngmen's Competition in Bamenda, Cameroon." *Urban Forum* 23:501–26.

Gable, Eric. 2002. "Bad Copies: The Colonial Aesthetic and the Manjaco-Portuguese Encounter." In *Images and Empires: Visuality in Colonial and Postcolonial Africa,* edited by P. S. Landau and D. D. Kaspin, 294–319. Berkeley: University of California Press.

Gates, Henry Louis. 2019. *Stony the Road: Reconstruction, White Supremacy, and the Rise of Jim Crow.* New York: Penguin Press.

Gatewood, Lucian B. 1974. "The Black Artisan in the U.S., 1890–1930." *Review of Black Political Economy* 5 (1):19–44.

Genova, James Eskridge. 2004. *Colonial Ambivalence, Cultural Authenticity, and the Limitations of Mimicry in French-Ruled West Africa, 1914–1956.* Washington, DC: Peter Lang.

Gervais, Djidji. 2011. "Historique du palais présidentiel." *L'Impartial,* August 6. http://gervaisdjidji.over-blog.fr/article-historique-du-palais-presidentiel-80971473.html.

Gervereau, Laurent. 1993a. "Africains et colonisation dans l'affiche politique française." In *Images et colonies,* edited by P. Blanchard and A. Chatelier, 61–66. Paris: Syros Achac.

Gervereau, Laurent. 1993b. "L'Exotisme." In *Images et colonies : Iconographie et propagande coloniale sur l'Afrique française de 1880 à 1962,* edited by N. Bancel, P. Blanchard, and L. Gervereau, 26–47. Paris: BDIC-ACHAC.

Gilroy, Paul. 1993. *The Black Atlantic: Modernity and Double Consciousness.* Cambridge, MA: Harvard University Press.

Gilroy, Paul. 2001. "Driving while Black." In *Car Cultures,* edited by D. Miller, 81–104. New York: Berg.

Gilroy, Paul. 2004. "Forward." In *Blackening Europe: The African American Presence,* edited by H. Raphael-Hernandez, xi–xxii. New York: Routledge.

Girard, Éliane, and Brigitte Kernel. 1993. *Colons : Statuettes habillées d'Afrique de l'ouest.* Paris: Syros Alternatives.

Gondola, Ch. Didier. 1999. "Dream and Drama: The Search for Elegance among Congolese Youth." *African Studies Review* 42 (1):23–48.

Gondola, Ch. Didier. 2004. "'But I Ain't African, I'm American!': Black American Exiles and the Construction of Racial Identities in Twentieth-Century France." In *Blackening Europe: The African American Presence,* edited by H. Raphael-Hernandez, 201–16. New York: Routledge.

Gondola, Ch. Didier. 2016. *Tropical Cowboys: Westerns, Violence, and Masculinity in Kinshasa.* Bloomington: Indiana University Press.

Gondola, Ch. Didier. 2019. Feedback notes from author. June 18.

Goodwin, Paul. 2009. "Introduction." In *Gentlemen of Bacongo*, edited by D. Tamagni. London: Trolley.

Gramsci, Antonio. (n.d.) 1971. *Selections from the Prison Notebooks*. Translated by Q. Hoare and G. Smith. New York: International Publishers.

Haeringer, Philippe. 2000. "Abidjan : Quatre cercles plus un." In *Villes en mouvement, une comparaison internationale*, edited by F. Dureau, V. Dupont, É. Lelièvre, J.-P. Lévy, and T. Lulle, 73–81. Paris: Coédition IRD Éditions/Économica.

Hale, Dana S. 2003. "French Images of Race on Product Trademarks during the Third Republic." In *The Color of Liberty: Histories of Race in France*, edited by S. Peabody and T. E. Stovall, 131–46. Durham, NC: Duke University Press.

Hall, Peter, and Michele Lamont. 2013. "Introduction." In *Social Resilience in the Neoliberal Era*, edited by P. Hall and M. Lamont, 1–33. Cambridge: Cambridge University Press.

Hall, Stuart. (1980) 1996. "Race, Articulation, and Societies Structured in Dominance." In *Black British Cultural Studies: A Reader*, edited by H. A. Baker, M. Diawara and R. H. Lindeborg, 16–60. Chicago: University of Chicago Press.

Hall, Stuart. 1986. "Gramsci's Relevance for the Study of Race and Ethnicity." *Journal of Communication Inquiry* 10 (2):5–27.

Hall, Stuart. 1993. "What Is This 'Black' in Black Popular Culture?" *Social Justice* 20 (1–2):104–14.

Hall, Stuart. 1997a. *Race, The Floating Signifier*. Interview by Sut Jhally. Northampton, MA: Media Education Foundation. http://www.mediaed.org/transcripts/Stuart-Hall-Race-the-Floating-Signifier-Transcript.pdf.

Hall, Stuart. 1997b. "The Spectacle of the 'Other.'" In *Representation: Cultural Representations and Signifying Practices*, edited by S. Hall, 223–90. Thousand Oaks, CA: Sage Publications; The Open University.

Hanchard, Michael. 1990. "Identity, Meaning and the African-American." *Social Text* 24:31–42.

Harris, Cheryl I. 1993. "Whiteness as Property." *Harvard Law Review* 106 (8):1707–91.

Harris, Donald J. 1972. "The Black Ghetto as Colony: A Theoretical Critique and Alternative Formulation." *Review of Black Political Economy* 2 (4):3–33.

Hart, Keith. 1973. "Informal Income Opportunities and Urban Employment in Ghana." *Journal of Modern African Studies* 11 (1):61–89.

Harvey, David. 2005. *A Brief History of Neoliberalism*. New York: Oxford University Press.

Hecht, Robert M. 1983. "The Ivory Coast Economic 'Miracle': What Benefits for Peasant Farmers?" *Journal of Modern African Studies* 21 (1):25–53.

Hegel, Georg Wilhelm Friedrich. (1956) 2004. *The Philosophy of History*. Translated by J. Sibree. Mineola, NY: Dover Publications.

Heller, Patrick. 1999. *The Labor of Development: Workers and the Transformation of Capitalism in Kerala, India*. Ithaca, NY: Cornell University Press.

Hirschmann, David. 1990. "The Black Consciousness Movement in South Africa." *Journal of Modern African Studies* 28 (1):1–22.

Hodeir, Catherine. 2002. "Decentering the Gaze at French Colonial Exhibitions." In *Images and Empires: Visuality in Colonial and Postcolonial Africa*, edited by P. Landau and D. Kaspin, 233–52. Berkeley: University of California Press.

Hodeir, Catherine, Michel Pierre, and Sylviane Leprun. 1993. "Les Expositions coloniales: Discours et images." In *Images et colonies: Iconographie et propagande coloniale sur l'Afrique française de 1880 à 1962*, edited by N. Bancel, P. Blanchard, and L. Gervereau, 129–39. Paris: BDIC-ACHAC.

Holo, Yann. 1993. "L'Œuvre civilisatrice de l'image à l'image." In *Images et colonies: Iconographie et propagande coloniale sur l'Afrique française de 1880 à 1962*, edited by N. Bancel, P. Blanchard, and L. Gervereau, 58–65. Paris: BDIC-ACHAC.

Honey, Michael Keith. 1999. *Black Workers Remember: An Oral History of Segregation, Unionism, and the Freedom Struggle*. Berkeley: University of California Press.

Honwana, Alcinda Manuel. 2012. *The Time of Youth: Work, Social Change and Politics in Africa*. Sterling, VA: Kumarian Press.

hooks, bell. 1992. *Black Looks: Race and Representation*. Boston, MA: South End Press.

hooks, bell. 2004. *We Real Cool: Black Men and Masculinity*. New York: Routledge.

Hopkinson, Natalie, and Natalie Y. Moore. 2006. *Deconstructing Tyrone: A New Look at Black Masculinity in the Hip-Hop Generation*. San Francisco, CA: Cleis Press.

Hugo, Charles. 1848. "Un coté de la question d'Afrique." *L'Evènement* 138 Bis (December 17). https://www.retronews.fr/journal/l-evenement-1848-1851/17-decembre-1848/2545/3668311/2.

Hugon, Anne. 1993. "Images et messages." In *Images et colonies*, edited by P. Blanchard and A. Chatelier, 51–60. Paris: Syros Achac.

Hunt, Nancy Rose. 2002. "Tintin and the Interruptions of Congolese Comics." In *Images and Empires: Visuality in Colonial and Postcolonial Africa*, edited by P. Landau and D. Kaspin, 90–123. Berkeley: University of California Press.

Hunter, Mark. 2010. *Love in the Time of AIDS: Inequality, Gender, and Rights in South Africa*. Bloomington: Indiana University Press.

Institut National de la Statistique. 2003. *Enquête 1–2–3: Premiers résultats de l'enquête emploi (Phase 1)*. Abidjan: Projet PARSTAT.

Jaffe, Rivke. 2012. "Talkin' 'bout the Ghetto: Popular Culture and Urban Imaginaries of Immobility." *International Journal of Urban and Regional Research* 36 (4):674–88.

Jarosz, Lucy. 1992. "Constructing the Dark Continent: Metaphor as Geographic Representation of Africa." *Geografiska Annaler. Series B, Human Geography* 74 (2):105–15.

Jeffrey, Craig. 2010. *Timepass: Youth, Class, and the Politics of Waiting in India*. Palo Alto, CA: Stanford University Press.

Jet Magazine. 1978. "Eldridge Cleaver Designs Pants 'For Men Only.'" *Jet Magazine* 55 (1):22–24. September 21.

Johnson, M. S., and Alford A. Young, Jr. 2016. "Diversity and Meaning in the Study of Black Fatherhood." *Du Bois Review* 13 (1): 5–23.

Johnson, Walter. 2013. *River of Dark Dreams: Slavery and Empire in the Cotton Kingdom*. Cambridge, MA: Harvard University Press.

Kaplan, Sara Clarke. 2009. "Our Founding (M)other: Erotic Love and Social Death in *Sally Hemings* and *The President's Daughter*." *Callaloo* 32 (3):773–91.

Keaton, Trica Danielle, T. Denean Sharpley-Whiting, and Tyler Stovall. 2012. "Blackness Matters, Made to Matter." In *Black France/France Noire: The History and Politics of Blackness*, edited by T. D. Keaton, T. D. Sharpley-Whiting and T. E. Stovall, 1–14. Durham, NC: Duke University Press.

Kelley, Robin D. G. 1994. *Race Rebels: Culture, Politics, and the Black Working Class*. New York: Free Press.

Kern-Foxworth, Marilyn. 1994. *Aunt Jemima, Uncle Ben, and Rastus: Blacks in Advertising, Yesterday, Today, and Tomorrow*. Westport, CT: Greenwood Press.

King, Anthony D. 2002. *Urbanism, Colonialism and the World-Economy: Cultural and Spatial Foundations of the World Urban System*. New York: Routledge.

Kohlhagen, Dominik. 2005–2006. "Frime, escroquerie et cosmopolitisme : Le succès du 'coupé-décalé' en Afrique et ailleurs." *Politique africaine* 100 (4):92–105.

Konan Kanga, Antoine. 1970. "Preface." *Abidjan: Perle des Lagunes*. Abidjan: Éditions Normand.

Konaté, Yacouba. 2002. "Génération zouglou." *Cahiers d'études africaines* 168:777–96.

Koulibaly, Mamadou. 2005. *Les servitudes du pacte colonial*. Abidjan: CEDA/NEI.

Kourouma, Ahmadou. (1998) 2004. *Waiting for the Wild Beasts to Vote*. Translated by F. Wynne. London: Vintage.

Krell, David Farrell. 2000. "The Bodies of Black Folk: From Kant and Hegel to Du Bois and Baldwin." *boundary 2* 27 (3):103–34.

Kulick, Don. 1995. "Introduction: The Sexual Life of Anthropologists: Erotic Subjectivity and Ethnographic Work." In *Taboo: Sex, Identity, and Erotic Subjectivity in Anthropological Fieldwork*, edited by D. Kulick and M. Wilson, 1–28. New York: Routledge.

Kulish, Nicholas. 2014. "Africans Open Fuller Wallets to the Future." *New York Times*, July 20. https://www.nytimes.com/2014/07/21/world/africa/economy-improves-as-middle-class-africans-open-wallets-to-the-future.html.

Künzler, Daniel, and Raffaele Poli. 2012. "The African Footballer as Visual Object and Figure of Success: Didier Drogba and Social Meaning." *Soccer and Society* 13 (2):207–21.

LaFeber, Walter. 1999. *Michael Jordan and the New Global Capitalism*. New York: W. W. Norton.

Land, F. Mitchell. 1995. "Reggae, Resistance and the State: Television and Popular Music in the Côte d'Ivoire." *Critical Studies in Mass Communication* 12:438–54.

Landau, Paul S. 2002. "Empires of the Visual: Photography and Colonial Administration in Africa." In *Images and Empires: Visuality in Colonial and Postcolonial Africa*, edited by P. Landau and D. Kaspin, 141–71. Berkeley: University of California Press.

Lea, David, and Annamarie Rowe. 2001. "Côte d'Ivoire." In *A Political Chronology of Africa*, edited by David Lea and Annamarie Rowe, 123–30. London: Europa Publications.

Leclerc, Georges-Louis, Comte de Buffon. (1785) 1828. *Natural History, General and Particular*. Translated by W. Smellie. London: Paternoster-Row.

Leong, Nancy. 2013. "Racial Capitalism." *Harvard Law Review* 126 (8):2153–225.

Leonhardt, Andrea. 2017. "A Night of Fashion and Black Dandies at the Brooklyn Museum." *Brooklyn Reader*, June 1. https://www.bkreader.com/2017/06/01/night-fashion-black-dandies-brooklyn-museum/.

Le Pape, Marc. 1997. *L'énergie sociale à Abidjan: Économie politique de la ville en Afrique noire, 1930–1995*. Paris: Karthala.

Le Pape, Marc, and Claudine Vidal. 1987. "L'école a tout prix: Stratégies éducatives dans la petite bourgeoisie d'Abidjan." *Actes de la recherche en sciences sociales* 70 (1):64–73.

Lindsay, Lisa A. 2003. *Working with Gender: Wage Labor and Social Change in Southwestern Nigeria*. Portsmouth, NH: Heinemann.

Lindsay, Lisa A., and Stephan F. Miescher. 2003. "Introduction: Men and Masculinities in Modern African History." In *Men and Masculinities in Modern Africa*, edited by L. A. Lindsay and S. F. Miescher, 1–29. Portsmouth, NH: Heinemann.

Locke, Catherine, and Dolf J. H. Te Lintelo. 2012. "Young Zambians 'Waiting' for Opportunities and 'Working Towards' Living Well: Life Course and Aspiration in Youth Transitions." *Journal of International Development* 24 (6):777–94.

Lonely Planet. 2006. *West Africa*. Oakland, CA: Lonely Planet Publications.

Loucou, Jean-Noël. 2012. *La Côte d'Ivoire coloniale, 1893–1960*. Abidjan: Éditions du CERAP.

Lowe, Lisa. 2015. *The Intimacies of Four Continents*. Durham, NC: Duke University Press.

Lugones, Maria. 2007. "Heterosexualism and the Colonial/Modern Gender System." *Hypatia* 22 (1):186–209.

Lumsden, Linda. 2009. "Good Mothers with Guns: Framing Black Womanhood in the Black Panther, 1968–1980." *Journalism and Mass Communication Quarterly* 86 (4):900–922.

Lyons, Michal, and Simon Snoxell. 2005. "Creating Urban Social Capital: Some Evidence from Informal Traders in Nairobi." *Urban Studies* 42 (7):1077–97.

Mains, Daniel. 2012. *Hope Is Cut: Youth, Unemployment, and the Future in Urban Ethiopia*. Philadelphia, PA: Temple University Press.

Mamdani, Mahmood. 1996. *Citizen and Subject: Contemporary Africa and the Legacy of Late Colonialism*. Princeton, NJ: Princeton University Press.

Manceron, Gilles, and Jean-Barthélemi Debost. 1993. "Conclusion." In *Images et colonies*, edited by P. Blanchard and A. Chatelier, 141–48. Paris: Syros Achac.

Martin, Michel. 2015. "Karim Abdul Jabbar: 'If It's Time To Speak Up, You Have To Speak Up.'" *National Public Radio*, November 1. https://www.npr.org/2015/11/01/453739566/kareem-abdul-jabbar-if-its-time-to-speak-up-you-have-to-speak-up.

Massire, Hugo. 2018. "Le Palais présidentiel d'Abidjan: la logique de l'opulence." *In Situ: Revue des patrimoines* 34. https://journals.openedition.org/insitu/15837.

Matlon, Jordanna. 2016. "Racial Capitalism and the Crisis of Black Masculinity." *American Sociological Review* 81 (5):1014–38.

Matory, J. Lorand. 2005. "Afro-Atlantic Culture: On the Live Dialogue between Africa and the Americas." In *Africana: The Encyclopedia of the African and African American Experience*, 2nd ed., edited by K. A. Appiah and H. L. Gates, Jr., 93–103. New York: Oxford University Press.

Mbembe, Achille. 1993. "Regards d'Afrique sur l'image et imaginaire colonial." In *Images et colonies*, edited by P. Blanchard and A. Chatelier, 133–37. Paris: Syros Achac.

Mbembe, Achille. 2001. *On the Postcolony*. Berkeley: University of California Press.

Mbembe, Achille. 2003. "Necropolitics." *Public Culture* 15 (1):11–40.

Mbembe, Achille. 2017. *Critique of Black Reason*. Durham, NC: Duke University Press.

Mbembe, Achille, and Janet Roitman. 1995. "Figures of the Subject in Times of Crisis." *Public Culture* 7 (2):323–52.

McCarren, Felicia. 2004. "Monsieur Hip-Hop." In *Blackening Europe: The African American Presence*, edited by H. Raphael-Hernandez, 35–52. New York: Routledge.

McClintock, Anne. 1995. *Imperial Leather: Race, Gender, and Sexuality in the Colonial Conquest*. New York: Routledge.

McIntyre, Michael, and Heidi J. Nast. 2011. "Bio(Necro)Polis: Marx, Surplus Populations, and the Spatial Dialectics of Reproduction and 'Race.'" *Antipode* 43 (5):1465–88.

Melamed, Jodi. 2015. "Racial Capitalism." *Critical Ethnic Studies* 1 (1):76–85.

Meriwether, James Hunter. 2002. *Proudly We Can Be Africans: Black Americans and Africa, 1935–1961*. Chapel Hill: University of North Carolina Press.

Migration Profiles Project. 2009. "Migration in Côte d'Ivoire: 2009 National Profile." Accessed September 2, 2021. https://publications.iom.int/books/migration-en-cote-divoire-profil-national-2009.

Miller, Monica L. 2009. *Slaves to Fashion: Black Dandyism and the Styling of Black Diasporic Identity*. Durham, NC: Duke University Press.

Mingst, Karen A. 1988. "The Ivory Coast at the Semi-Periphery of the World-Economy." *International Studies Quarterly* 32 (3):259–74.

Ministère des Colonies. 1912. "Rapport au président de la République française." *Journal officiel de la République française* 147:4918–19.

Mitter, Siddhartha. 2015. "The French Are Back in Booming Côte d'Ivoire—But So Is Everyone Else." *Quartz Africa*, October 21. https://qz.com/africa/529441/the-french-are-back-in-booming-cote-divoire-but-so-is-everyone-else/.

Morrell, Robert, and Rachel Jewkes. 2011. "Carework and Caring: A Path to Gender Equitable Practices among Men in South Africa?" *International Journal for Equity and Health* 10 (17):1–10.

Morrell, Robert, and Lahoucine Ouzgane. 2005. "African Masculinities: An Introduction." In *African Masculinities: Men in Africa from the Late Nineteenth Century to the Present*, edited by L. Ouzgane and R. Morrell, 1–20. New York: Palgrave Macmillan.

Morisset, Jacques. 2015. "The Challenge of Creating Quality Jobs in Côte d'Ivoire." *Brookings*, December 17. https://www.brookings.edu/blog/future-development/2015/12/17/the-challenge-of-creating-quality-jobs-in-cote-divoire/.

Mouiche, Ibrahim. 2008. "L'état moderne africain et le patriarcat public." In *Masculinities in Contemporary Africa*, edited by E. Uchendu, 133–62. Dakar: CODESRIA (Council for the Development of Social Science Research in Africa).

Mudimbe, V. Y. 1994. *The Idea of Africa*. Bloomington: Indiana University Press.

Mudimbe-Boyi, Elisabeth. 2012. "Black France: Myth or Reality? Problems of Identity and Identification." In *Black France/France Noire: The History and Politics of Blackness*, edited by T. D. Keaton, T. D. Sharpley-Whiting and T. E. Stovall, 17–31. Durham, NC: Duke University Press.

Murphy, Libby. 2015. "A Brief History of Le Système D." *Contemporary French Civilization* 40 (3):351–371.

Myers, Joe. 2016. "Which Are the World's Fastest Growing Economies?" *World Economic Forum*, April 18. https://www.weforum.org/agenda/2016/04/worlds-fastest-growing-economies/.

Mytelka, Lynn Krieger. 1984. "Foreign Business and Economic Development." In *The Political Economy of Ivory Coast*, edited by I. W. Zartman and C. L. Delgado, 149–73. New York: Praeger.

Naipaul, V. S. 1984. *Finding the Center: Two Narratives*. New York: Knopf.

N'Diaye, Boubacar. 2001. *The Challenge of Institutionalizing Civilian Control: Botswana, Ivory Coast, and Kenya in Comparative Perspective*. Lanham, MD: Lexington Books.

Neal, Mark Anthony. 2006. *New Black Man*. New York: Routledge.

Neal, Mark Anthony. 2013a. "Nigga: The 21st-Century Theoretical Superhero." *Cultural Anthropology* 28 (3):556–63.

Neal, Mark Anthony. 2013b. *Looking for Leroy: Illegible Black Masculinities*: New York: New York University Press.

Newell, Sasha. 2009a. "Enregistering Modernity, Bluffing Criminality: How Nouchi Speech Reinvented (and Fractured) the Nation." *Journal of Linguistic Anthropology* 19 (2):157–84.

Newell, Sasha. 2009b. "Godrap Girls, Draou Boys, and the Sexual Economy of the Bluff in Abidjan, Côte d'Ivoire." *Ethnos* 74 (3):379–402.

Newell, Sasha. 2012. *The Modernity Bluff: Crime, Consumption, and Citizenship in Côte d'Ivoire*. Chicago: University of Chicago Press.

Newell, Sasha. 2019. "Sagacité: On Celebrity and Criminality in Côte d'Ivoire, 1987–2017." In *Most Wanted: The Popular Culture of Illegality*, edited by R. Jaffe and M. Oosterbaan, 115–121. Amsterdam: Amsterdam University Press.

Newton, Huey P. 1980. "War against the Panthers: A Study of Repression in America." PhD diss., University of California, Santa Cruz.

Nyankawindermera, Albert, and Benjamin Zanou. 2001. *Migration et réparation spatiale de la population en Côte d'Ivoire*. Abidjan: École Nationale Supérieure de Statistique et d'Économie Appliquée.

Ongiri, Amy Abugo. 2009. *Spectacular Blackness: The Cultural Politics of the Black Power Movement and the Search for a Black Aesthetic*. Charlottesville: University of Virginia Press.

Opoku, Kwame. 1974. "Traditional Law under French Colonial Rule." *Law and Politics in Africa, Asia and Latin America* 7 (2):139–53.

Ouattara, Aminata. 1985. "L'influence des Américains noirs sur les Ivoiriens dans la région d'Abidjan: À travers les mass-media de 1981–1984." *Kasa Bya Kasa* 5:70–97.

Packer, George. 2003. "Letter from Ivory Coast: Gangsta War." *New Yorker*, October 27. https://www.newyorker.com/magazine/2003/11/03/gangsta-war.

Palermo, Lynn E. 2003. "Identity under Construction: Representing the Colonies at the Paris Exposition Universelle of 1889." In *The Color of Liberty: Histories of Race in France*, edited by S. Peabody and T. E. Stovall, 285–301. Durham, NC: Duke University Press.

Patterson, Tiffany Ruby, and Robin D. G. Kelley. 2000. "Unfinished Migrations: Reflections on the African Diaspora and the Making of the Modern World." *African Studies Review* 43 (1):11–45.

Peabody, Sue, and Tyler Edward Stovall. 2003. "Introduction: Race, France, Histories." In *The Color of Liberty: Histories of Race in France*, edited by S. Peabody and T. E. Stovall, 1–7. Durham, NC: Duke University Press.

Piccolino, Guilia. 2011. "David against Goliath in Côte d'Ivoire? Laurent Gbagbo's War against Global Governance." *African Affairs* 111 (442):1–23.

Pierre, Jemima. 2013. *The Predicament of Blackness: Postcolonial Ghana and the Politics of Race*. Chicago: University of Chicago Press.

Pieterse, Jan Nederveen. 1992. *White on Black: Images of Africa and Blacks in Western Popular Culture*. New Haven, CT: Yale University Press.

Politique Africaine. 2012. "Parlements de la rue: Espaces publics de la parole et pratiques de la citoyenneté en Afrique." 127 (3).

Prahalad, C. K. 2006. *The Fortune at the Bottom of the Pyramid: Eradicating Poverty through Profits*. Upper Saddle River, NJ: Wharton School Publishing.

Proteau, Laurence. 1997. "Dévoilement de l'illusion d'une promotion sociale pour tous par l'école: Un 'moment critique'." In *Le modèle ivoirien en questions: Crises, ajustements, recompositions (Hommes et sociétés)*, edited by B. Contamin and H. Memel-Fotê, 635–53. Paris: Karthala et Orstom.

Radhakrishnan, Smitha, and Cinzia Solari. 2015. "Empowered Women, Failed Patriarchs: Neoliberalism and Global Gender Anxieties." *Sociology Compass* 9 (9):784–802.

Ralph, Michael. 2008. "Killing Time." *Social Text* 26 (4):1–29.

Ranganathan, Malini. 2016. "Thinking with Flint: Racial Liberalism and the Roots of an American Water Tragedy." *Capitalism Nature Socialism* 27 (3):17–33.

Ratele, Kopano. 2015. "Working through Resistance in Engaging Boys and Men towards Gender Equality and Progressive Masculinities." *Culture, Health, and Sexuality* 17 (supp. 2):144–58.

Ravenhill, Philip L. 1980. *Baule Statuary Art: Meaning and Modernization*. Philadelphia, PA: Institute for the Study of Human Issues.

Régent, Frédéric. n.d. "La France et ses esclaves: de la colonisation aux abolitions (1620–1848)." *Potomitan*. Accessed January 5, 2021. https://www.potomitan.info/bibliographie/regent.php.

République de Côte d'Ivoire. 2007. *La Côte d'Ivoire en chiffres*. Abidjan: Ministère de l'Économie et des Finances-Direction Générale de l'Économie.

ReseauIvoire. n.d. "La Place de la République." *Rezoivoire.net*. Accessed March 3, 2021. https://rezoivoire.net/ivoire/patrimoine/2295/la-place-de-la-republique.html#. YD-lNF1Kg-S.

Reynolds, Glenn. 2010. "'Africa Joins the World': The Missionary Imagination and the Africa Motion Picture Project in Central Africa, 1937–9." *Journal of Social History* 44 (2):459–79.

Reynolds, Glenn. 2015. *Colonial Cinema in Africa: Origins, Images, Audiences*. Jefferson, NC: MacFarland.

Ridler, Neil B. 1985. "Comparative Advantage as a Development Model: The Ivory Coast." *Journal of Modern African Studies* 23 (3):407–17.

Robinson, Cedric J. (1983) 2000. *Black Marxism: The Making of the Black Radical Tradition*. Chapel Hill: University of North Carolina Press.

Rodney, Walter. (1972) 2018. *How Europe Underdeveloped Africa*. New York: Verso.

Roitman, Janet. 2012. "Crisis." *Political Concepts: A Critical Lexicon*. Accessed November 8, 2013. http://www.politicalconcepts.org/issue1/crisis/.

Roubaud, François, and Constance Torelli. 2013. "Employment, Unemployment, and Working Conditions in the Urban Labor Markets of Sub-Saharan Africa: Main Stylized Facts." In *Urban Labor Markets in Sub-Saharan Africa*, edited by P. De Vreyer and F. Roubaud, 37–79. Washington, DC: Agence Française de Développement and the World Bank.

Roy, Ananya. 2003. *City Requiem, Calcutta: Gender and the Politics of Poverty*. Minneapolis: University of Minnesota Press.

Roy, Ananya. 2012. "Subjects of Risk: Technologies of Gender in the Making of Millennial Modernity." *Public Culture* 24 (1):131–55.

Runstedtler, Theresa. 2012. *Jack Johnson, Rebel Sojourner: Boxing in the Shadow of the Global Color Line*. Berkeley: University of California Press.

Sandbrook, Richard, and Judith Barker. 1985. *The Politics of Africa's Economic Stagnation*. New York: Cambridge University Press.

Sartre, Jean-Paul. (1948) 1964–65. "Black Orpheus." Translated by J. MacCombie. *Massachusetts Review* 6 (1):13–52.

Schilling, Hannah, and Ousmane Dembele. 2019. "Young Mobile Phone Entrepreneurs in Abidjan: Entrepreneurial Social Ties at the Service of Economic Exploitation." *Politique Africaine* 152 (1):181–201.

Schneider, William H. 1982. *An Empire for the Masses: The French Popular Image of Africa, 1870–1900*. Westport, CT: Greenwood Press.

Schumann, Anne. 2015. "Music at War: Reggae Musicians as Political Actors in the Ivoirian Crisis." *Journal of African Cultural Studies* 27 (3):342–55.

Semley, Lorelle D. 2014. "'Evolution Revolution' and the Journey from African Colonial Subject to French Citizen." *Law and History Review* 32 (2):267–307.

Shaw, Timothy M., and Malcolm J. Grieve. 1978. "The Political Economy of Resources: Africa's Future in the Global Environment." *Journal of Modern African Studies* 16 (1):1–32.

Sheehan, Brian. 2013. *Loveworks*. Brooklyn, NY: powerHouse Books.

Shilliam, Robbie. 2018. *Race and the Undeserving Poor: From Abolition to Brexit*. Newcastle upon Tyne, UK: Agenda Publishing.

Shin, Andrew, and Barbara Judson. 1998. "Beneath the Black Aesthetic: James Baldwin's Primer of Black American Masculinity." *African American Review* 32 (3):247–61.

Shipley, Jesse Weaver. 2013. *Living the Hiplife: Celebrity and Entrepreneurship in Ghanaian Popular Music*. Durham, NC: Duke University Press.

Silberschmidt, Margrethe. 2005. "Poverty, Male Disempowerment, and Male Sexuality: Rethinking Men and Masculinities in Rural and Urban East Africa." In *African Masculinities: Men in Africa from the Late Nineteenth Century to the Present*, edited by L. Ouzgane and R. Morrell, 189–203. New York: Palgrave Macmillan.

Simiyu Njororai, Wycliffe W. 2014. "Iconic Figures in African Football: From Roger Milla to Didier Drogba." *Soccer and Society* 15 (5):761–79.

Simone, AbdouMaliq. 2001. "On the Worlding of African Cities." *African Studies Review* 44 (2):15–41.

Simone, AbdouMaliq. 2004a. *For the City Yet to Come: Changing African Life in Four Cities*. Durham, NC: Duke University Press.

Simone, AbdouMaliq. 2004b. "People as Infrastructure: Intersecting Fragments in Johannesburg." *Public Culture* 16 (3):407–429.

Simone, AbdouMaliq. 2010. *City Life from Jakarta to Dakar: Movements at the Crossroads*. New York: Routledge.

Singh, Nikhil. 2016. "On Race, Violence, and So-Called Primitive Accumulation." *Social Text* 34 (3):27–50.

Singh, Simboonath. 2004. "Resistance, Essentialism, and Empowerment in Black Nationalist Discourse in the African Diaspora: A Comparison of the Back to Africa, Black Power, and Rastafari Movements." *Journal of African American Studies* 8 (3):18–36.

Skogseth, Geir. 2006. "Côte d'Ivoire: Ethnicity, *Ivoirité* and Conflict." *LandInfo*, November 2. https://landinfo.no/asset/514/1/514_1.pdf.

Smith, Daniel Jordan. 2017. *To Be a Man Is Not a One-Day Job: Masculinity, Money, and Intimacy in Nigeria*. Chicago: University of Chicago Press.

Spence, Lester K. 2015. *Knocking the Hustle: Against the Neoliberal Turn in Black Politics*. New York: Punctum Books.

Spencer, Robyn C. 2016. *The Revolution Has Come: Black Power, Gender, and the Black Panther Party in Oakland*. Durham, NC: Duke University Press.

Springer, Kimberly. 2006. "Black Feminists Respond to Black Power Masculinism." In *The Black Power Movement: Rethinking the Civil Rights–Black Power Era*, edited by P. E. Joseph, 105–18. New York: Routledge.

Standing, Guy. 1999. "Global Feminization through Flexible Labor: A Theme Revisited." *World Development* 27 (3):583–602.

Steck, Jean-Fabien. 2005. "Abidjan et le Plateau: Quels modèles urbains pour la vitrine du 'miracle' ivoirien?" *Géocarrefour* 80 (3):215–26.

Steck, Jean-Fabien. 2008. "Yopougon, Yop City, Poy . . . périphérie et modèle urbain ivoirien." *Autrepart* (3):227–44.

Stovall, Tyler Edward. 1996. *Paris Noir: African Americans in the City of Light*. Boston, MA: Houghton Mifflin Harcourt.

Stovall, Tyler Edward. 2003. "From Red Belt to Black Belt: Race, Class, and Urban Marginality in Twentieth-Century Paris." In *The Color of Liberty: Histories of Race in France*, edited by S. Peabody and T. E. Stovall, 351–69. Durham, NC: Duke University Press.

Strother, Zoe S. 1999. "Display of the Body Hottentot." In *Africans on Stage: Studies in Ethnological Show Business*, edited by B. Lindfors, 1–61. Bloomington: Indiana University Press.

Swanson, Maynard W. 1977. "The Sanitation Syndrome: Bubonic Plague and Urban Native Policy in the Cape Colony, 1900–1909." *Journal of African History* 18 (3):387–410.

Sylvanus, Nina. 2007. "The Fabric of Africanity: Tracing the Global Threads of Authenticity." *Anthropological Theory* 7 (2):201–16.

Tadiar, Neferti X. M. 2012. "Life-Times in Fate Playing." *South Atlantic Quarterly* 111 (4):783–802.

Tamagni, Daniele. 2009. *Gentlemen of Bacongo*. London: Trolley Books.

Tate, Greg. 2003. "Nigs R Us, or How Blackfolk Became Fetish Objects." In *Everything but the Burden: What White People Are Taking from Black Culture*, edited by G. Tate, 1–14. New York: Broadway Books.

Tate, Greg. 2005. "Visible Man." *Nation*, February 10. https://www.thenation.com/article/archive/visible-man/.

Théroux-Bénoni, Lori-Anne. 2009. "Manufacturing Conflict? An Ethnographic Study of the News Community in Abidjan." PhD diss., University of Toronto.

Thomann, Matthew. 2016. "Zones of Difference, Boundaries of Access: Moral Geography and Community Mapping in Abidjan, Côte d'Ivoire." *Journal of Homosexuality* 63 (3):426–436.

Thomann, Matthew, and Robbie Corey-Boulet. 2017. "Violence, Exclusion and Resilience among Ivoirian Travestis." *Critical African Studies* 9 (1):106–23.

Thomann, Matthew, and Ashley Currier. 2019. "Sex and Money in West Africa: The 'Money' Problem in West African Sexual Diversity Politics." In *Routledge Handbook of Queer African Studies*, edited by S. N. Nyeck, 200–212. New York: Routledge.

Thomas, Hank Willis. 2016. "What Goes without Saying." In *Visualizing Slavery: Art across the African Diaspora*, edited by C. M. Bernier and H. Durkin, 34–47. Lancaster, UK: Liverpool University Press.

Tirefort, Alain. 2013–2014. "Ivoiriens en images: La carte postale du premier quart du vingtième siècle." *I&M Bulletin* 39:25–37.

Toungara, Jeanne Maddox. 1990. "The Apotheosis of Côte d'Ivoire's Nana Houphouët-Boigny." *Journal of Modern African Studies* 28 (1):23–54.

Touré, Abdou. 1981. *La civilisation quotidienne en Côte d'Ivoire : Procès d'occidentalisation*. Paris: Karthala.

Trading Economics. n.d. "Cocoa | 1959–2018." Accessed October 20, 2018. https://tradingeconomics.com/commodity/cocoa.

Trial International. 2016. Charles Ble Goudé. Trial Watch Database. Accessed December 10, 2019. https://trialinternational.org/latest-post/charles-ble-goude/.

Tsing, Anna Lowenhaupt. 2005. *Friction: An Ethnography of Global Connection*. Princeton, NJ: Princeton University Press.

Tyner, James A. 2007. "Urban Revolutions and the Spaces of Black Radicalism." In *Black Geographies and the Politics of Place*, edited by K. McKittrick and C. Woods, 218–32. Cambridge: South End Press.

Union Économique et Monétaire Ouest-Africaine (West African Economic and Monetary Union). 2001–2002. "Le marché du travail dans la principale agglomération de sept pays de l'UEMOA." OuagFidelgou: UEMOA, PARSTAT.

United Nations Development Programme. 2011. "Sustainability and Equity: A Better Future for All." *Human Development Report 2011*. Accessed June 10, 2020. http://hdr.undp.org/sites/default/files/reports/271/hdr_2011_en_complete.pdf.

United Nations Development Programme. 2016. "Income Gini Coefficient." In *United Nations Development Programme Human Development Reports*. Accessed March 15, 2017. http://hdr.undp.org/en/content/income-gini-coefficient.

United Nations Population Division. 2009. "World Urbanization Prospects: The 2009 Revision." New York: United Nations Department of Economic and Social Affairs.

United States Government Accountability Office (GAO). 1998. "Developing Countries: Status of the Heavily Indebted Poor Countries Debt Relief Initiative." NSIAD-98–229. September 30. https://www.gao.gov/products/NSIAD-98–229.

Urban, Yerri. 2009. "Race et nationalité dans le droit colonial Français (1865–1955)." Faculté de droit, Université de Bourgogne.

Utas, Mats. 2012. "Introduction: Bigmanity and Network Governance in African Conflicts." In *African Conflicts and Informal Power: Big Men and Networks*, edited by M. Utas, 1–31. London: Zed Books; Nordiska Afrikainstitutet.

Vermeil, Elodie, Dominique Auzias, and Jean-Paul Labourdette. 2008. *Petit futé Côte d'Ivoire*. Paris: Nouvelles Éditions de l'Université.

Verschave, François-Xavier. 1998. *La Françafrique: Le plus long scandale de la République*. Paris: Stock.

Vogel, Jermone. 1991. "Culture, Politics, and National Identity in Côte d'Ivoire." *Social Research* 58 (2):439–56.

Wacquant, Loïc. 2000. "The New 'Peculiar Institution': On the Prison as Surrogate Ghetto." *Theoretical Criminology* 4 (3):377–89.

Wallace, Michelle. (1978) 1999. *Black Macho and the Myth of the Superwoman*. New York: Verso Books.

Wallerstein, Immanuel Maurice. 1959. "The Emergence of Two West African Nations: Ghana and the Ivory Coast." PhD diss., Columbia University.

Wallerstein, Immanuel Maurice. 1974. "Dependence in an Interdependent World: The Limited Possibilities of Transformation within the Capitalist World Economy." *African Studies Review* 17 (1):1–26.

Wa-Mungai, Mbugua. 2010. "Dynamics of Popular Transgression: The Speed Culture of Nairobi Matatu." In *Popular Snapshots and Tracks to the Past: Cape Town, Nairobi, Lubumbashi*, edited by D. de Lame and C. Rassool, 117–40. Tervuren, Belgium: Royal Museum for Central Africa.

Wan, Marilyn. 1992. *Naturalized Seeing/Colonial Vision: Interrogating the Display of Races in Late Nineteenth Century France*. MA thesis, University of British Columbia.

Watts, Michael. 2005. "Baudelaire over Berea, Simmel over Sandton?" *Public Culture* 17 (1):181–92.

Weems, Robert E. 1998. *Desegregating the Dollar: African American Consumerism in the Twentieth Century*. New York: New York University Press.

Weinstein, Brian. 1978. "Governor-General Félix Eboué (1884–1944)." In *African Proconsuls: European Governors in Africa*, edited by L. H. Gann and P. Duignan, 157–184. New York: Free Press/Collier Macmillan & Hoover Institution.

Weiss, Brad. 2009. *Street Dreams and Hip-Hop Barbershops: Global Fantasy in Urban Tanzania*. Bloomington: Indiana University Press.

Werewere-Liking. 1987. *Statues colons : Statuettes peintes d'Afrique de l'Ouest*. Abidjan: Nouvelles Éditions Africaines.

Widner, Jennifer A. 1991. "The 1990 Elections in Côte d'Ivoire." *Issue: A Journal of Opinion* 20 (1):31–40.

Wilder, Gary. 2003. "Panafricanism and the Republican Political Sphere." In *The Color of Liberty: Histories of Race in France*, edited by S. Peabody and T. E. Stovall, 237–58. Durham, NC: Duke University Press.

Williams, Eric. (1944) 1994. *Capitalism and Slavery*. Chapel Hill: University of North Carolina Press.

Wilson, Francis. 2006. "On Being a Father and Poor in Southern Africa Today." In *Baba: Men and Fatherhood in South Africa*, edited by R. Morrell and L. Richter, 26–37. Cape Town, South Africa: HSRC.

Woods, Dwayne. 1988. "State Action and Class Interests in the Ivory Coast." *African Studies Review* 31 (1):93–116.

Woods, Dwayne. 1999. "The Politics of Organising the Countryside: Rural Cooperatives in Côte d'Ivoire." *Journal of Modern African Studies* 37 (3):489–506.

World Bank. 2018. "GDP Per Capita Growth (Annual %) (2000–2010)." World Bank National Accounts Data and OECD National Accounts Data Files. https://data. worldbank.org/indicator/NY.GDP.PCAP.KD.ZG?end=2010&locations=CI&start= 2000.

World Bank Development Research Group. 2017a. "Poverty Headcount Ratio at $1.90 a Day (2011 Ppp) (% of Population). Côte d'Ivoire." http://data.worldbank.org/ indicator/SI.POV.DDAY?locations=CI.

World Bank Development Research Group. 2017b. "Poverty Headcount Ratio at $3.10 a Day (2011 Ppp) (% of Population). Côte d'Ivoire." http://data.worldbank.org/ indicator/SI.POV.2DAY?locations=CI.

World Bank Group. 2014. *Doing Business 2015: Going beyond Efficiency*. Washington, DC: International Bank for Reconstruction and Development/ World Bank. Accessed May 25, 2020. https://www.doingbusiness.org/content/dam/doingBusiness/media/ Annual-Reports/English/DB15-Full-Report.pdf.

Wren, Christopher S. 1989. "De Klerk Gets Full Welcome in Ivory Coast." *New York Times*, December 3. https://www.nytimes.com/1989/12/03/world/de-klerk-gets-full-welcome-in-ivory-coast.html.

Wright, Melissa W. 2006. *Disposable Women and Other Myths of Global Capitalism*. New York: Routledge.

Wright, Richard. 1956. "Tradition and Industrialization: The Plight of the Tragic Elite in Africa." *Présence Africaine* 8/10:347–360.

Yates, Michelle. 2011. "The Human-as-Waste, the Labor Theory of Value and Disposability in Contemporary Capitalism." *Antipode* 43 (5):1679–95.

Zartman, I. William, and Christopher L. Delgado. 1984. *The Political Economy of Ivory Coast*. New York: Praeger.

Zolberg, Aristide. 1967. "Patterns of National Integration." *Journal of Modern African Studies* 5 (4):449–67.

Index